SINISTERDEXTER

MURDER 101

SINISTER DEXTER CREATED BY

DAN ABNETT AND DAVID MILLGATE

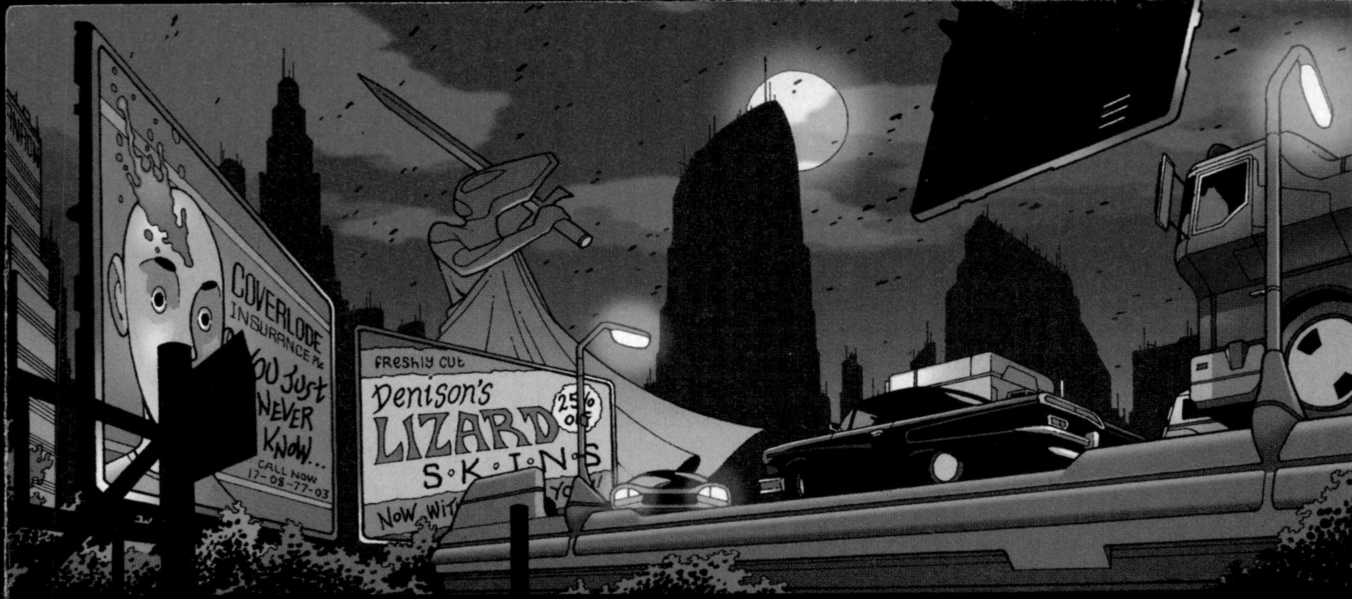
COVERLODE
INSURANCE Plc
YOU Just NEVER KNOW...
CALL NOW
17-08-77-03
FRESHLY CUT
Denison's
LIZARD
S·K·I·N·S
25% off

GREATEST HITS!

... And this is Downlode, the city that sleeps when it's dead...

Finnigan Sinister and Ramone Dexter, the two coolest gunsharks in the 'lode, pulled the hit of their lives — knocking off the crime boss and de facto lord of the city, "Holy" Moses Tannenbaum. At first, the boys figured that Moses himself had put out the contract — for whatever reason — but then they discovered that the hit had been ordered by Moses's wife, Demi Octavo, as repayment for the contract he put out on her lover.

The hit on Tannenbaum created a power vacuum in Downlode's underworld — a vacuum that was quickly filled when the "Czar" of the local Russian mafia nuked several of the other local crimelords. Naturally, he managed to involve Finnigan and Ramone, but it was clear that the boys didn't need his help to find trouble, especially after they helped a crooked taxman avoid a fatal golden handshake from his local "family," prompting one of the most devastating bloodbaths Downlode had ever seen.

When the smoke had cleared, the boys realized that they needed to get out of town, and fast. Calling in the favor they did for the Czar, they headed to Asbestopol, the hottest resort in Central Europe — and straight into the middle of a local gang war between Kilopatra, proprietor of the Bawdwalk — the hottest joint in Asbestopol — and Philly O'Fisch, a would-be local criminal kingpin.

Following an unexpected reunion with Demi Octavo — who, like the boys, had been running ever since Tannenbaum went down — they offed Fisch and escaped his goons, including the legendary hitman Tony Lacuna and a very annoyed cyber-gator. Of course, it didn't take long for the boys to realize that the Czar had set them up.

One return to Downlode and a visit home later, and suddenly Demi Octavo had become the queen of Downlode's underworld — with two friendly hitmen to protect her against all comers...

MURDER 101

Script: Dan Abnett

Art: Simon Davis

Letters: Ellie De Ville

Originally published in *2000 AD* Progs 1051-1061

SINISTERDEXTER

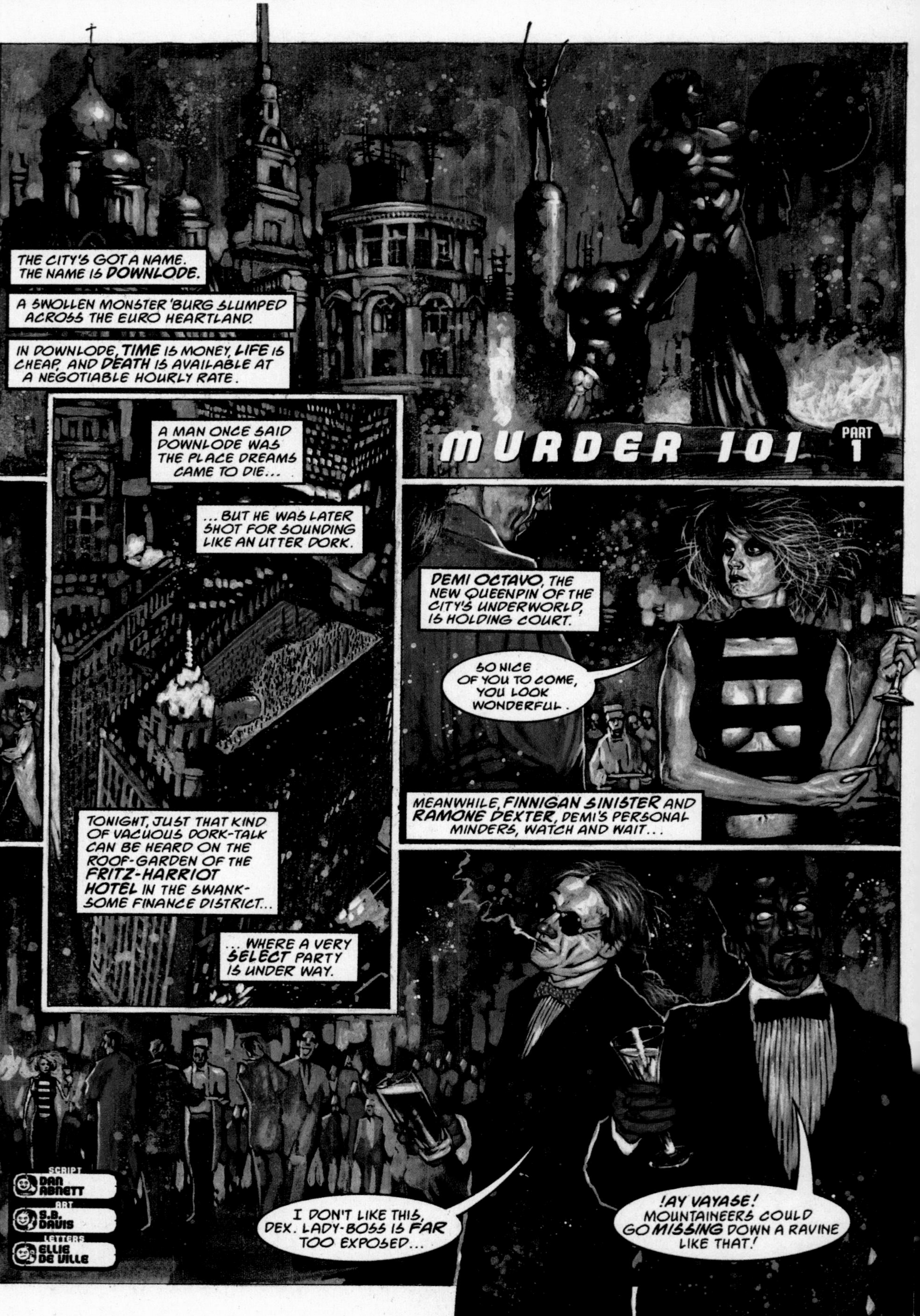
THE CITY'S GOT A NAME. THE NAME IS DOWNLODE.
A SWOLLEN MONSTER 'BURG SLUMPED ACROSS THE EURO HEARTLAND.
IN DOWNLODE, TIME IS MONEY, LIFE IS CHEAP, AND DEATH IS AVAILABLE AT A NEGOTIABLE HOURLY RATE.
MURDER 101 PART 1
A MAN ONCE SAID DOWNLODE WAS THE PLACE DREAMS CAME TO DIE...
...BUT HE WAS LATER SHOT FOR SOUNDING LIKE AN UTTER DORK.
TONIGHT, JUST THAT KIND OF VACUOUS DORK-TALK CAN BE HEARD ON THE ROOF-GARDEN OF THE FRITZ-HARRIOT HOTEL IN THE SWANK-SOME FINANCE DISTRICT...
...WHERE A VERY SELECT PARTY IS UNDER WAY.
DEMI OCTAVO, THE NEW QUEENPIN OF THE CITY'S UNDERWORLD, IS HOLDING COURT.
SO NICE OF YOU TO COME, YOU LOOK WONDERFUL.
MEANWHILE, FINNIGAN SINISTER AND RAMONE DEXTER, DEMI'S PERSONAL MINDERS, WATCH AND WAIT...
SCRIPT DAN ABNETT
ART S.B. DAVIS
LETTERS ELLIE DE VILLE
I DON'T LIKE THIS, DEX. LADY-BOSS IS FAR TOO EXPOSED...
!AY VAYASE! MOUNTAINEERS COULD GO MISSING DOWN A RAVINE LIKE THAT!

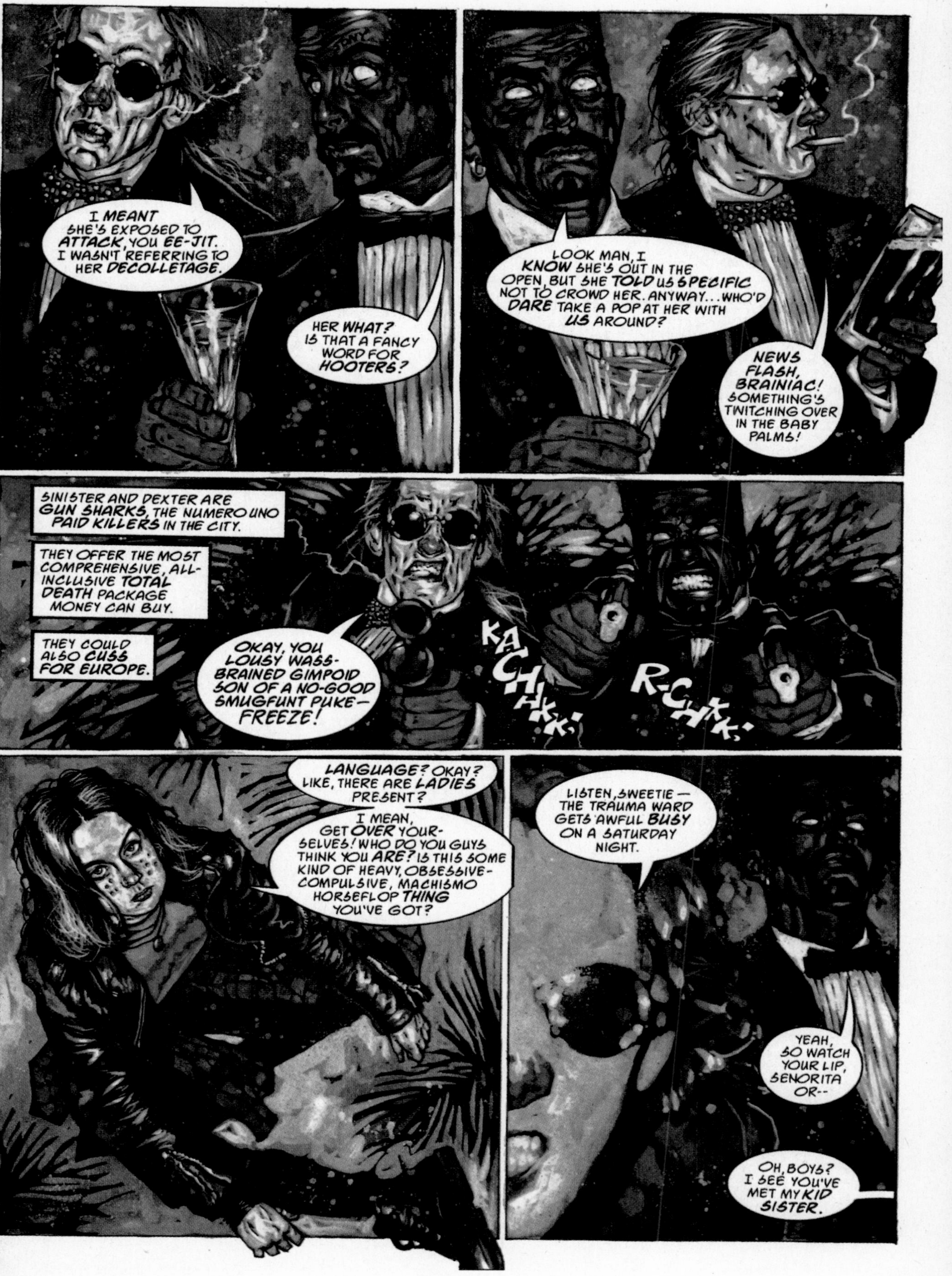

I MEANT SHE'S EXPOSED TO ATTACK, YOU EE-JIT. I WASN'T REFERRING TO HER DECOLLETAGE.
HER WHAT? IS THAT A FANCY WORD FOR HOOTERS?
LOOK MAN, I KNOW SHE'S OUT IN THE OPEN, BUT SHE TOLD US SPECIFIC NOT TO CROWD HER. ANYWAY... WHO'D DARE TAKE A POP AT HER WITH US AROUND?
NEWS FLASH, BRAINIAC! SOMETHING'S TWITCHING OVER IN THE BABY PALMS!
SINISTER AND DEXTER ARE GUN SHARKS, THE NUMERO UNO PAID KILLERS IN THE CITY.
THEY OFFER THE MOST COMPREHENSIVE, ALL-INCLUSIVE TOTAL DEATH PACKAGE MONEY CAN BUY.
THEY COULD ALSO CUSS FOR EUROPE.
OKAY, YOU LOUSY WASS-BRAINED GIMPOID SON OF A NO-GOOD SMUGFUNT PUKE—FREEZE!
KA-CHKK!
R-CHKK!
LANGUAGE? OKAY? LIKE, THERE ARE LADIES PRESENT?
I MEAN, GET OVER YOURSELVES! WHO DO YOU GUYS THINK YOU ARE? IS THIS SOME KIND OF HEAVY, OBSESSIVE-COMPULSIVE, MACHISMO HORSEFLOP THING YOU'VE GOT?
LISTEN, SWEETIE — THE TRAUMA WARD GETS AWFUL BUSY ON A SATURDAY NIGHT.
YEAH, SO WATCH YOUR LIP, SENORITA OR--
OH, BOYS? I SEE YOU'VE MET MY KID SISTER.

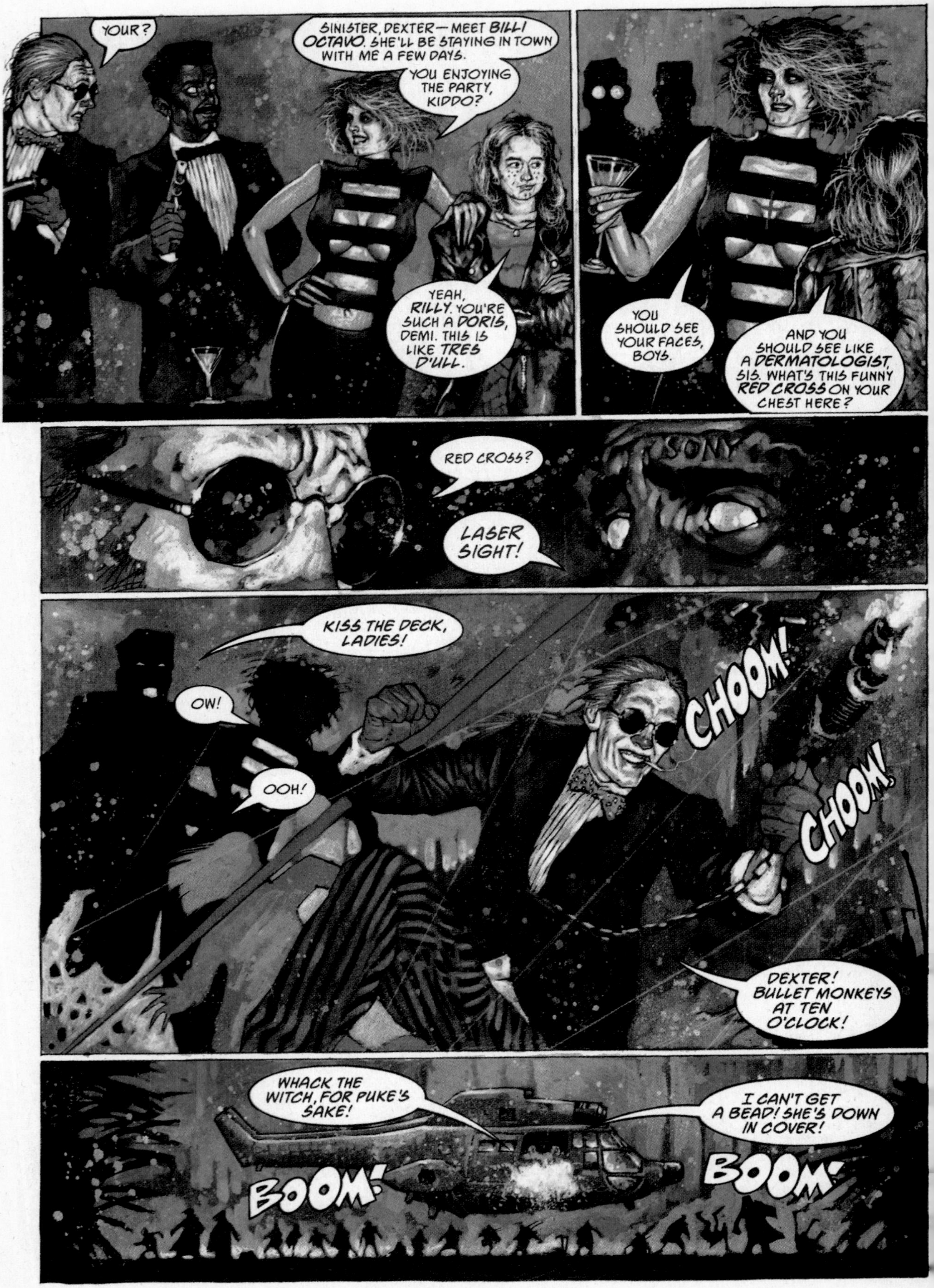
YOUR?
SINISTER, DEXTER— MEET BILLI OCTAVO. SHE'LL BE STAYING IN TOWN WITH ME A FEW DAYS.
YOU ENJOYING THE PARTY, KIDDO?
YEAH, RILLY. YOU'RE SUCH A DORIS, DEMI. THIS IS LIKE TRES D'ULL.
YOU SHOULD SEE YOUR FACES, BOYS.
AND YOU SHOULD SEE LIKE A DERMATOLOGIST, SIS. WHAT'S THIS FUNNY RED CROSS ON YOUR CHEST HERE?
SONY
RED CROSS?
LASER SIGHT!
KISS THE DECK, LADIES!
OW!
OOH!
CHOOM!
CHOOM!
DEXTER! BULLET MONKEYS AT TEN O'CLOCK!
WHACK THE WITCH, FOR PUKE'S SAKE!
I CAN'T GET A BEAD! SHE'S DOWN IN COVER!
BOOM!
BOOM!

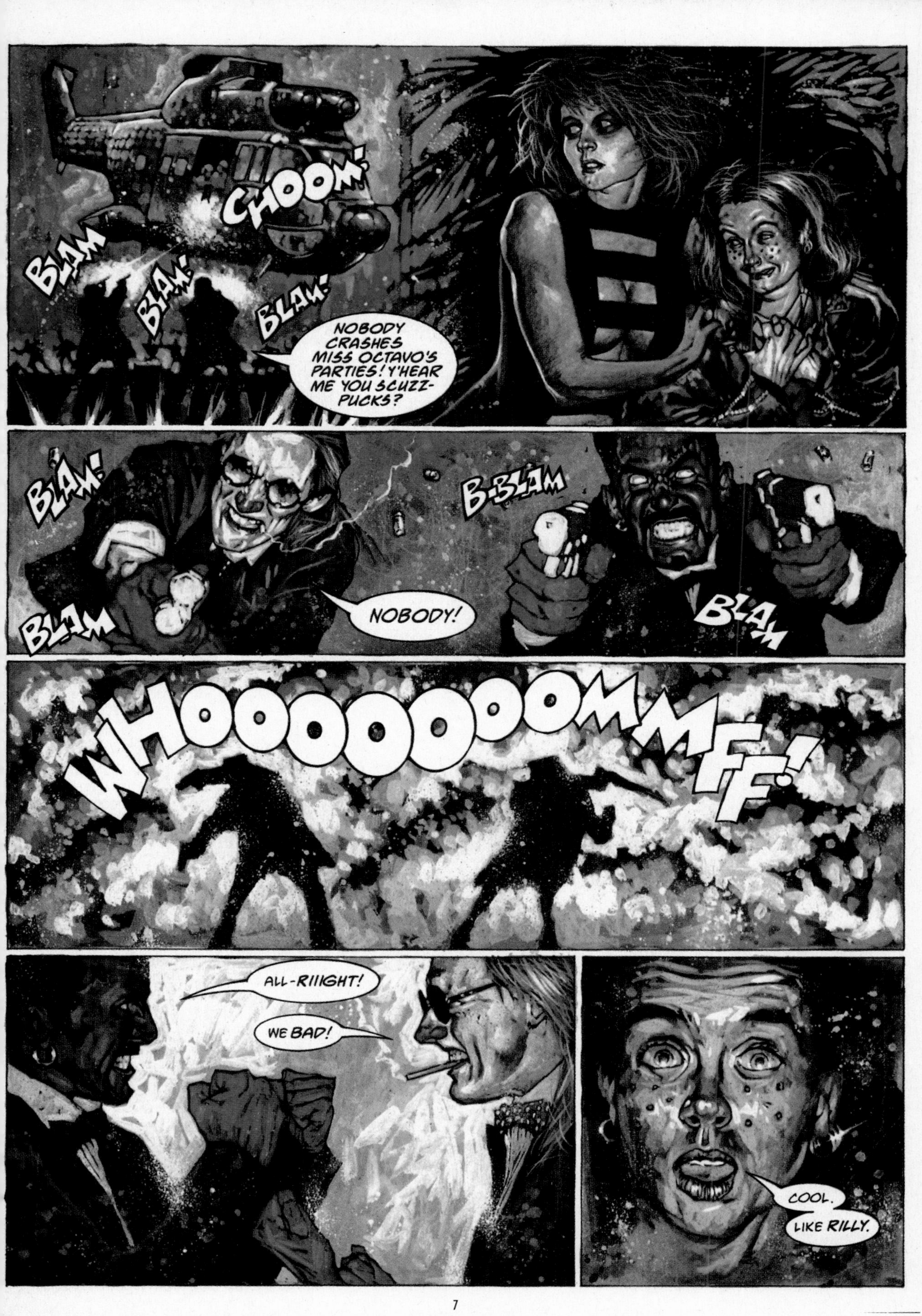
CHOOM!
BLAM
BLAM!
BLAM!
NOBODY CRASHES MISS OCTAVO'S PARTIES! Y'HEAR ME YOU SCUZZ-PUCKS?
BLAM!
B-BLAM
BLAM
NOBODY!
BLAM
WHOOOOOOOMMFF!
ALL-RIIIGHT!
WE BAD!
COOL.
LIKE RILLY.

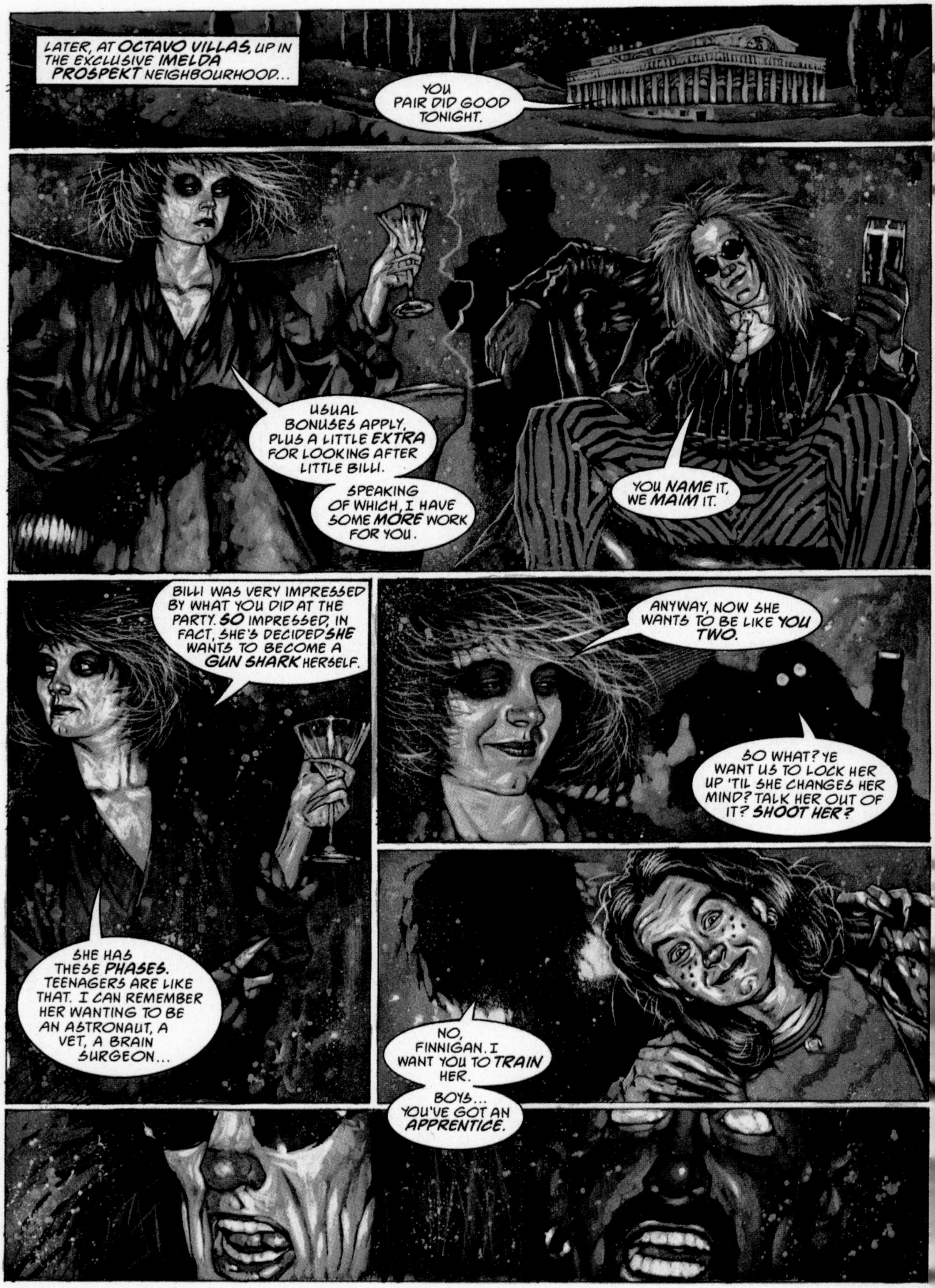
LATER, AT OCTAVO VILLAS, UP IN THE EXCLUSIVE IMELDA PROSPEKT NEIGHBOURHOOD...
YOU PAIR DID GOOD TONIGHT.
USUAL BONUSES APPLY, PLUS A LITTLE EXTRA FOR LOOKING AFTER LITTLE BILLI.
SPEAKING OF WHICH, I HAVE SOME MORE WORK FOR YOU.
YOU NAME IT, WE MAIM IT.
BILLI WAS VERY IMPRESSED BY WHAT YOU DID AT THE PARTY. SO IMPRESSED, IN FACT, SHE'S DECIDED SHE WANTS TO BECOME A GUN SHARK HERSELF.
SHE HAS THESE PHASES. TEENAGERS ARE LIKE THAT. I CAN REMEMBER HER WANTING TO BE AN ASTRONAUT, A VET, A BRAIN SURGEON...
ANYWAY, NOW SHE WANTS TO BE LIKE YOU TWO.
SO WHAT? YE WANT US TO LOCK HER UP 'TIL SHE CHANGES HER MIND? TALK HER OUT OF IT? SHOOT HER?
NO, FINNIGAN. I WANT YOU TO TRAIN HER.
BOYS... YOU'VE GOT AN APPRENTICE.

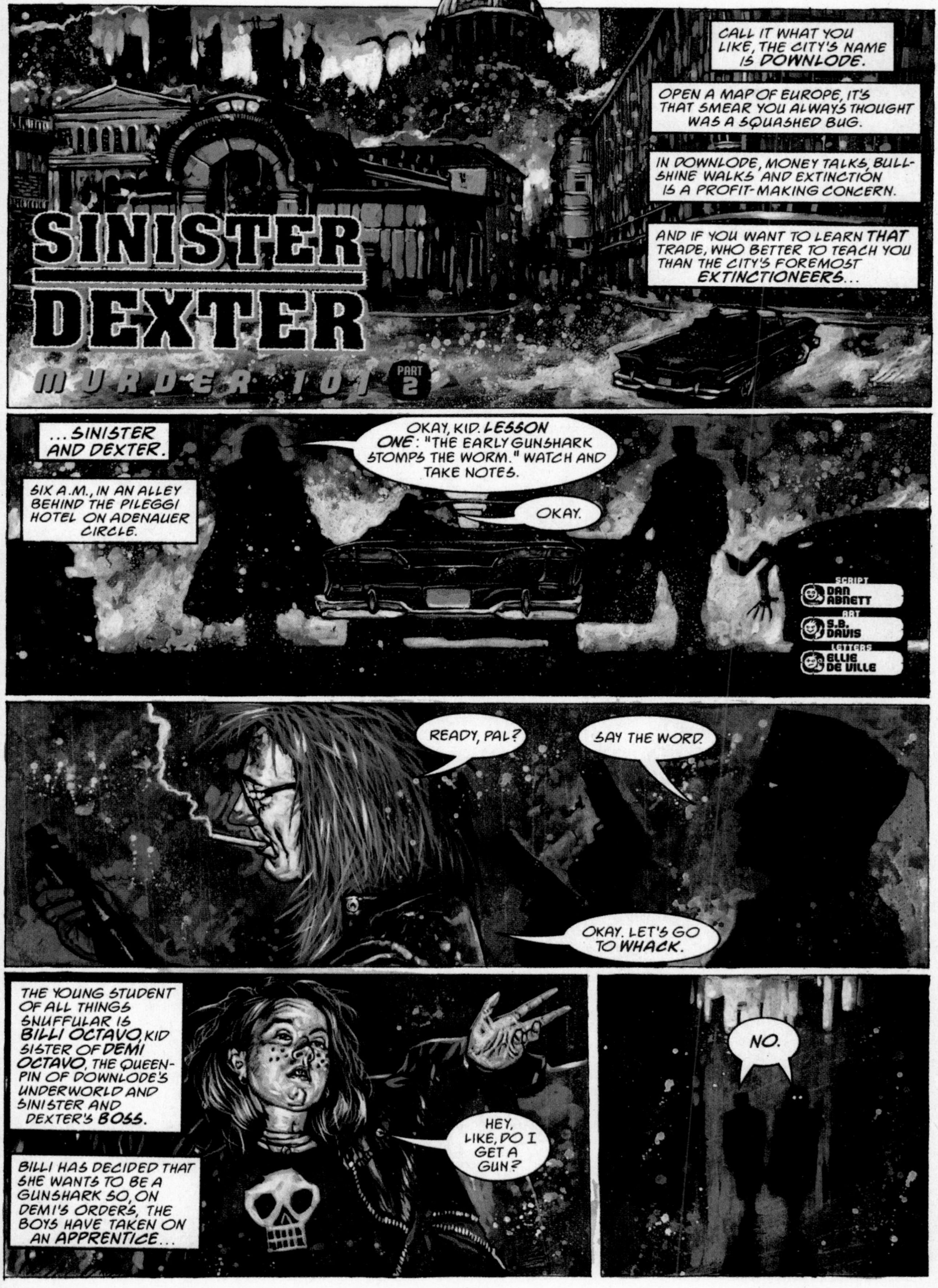
SINISTER DEXTER
MURDER 101 PART 2
CALL IT WHAT YOU LIKE, THE CITY'S NAME IS DOWNLODE.
OPEN A MAP OF EUROPE, IT'S THAT SMEAR YOU ALWAYS THOUGHT WAS A SQUASHED BUG.
IN DOWNLODE, MONEY TALKS, BULL-SHINE WALKS AND EXTINCTION IS A PROFIT-MAKING CONCERN.
AND IF YOU WANT TO LEARN THAT TRADE, WHO BETTER TO TEACH YOU THAN THE CITY'S FOREMOST EXTINCTIONEERS...
...SINISTER AND DEXTER.
SIX A.M., IN AN ALLEY BEHIND THE PILEGGI HOTEL ON ADENAUER CIRCLE.
OKAY, KID. LESSON ONE: "THE EARLY GUNSHARK STOMPS THE WORM." WATCH AND TAKE NOTES.
OKAY.
SCRIPT DAN ABNETT
ART S.B. DAVIS
LETTERS ELLIE DE VILLE
READY, PAL?
SAY THE WORD.
OKAY. LET'S GO TO WHACK.
THE YOUNG STUDENT OF ALL THINGS SNUFFULAR IS BILLI OCTAVO, KID SISTER OF DEMI OCTAVO, THE QUEEN-PIN OF DOWNLODE'S UNDERWORLD AND SINISTER AND DEXTER'S BOSS.
BILLI HAS DECIDED THAT SHE WANTS TO BE A GUNSHARK SO, ON DEMI'S ORDERS, THE BOYS HAVE TAKEN ON AN APPRENTICE...
HEY, LIKE, DO I GET A GUN?
NO.

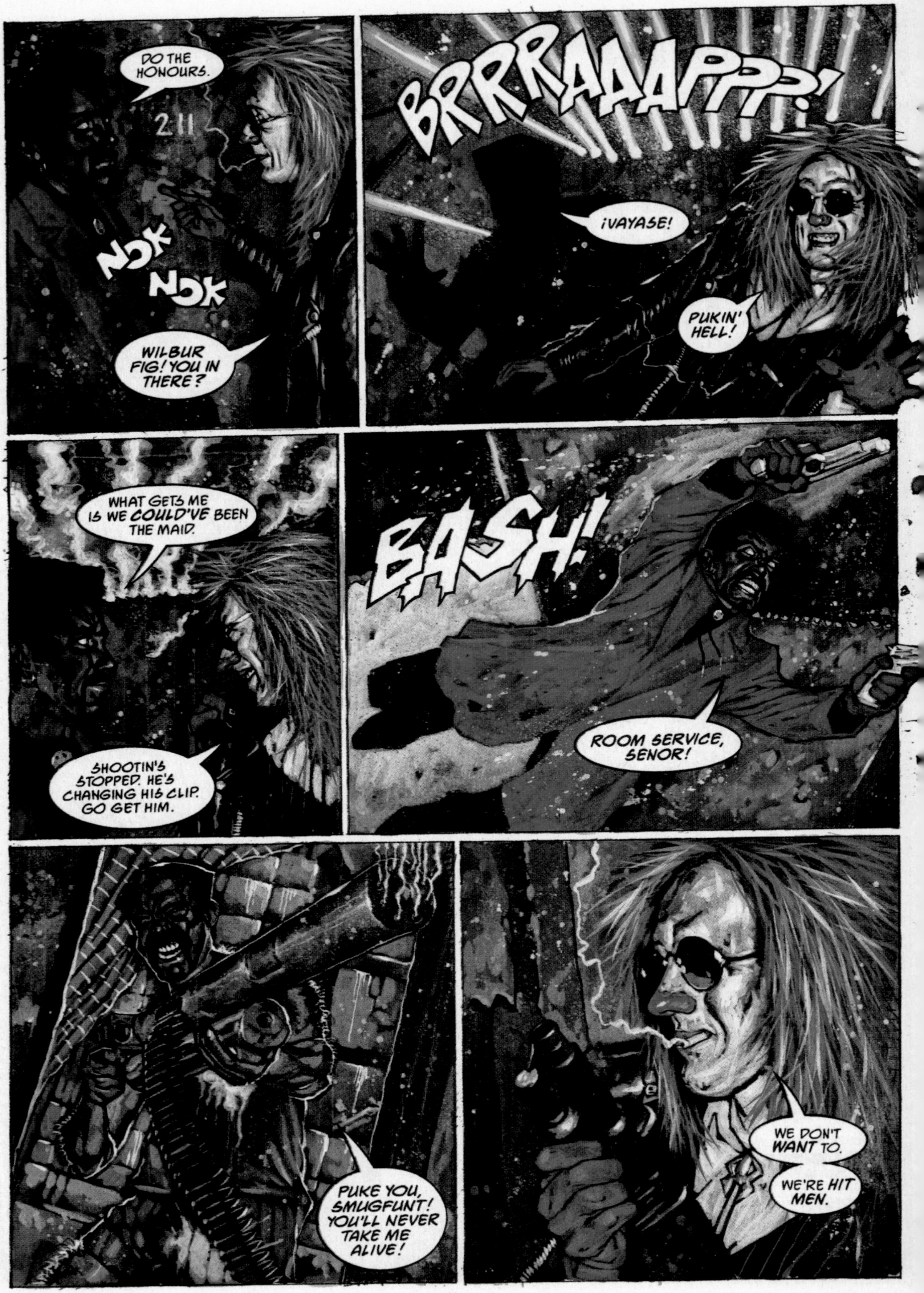
DO THE HONOURS.
211
NOK NOK
WILBUR FIG! YOU IN THERE?
BRRRAAAPPP!
¡VAYASE!
PUKIN' HELL!
WHAT GETS ME IS WE COULD'VE BEEN THE MAID.
SHOOTIN'S STOPPED. HE'S CHANGING HIS CLIP. GO GET HIM.
BASH!
ROOM SERVICE, SENOR!
PUKE YOU, SMUGFUNT! YOU'LL NEVER TAKE ME ALIVE!
WE DON'T WANT TO.
WE'RE HIT MEN.

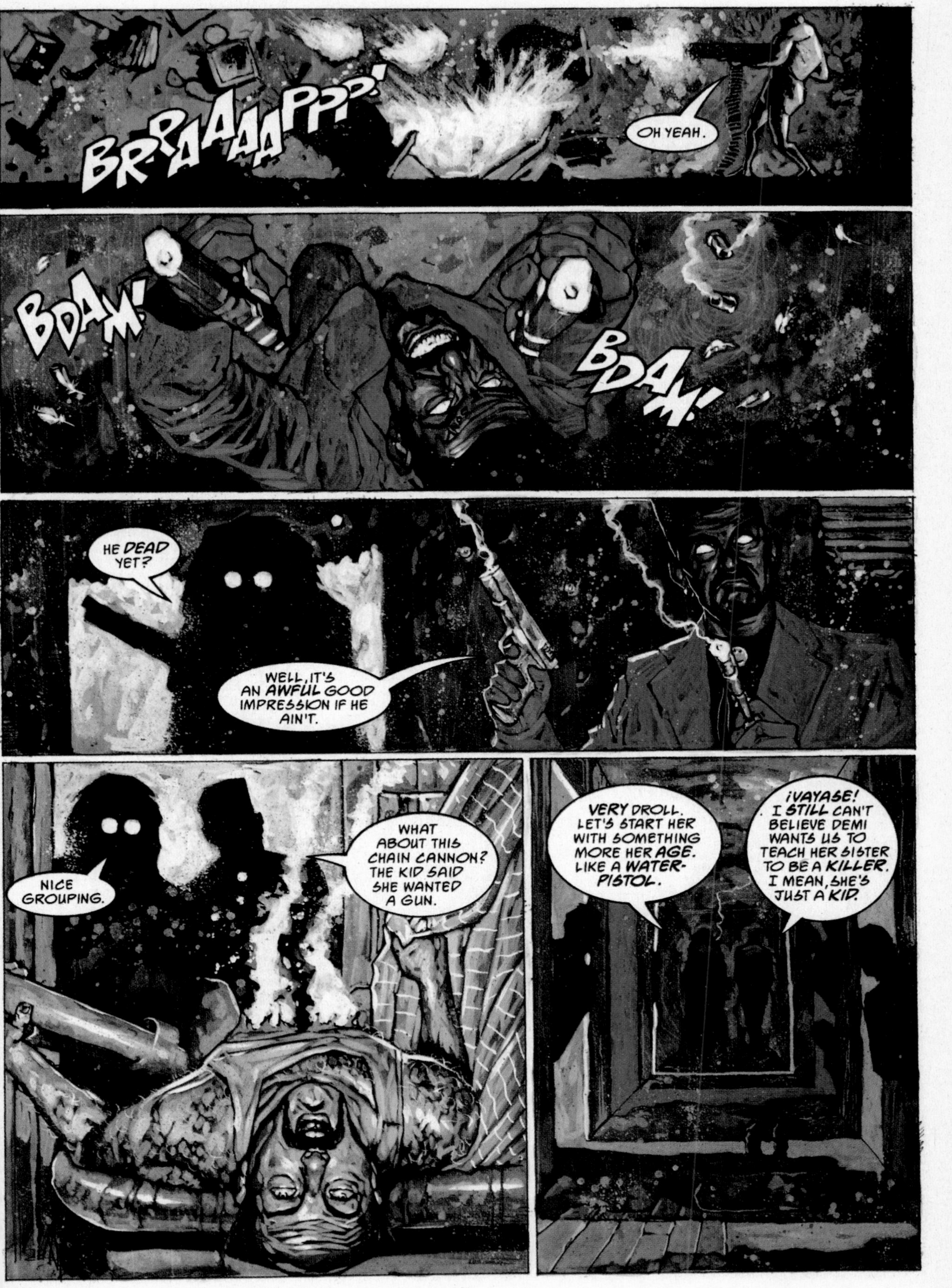
BRRAAAAPPPP!
OH YEAH.
BDAM!
BDAM!
HE DEAD YET?
WELL, IT'S AN AWFUL GOOD IMPRESSION IF HE AIN'T.
NICE GROUPING.
WHAT ABOUT THIS CHAIN CANNON? THE KID SAID SHE WANTED A GUN.
VERY DROLL. LET'S START HER WITH SOMETHING MORE HER AGE. LIKE A WATER-PISTOL.
¡VAYASE! I STILL CAN'T BELIEVE DEMI WANTS US TO TEACH HER SISTER TO BE A KILLER. I MEAN, SHE'S JUST A KID.

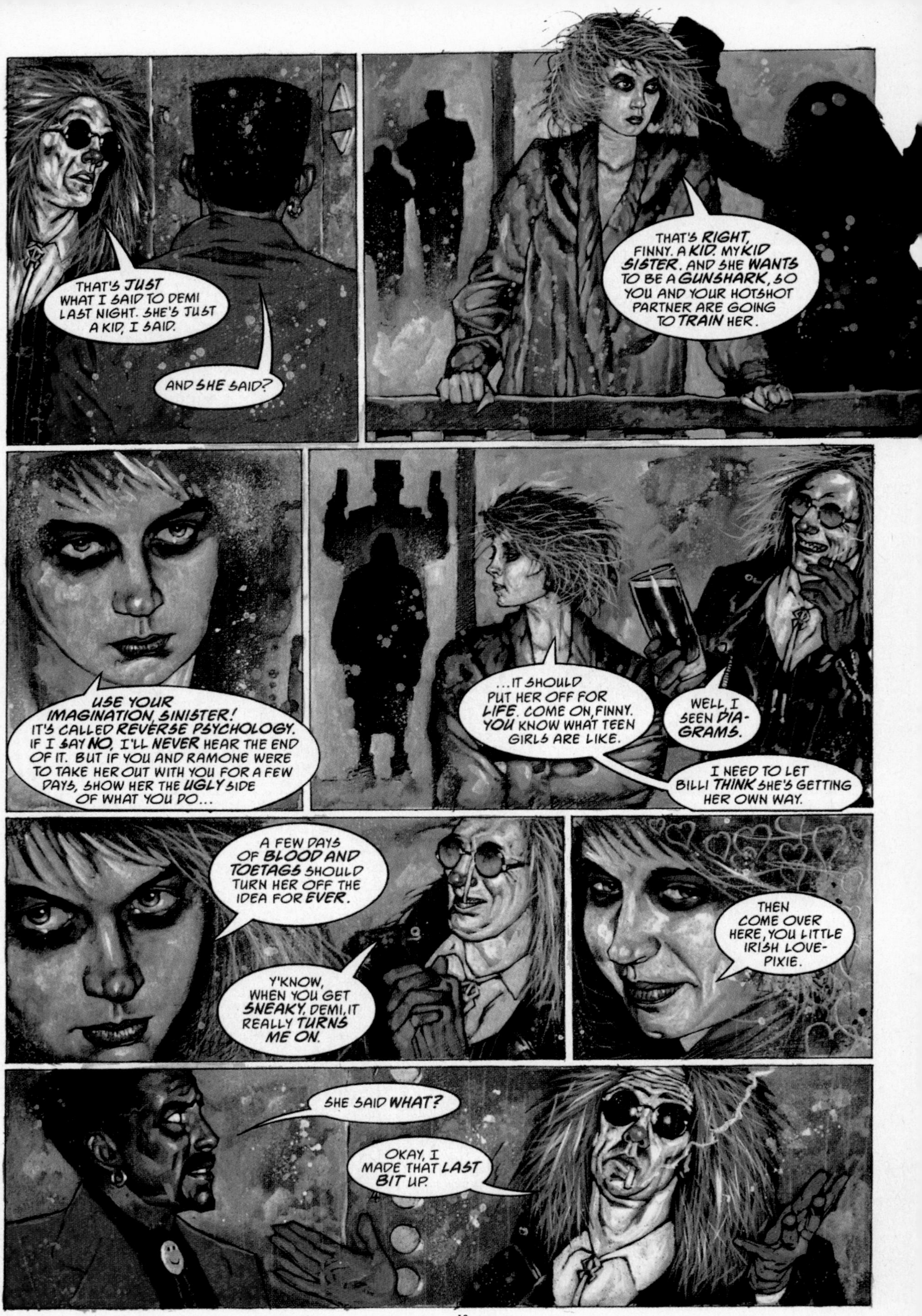
THAT'S JUST WHAT I SAID TO DEMI LAST NIGHT. SHE'S JUST A KID, I SAID.
AND SHE SAID?
THAT'S RIGHT, FINNY. A KID. MY KID SISTER. AND SHE WANTS TO BE A GUNSHARK, SO YOU AND YOUR HOTSHOT PARTNER ARE GOING TO TRAIN HER.
USE YOUR IMAGINATION, SINISTER! IT'S CALLED REVERSE PSYCHOLOGY. IF I SAY NO, I'LL NEVER HEAR THE END OF IT. BUT IF YOU AND RAMONE WERE TO TAKE HER OUT WITH YOU FOR A FEW DAYS, SHOW HER THE UGLY SIDE OF WHAT YOU DO...
...IT SHOULD PUT HER OFF FOR LIFE. COME ON, FINNY. YOU KNOW WHAT TEEN GIRLS ARE LIKE.
WELL, I SEEN DIA-GRAMS.
I NEED TO LET BILLI THINK SHE'S GETTING HER OWN WAY.
A FEW DAYS OF BLOOD AND TOETAGS SHOULD TURN HER OFF THE IDEA FOR EVER.
Y'KNOW, WHEN YOU GET SNEAKY, DEMI, IT REALLY TURNS ME ON.
THEN COME OVER HERE, YOU LITTLE IRISH LOVE-PIXIE.
SHE SAID WHAT?
OKAY, I MADE THAT LAST BIT UP.

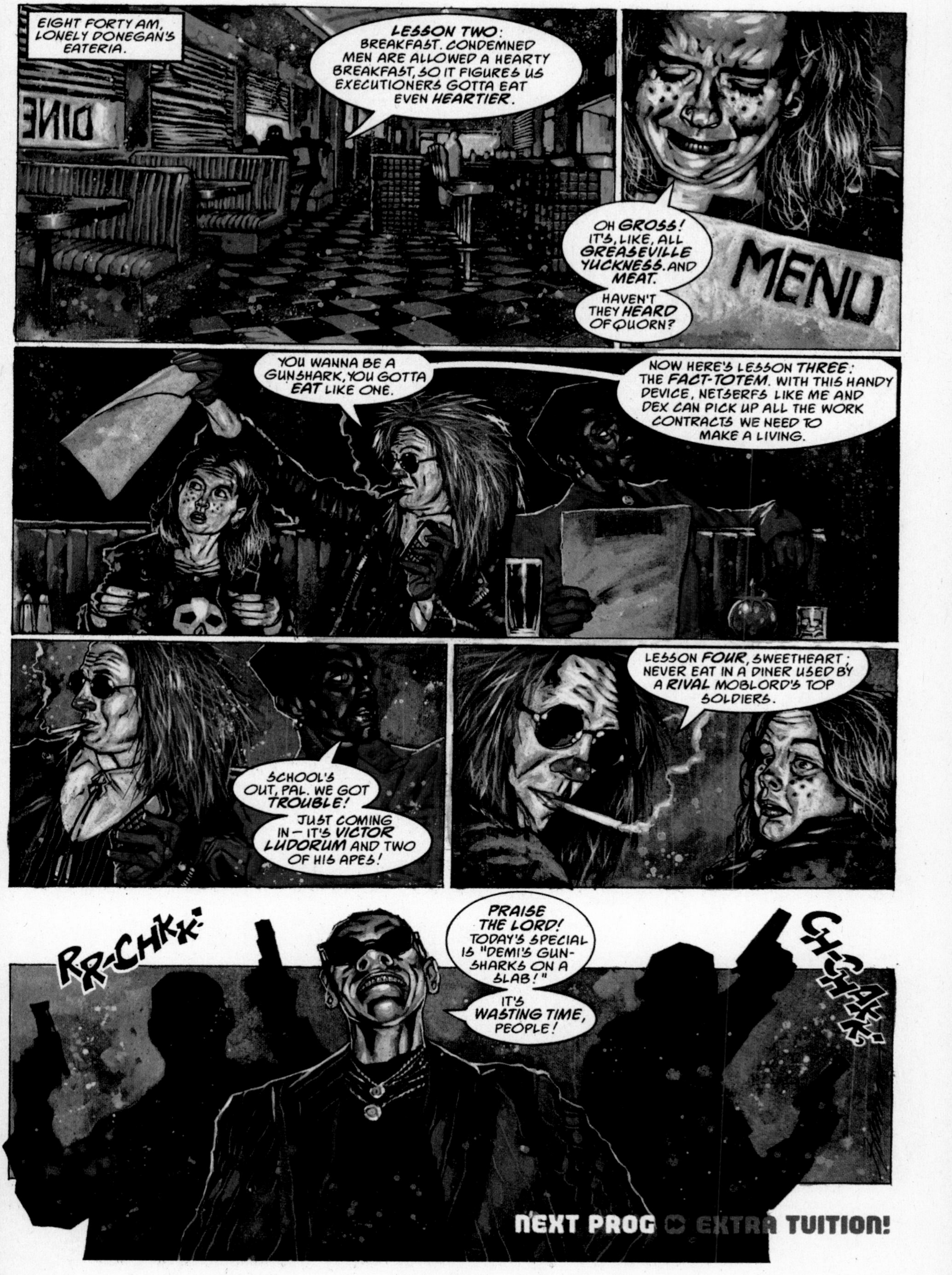

EIGHT FORTY AM, LONELY DONEGAN'S EATERIA.
LESSON TWO: BREAKFAST. CONDEMNED MEN ARE ALLOWED A HEARTY BREAKFAST, SO IT FIGURES US EXECUTIONERS GOTTA EAT EVEN HEARTIER.
DINE
OH GROSS! IT'S, LIKE, ALL GREASEVILLE YUCKNESS. AND MEAT.
HAVEN'T THEY HEARD OF QUORN?
MENU
YOU WANNA BE A GUNSHARK, YOU GOTTA EAT LIKE ONE.
NOW HERE'S LESSON THREE: THE FACT-TOTEM. WITH THIS HANDY DEVICE, NETSERFS LIKE ME AND DEX CAN PICK UP ALL THE WORK CONTRACTS WE NEED TO MAKE A LIVING.
SCHOOL'S OUT, PAL. WE GOT TROUBLE!
JUST COMING IN – IT'S VICTOR LUDORUM AND TWO OF HIS APES!
LESSON FOUR, SWEETHEART: NEVER EAT IN A DINER USED BY A RIVAL MOBLORD'S TOP SOLDIERS.
RR-CHKK-
PRAISE THE LORD! TODAY'S SPECIAL IS "DEMI'S GUN-SHARKS ON A SLAB!"
IT'S WASTING TIME, PEOPLE!
CH-CHAK-
NEXT PROG ⊃ EXTRA TUITION!

GIVE IT A NAME, THE NAME IS *DOWNLODE*.

A BILLION-POP *UBER-OPOLIS* SPRAWLING LIKE A THREAD-VEINED *ODALISQUE* ACROSS THE CHAISE LONGUE OF EUROPE, WHERE...

...AH *SCREW IT*. IT'S TOO EARLY FOR POETRY. DOWN AT LONELY DONEGAN'S EATERIE, FOLKS ARE GETTING *DEAD*.

SCRIPT
DAN ABNETT

ART
S.B. DAVIS

LETTERS
ELLIE DE VILLE

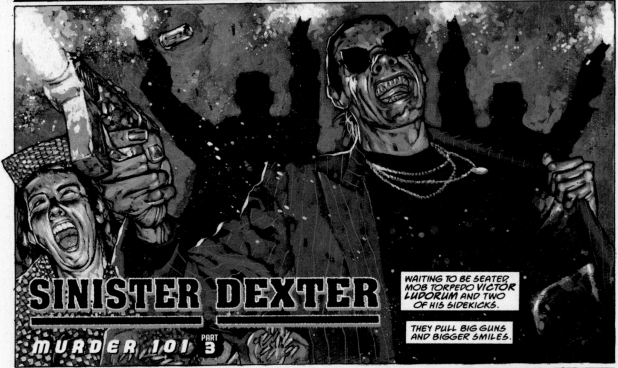

SINISTER DEXTER

MURDER 101 PART 3

WAITING TO BE SEATED, MOB TORPEDO *VICTOR LUDORUM* AND TWO OF HIS SIDEKICKS.

THEY PULL BIG GUNS AND BIGGER SMILES.

AT TABLE SIX, THE CITY'S TOP CONTRACT-A-WHACK EXPERTS, *FINNIGAN SINISTER* AND *RAMONE DEXTER*.

THEY CURSE LUCK, CHANCE, PROBABILITY MATH, AND THE GREAT LAWGIVER MURPHY.

AND THIS IS *BILLI*, KID SISTER OF DOWNLODE'S CRIME QUEENPIN, *DEMI OCTAVO*. ALL SHE *WANTS* IS TO BE A GUN SHARK.

ALL SHE MAY *GET* IS KILLED BEFORE THE BILL ARRIVES.

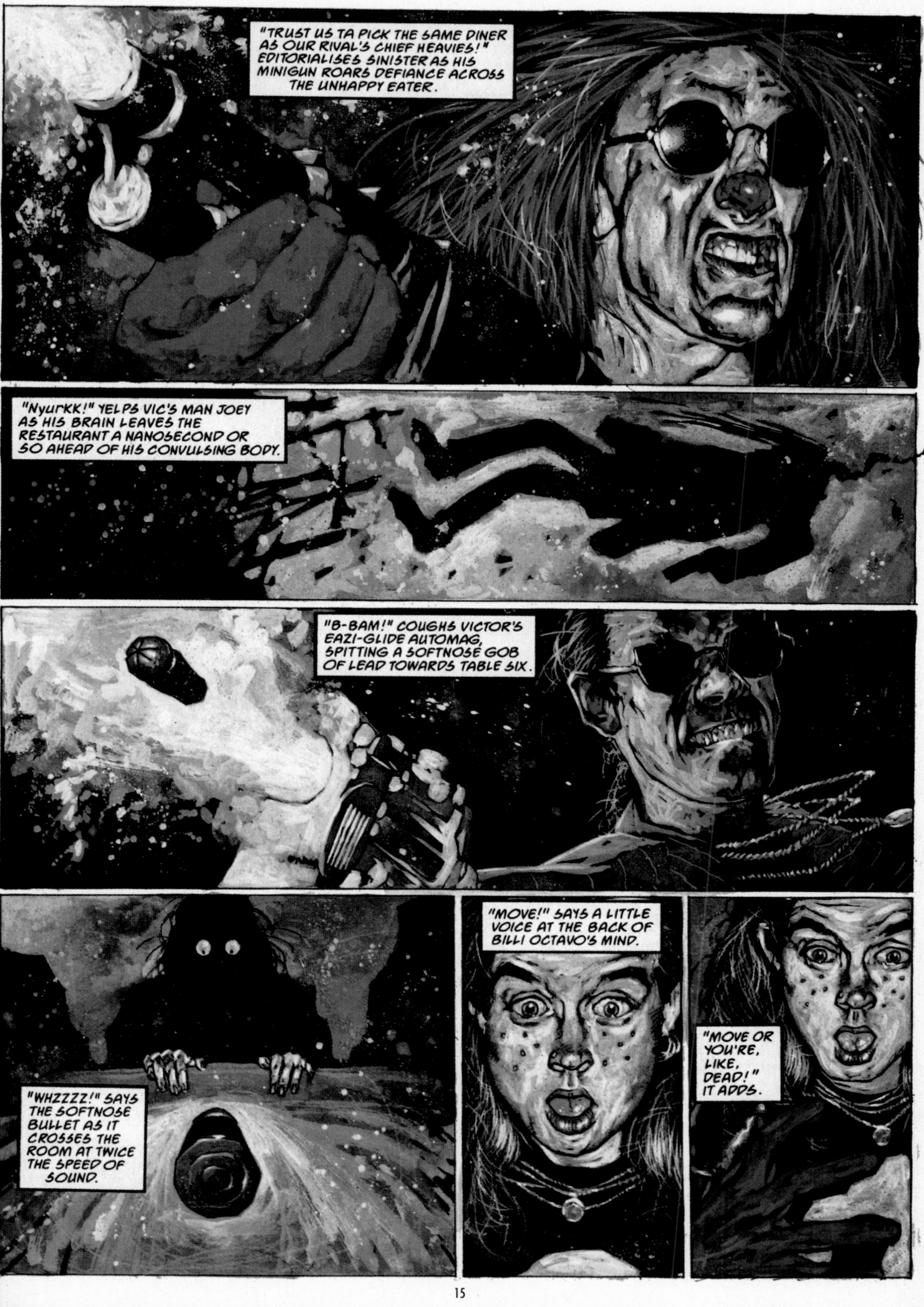
"TRUST US TA PICK THE SAME DINER AS OUR RIVAL'S CHIEF HEAVIES!" EDITORIALISES SINISTER AS HIS MINIGUN ROARS DEFIANCE ACROSS THE UNHAPPY EATER.
"Nyurkk!" YELPS VIC'S MAN JOEY AS HIS BRAIN LEAVES THE RESTAURANT A NANOSECOND OR SO AHEAD OF HIS CONVULSING BODY.
"B-BAM!" COUGHS VICTOR'S EAZI-GLIDE AUTOMAG, SPITTING A SOFTNOSE GOB OF LEAD TOWARDS TABLE SIX.
"WHZZZZ!" SAYS THE SOFTNOSE BULLET AS IT CROSSES THE ROOM AT TWICE THE SPEED OF SOUND.
"MOVE!" SAYS A LITTLE VOICE AT THE BACK OF BILLI OCTAVO'S MIND.
"MOVE OR YOU'RE, LIKE, DEAD!" IT ADDS.

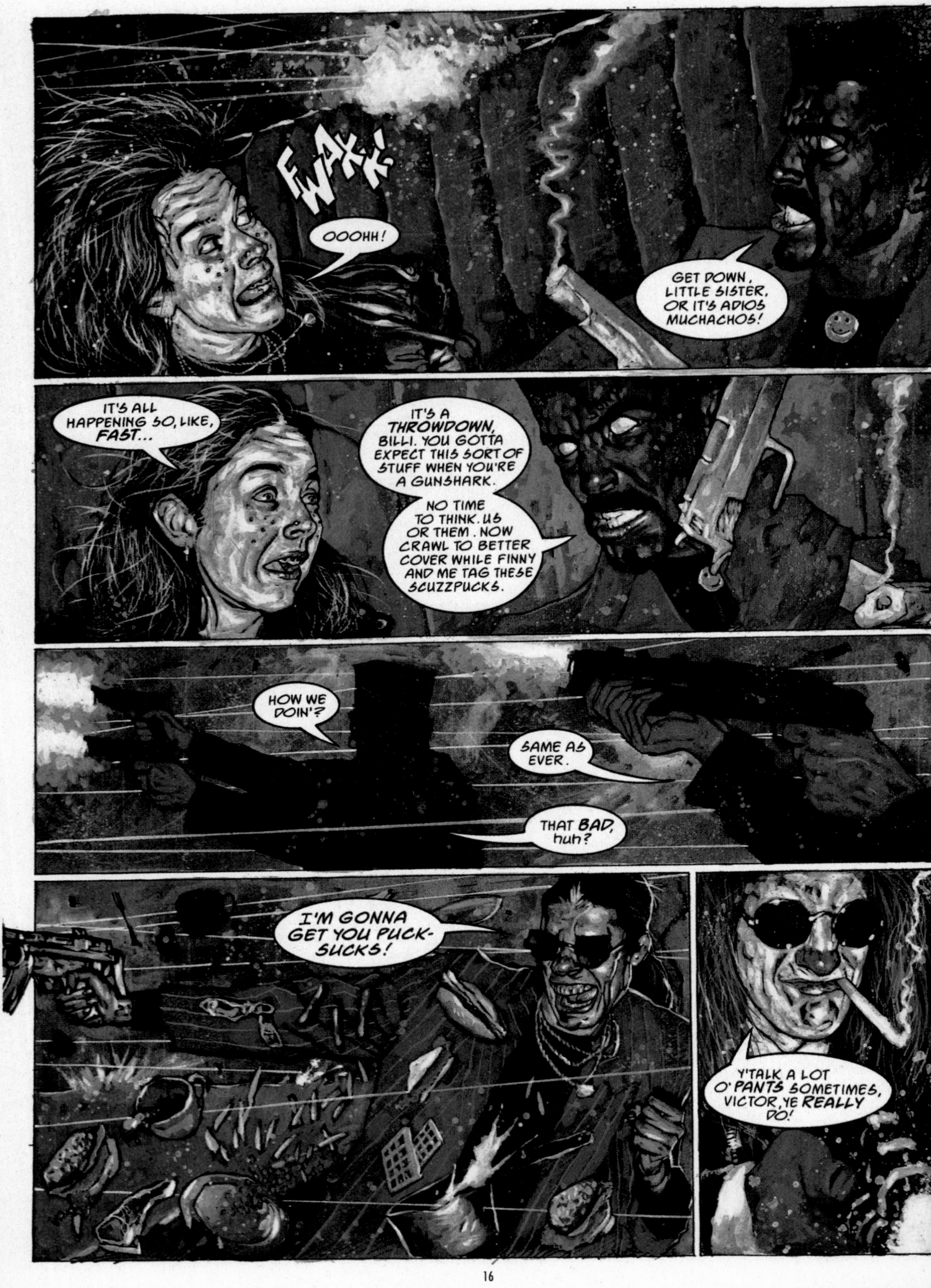
FWAXX!
OOOHH!
GET DOWN, LITTLE SISTER, OR IT'S ADIOS MUCHACHOS!
IT'S ALL HAPPENING SO, LIKE, FAST...
IT'S A THROWDOWN, BILLI. YOU GOTTA EXPECT THIS SORT OF STUFF WHEN YOU'RE A GUNSHARK.
NO TIME TO THINK. US OR THEM. NOW CRAWL TO BETTER COVER WHILE FINNY AND ME TAG THESE SCUZZPUCKS.
HOW WE DOIN'?
SAME AS EVER.
THAT BAD, huh?
I'M GONNA GET YOU PUCK-SUCKS!
Y'TALK A LOT O'PANTS SOMETIMES, VICTOR, YE REALLY DO!

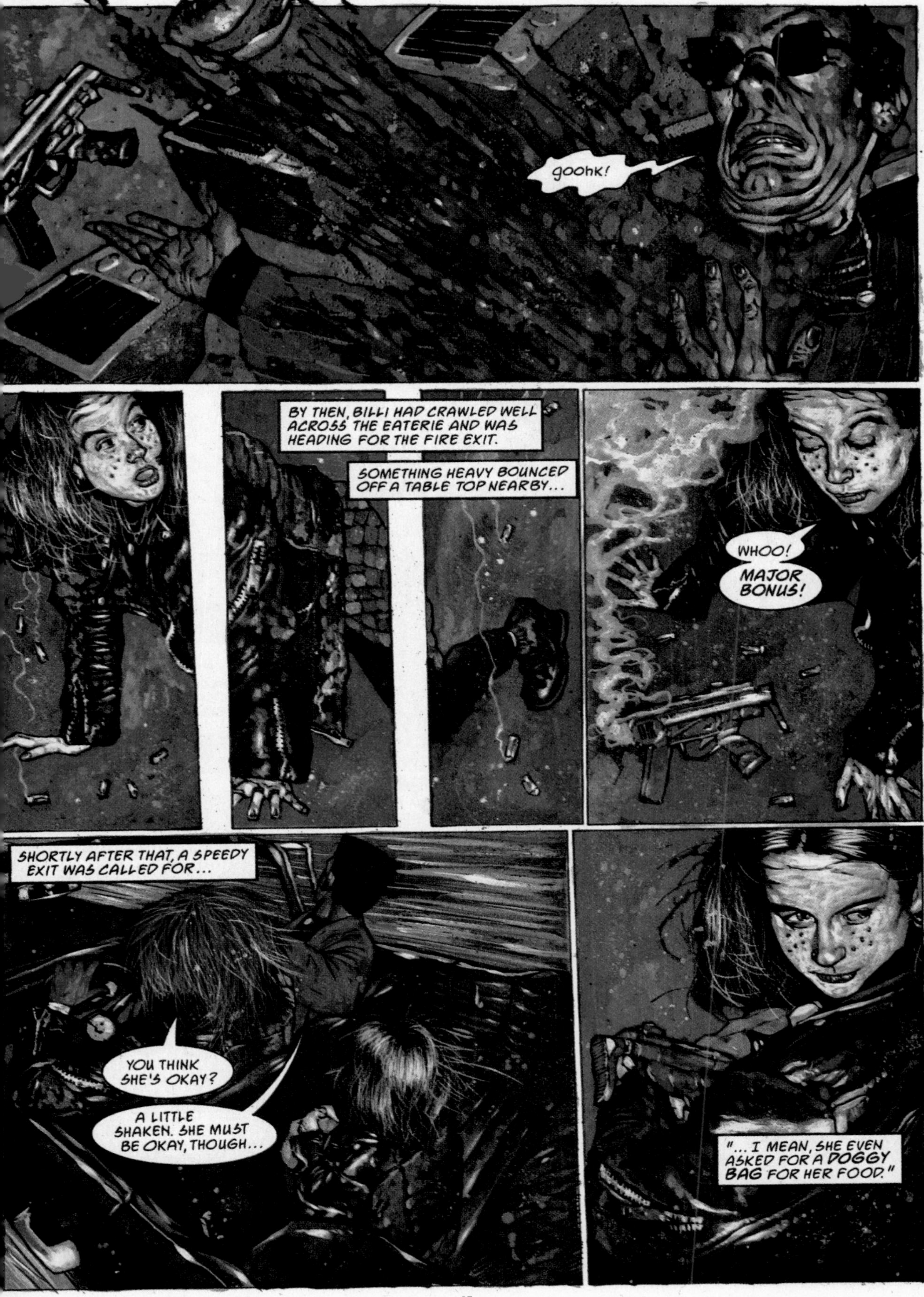
gOOhK!
BY THEN, BILLI HAD CRAWLED WELL ACROSS THE EATERIE AND WAS HEADING FOR THE FIRE EXIT.
SOMETHING HEAVY BOUNCED OFF A TABLE TOP NEARBY...
WHOO! MAJOR BONUS!
SHORTLY AFTER THAT, A SPEEDY EXIT WAS CALLED FOR...
YOU THINK SHE'S OKAY?
A LITTLE SHAKEN. SHE MUST BE OKAY, THOUGH...
"... I MEAN, SHE EVEN ASKED FOR A DOGGY BAG FOR HER FOOD."

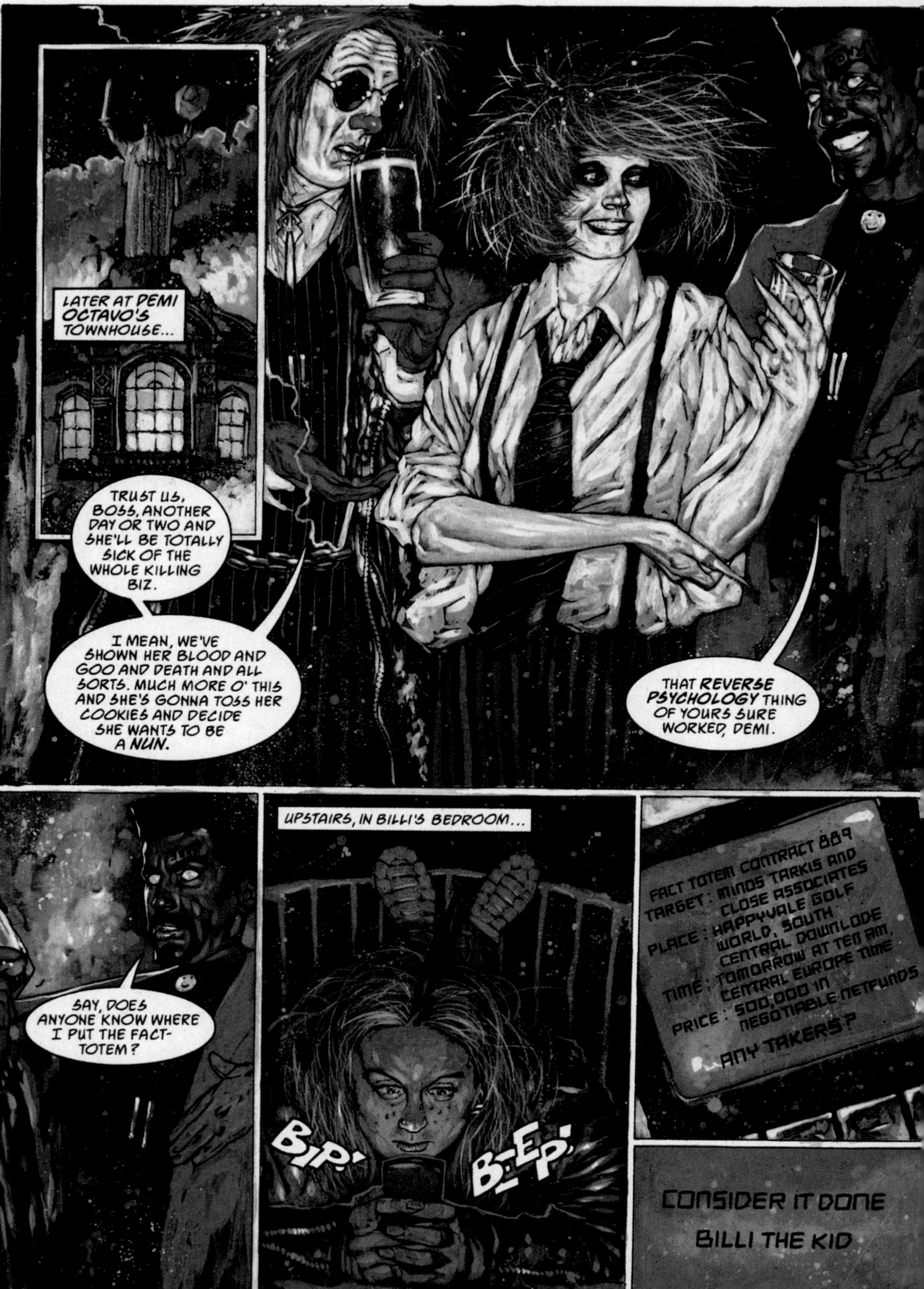
LATER AT DEMI OCTAVO'S TOWNHOUSE...
TRUST US, BOSS, ANOTHER DAY OR TWO AND SHE'LL BE TOTALLY SICK OF THE WHOLE KILLING BIZ.
I MEAN, WE'VE SHOWN HER BLOOD AND GOO AND DEATH AND ALL SORTS. MUCH MORE O' THIS AND SHE'S GONNA TOSS HER COOKIES AND DECIDE SHE WANTS TO BE A NUN.
THAT REVERSE PSYCHOLOGY THING OF YOURS SURE WORKED, DEMI.
SAY, DOES ANYONE KNOW WHERE I PUT THE FACT-TOTEM?
UPSTAIRS, IN BILLI'S BEDROOM...
BIP!
BEEP!
FACT TOTEM CONTRACT 889
TARGET: MINOS TARKIS AND CLOSE ASSOCIATES
PLACE: HAPPYVALE GOLF WORLD, SOUTH CENTRAL DOWNLODE
TIME: TOMORROW AT TEN AM, CENTRAL EUROPE TIME
PRICE: 500,000 IN NEGOTIABLE NETFUNDS
ANY TAKERS?
CONSIDER IT DONE
BILLI THE KID

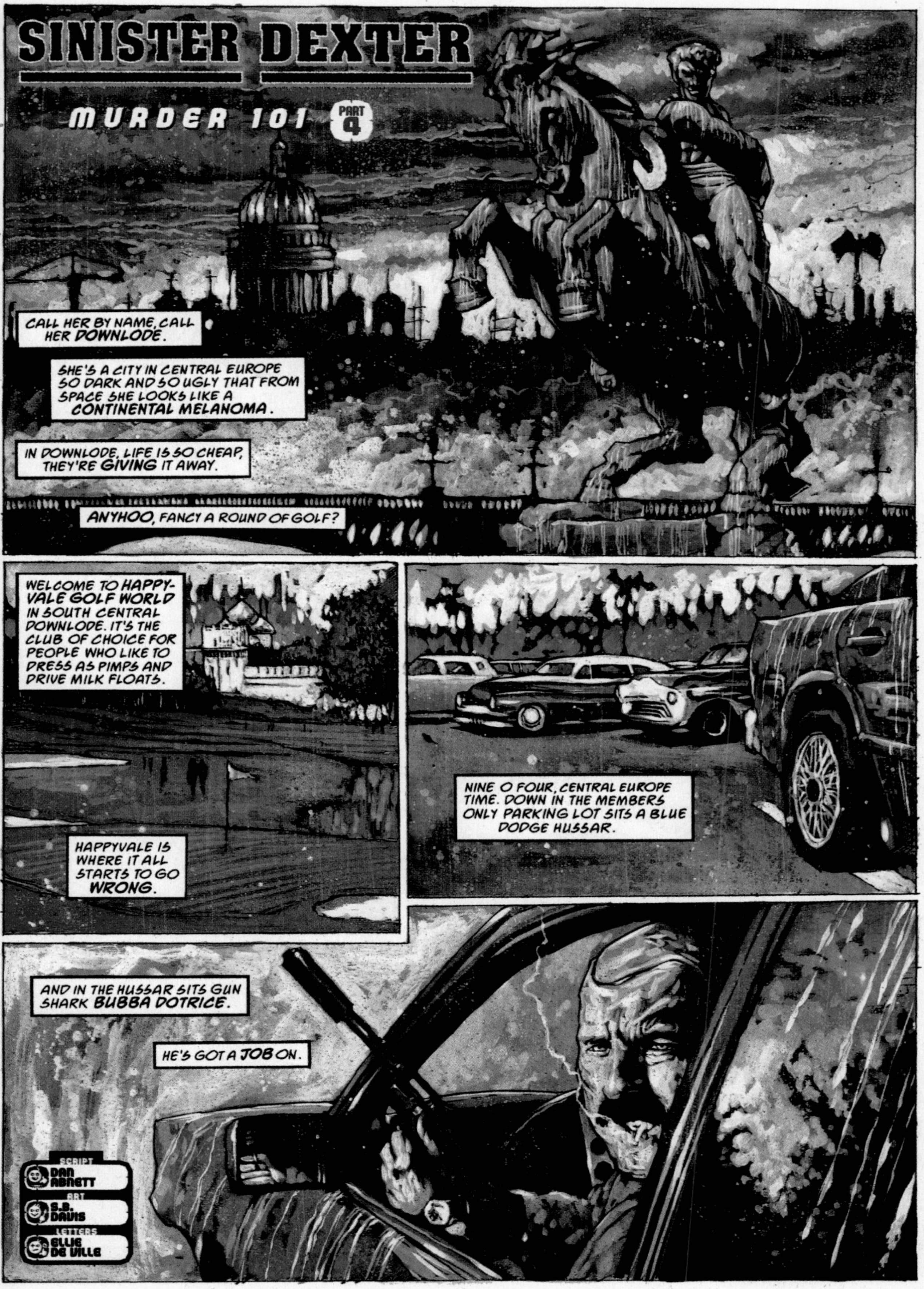
SINISTER DEXTER
MURDER 101 PART 4
CALL HER BY NAME, CALL HER DOWNLODE.
SHE'S A CITY IN CENTRAL EUROPE SO DARK AND SO UGLY THAT FROM SPACE SHE LOOKS LIKE A CONTINENTAL MELANOMA.
IN DOWNLODE, LIFE IS SO CHEAP, THEY'RE GIVING IT AWAY.
ANYHOO, FANCY A ROUND OF GOLF?
WELCOME TO HAPPY-VALE GOLF WORLD IN SOUTH CENTRAL DOWNLODE. IT'S THE CLUB OF CHOICE FOR PEOPLE WHO LIKE TO DRESS AS PIMPS AND DRIVE MILK FLOATS.
HAPPYVALE IS WHERE IT ALL STARTS TO GO WRONG.
NINE O FOUR, CENTRAL EUROPE TIME. DOWN IN THE MEMBERS ONLY PARKING LOT SITS A BLUE DODGE HUSSAR.
AND IN THE HUSSAR SITS GUN SHARK BUBBA DOTRICE.
HE'S GOT A JOB ON.
SCRIPT
DAN ABNETT
ART
S.B. DAVIS
LETTERS
ELLIE DE VILLE

AT NINE THIRTY FOUR, *MINOS TARKIS*, HIGH KING OF THE ADRIATIC PORN EMPIRE, ARRIVES FOR A ROUND WITH THE CLUB PRO.

AT NINE FORTY TWO, TARKIS AND HIS GOONS GET INTO A HEATED DEBATE WITH A PARTY OF AD MEN ABOUT WHO HAD BOOKED WHICH CADDY.

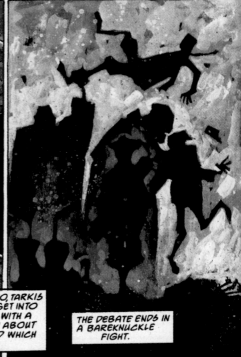

THE DEBATE ENDS IN A BAREKNUCKLE FIGHT.

WHICH IS WHY MINOS TARKIS DOESN'T MAKE IT OUT ONTO THE COURSE AT THE APPOINTED TIME.

THIS DOESN'T PLEASE BUBBA DOTRICE MUCH. HE IS WORKING TO A *TIGHT SCHEDULE* OBTAINED THE NIGHT BEFORE FROM HIS *FACT-TOTEM*, A NET LINK FOR CONTRACT KILLERS ACROSS THE CITY...

IT HAD SAID...

FACT-TOTEM CONTRACT 886
TARGET: MINOS TARKIS AND
CLOSE ASSOCIATES
PLACE: HAPPY VALLEY WORLD,
SOUTH CENTRAL DOWNLOE
TIME: TOMORROW, 10:10AM,
CENTRAL EUROPE TIME
PRICE: 500,000 IN NEGOTIABLE
NETFUNDS

ANY TAKERS?

DOTRICE ISN'T THE ONLY ONE.

THANKS TO THAT FACT-TOTEM MESSAGE, THE BUNKER AT THE SEVENTH HAS BECOME A LITTLE MORE *HAZARDOUS* THAN USUAL.

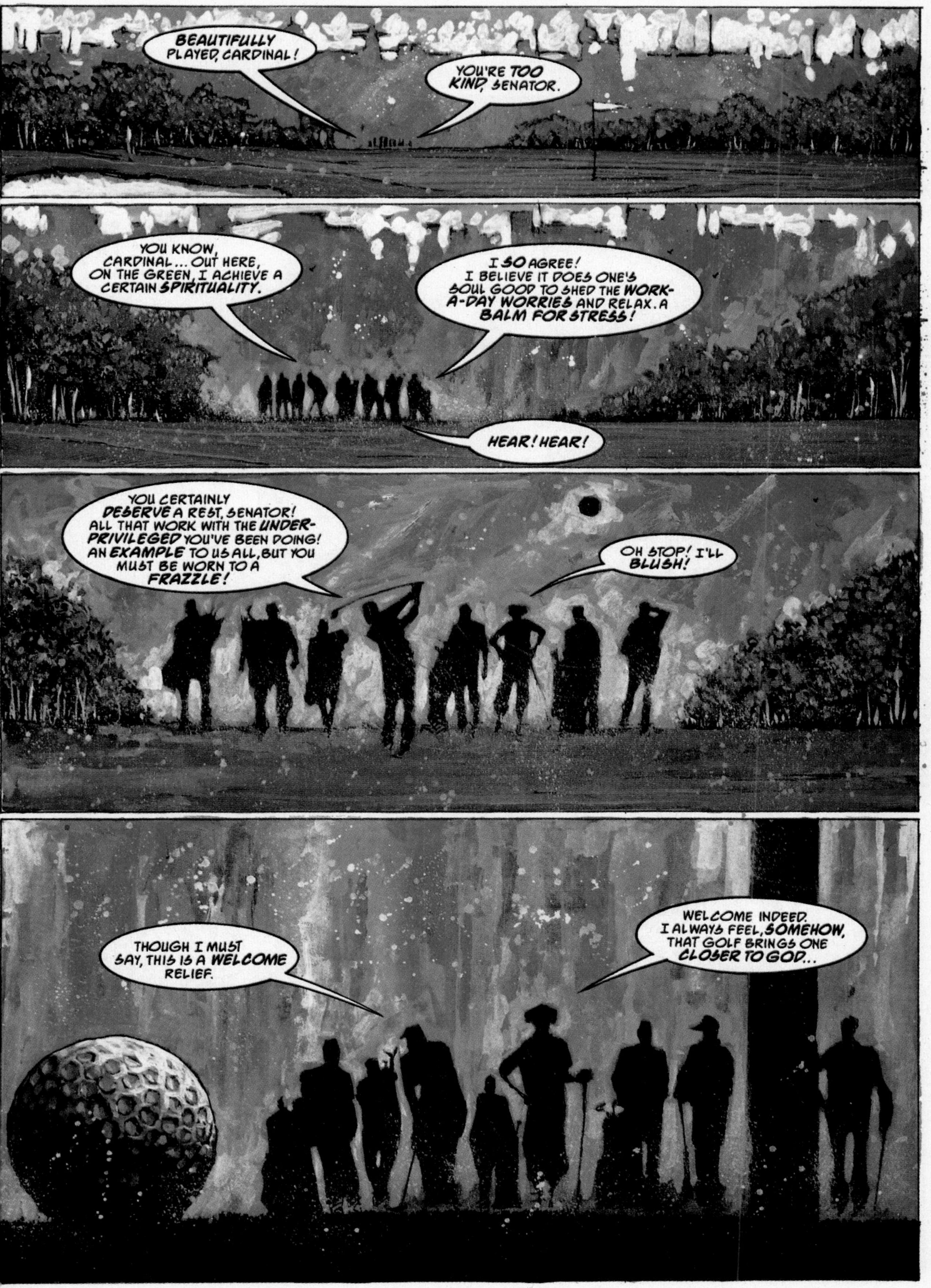
BEAUTIFULLY PLAYED, CARDINAL!
YOU'RE TOO KIND, SENATOR.
YOU KNOW, CARDINAL... OUT HERE, ON THE GREEN, I ACHIEVE A CERTAIN SPIRITUALITY.
I SO AGREE! I BELIEVE IT DOES ONE'S SOUL GOOD TO SHED THE WORK-A-DAY WORRIES AND RELAX. A BALM FOR STRESS!
HEAR! HEAR!
YOU CERTAINLY DESERVE A REST, SENATOR! ALL THAT WORK WITH THE UNDER-PRIVILEGED YOU'VE BEEN DOING! AN EXAMPLE TO US ALL, BUT YOU MUST BE WORN TO A FRAZZLE!
OH STOP! I'LL BLUSH!
THOUGH I MUST SAY, THIS IS A WELCOME RELIEF.
WELCOME INDEED. I ALWAYS FEEL, SOMEHOW, THAT GOLF BRINGS ONE CLOSER TO GOD...

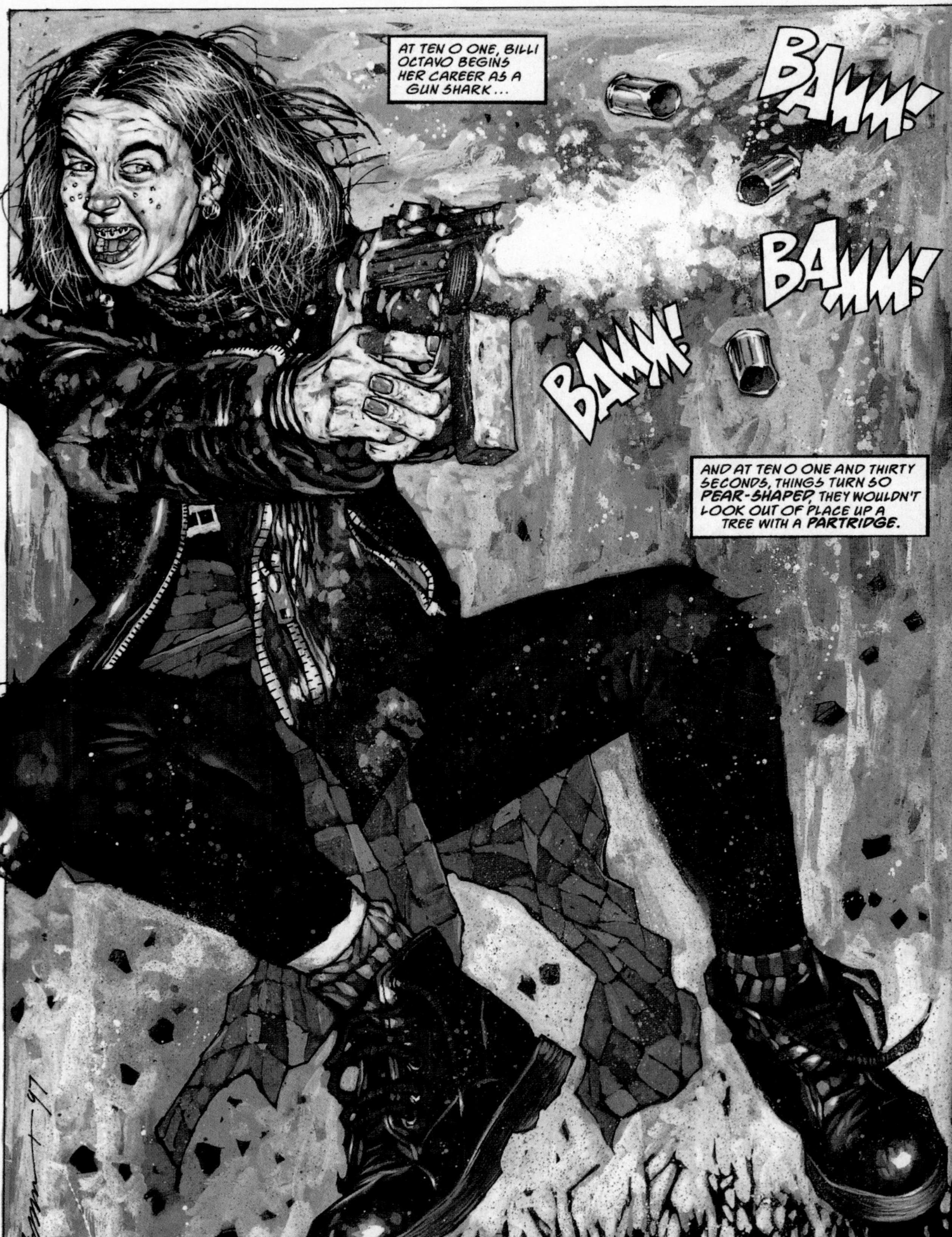
AT TEN O ONE, BILLI OCTAVO BEGINS HER CAREER AS A GUN SHARK...
BAMM!
BAMM!
BAMM!
AND AT TEN O ONE AND THIRTY SECONDS, THINGS TURN SO PEAR-SHAPED, THEY WOULDN'T LOOK OUT OF PLACE UP A TREE WITH A PARTRIDGE.

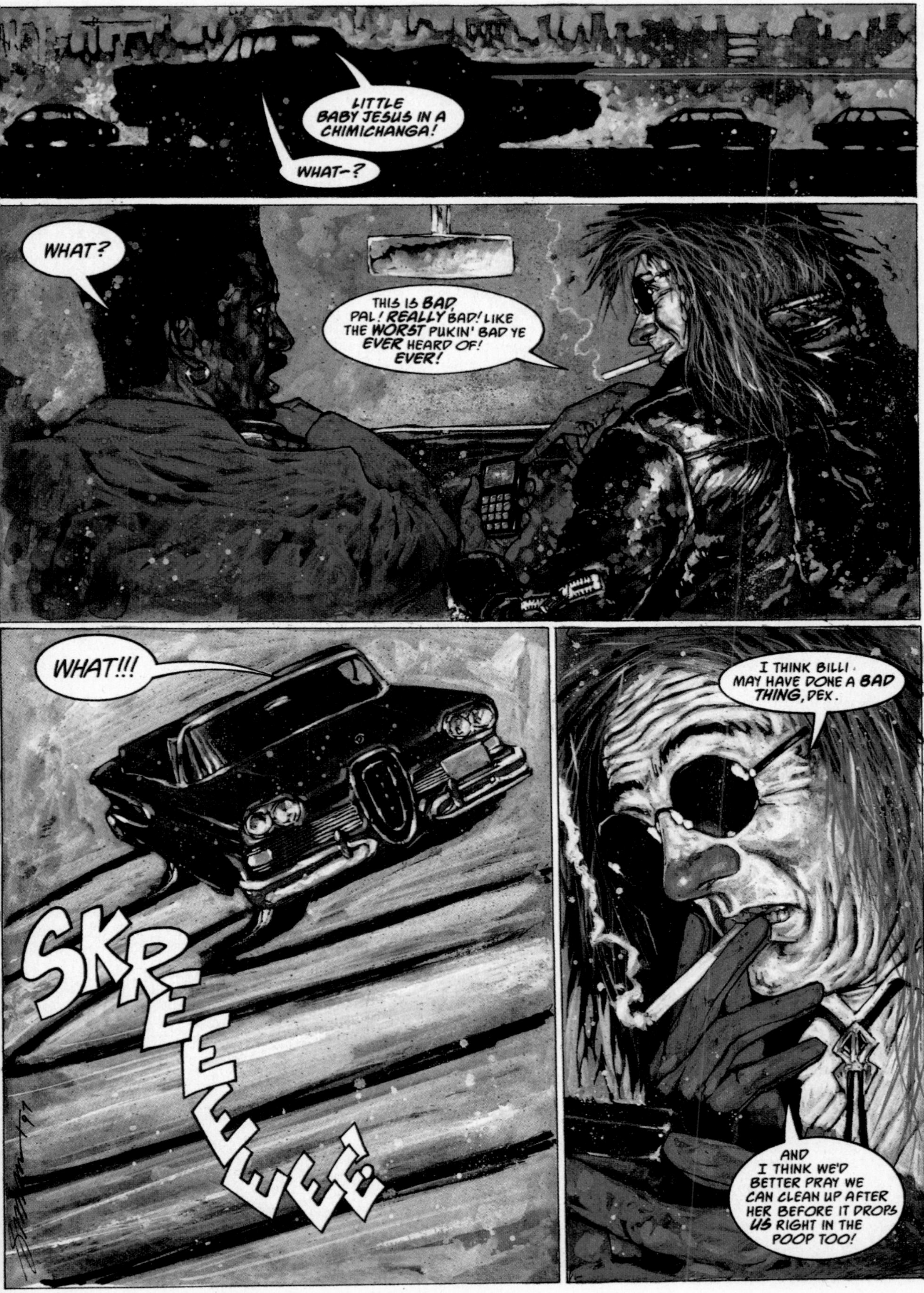
LITTLE BABY JESUS IN A CHIMICHANGA!
WHAT-?
WHAT?
THIS IS BAD PAL! REALLY BAD! LIKE THE WORST PUKIN' BAD YE EVER HEARD OF! EVER!
WHAT!!!
SKREEEEEE!
I THINK BILLI MAY HAVE DONE A BAD THING, DEX.
AND I THINK WE'D BETTER PRAY WE CAN CLEAN UP AFTER HER BEFORE IT DROPS US RIGHT IN THE POOP TOO!

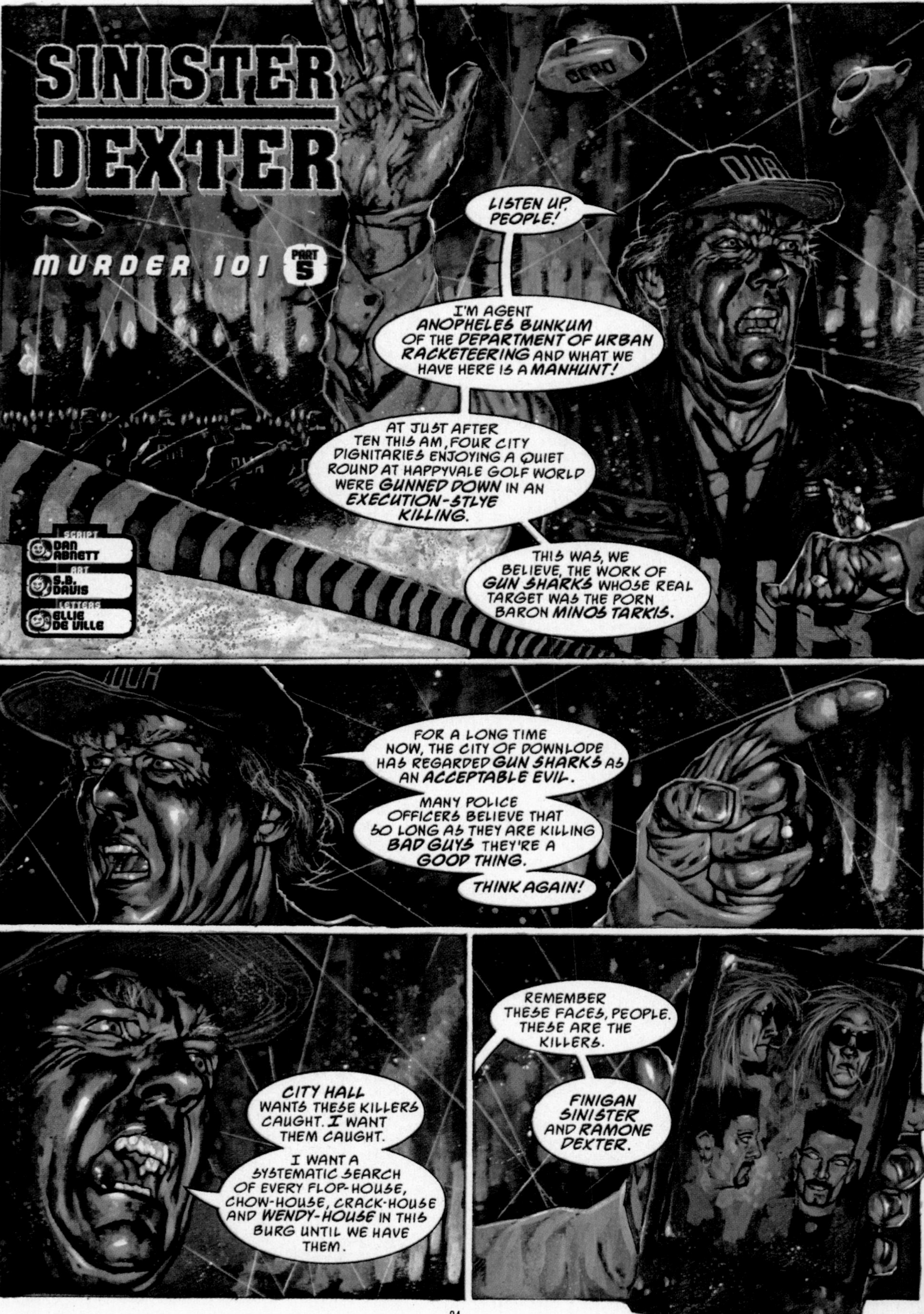
SINISTER DEXTER
MURDER 101 PART 5
SCRIPT DAN ABNETT
ART S.B. DAVIS
LETTERS ELLIE DE VILLE
LISTEN UP, PEOPLE!
I'M AGENT ANOPHELES BUNKUM OF THE DEPARTMENT OF URBAN RACKETEERING AND WHAT WE HAVE HERE IS A MANHUNT!
AT JUST AFTER TEN THIS AM, FOUR CITY DIGNITARIES ENJOYING A QUIET ROUND AT HAPPYVALE GOLF WORLD WERE GUNNED DOWN IN AN EXECUTION-STLYE KILLING.
THIS WAS, WE BELIEVE, THE WORK OF GUN SHARKS WHOSE REAL TARGET WAS THE PORN BARON MINOS TARKIS.
FOR A LONG TIME NOW, THE CITY OF DOWNLODE HAS REGARDED GUN SHARKS AS AN ACCEPTABLE EVIL.
MANY POLICE OFFICERS BELIEVE THAT SO LONG AS THEY ARE KILLING BAD GUYS THEY'RE A GOOD THING.
THINK AGAIN!
CITY HALL WANTS THESE KILLERS CAUGHT. I WANT THEM CAUGHT.
I WANT A SYSTEMATIC SEARCH OF EVERY FLOP-HOUSE, CHOW-HOUSE, CRACK-HOUSE AND WENDY-HOUSE IN THIS BURG UNTIL WE HAVE THEM.
REMEMBER THESE FACES, PEOPLE. THESE ARE THE KILLERS.
FINIGAN SINISTER AND RAMONE DEXTER.

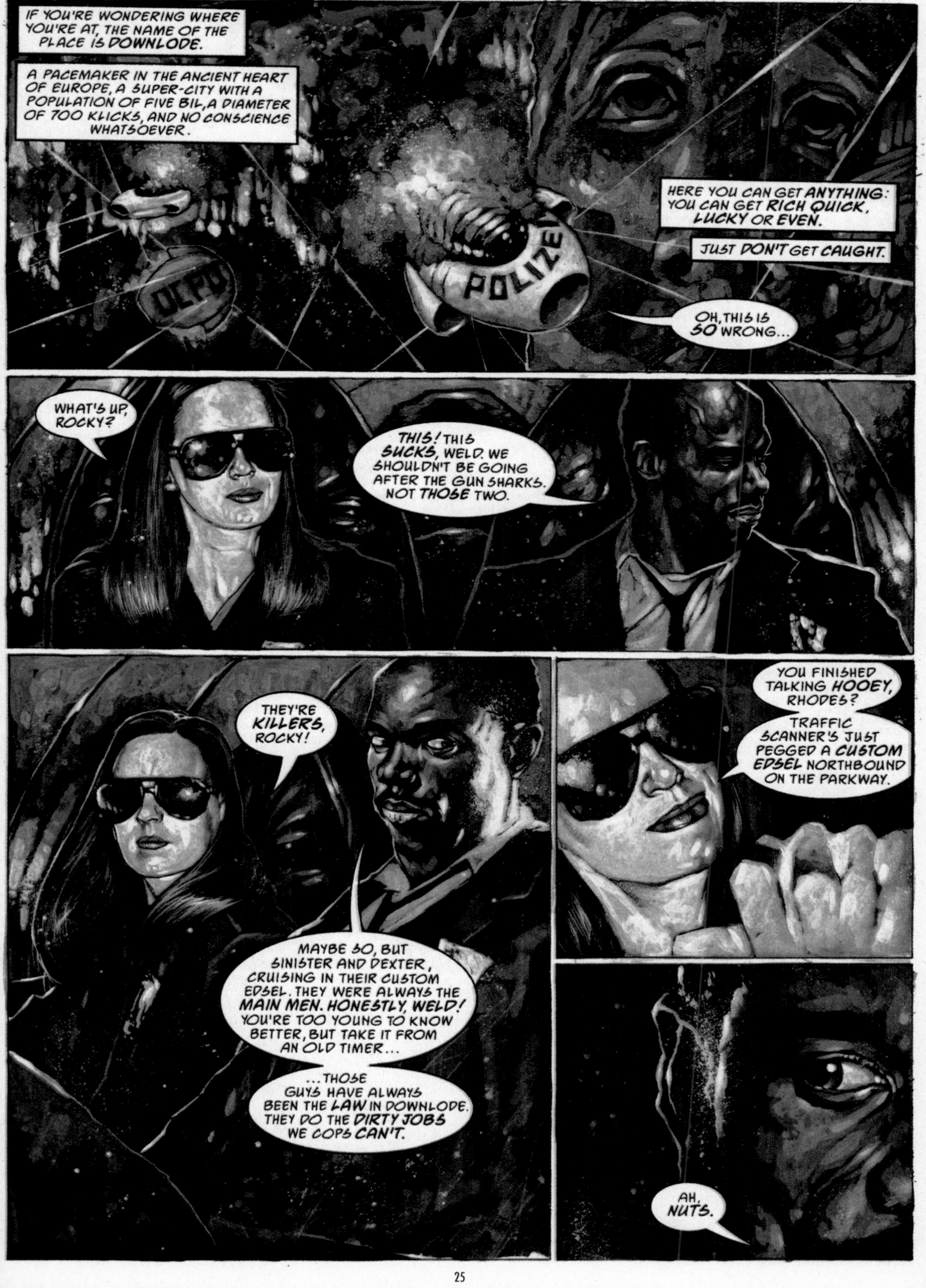
IF YOU'RE WONDERING WHERE YOU'RE AT, THE NAME OF THE PLACE IS DOWNLODE.
A PACEMAKER IN THE ANCIENT HEART OF EUROPE, A SUPER-CITY WITH A POPULATION OF FIVE BIL, A DIAMETER OF 700 KLICKS, AND NO CONSCIENCE WHATSOEVER.
HERE YOU CAN GET ANYTHING: YOU CAN GET RICH QUICK, LUCKY OR EVEN.
JUST DON'T GET CAUGHT.
POLIZEI
OH, THIS IS SO WRONG...
WHAT'S UP, ROCKY?
THIS! THIS SUCKS, WELD. WE SHOULDN'T BE GOING AFTER THE GUN SHARKS. NOT THOSE TWO.
THEY'RE KILLERS, ROCKY!
MAYBE SO, BUT SINISTER AND DEXTER, CRUISING IN THEIR CUSTOM EDSEL. THEY WERE ALWAYS THE MAIN MEN. HONESTLY, WELD! YOU'RE TOO YOUNG TO KNOW BETTER, BUT TAKE IT FROM AN OLD TIMER...
...THOSE GUYS HAVE ALWAYS BEEN THE LAW IN DOWNLODE. THEY DO THE DIRTY JOBS WE COPS CAN'T.
YOU FINISHED TALKING HOOEY, RHODES?
TRAFFIC SCANNER'S JUST PEGGED A CUSTOM EDSEL NORTHBOUND ON THE PARKWAY.
AH, NUTS.

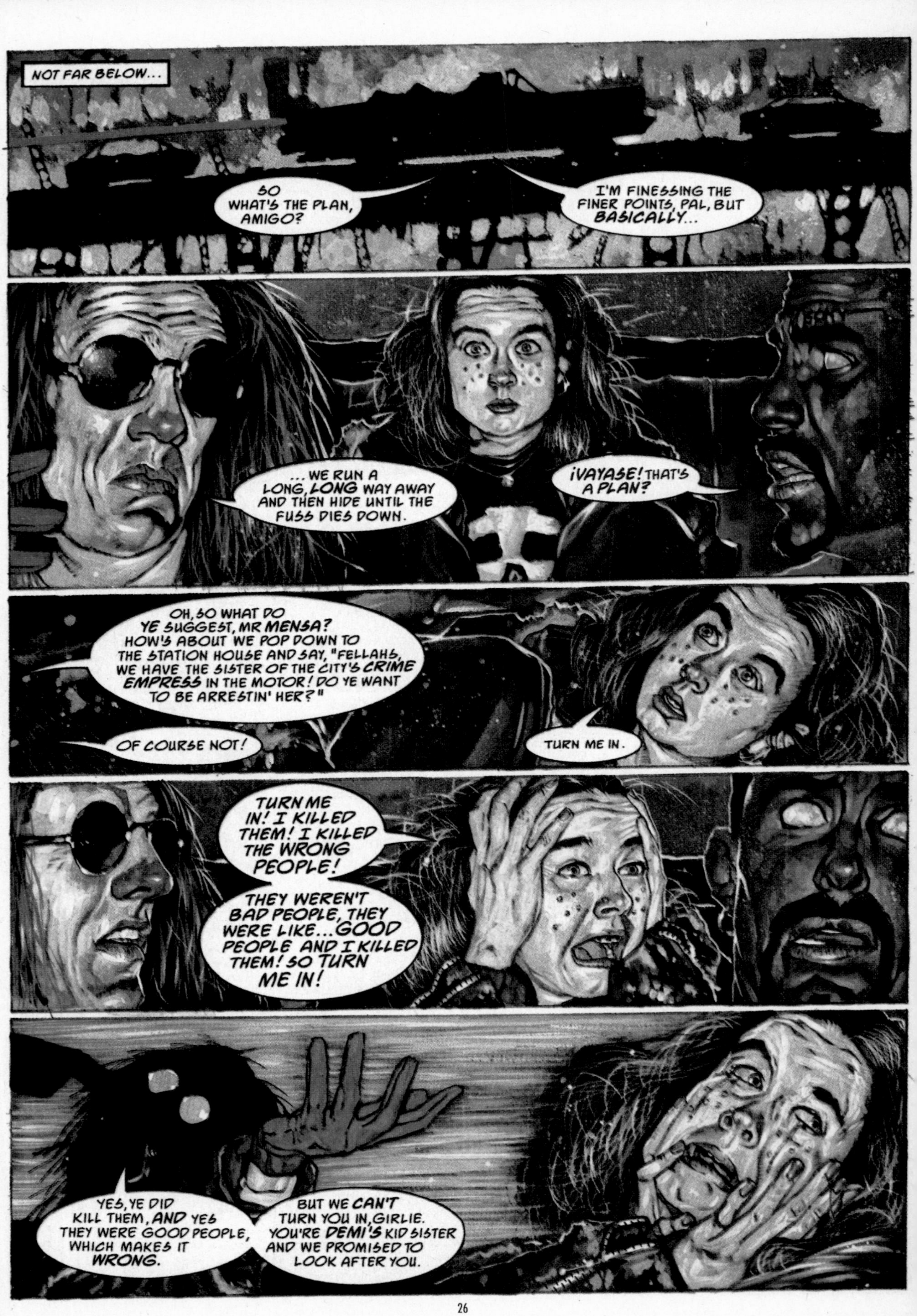
NOT FAR BELOW...
SO WHAT'S THE PLAN, AMIGO?
I'M FINESSING THE FINER POINTS, PAL, BUT BASICALLY...
...WE RUN A LONG, LONG WAY AWAY AND THEN HIDE UNTIL THE FUSS DIES DOWN.
¡VAYASE! THAT'S A PLAN?
OH, SO WHAT DO YE SUGGEST, MR MENSA? HOW'S ABOUT WE POP DOWN TO THE STATION HOUSE AND SAY, "FELLAHS, WE HAVE THE SISTER OF THE CITY'S CRIME EMPRESS IN THE MOTOR! DO YE WANT TO BE ARRESTIN' HER?"
OF COURSE NOT!
TURN ME IN.
TURN ME IN! I KILLED THEM! I KILLED THE WRONG PEOPLE!
THEY WEREN'T BAD PEOPLE, THEY WERE LIKE...GOOD PEOPLE AND I KILLED THEM! SO TURN ME IN!
YES, YE DID KILL THEM, AND YES THEY WERE GOOD PEOPLE, WHICH MAKES IT WRONG.
BUT WE CAN'T TURN YOU IN, GIRLIE. YOU'RE DEMI'S KID SISTER AND WE PROMISED TO LOOK AFTER YOU.

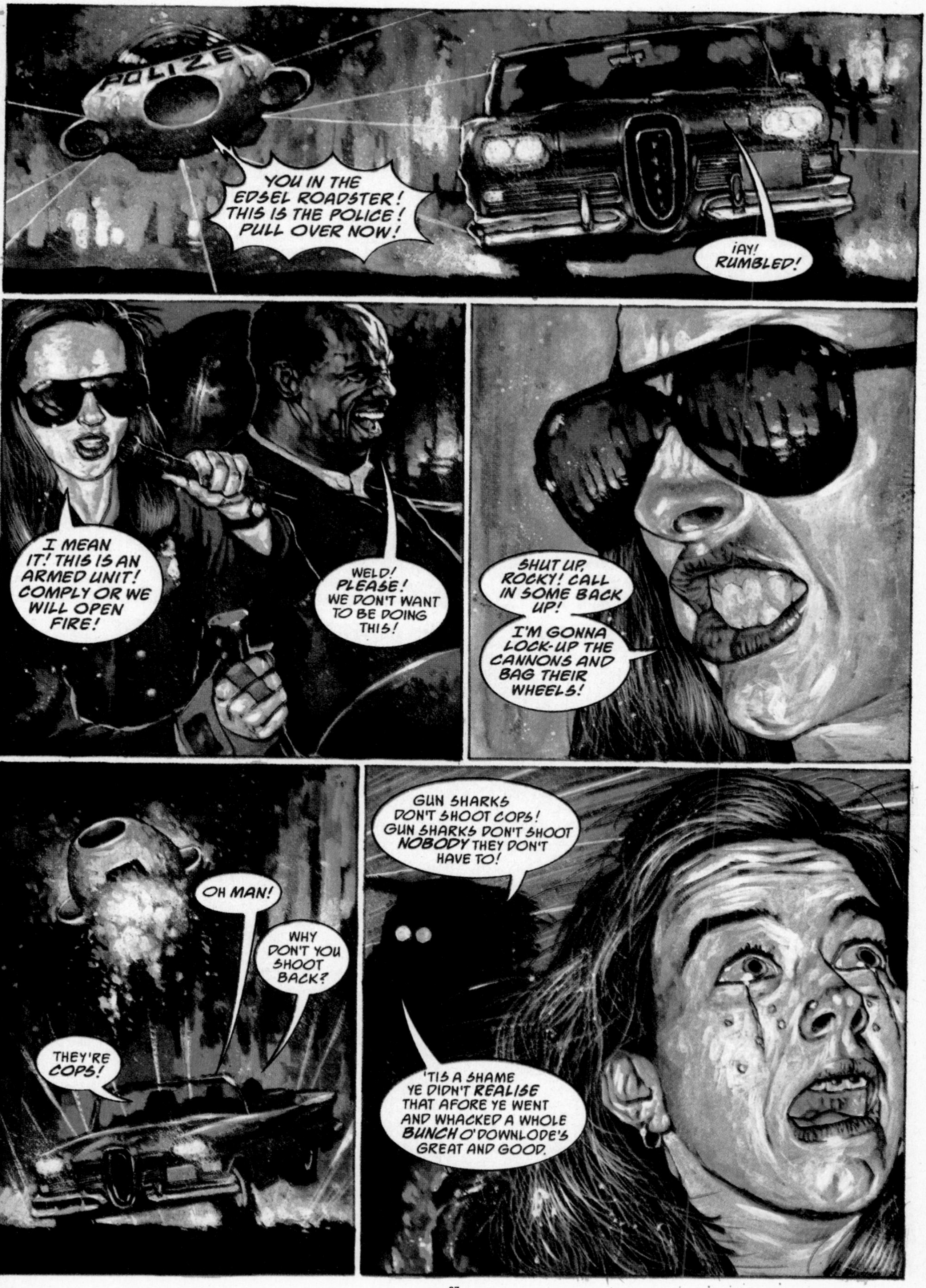
POLIZEI
YOU IN THE EDSEL ROADSTER! THIS IS THE POLICE! PULL OVER NOW!
¡AY! RUMBLED!
I MEAN IT! THIS IS AN ARMED UNIT! COMPLY OR WE WILL OPEN FIRE!
WELD! PLEASE! WE DON'T WANT TO BE DOING THIS!
SHUT UP, ROCKY! CALL IN SOME BACK UP!
I'M GONNA LOCK-UP THE CANNONS AND BAG THEIR WHEELS!
OH MAN!
WHY DON'T YOU SHOOT BACK?
THEY'RE COPS!
GUN SHARKS DON'T SHOOT COPS! GUN SHARKS DON'T SHOOT NOBODY THEY DON'T HAVE TO!
'TIS A SHAME YE DIDN'T REALISE THAT AFORE YE WENT AND WHACKED A WHOLE BUNCH O' DOWNLODE'S GREAT AND GOOD.

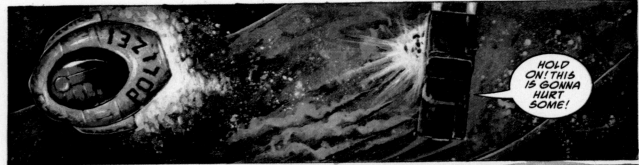

HOLD ON! THIS IS GONNA HURT SOME!

WHOOMMCHH!

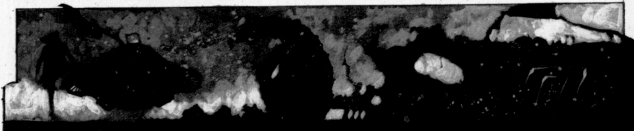

YOU IN THE CAR! I'M TRACY WELD OF THE D.C.P.D. SOUTH CENTRAL HOMICIDE!

SURRENDER YOUR WEAPONS AND STEP OUT WHERE I CAN SEE YOU!

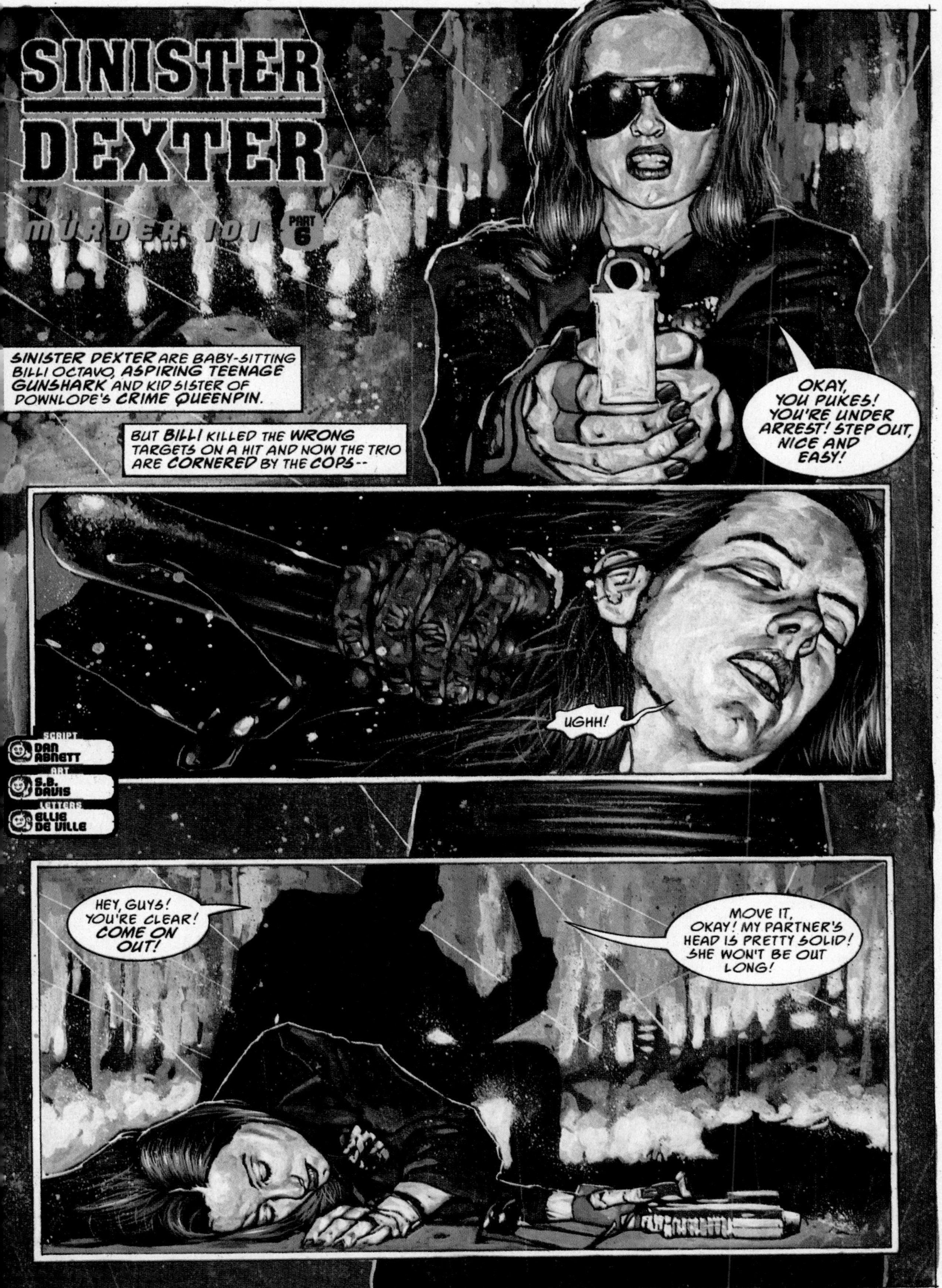
SINISTER DEXTER
MURDER 101 PART 6
SINISTER DEXTER ARE BABY-SITTING BILLI OCTAVO, ASPIRING TEENAGE GUNSHARK AND KID SISTER OF DOWNLODE'S CRIME QUEENPIN.
BUT BILLI KILLED THE WRONG TARGETS ON A HIT AND NOW THE TRIO ARE CORNERED BY THE COPS--
OKAY, YOU PUKES! YOU'RE UNDER ARREST! STEP OUT, NICE AND EASY!
UGHH!
SCRIPT DAN ABNETT
ART S.B. DAVIS
LETTERS ELLIE DE VILLE
HEY, GUYS! YOU'RE CLEAR! COME ON OUT!
MOVE IT, OKAY! MY PARTNER'S HEAD IS PRETTY SOLID! SHE WON'T BE OUT LONG!

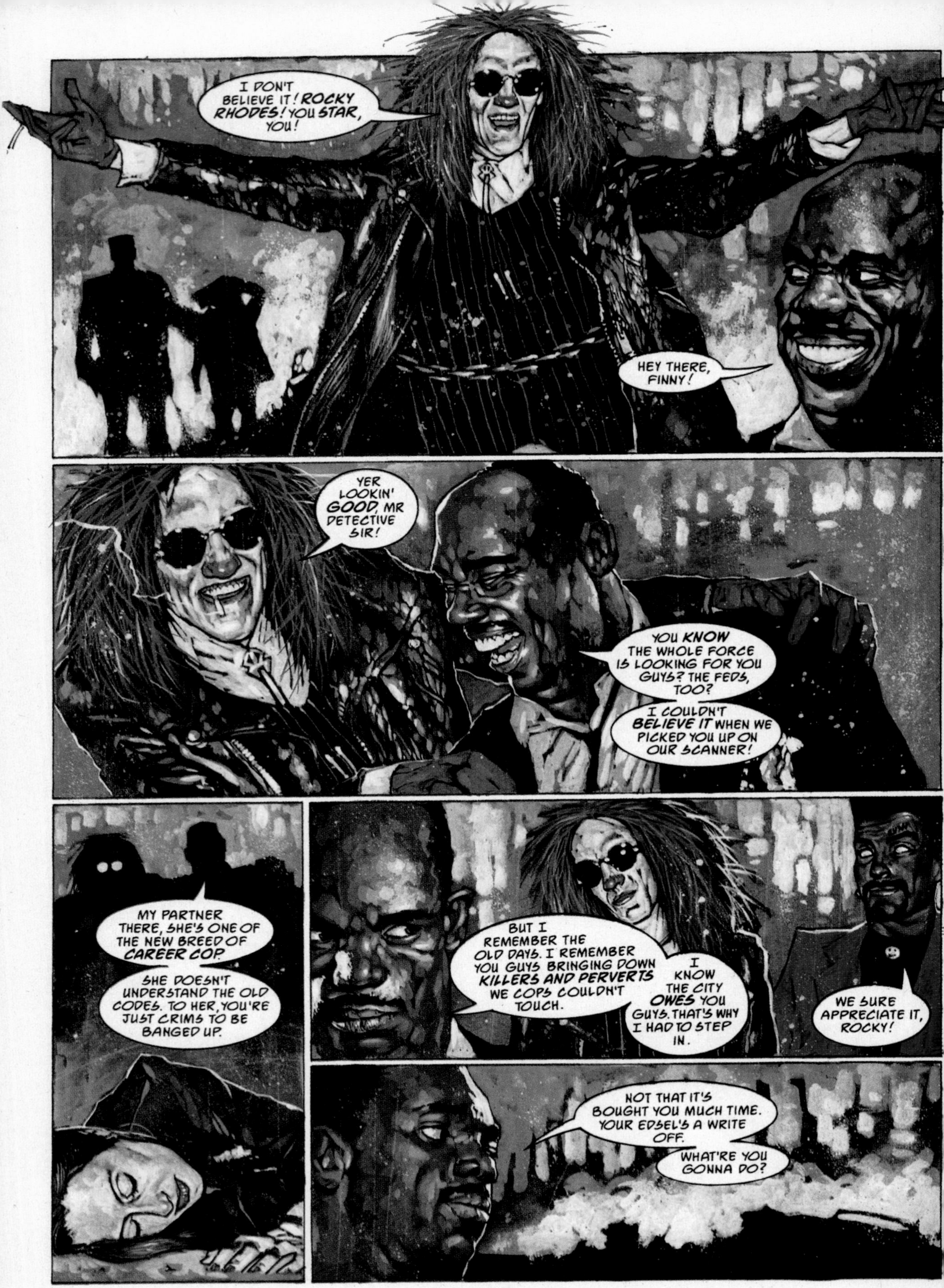
I DON'T BELIEVE IT! ROCKY RHODES! YOU STAR, YOU!
HEY THERE, FINNY!
YER LOOKIN' GOOD, MR DETECTIVE SIR!
YOU KNOW THE WHOLE FORCE IS LOOKING FOR YOU GUYS? THE FEDS, TOO?
I COULDN'T BELIEVE IT WHEN WE PICKED YOU UP ON OUR SCANNER!
MY PARTNER THERE, SHE'S ONE OF THE NEW BREED OF CAREER COP.
SHE DOESN'T UNDERSTAND THE OLD CODES. TO HER, YOU'RE JUST CRIMS TO BE BANGED UP.
BUT I REMEMBER THE OLD DAYS. I REMEMBER YOU GUYS BRINGING DOWN KILLERS AND PERVERTS WE COPS COULDN'T TOUCH.
I KNOW THE CITY OWES YOU GUYS. THAT'S WHY I HAD TO STEP IN.
WE SURE APPRECIATE IT, ROCKY!
NOT THAT IT'S BOUGHT YOU MUCH TIME. YOUR EDSEL'S A WRITE OFF.
WHAT'RE YOU GONNA DO?

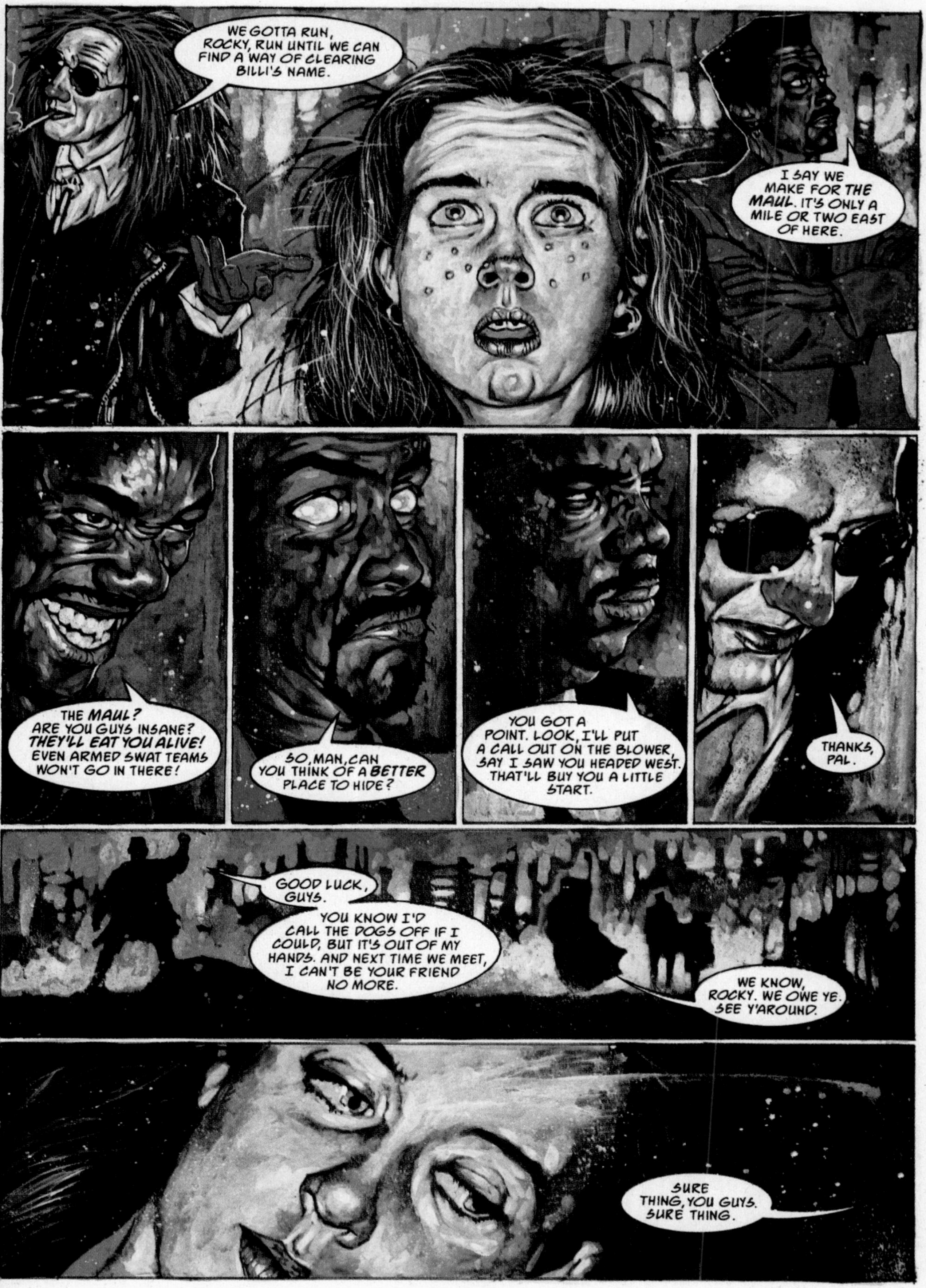

WE GOTTA RUN, ROCKY, RUN UNTIL WE CAN FIND A WAY OF CLEARING BILLI'S NAME.
I SAY WE MAKE FOR THE MAUL. IT'S ONLY A MILE OR TWO EAST OF HERE.
THE MAUL? ARE YOU GUYS INSANE? THEY'LL EAT YOU ALIVE! EVEN ARMED SWAT TEAMS WON'T GO IN THERE!
SO, MAN, CAN YOU THINK OF A BETTER PLACE TO HIDE?
YOU GOT A POINT. LOOK, I'LL PUT A CALL OUT ON THE BLOWER, SAY I SAW YOU HEADED WEST. THAT'LL BUY YOU A LITTLE START.
THANKS, PAL.
GOOD LUCK, GUYS.
YOU KNOW I'D CALL THE DOGS OFF IF I COULD, BUT IT'S OUT OF MY HANDS. AND NEXT TIME WE MEET, I CAN'T BE YOUR FRIEND NO MORE.
WE KNOW, ROCKY. WE OWE YE. SEE Y'AROUND.
SURE THING, YOU GUYS. SURE THING.

THEY WERE REPORTED HEADING WEST OFF THE PARKWAY, AGENT BUNKUM.

WAS THAT A POSITIVE MAKE?

YES, SIR.

THEN LET'S SHAKE IT, PEOPLE! MOBILISE AND CLOSE THAT NET!

GO! GO! GO!

YO, FELLAH?

I'M A LITTLE BUSY RIGHT NOW, FRIEND.

YOU WON'T CATCH 'EM, FELLAH. NOT YUH OR ANY OF YUH FANCY *SEARCH PATTERNS* AND *CRIMINAL PROFILING*.

AND WHY NOT?

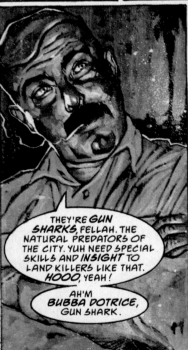

THEY'RE *GUN SHARKS*, FELLAH. THE NATURAL PREDATORS OF THE CITY. YUH NEED SPECIAL SKILLS AND *INSIGHT* TO LAND KILLERS LIKE THAT. *HOOO*, YEAH!

AH'M *BUBBA DOTRICE*, GUN SHARK.

AH WAS AFTER THAT TARKIS CONTRACT AT HAPPYVALE THIS AM. THANKS TO THAT PAIR, AH LOST OUT ON *FIVE HUND'D THOUSAND BIG ONES*.

AH FIGURE AH CAN HELP Y'ALL. AND AH FIGURE, HEY! IT'S PAY-BACK TIME.

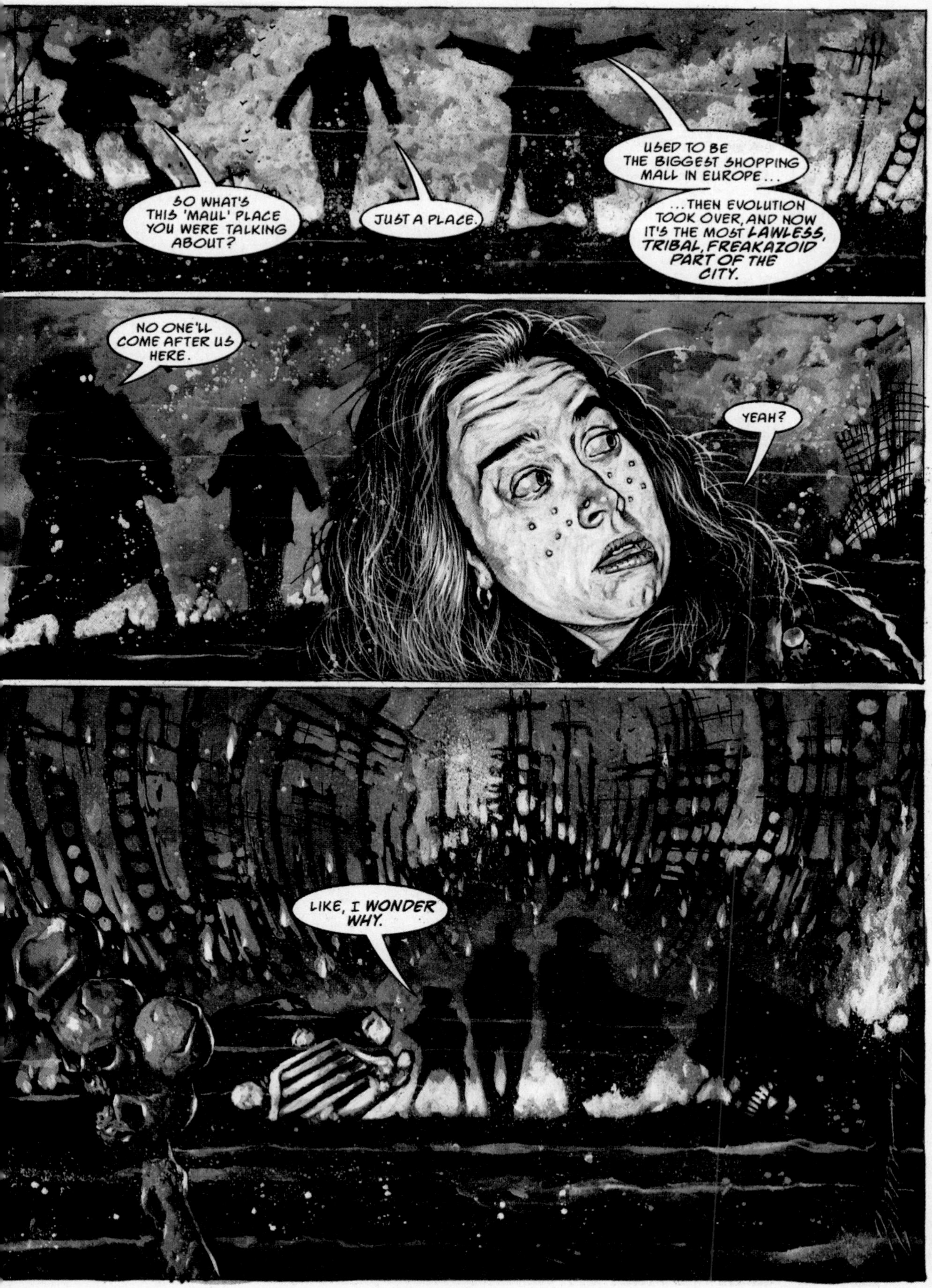
SO WHAT'S THIS 'MAUL' PLACE YOU WERE TALKING ABOUT?
JUST A PLACE.
USED TO BE THE BIGGEST SHOPPING MALL IN EUROPE...
...THEN EVOLUTION TOOK OVER, AND NOW IT'S THE MOST LAWLESS, TRIBAL, FREAKAZOID PART OF THE CITY.
NO ONE'LL COME AFTER US HERE.
YEAH?
LIKE, I WONDER WHY.

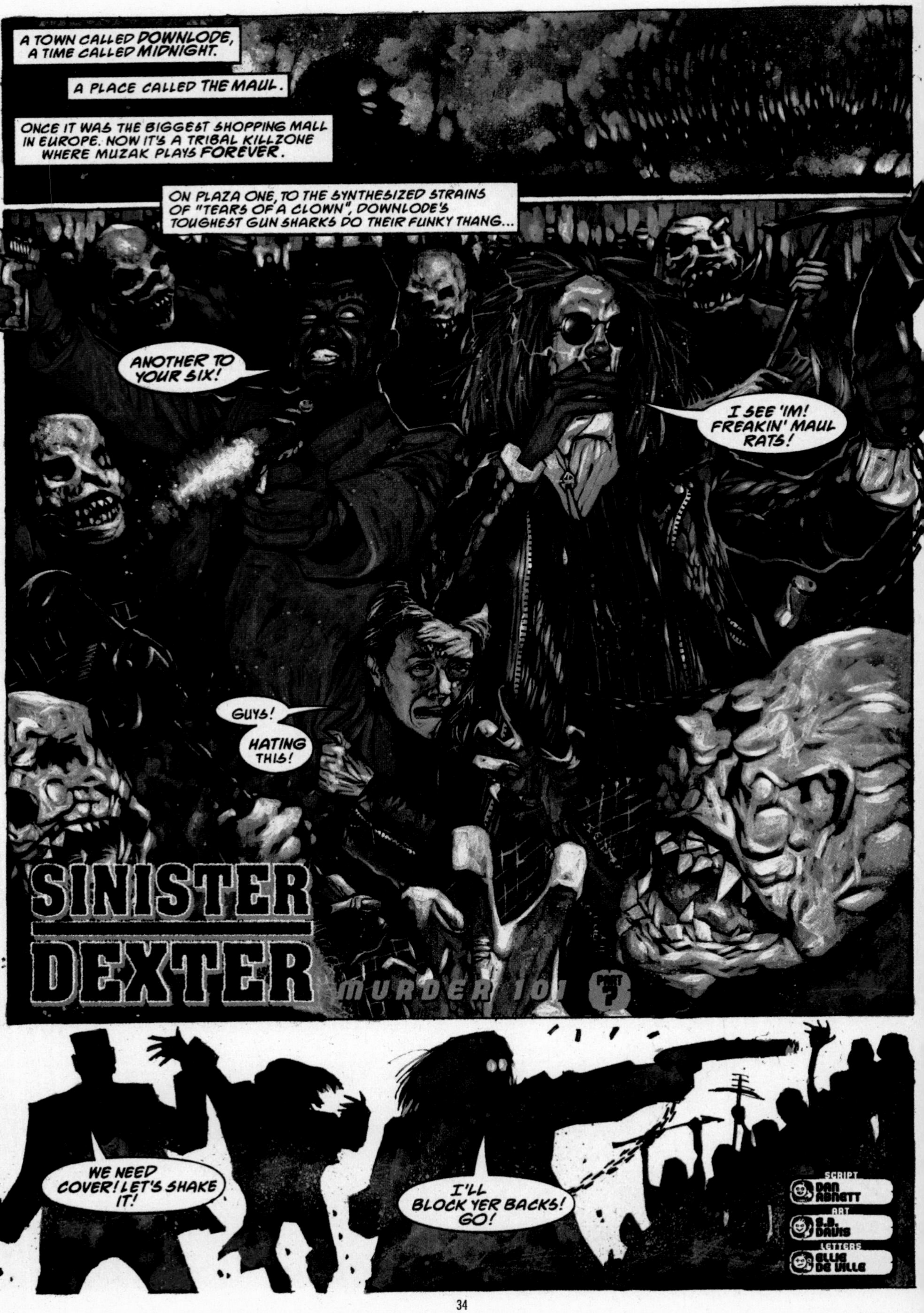
A TOWN CALLED DOWNLODE, A TIME CALLED MIDNIGHT.
A PLACE CALLED THE MAUL.
ONCE IT WAS THE BIGGEST SHOPPING MALL IN EUROPE. NOW IT'S A TRIBAL KILLZONE WHERE MUZAK PLAYS FOREVER.
ON PLAZA ONE, TO THE SYNTHESIZED STRAINS OF "TEARS OF A CLOWN", DOWNLODE'S TOUGHEST GUN SHARKS DO THEIR FUNKY THANG...
ANOTHER TO YOUR SIX!
I SEE 'IM! FREAKIN' MAUL RATS!
GUYS!
HATING THIS!
SINISTER DEXTER
MURDER 101
PART 7
WE NEED COVER! LET'S SHAKE IT!
I'LL BLOCK YER BACKS! GO!
SCRIPT DAN ABNETT
ART S.B. DAVIS
LETTERS ELLIE DE VILLE

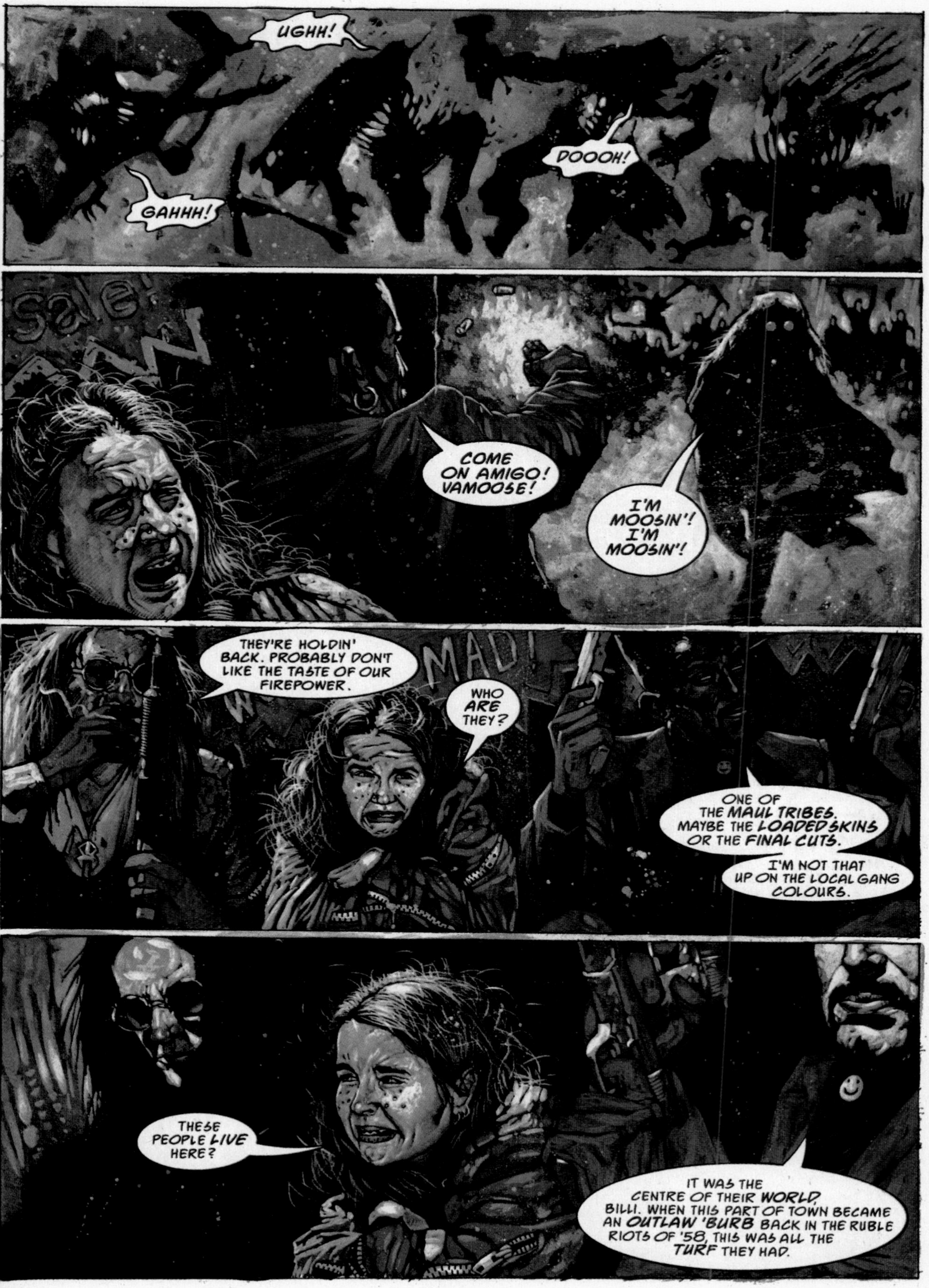
UGHH!
GAHHH!
DOOOH!
Sale!
COME ON AMIGO! VAMOOSE!
I'M MOOSIN'! I'M MOOSIN'!
THEY'RE HOLDIN' BACK. PROBABLY DON'T LIKE THE TASTE OF OUR FIREPOWER.
MAD!
WHO ARE THEY?
ONE OF THE MAUL TRIBES. MAYBE THE LOADED SKINS OR THE FINAL CUTS.
I'M NOT THAT UP ON THE LOCAL GANG COLOURS.
THESE PEOPLE LIVE HERE?
IT WAS THE CENTRE OF THEIR WORLD, BILLI. WHEN THIS PART OF TOWN BECAME AN OUTLAW 'BURB BACK IN THE RUBLE RIOTS OF '58, THIS WAS ALL THE TURF THEY HAD.

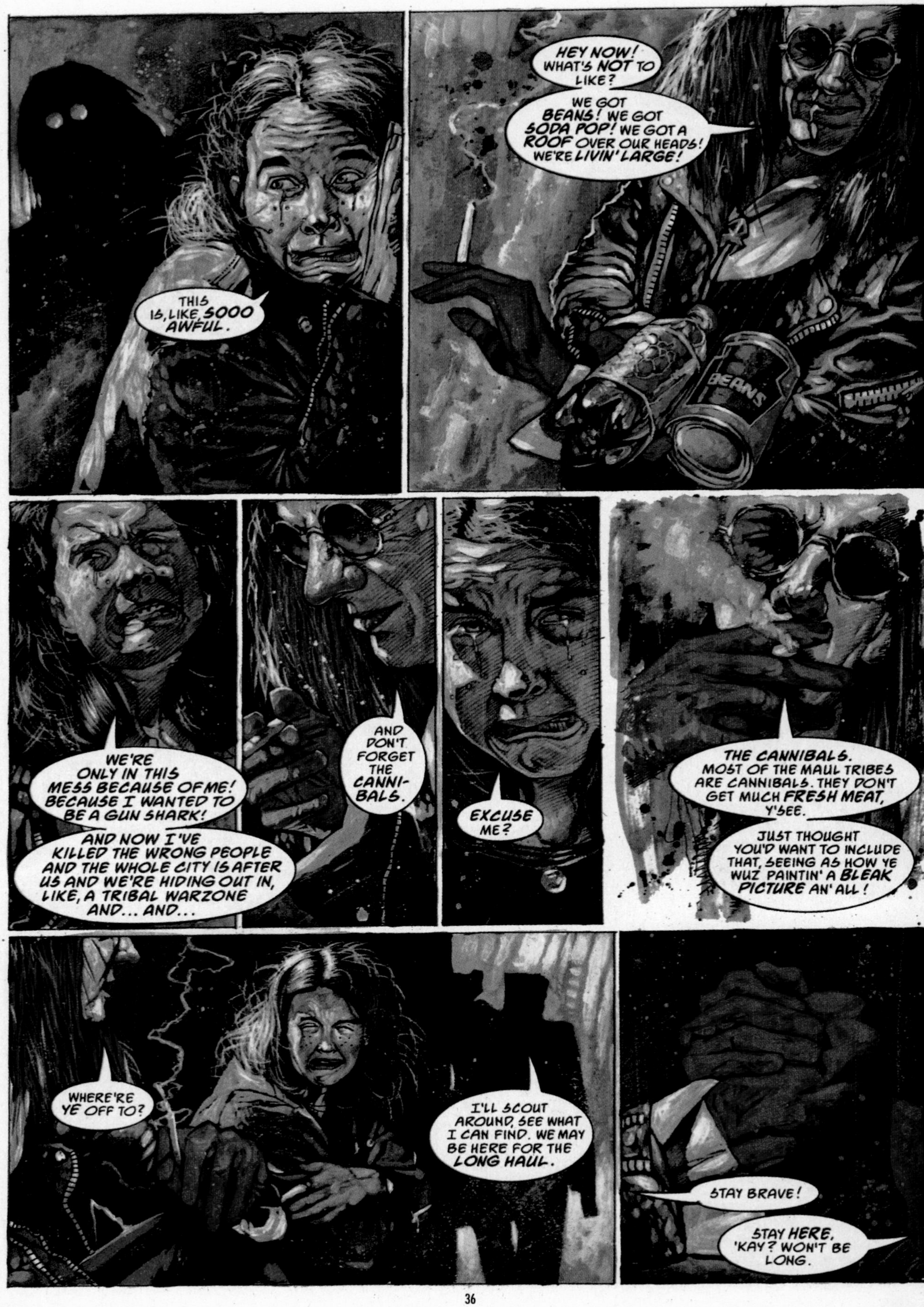
THIS IS, LIKE, SOOO AWFUL.
HEY NOW! WHAT'S NOT TO LIKE?
WE GOT BEANS! WE GOT SODA POP! WE GOT A ROOF OVER OUR HEADS! WE'RE LIVIN' LARGE!
BEANS
WE'RE ONLY IN THIS MESS BECAUSE OF ME! BECAUSE I WANTED TO BE A GUN SHARK!
AND NOW I'VE KILLED THE WRONG PEOPLE AND THE WHOLE CITY IS AFTER US AND WE'RE HIDING OUT IN, LIKE, A TRIBAL WARZONE AND... AND...
AND DON'T FORGET THE CANNI-BALS.
EXCUSE ME?
THE CANNIBALS. MOST OF THE MAUL TRIBES ARE CANNIBALS. THEY DON'T GET MUCH FRESH MEAT, Y'SEE.
JUST THOUGHT YOU'D WANT TO INCLUDE THAT, SEEING AS HOW YE WUZ PAINTIN' A BLEAK PICTURE AN' ALL!
WHERE'RE YE OFF TO?
I'LL SCOUT AROUND, SEE WHAT I CAN FIND. WE MAY BE HERE FOR THE LONG HAUL.
STAY BRAVE!
STAY HERE, 'KAY? WON'T BE LONG.

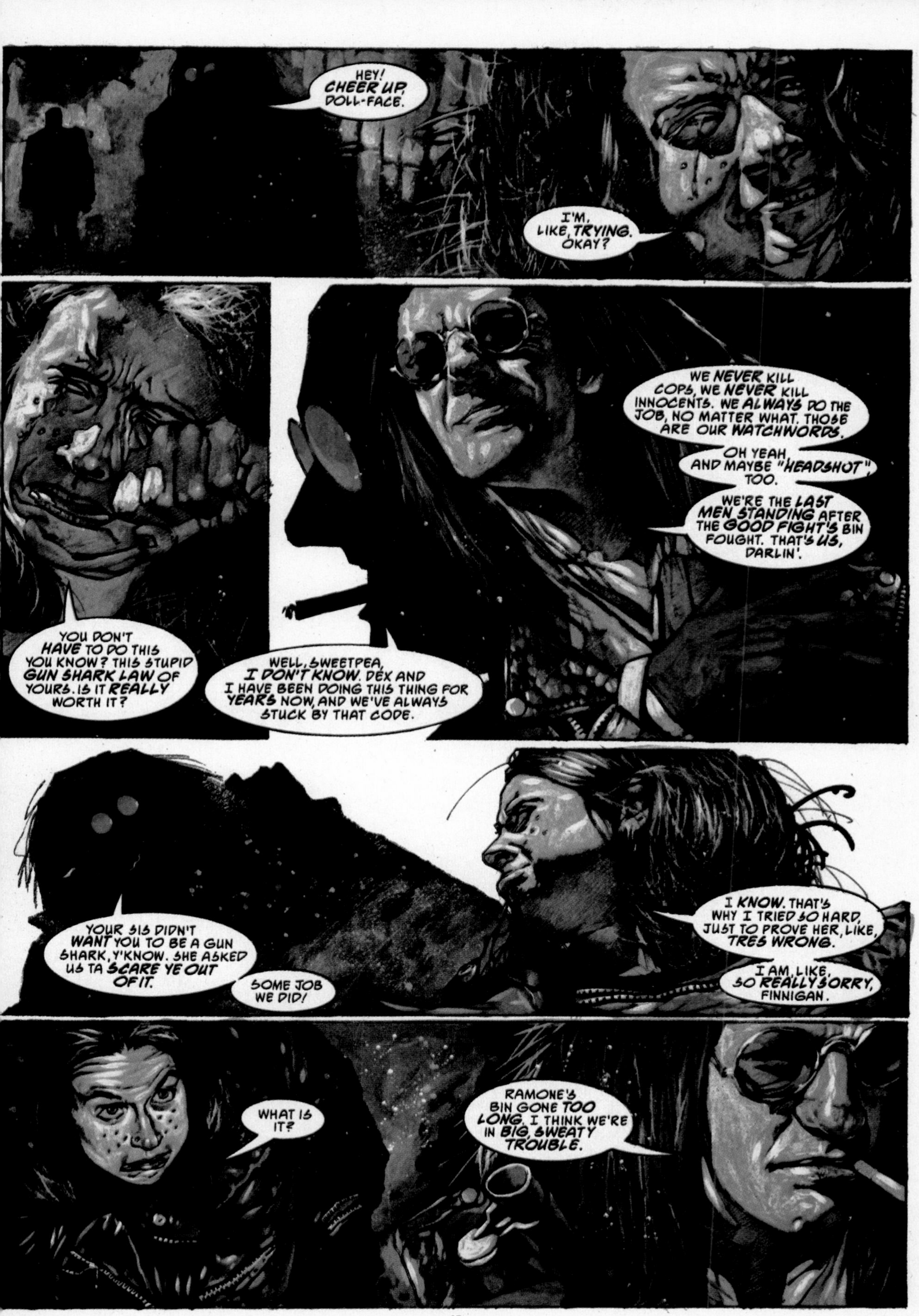
HEY! CHEER UP, DOLL-FACE.
I'M, LIKE, TRYING. OKAY?
YOU DON'T HAVE TO DO THIS YOU KNOW? THIS STUPID GUN SHARK LAW OF YOURS. IS IT REALLY WORTH IT?
WELL, SWEETPEA, I DON'T KNOW. DEX AND I HAVE BEEN DOING THIS THING FOR YEARS NOW, AND WE'VE ALWAYS STUCK BY THAT CODE.
WE NEVER KILL COPS, WE NEVER KILL INNOCENTS. WE ALWAYS DO THE JOB, NO MATTER WHAT. THOSE ARE OUR WATCHWORDS.
OH YEAH, AND MAYBE "HEADSHOT", TOO.
WE'RE THE LAST MEN STANDING AFTER THE GOOD FIGHT'S BIN FOUGHT. THAT'S US, DARLIN'.
YOUR SIS DIDN'T WANT YOU TO BE A GUN SHARK, Y'KNOW. SHE ASKED US TA SCARE YE OUT OF IT.
SOME JOB WE DID!
I KNOW. THAT'S WHY I TRIED SO HARD, JUST TO PROVE HER, LIKE, TRES WRONG.
I AM, LIKE, SO REALLY SORRY, FINNIGAN.
WHAT IS IT?
RAMONE'S BIN GONE TOO LONG. I THINK WE'RE IN BIG, SWEATY TROUBLE.

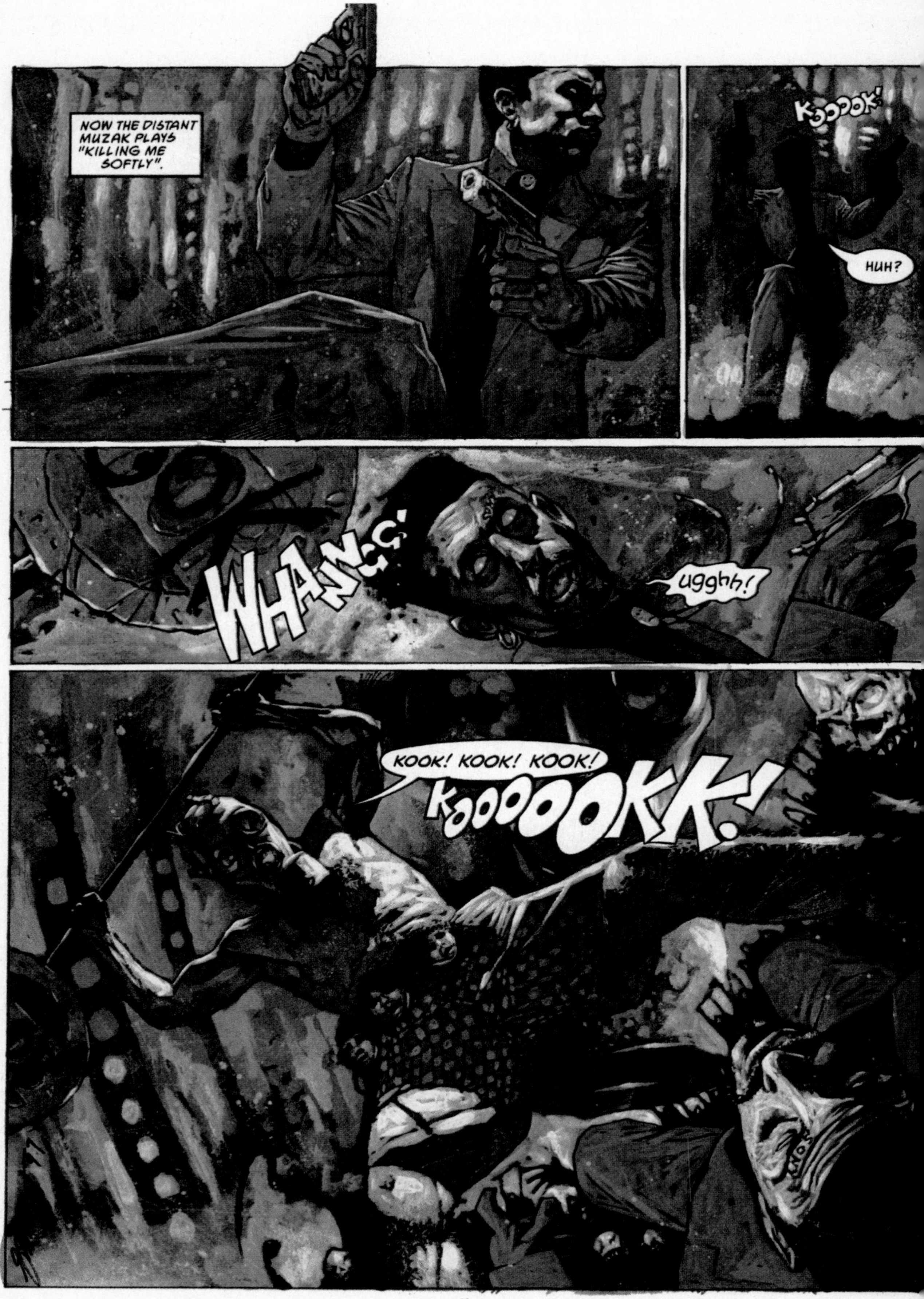
NOW THE DISTANT MUZAK PLAYS "KILLING ME SOFTLY".
KOOOOK!
HUH?
WHANGG!
ugghh!
KOOK! KOOK! KOOK!
KOOOOOKK!

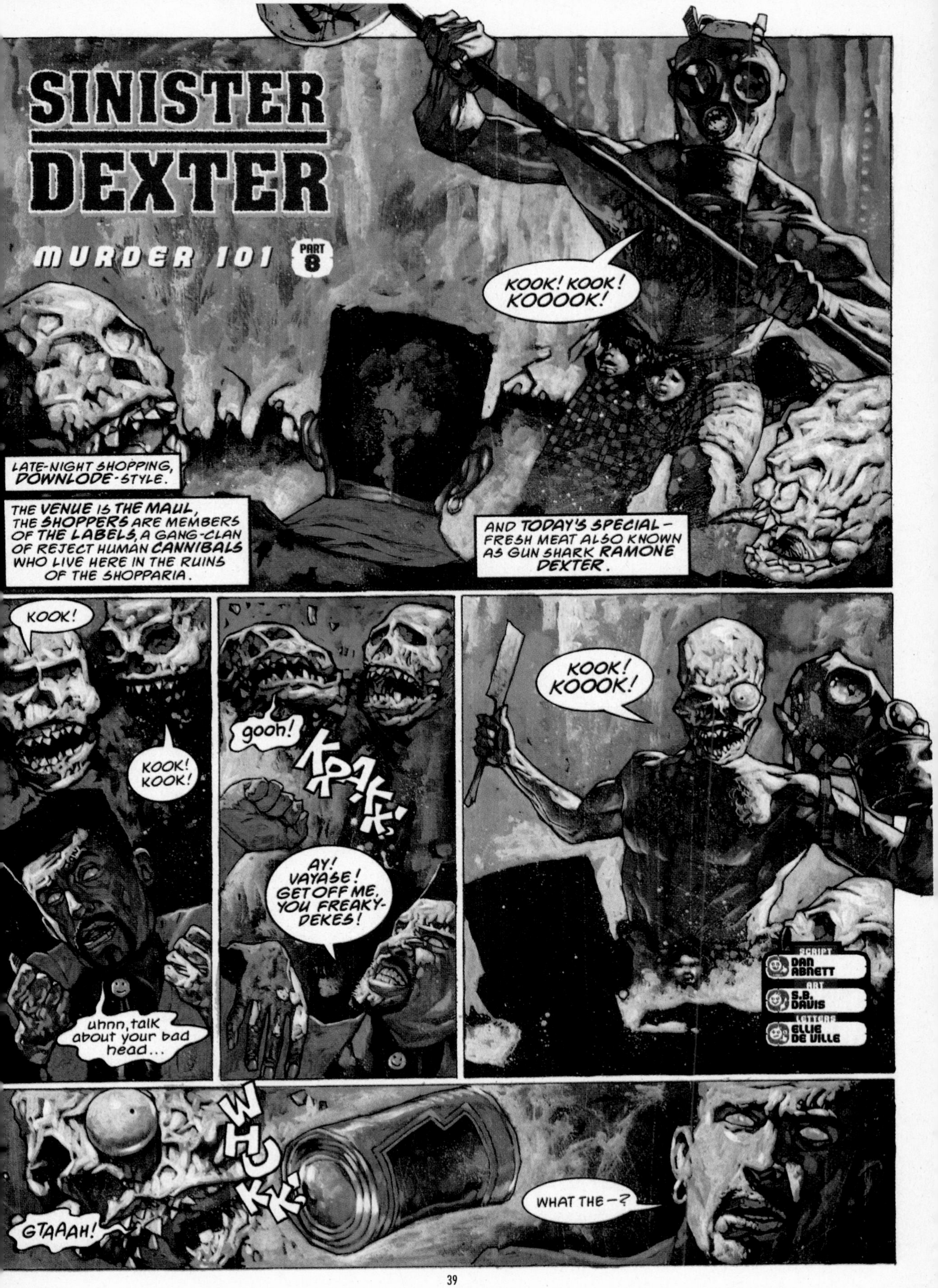
SINISTER DEXTER
MURDER 101 PART 8
KOOK! KOOK! KOOOOK!
LATE-NIGHT SHOPPING, DOWNLODE-STYLE.
THE VENUE IS THE MAUL, THE SHOPPERS ARE MEMBERS OF THE LABELS, A GANG-CLAN OF REJECT HUMAN CANNIBALS WHO LIVE HERE IN THE RUINS OF THE SHOPPARIA.
AND TODAY'S SPECIAL — FRESH MEAT ALSO KNOWN AS GUN SHARK RAMONE DEXTER.
KOOK!
KOOK! KOOK!
uhnn, talk about your bad head...
gooh!
KRAKK!
AY! VAYASE! GET OFF ME, YOU FREAKY-DEKES!
KOOK! KOOOK!
SCRIPT DAN ABNETT
ART S.B. DAVIS
LETTERS ELLIE DE VILLE
WHUKK!
GTAAAH!
WHAT THE —?

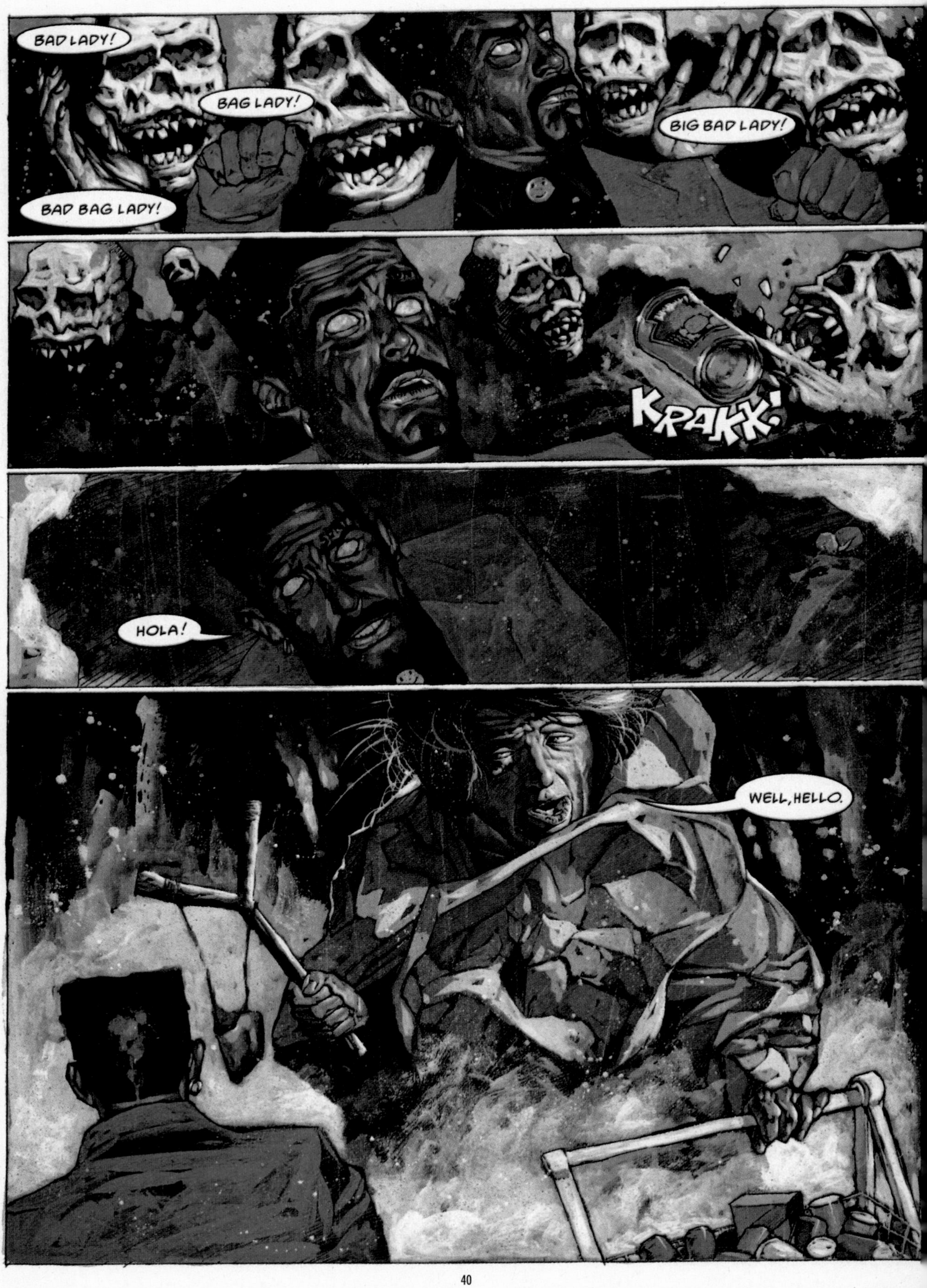
BAD LADY!
BAG LADY!
BIG BAD LADY!
BAD BAG LADY!
KRAKK!
HOLA!
WELL, HELLO.

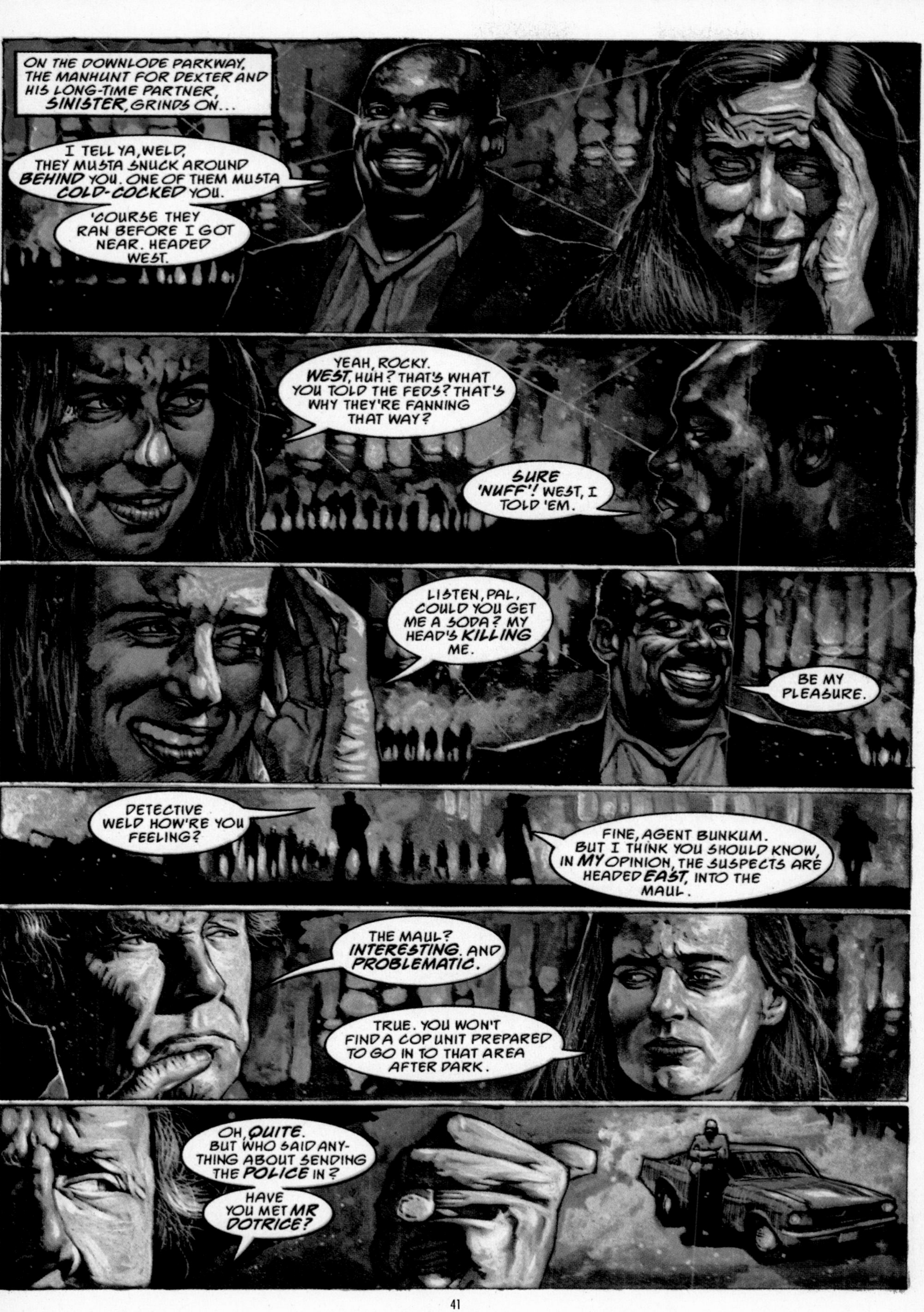
ON THE DOWNLODE PARKWAY, THE MANHUNT FOR DEXTER AND HIS LONG-TIME PARTNER, SINISTER, GRINDS ON...
I TELL YA, WELD, THEY MUSTA SNUCK AROUND BEHIND YOU. ONE OF THEM MUSTA COLD-COCKED YOU.
'COURSE THEY RAN BEFORE I GOT NEAR. HEADED WEST.
YEAH, ROCKY. WEST, HUH? THAT'S WHAT YOU TOLD THE FEDS? THAT'S WHY THEY'RE FANNING THAT WAY?
SURE 'NUFF'! WEST, I TOLD 'EM.
LISTEN, PAL, COULD YOU GET ME A SODA? MY HEAD'S KILLING ME.
BE MY PLEASURE.
DETECTIVE WELD HOW'RE YOU FEELING?
FINE, AGENT BUNKUM. BUT I THINK YOU SHOULD KNOW, IN MY OPINION, THE SUSPECTS ARE HEADED EAST, INTO THE MAUL.
THE MAUL? INTERESTING. AND PROBLEMATIC.
TRUE. YOU WON'T FIND A COP UNIT PREPARED TO GO IN TO THAT AREA AFTER DARK.
OH, QUITE. BUT WHO SAID ANYTHING ABOUT SENDING THE POLICE IN?
HAVE YOU MET MR DOTRICE?

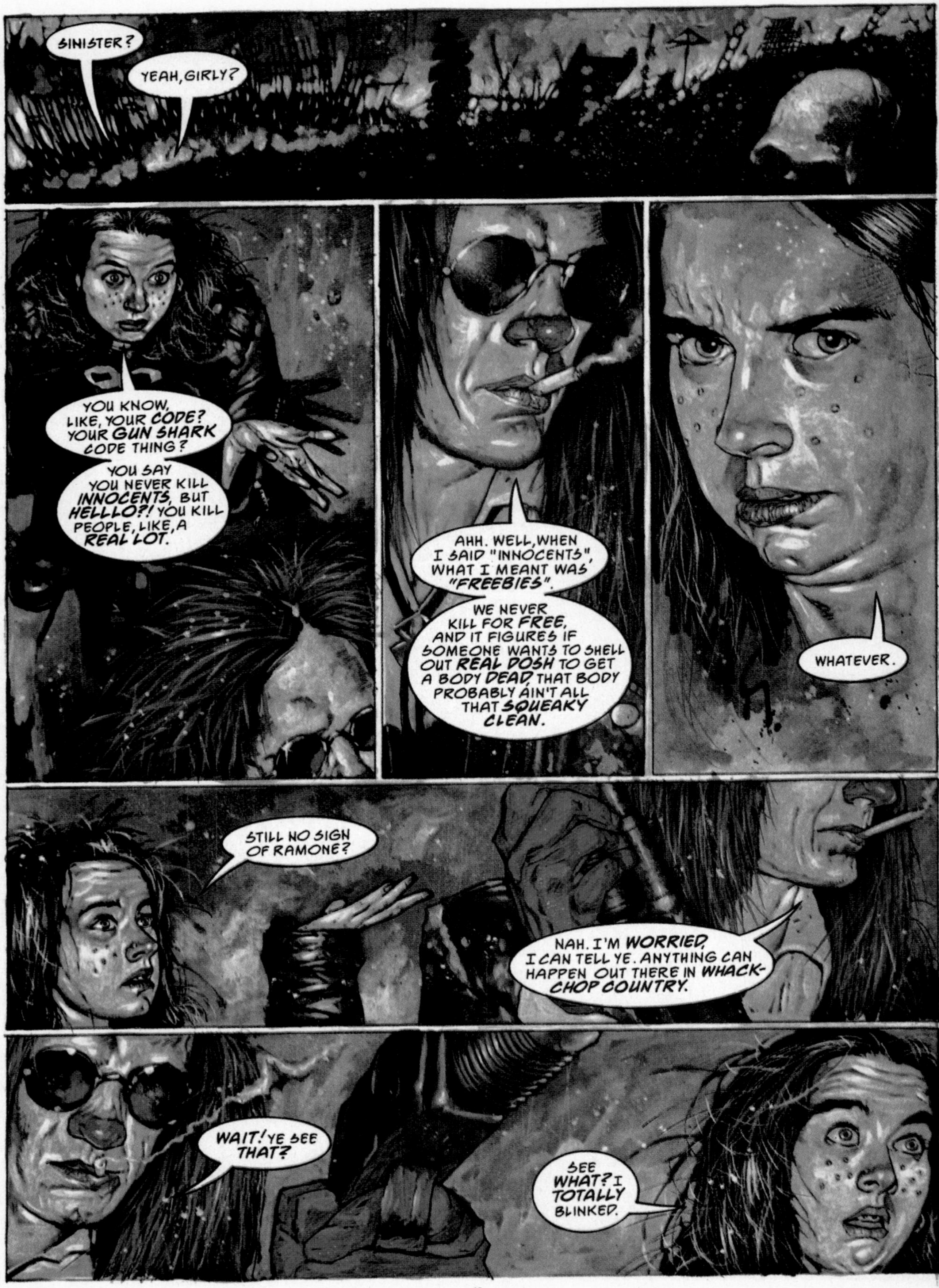
SINISTER?
YEAH, GIRLY?
YOU KNOW, LIKE, YOUR CODE? YOUR GUN SHARK CODE THING?
YOU SAY YOU NEVER KILL INNOCENTS, BUT HELLLO?! YOU KILL PEOPLE, LIKE, A REAL LOT.
AHH. WELL, WHEN I SAID "INNOCENTS", WHAT I MEANT WAS "FREEBIES".
WE NEVER KILL FOR FREE, AND IT FIGURES IF SOMEONE WANTS TO SHELL OUT REAL DOSH TO GET A BODY DEAD, THAT BODY PROBABLY AIN'T ALL THAT SQUEAKY CLEAN.
WHATEVER.
STILL NO SIGN OF RAMONE?
NAH. I'M WORRIED, I CAN TELL YE. ANYTHING CAN HAPPEN OUT THERE IN WHACK-CHOP COUNTRY.
WAIT! YE SEE THAT?
SEE WHAT? I TOTALLY BLINKED.

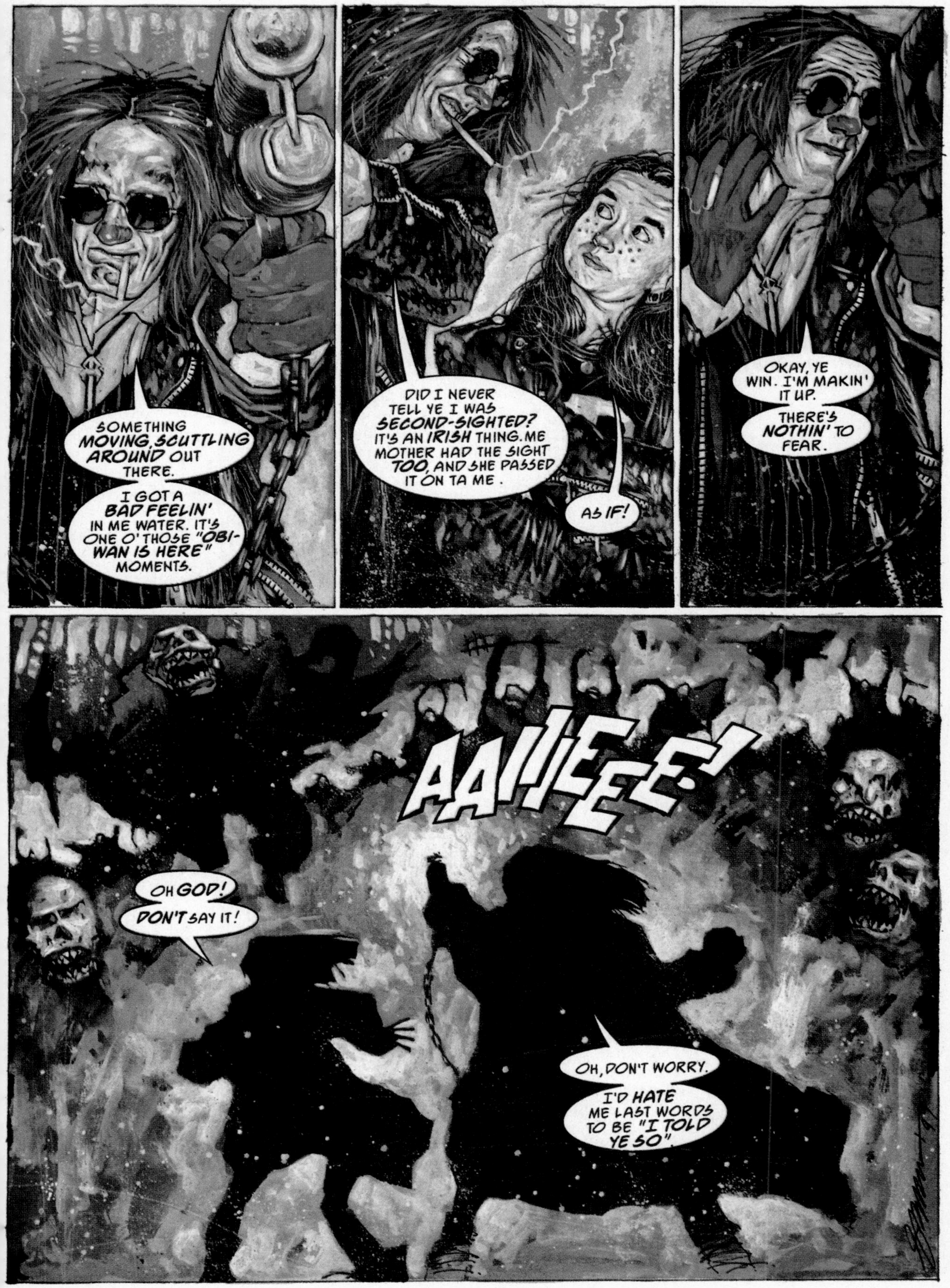
SOMETHING MOVING, SCUTTLING AROUND OUT THERE.
I GOT A BAD FEELIN' IN ME WATER. IT'S ONE O' THOSE "OBI-WAN IS HERE" MOMENTS.
DID I NEVER TELL YE I WAS SECOND-SIGHTED? IT'S AN IRISH THING. ME MOTHER HAD THE SIGHT TOO, AND SHE PASSED IT ON TA ME.
AS IF!
OKAY, YE WIN. I'M MAKIN' IT UP.
THERE'S NOTHIN' TO FEAR.
AAIIEEE!
OH GOD! DON'T SAY IT!
OH, DON'T WORRY.
I'D HATE ME LAST WORDS TO BE "I TOLD YE SO".

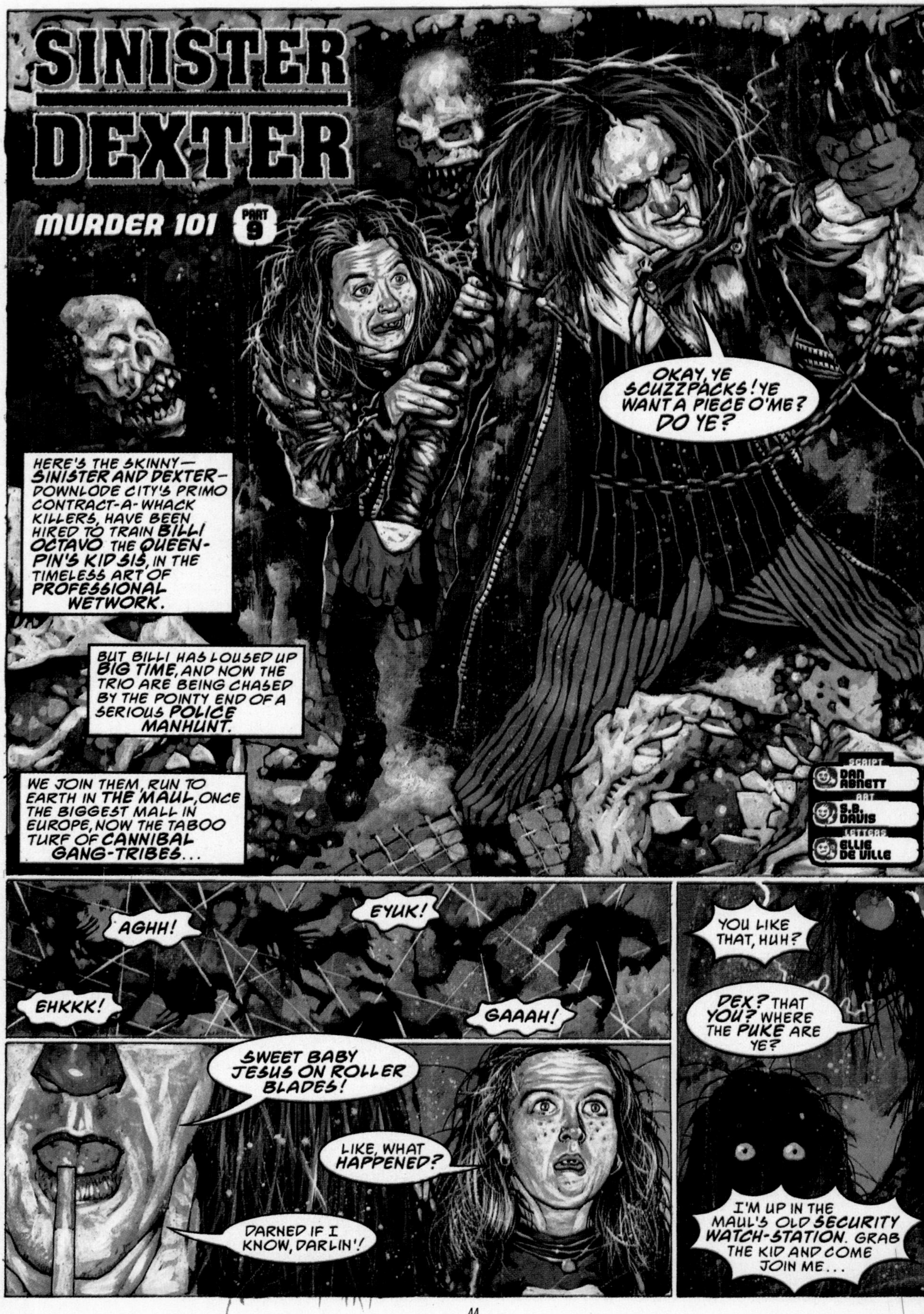
SINISTER DEXTER
MURDER 101 PART 9
OKAY, YE SCUZZPACKS! YE WANT A PIECE O'ME? DO YE?
HERE'S THE SKINNY— SINISTER AND DEXTER— DOWNLODE CITY'S PRIMO CONTRACT-A-WHACK KILLERS, HAVE BEEN HIRED TO TRAIN BILLI OCTAVO THE QUEEN-PIN'S KID SIS, IN THE TIMELESS ART OF PROFESSIONAL WETWORK.
BUT BILLI HAS LOUSED UP BIG TIME, AND NOW THE TRIO ARE BEING CHASED BY THE POINTY END OF A SERIOUS POLICE MANHUNT.
WE JOIN THEM, RUN TO EARTH IN THE MAUL, ONCE THE BIGGEST MALL IN EUROPE, NOW THE TABOO TURF OF CANNIBAL GANG-TRIBES...
SCRIPT DAN ABNETT
ART S.B. DAVIS
LETTERS ELLIE DE VILLE
AGHH!
EYUK!
EHKKK!
GAAAH!
SWEET BABY JESUS ON ROLLER BLADES!
LIKE, WHAT HAPPENED?
DARNED IF I KNOW, DARLIN'!
YOU LIKE THAT, HUH?
DEX? THAT YOU? WHERE THE PUKE ARE YE?
I'M UP IN THE MAUL'S OLD SECURITY WATCH-STATION. GRAB THE KID AND COME JOIN ME...

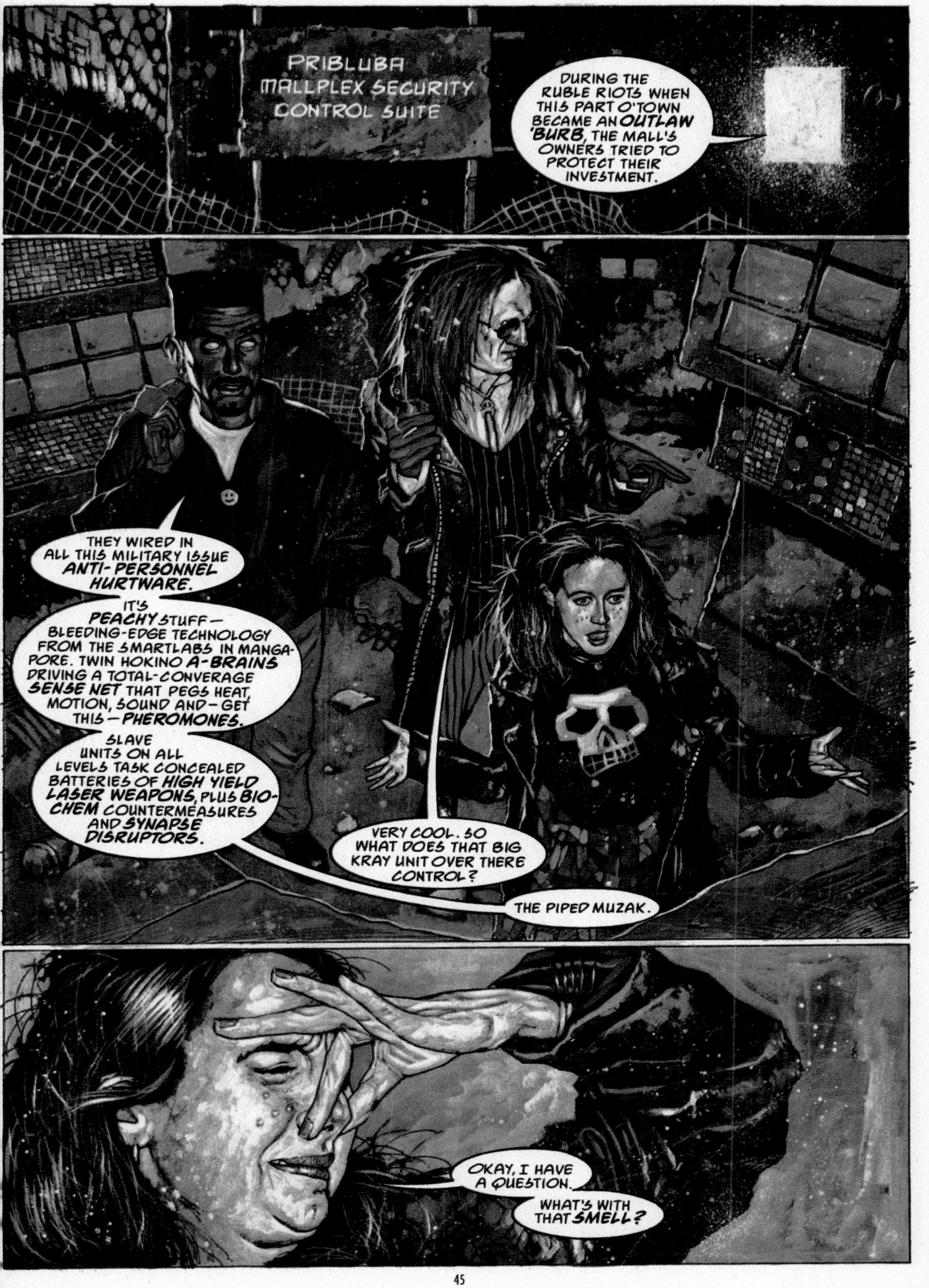
PRIBLUBA MALLPLEX SECURITY CONTROL SUITE
DURING THE RUBLE RIOTS WHEN THIS PART O'TOWN BECAME AN OUTLAW 'BURB, THE MALL'S OWNERS TRIED TO PROTECT THEIR INVESTMENT.
THEY WIRED IN ALL THIS MILITARY ISSUE ANTI-PERSONNEL HURTWARE.
IT'S PEACHY STUFF— BLEEDING-EDGE TECHNOLOGY FROM THE SMARTLABS IN MANGAPORE. TWIN HOKINO A-BRAINS DRIVING A TOTAL-CONVERAGE SENSE NET THAT PEGS HEAT, MOTION, SOUND AND—GET THIS—PHEROMONES.
SLAVE UNITS ON ALL LEVELS TASK CONCEALED BATTERIES OF HIGH YIELD LASER WEAPONS, PLUS BIO-CHEM COUNTERMEASURES AND SYNAPSE DISRUPTORS.
VERY COOL. SO WHAT DOES THAT BIG KRAY UNIT OVER THERE CONTROL?
THE PIPED MUZAK.
OKAY, I HAVE A QUESTION.
WHAT'S WITH THAT SMELL?

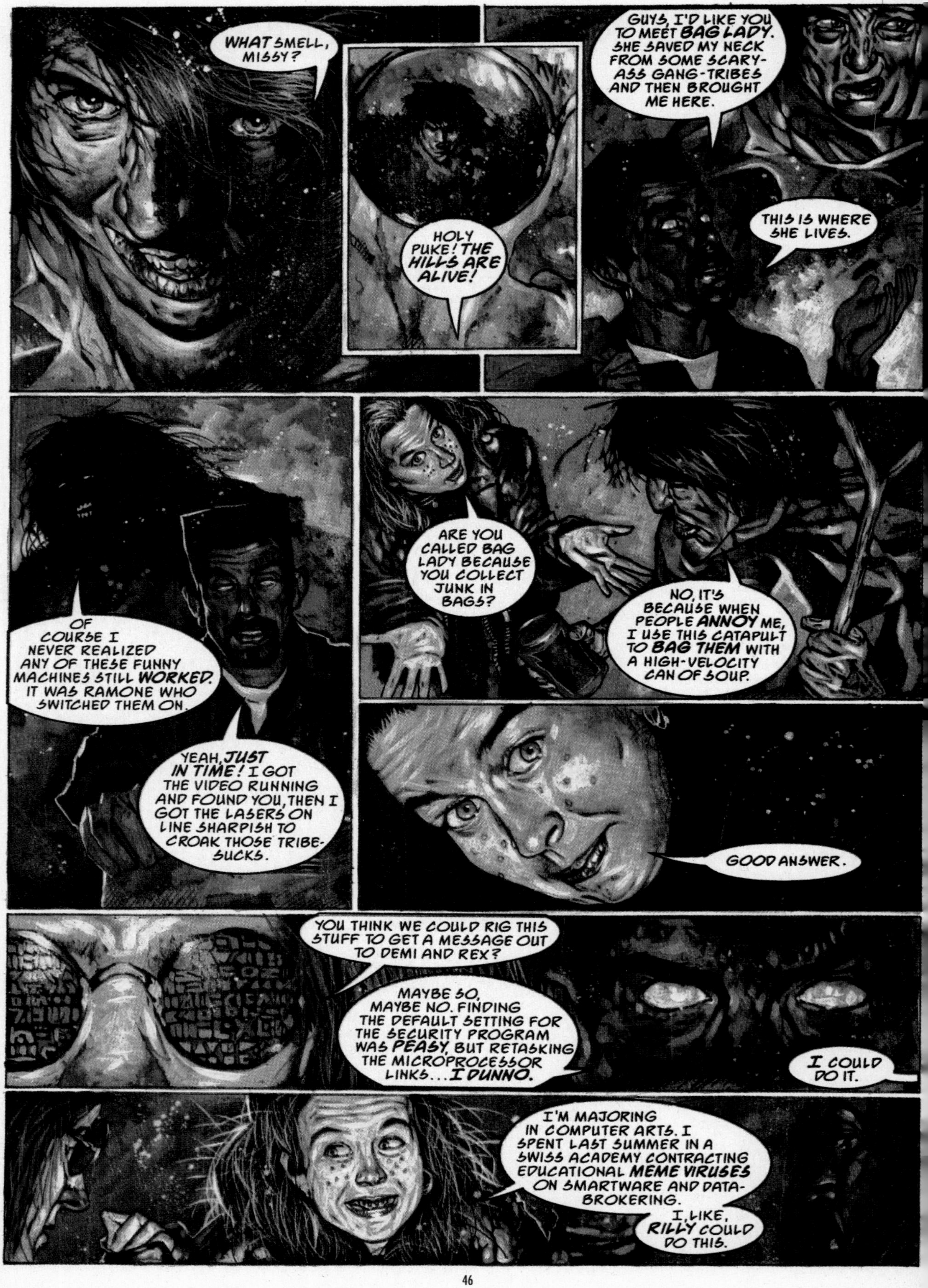
WHAT SMELL, MISSY?
HOLY PUKE! THE HILLS ARE ALIVE!
GUYS, I'D LIKE YOU TO MEET BAG LADY. SHE SAVED MY NECK FROM SOME SCARY-ASS GANG-TRIBES AND THEN BROUGHT ME HERE.
THIS IS WHERE SHE LIVES.
OF COURSE I NEVER REALIZED ANY OF THESE FUNNY MACHINES STILL WORKED. IT WAS RAMONE WHO SWITCHED THEM ON.
YEAH, JUST IN TIME! I GOT THE VIDEO RUNNING AND FOUND YOU, THEN I GOT THE LASERS ON LINE SHARPISH TO CROAK THOSE TRIBE-SUCKS.
ARE YOU CALLED BAG LADY BECAUSE YOU COLLECT JUNK IN BAGS?
NO, IT'S BECAUSE WHEN PEOPLE ANNOY ME, I USE THIS CATAPULT TO BAG THEM WITH A HIGH-VELOCITY CAN OF SOUP.
GOOD ANSWER.
YOU THINK WE COULD RIG THIS STUFF TO GET A MESSAGE OUT TO DEMI AND REX?
MAYBE SO, MAYBE NO. FINDING THE DEFAULT SETTING FOR THE SECURITY PROGRAM WAS PEASY, BUT RETASKING THE MICROPROCESSOR LINKS... I DUNNO.
I COULD DO IT.
I'M MAJORING IN COMPUTER ARTS. I SPENT LAST SUMMER IN A SWISS ACADEMY CONTRACTING EDUCATIONAL MEME VIRUSES ON SMARTWARE AND DATA-BROKERING.
I, LIKE, RILLY COULD DO THIS.

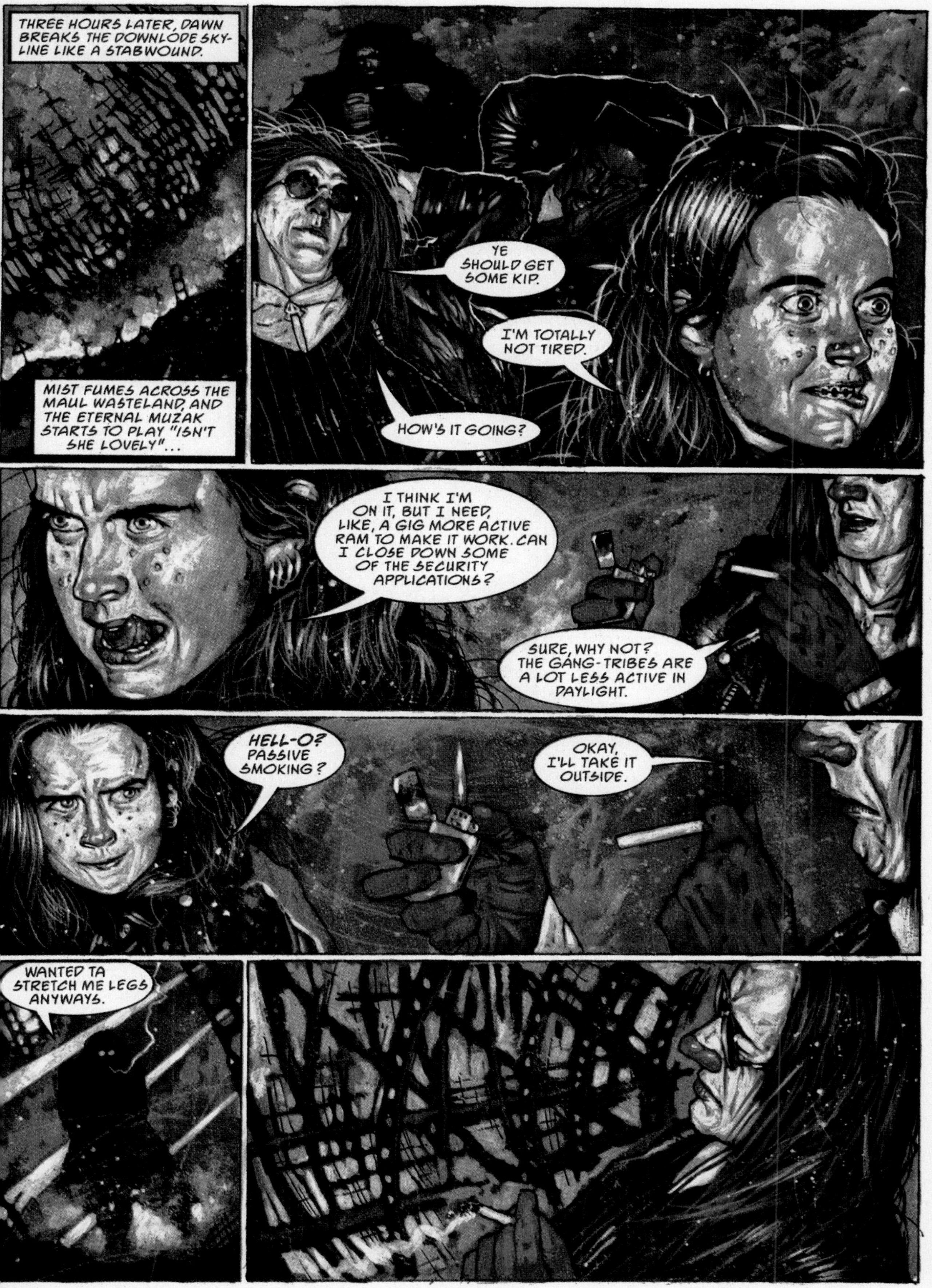
THREE HOURS LATER, DAWN BREAKS THE DOWNLODE SKY-LINE LIKE A STABWOUND.
MIST FUMES ACROSS THE MAUL WASTELAND, AND THE ETERNAL MUZAK STARTS TO PLAY "ISN'T SHE LOVELY"...
YE SHOULD GET SOME KIP.
I'M TOTALLY NOT TIRED.
HOW'S IT GOING?
I THINK I'M ON IT, BUT I NEED, LIKE, A GIG MORE ACTIVE RAM TO MAKE IT WORK. CAN I CLOSE DOWN SOME OF THE SECURITY APPLICATIONS?
SURE, WHY NOT? THE GANG-TRIBES ARE A LOT LESS ACTIVE IN DAYLIGHT.
HELL-O? PASSIVE SMOKING?
OKAY, I'LL TAKE IT OUTSIDE.
WANTED TA STRETCH ME LEGS ANYWAYS.

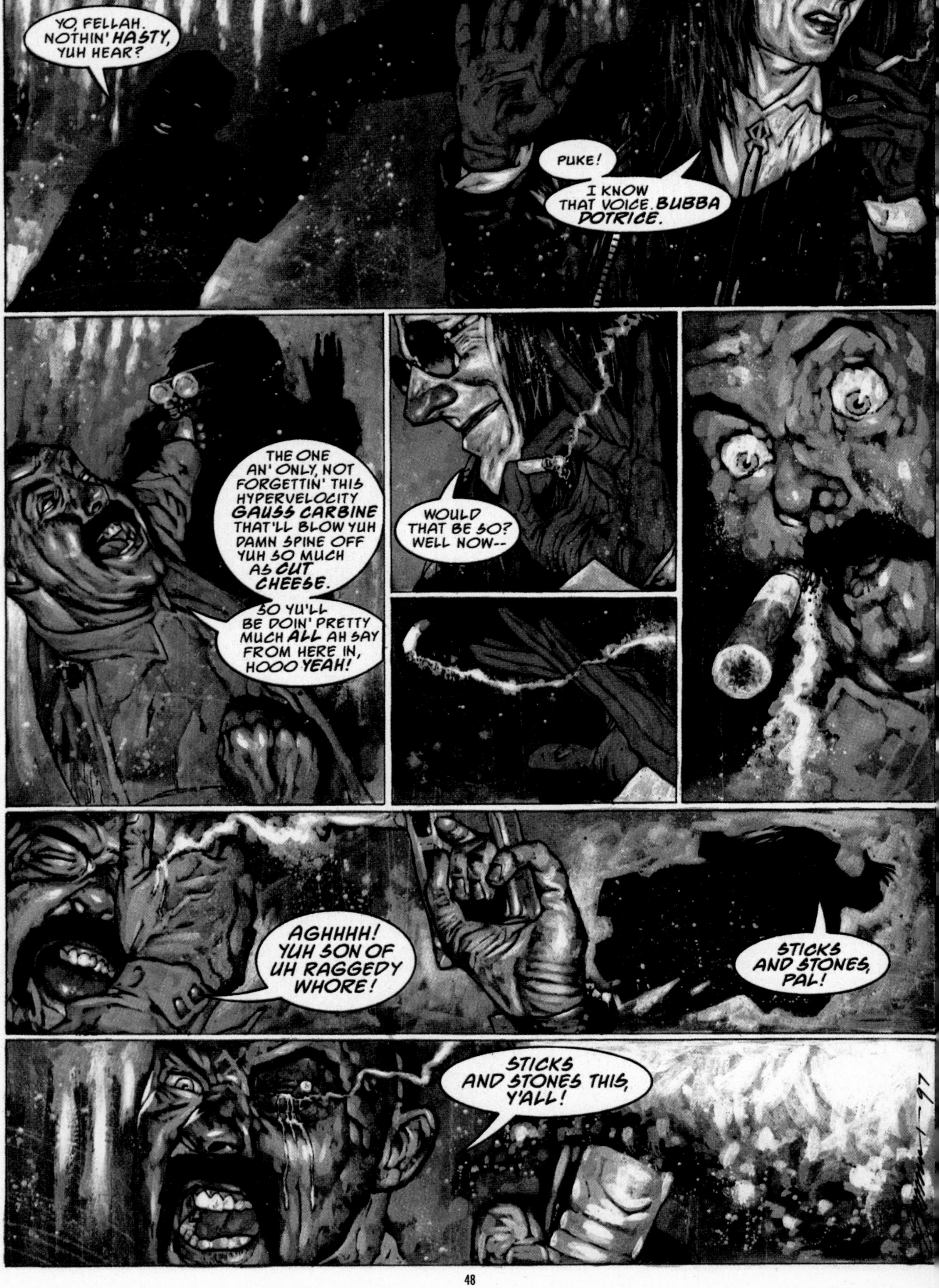
YO, FELLAH. NOTHIN' HASTY, YUH HEAR?
PUKE!
I KNOW THAT VOICE. BUBBA DOTRICE.
THE ONE AN' ONLY, NOT FORGETTIN' THIS HYPERVELOCITY GAUSS CARBINE THAT'LL BLOW YUH DAMN SPINE OFF YUH SO MUCH AS CUT CHEESE.
SO YU'LL BE DOIN' PRETTY MUCH ALL AH SAY FROM HERE IN, HOOO YEAH!
WOULD THAT BE SO? WELL NOW--
AGHHHH! YUH SON OF UH RAGGEDY WHORE!
STICKS AND STONES, PAL!
STICKS AND STONES THIS, Y'ALL!

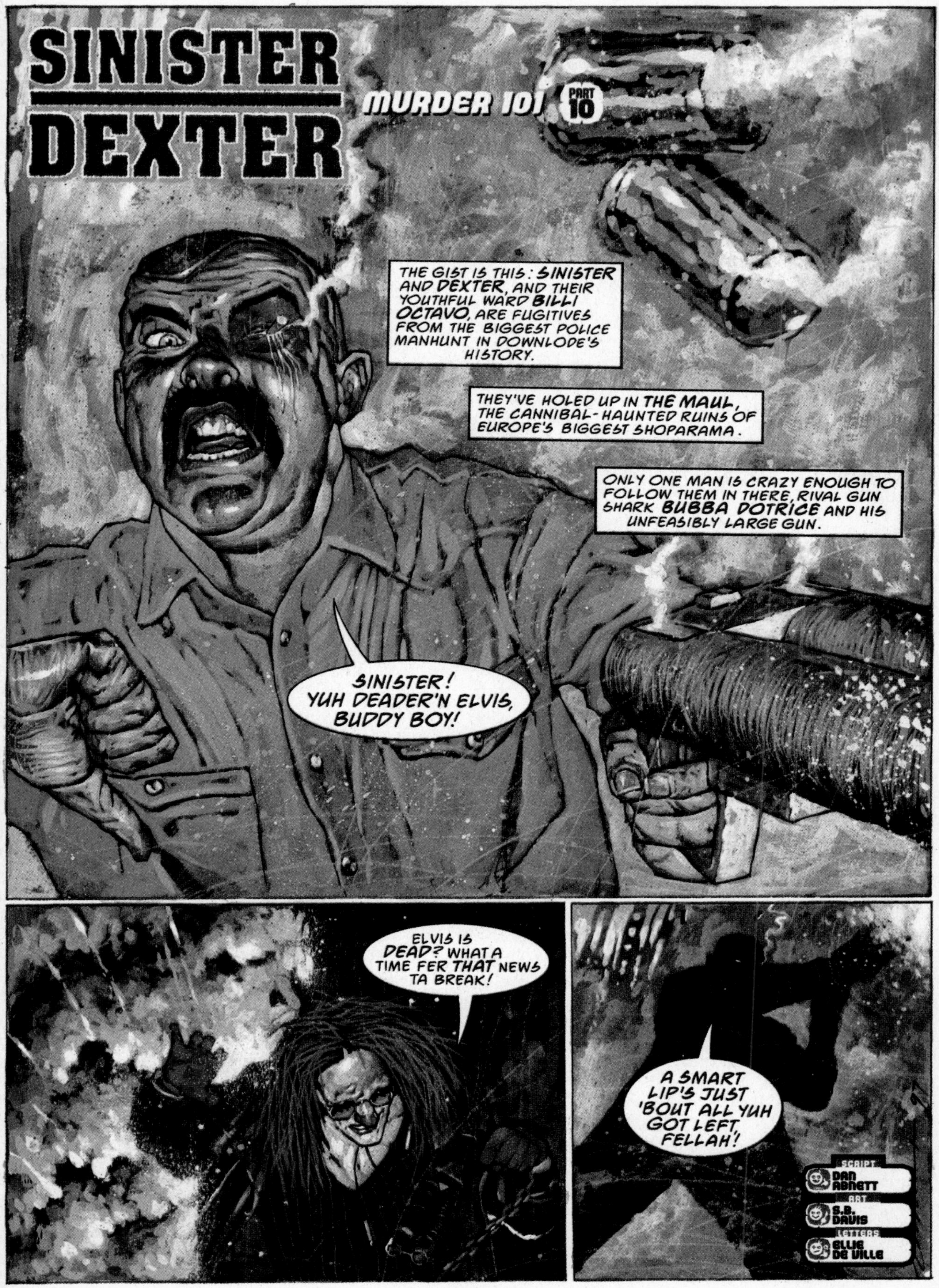
SINISTER DEXTER
MURDER 101 PART 10
THE GIST IS THIS: SINISTER AND DEXTER, AND THEIR YOUTHFUL WARD BILLI OCTAVO, ARE FUGITIVES FROM THE BIGGEST POLICE MANHUNT IN DOWNLODE'S HISTORY.
THEY'VE HOLED UP IN THE MAUL, THE CANNIBAL-HAUNTED RUINS OF EUROPE'S BIGGEST SHOPARAMA.
ONLY ONE MAN IS CRAZY ENOUGH TO FOLLOW THEM IN THERE, RIVAL GUN SHARK BUBBA DOTRICE AND HIS UNFEASIBLY LARGE GUN.
SINISTER! YUH DEADER'N ELVIS, BUDDY BOY!
ELVIS IS DEAD? WHAT A TIME FER THAT NEWS TA BREAK!
A SMART LIP'S JUST 'BOUT ALL YUH GOT LEFT, FELLAH!
SCRIPT DAN ABNETT
ART S.B. DAVIS
LETTERS ELLIE DE VILLE

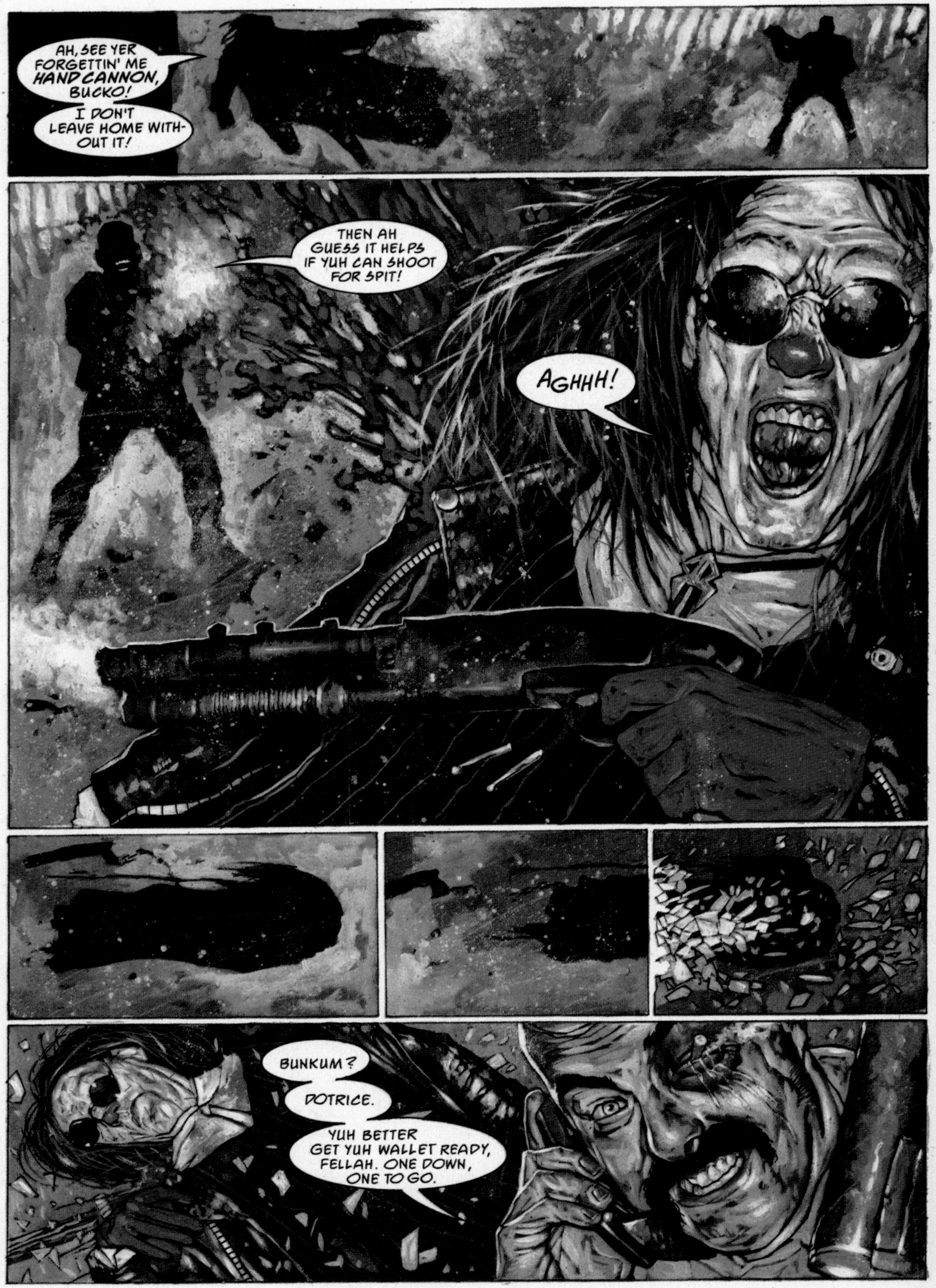
AH, SEE YER FORGETTIN' ME HAND CANNON, BUCKO!
I DON'T LEAVE HOME WITH-OUT IT!
THEN AH GUESS IT HELPS IF YUH CAN SHOOT FOR SPIT!
AGHHH!
BUNKUM?
DOTRICE.
YUH BETTER GET YUH WALLET READY, FELLAH. ONE DOWN, ONE TO GO.

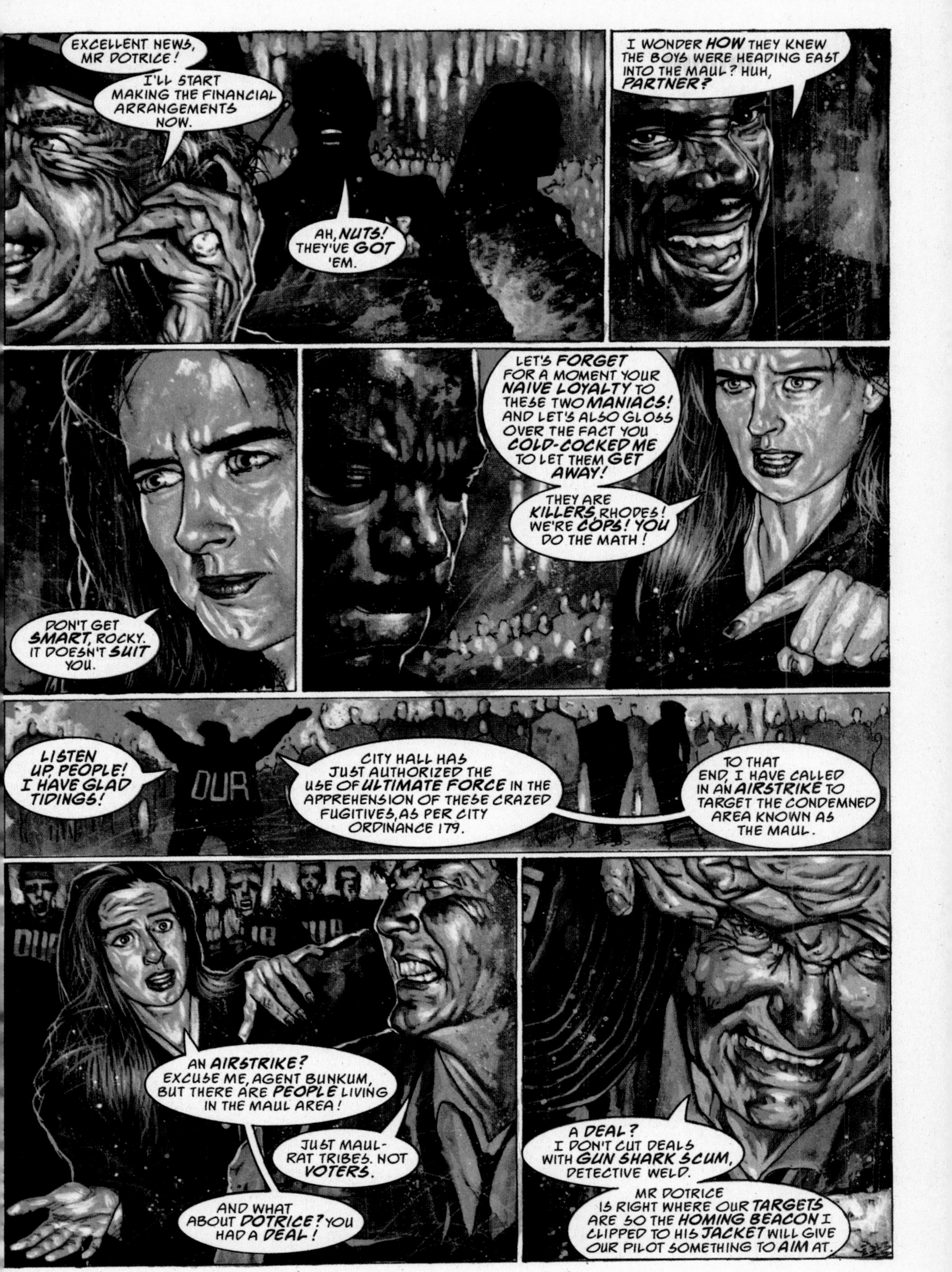
EXCELLENT NEWS, MR DOTRICE!
I'LL START MAKING THE FINANCIAL ARRANGEMENTS NOW.
AH, NUTS! THEY'VE GOT 'EM.
I WONDER HOW THEY KNEW THE BOYS WERE HEADING EAST INTO THE MAUL? HUH, PARTNER?
DON'T GET SMART, ROCKY. IT DOESN'T SUIT YOU.
LET'S FORGET FOR A MOMENT YOUR NAIVE LOYALTY TO THESE TWO MANIACS! AND LET'S ALSO GLOSS OVER THE FACT YOU COLD-COCKED ME TO LET THEM GET AWAY!
THEY ARE KILLERS, RHODES! WE'RE COPS! YOU DO THE MATH!
LISTEN UP, PEOPLE! I HAVE GLAD TIDINGS!
CITY HALL HAS JUST AUTHORIZED THE USE OF ULTIMATE FORCE IN THE APPREHENSION OF THESE CRAZED FUGITIVES, AS PER CITY ORDINANCE 179.
TO THAT END, I HAVE CALLED IN AN AIRSTRIKE TO TARGET THE CONDEMNED AREA KNOWN AS THE MAUL.
DUR
AN AIRSTRIKE? EXCUSE ME, AGENT BUNKUM, BUT THERE ARE PEOPLE LIVING IN THE MAUL AREA!
JUST MAUL-RAT TRIBES. NOT VOTERS.
AND WHAT ABOUT DOTRICE? YOU HAD A DEAL!
A DEAL? I DON'T CUT DEALS WITH GUN SHARK SCUM, DETECTIVE WELD.
MR DOTRICE IS RIGHT WHERE OUR TARGETS ARE SO THE HOMING BEACON I CLIPPED TO HIS JACKET WILL GIVE OUR PILOT SOMETHING TO AIM AT.

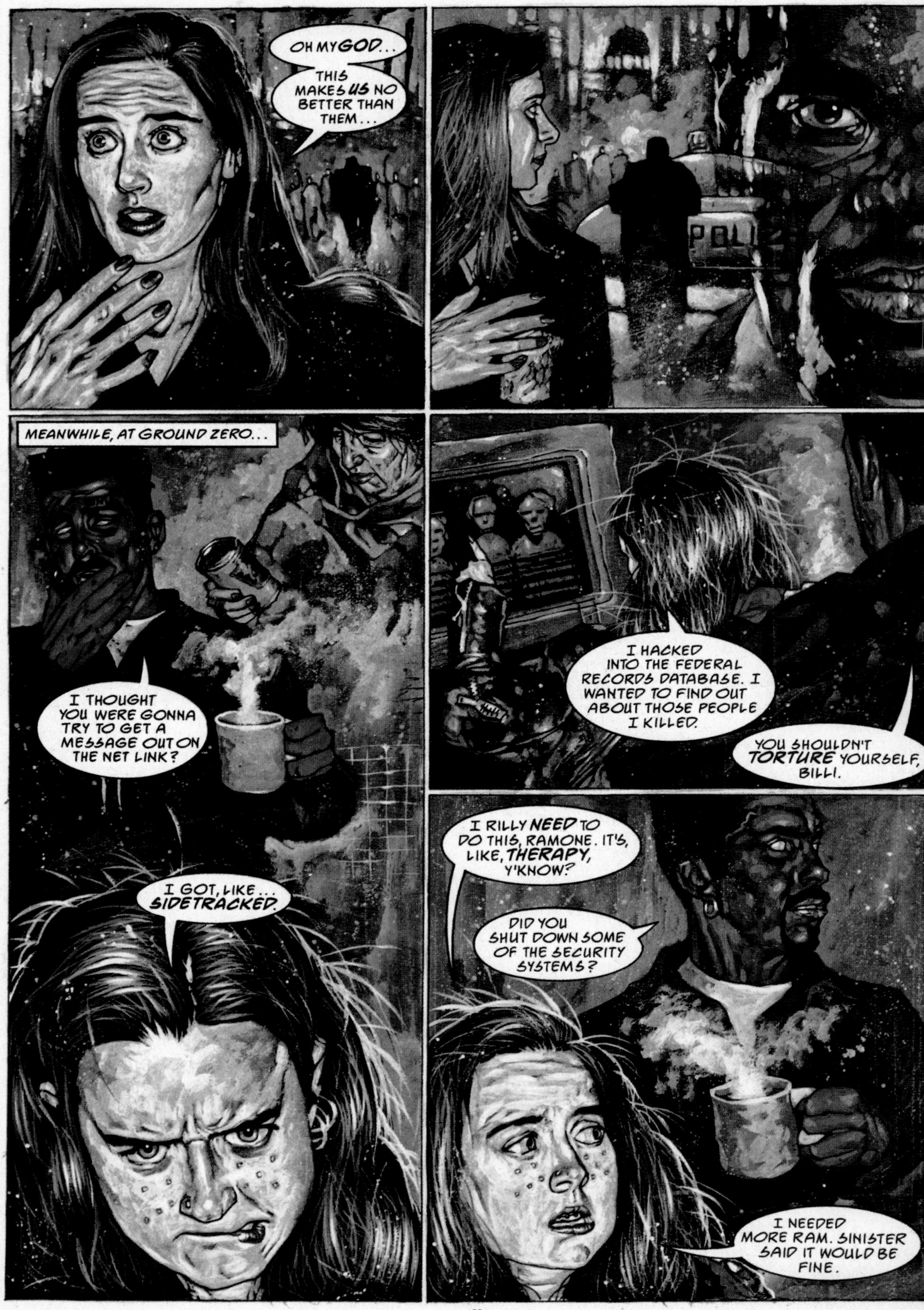
OH MY GOD...
THIS MAKES US NO BETTER THAN THEM...
MEANWHILE, AT GROUND ZERO...
I THOUGHT YOU WERE GONNA TRY TO GET A MESSAGE OUT ON THE NET LINK?
I HACKED INTO THE FEDERAL RECORDS DATABASE. I WANTED TO FIND OUT ABOUT THOSE PEOPLE I KILLED.
YOU SHOULDN'T TORTURE YOURSELF, BILLI.
I GOT, LIKE ... SIDETRACKED.
I RILLY NEED TO DO THIS, RAMONE. IT'S, LIKE, THERAPY, Y'KNOW?
DID YOU SHUT DOWN SOME OF THE SECURITY SYSTEMS?
I NEEDED MORE RAM. SINISTER SAID IT WOULD BE FINE.

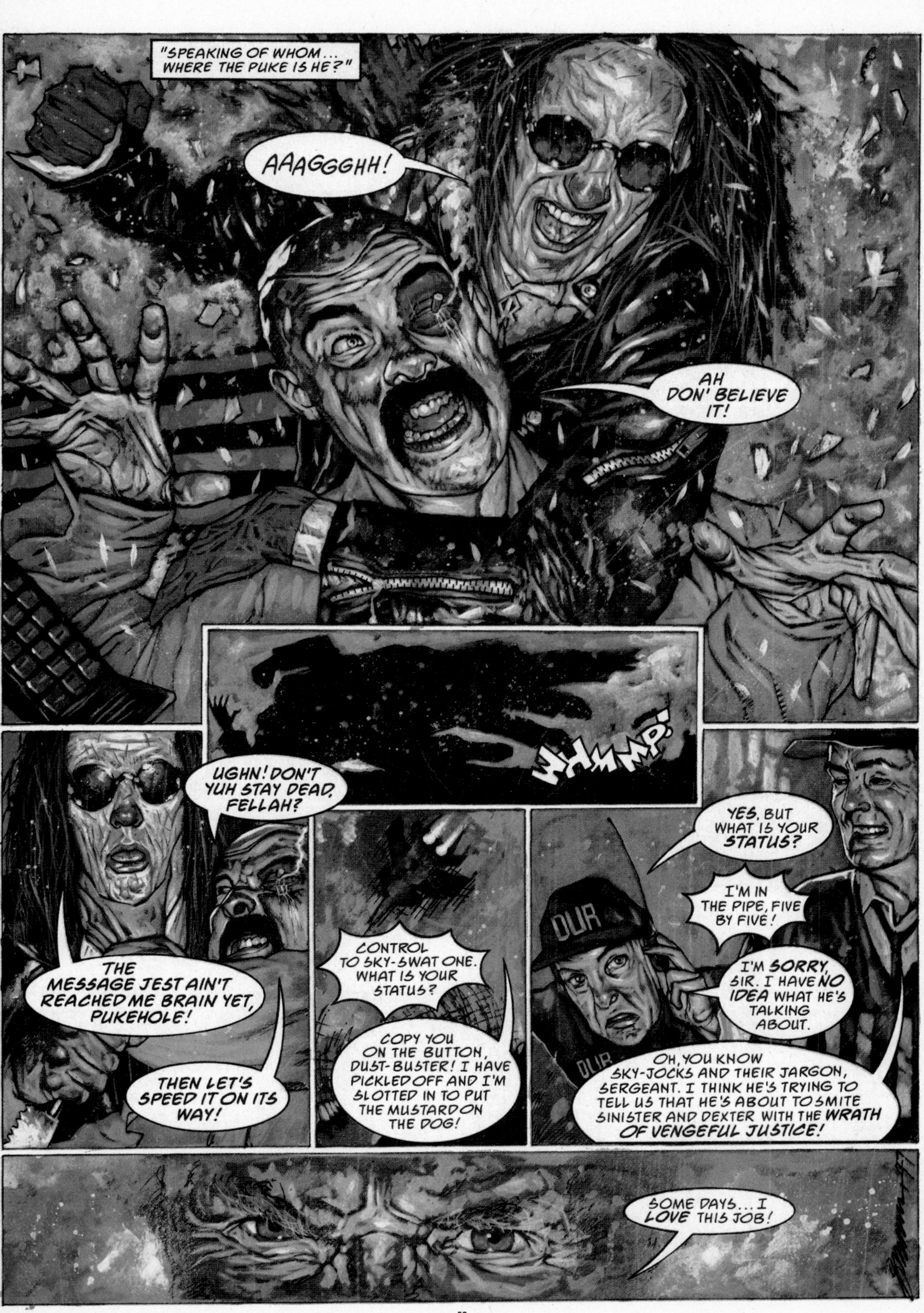
"SPEAKING OF WHOM... WHERE THE PUKE IS HE?"
AAAGGGHH!
AH DON' BELIEVE IT!
WHUMP!
UGHN! DON'T YUH STAY DEAD, FELLAH?
THE MESSAGE JEST AIN'T REACHED ME BRAIN YET, PUKEHOLE!
THEN LET'S SPEED IT ON ITS WAY!
CONTROL TO SKY-SWAT ONE. WHAT IS YOUR STATUS?
COPY YOU ON THE BUTTON, DUST-BUSTER! I HAVE PICKLED OFF AND I'M SLOTTED IN TO PUT THE MUSTARD ON THE DOG!
YES, BUT WHAT IS YOUR STATUS?
I'M IN THE PIPE, FIVE BY FIVE!
I'M SORRY, SIR. I HAVE NO IDEA WHAT HE'S TALKING ABOUT.
OH, YOU KNOW SKY-JOCKS AND THEIR JARGON, SERGEANT. I THINK HE'S TRYING TO TELL US THAT HE'S ABOUT TO SMITE SINISTER AND DEXTER WITH THE WRATH OF VENGEFUL JUSTICE!
SOME DAYS... I LOVE THIS JOB!

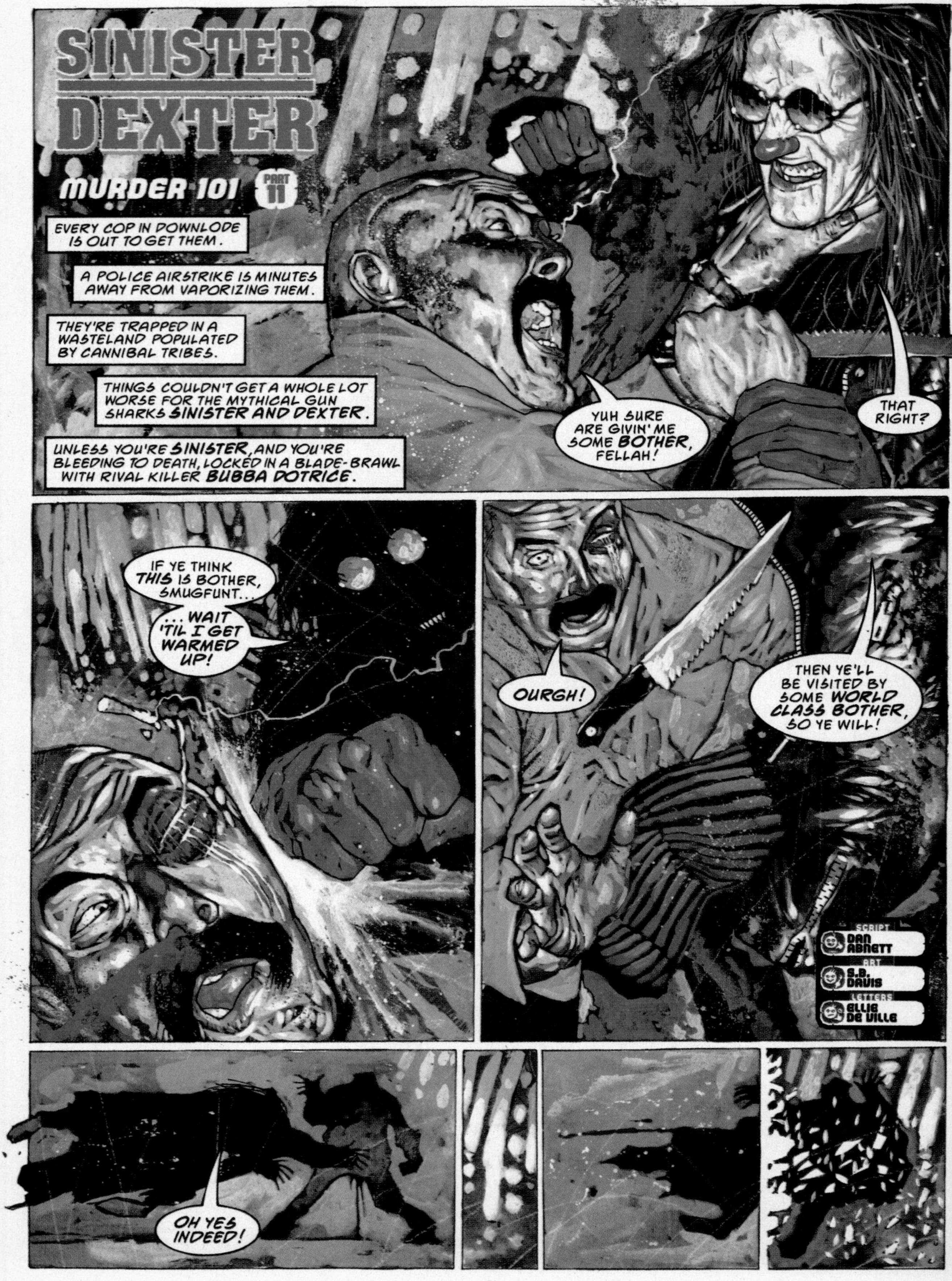
SINISTER DEXTER
MURDER 101 PART 11
EVERY COP IN DOWNLODE IS OUT TO GET THEM.
A POLICE AIRSTRIKE IS MINUTES AWAY FROM VAPORIZING THEM.
THEY'RE TRAPPED IN A WASTELAND POPULATED BY CANNIBAL TRIBES.
THINGS COULDN'T GET A WHOLE LOT WORSE FOR THE MYTHICAL GUN SHARKS SINISTER AND DEXTER.
UNLESS YOU'RE SINISTER, AND YOU'RE BLEEDING TO DEATH, LOCKED IN A BLADE-BRAWL WITH RIVAL KILLER BUBBA DOTRICE.
YUH SURE ARE GIVIN' ME SOME BOTHER, FELLAH!
THAT RIGHT?
IF YE THINK THIS IS BOTHER, SMUGFUNT...
...WAIT 'TIL I GET WARMED UP!
OURGH!
THEN YE'LL BE VISITED BY SOME WORLD CLASS BOTHER, SO YE WILL!
SCRIPT DAN ABNETT
ART S.B. DAVIS
LETTERS ELLIE DE VILLE
OH YES INDEED!

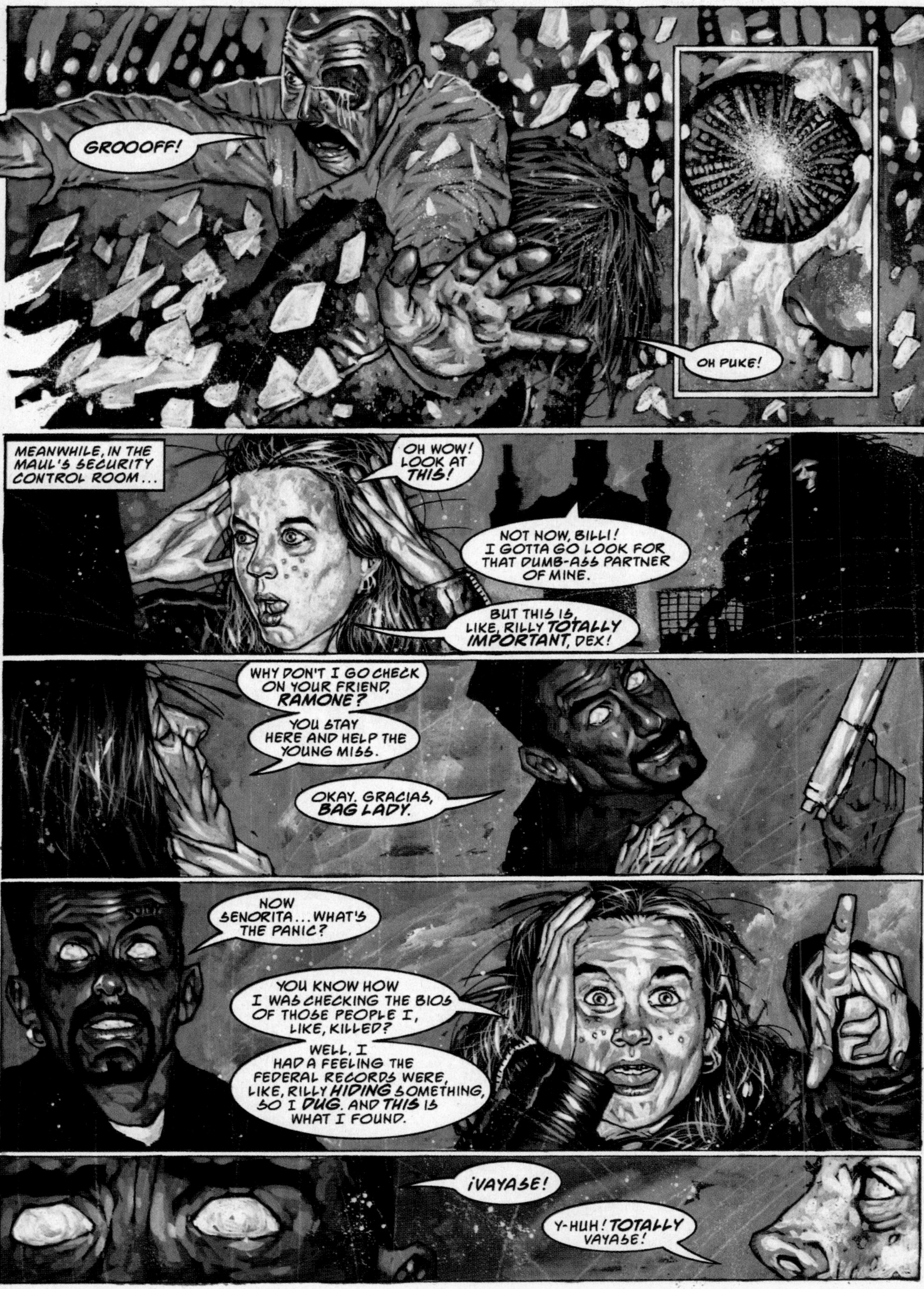
GROOOFF!
OH PUKE!
MEANWHILE, IN THE MAUL'S SECURITY CONTROL ROOM...
OH WOW! LOOK AT THIS!
NOT NOW, BILLI! I GOTTA GO LOOK FOR THAT DUMB-ASS PARTNER OF MINE.
BUT THIS IS, LIKE, RILLY TOTALLY IMPORTANT, DEX!
WHY DON'T I GO CHECK ON YOUR FRIEND, RAMONE?
YOU STAY HERE AND HELP THE YOUNG MISS.
OKAY. GRACIAS, BAG LADY.
NOW SENORITA... WHAT'S THE PANIC?
YOU KNOW HOW I WAS CHECKING THE BIOS OF THOSE PEOPLE I, LIKE, KILLED?
WELL, I HAD A FEELING THE FEDERAL RECORDS WERE, LIKE, RILLY HIDING SOMETHING, SO I DUG. AND THIS IS WHAT I FOUND.
¡VAYASE!
Y-HUH! TOTALLY VAYASE!

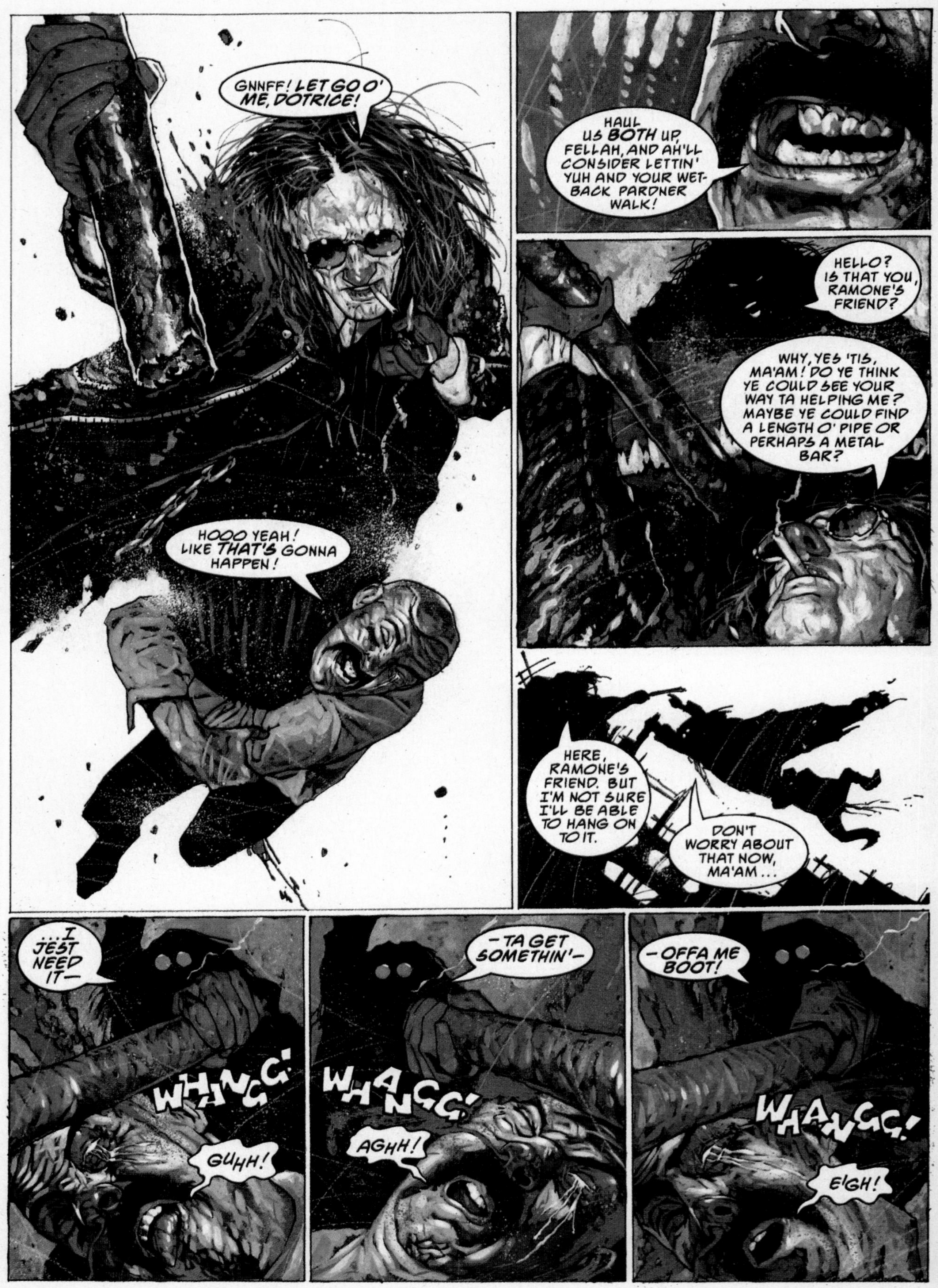
GNNFF! LET GO O' ME, DOTRICE!
HOOO YEAH! LIKE THAT'S GONNA HAPPEN!
HAUL US BOTH UP, FELLAH, AND AH'LL CONSIDER LETTIN' YUH AND YOUR WET-BACK PARDNER WALK!
HELLO? IS THAT YOU, RAMONE'S FRIEND?
WHY, YES 'TIS, MA'AM! DO YE THINK YE COULD SEE YOUR WAY TA HELPING ME? MAYBE YE COULD FIND A LENGTH O' PIPE OR PERHAPS A METAL BAR?
HERE, RAMONE'S FRIEND. BUT I'M NOT SURE I'LL BE ABLE TO HANG ON TO IT.
DON'T WORRY ABOUT THAT NOW, MA'AM...
...I JEST NEED IT—
WHANGG!
GUHH!
—TA GET SOMETHIN'—
WHANGG!
AGHH!
—OFFA ME BOOT!
WHANGG!
EIGH!

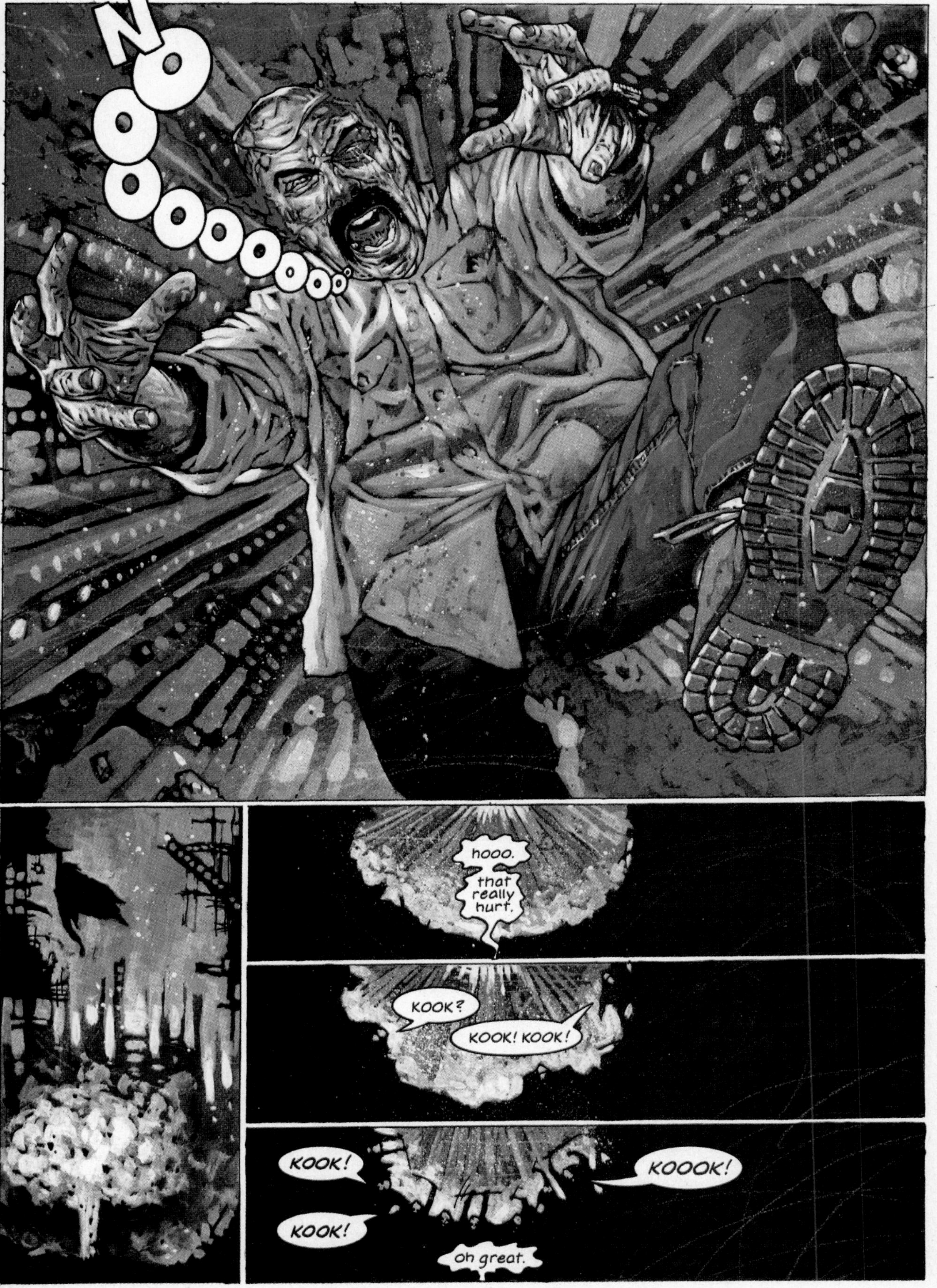
NOOOOOOOOOOOO
hooo. that really hurt.
KOOK?
KOOK! KOOK!
KOOK!
KOOOK!
KOOK!
oh great.

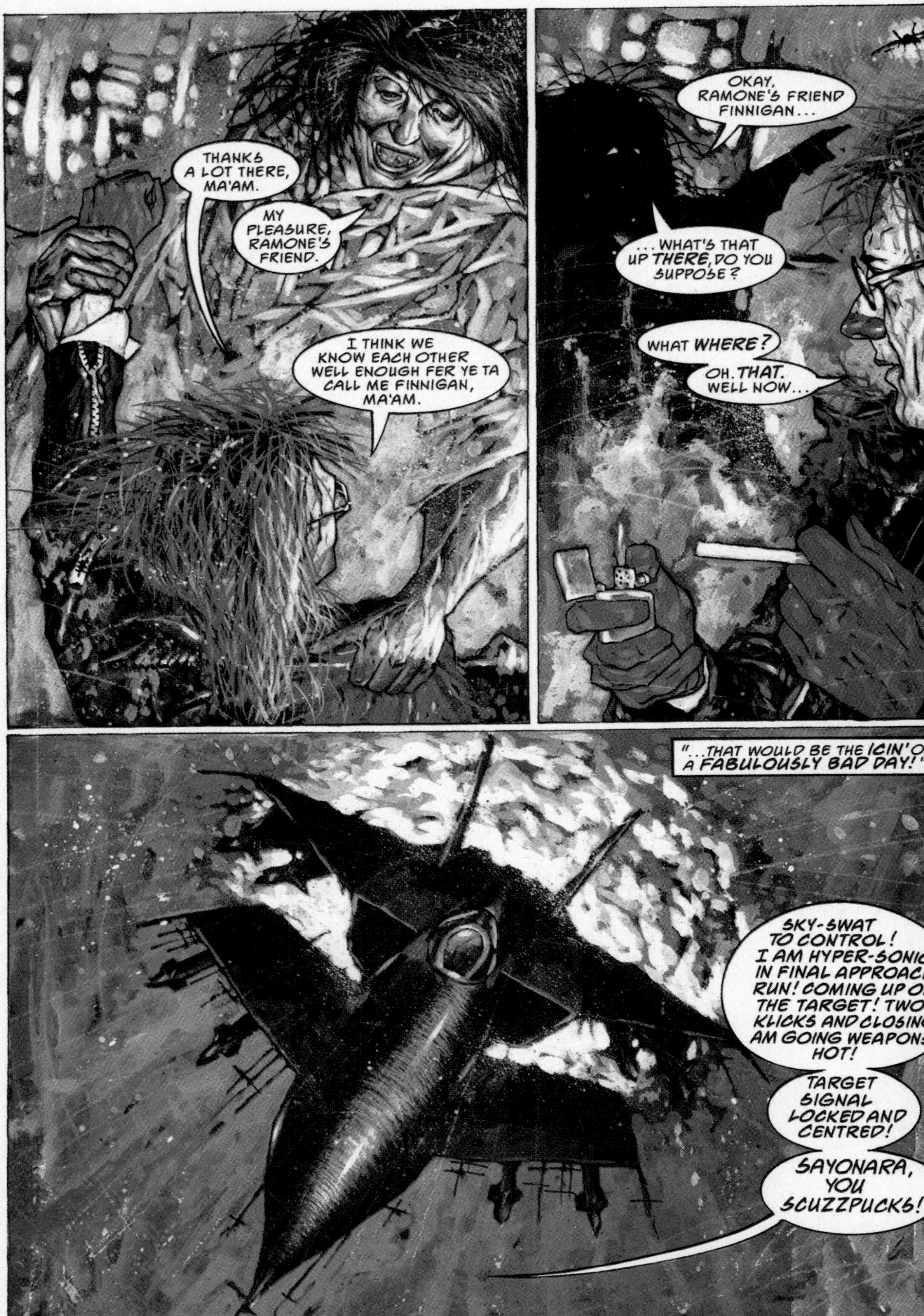
THANKS A LOT THERE, MA'AM.
MY PLEASURE, RAMONE'S FRIEND.
I THINK WE KNOW EACH OTHER WELL ENOUGH FER YE TA CALL ME FINNIGAN, MA'AM.
OKAY, RAMONE'S FRIEND FINNIGAN...
...WHAT'S THAT UP THERE, DO YOU SUPPOSE?
WHAT WHERE?
OH. THAT. WELL NOW...
"...THAT WOULD BE THE ICIN' ON A FABULOUSLY BAD DAY!"
SKY-SWAT TO CONTROL! I AM HYPER-SONIC IN FINAL APPROACH RUN! COMING UP ON THE TARGET! TWO KLICKS AND CLOSING! AM GOING WEAPONS HOT!
TARGET SIGNAL LOCKED AND CENTRED!
SAYONARA, YOU SCUZZPUCKS!

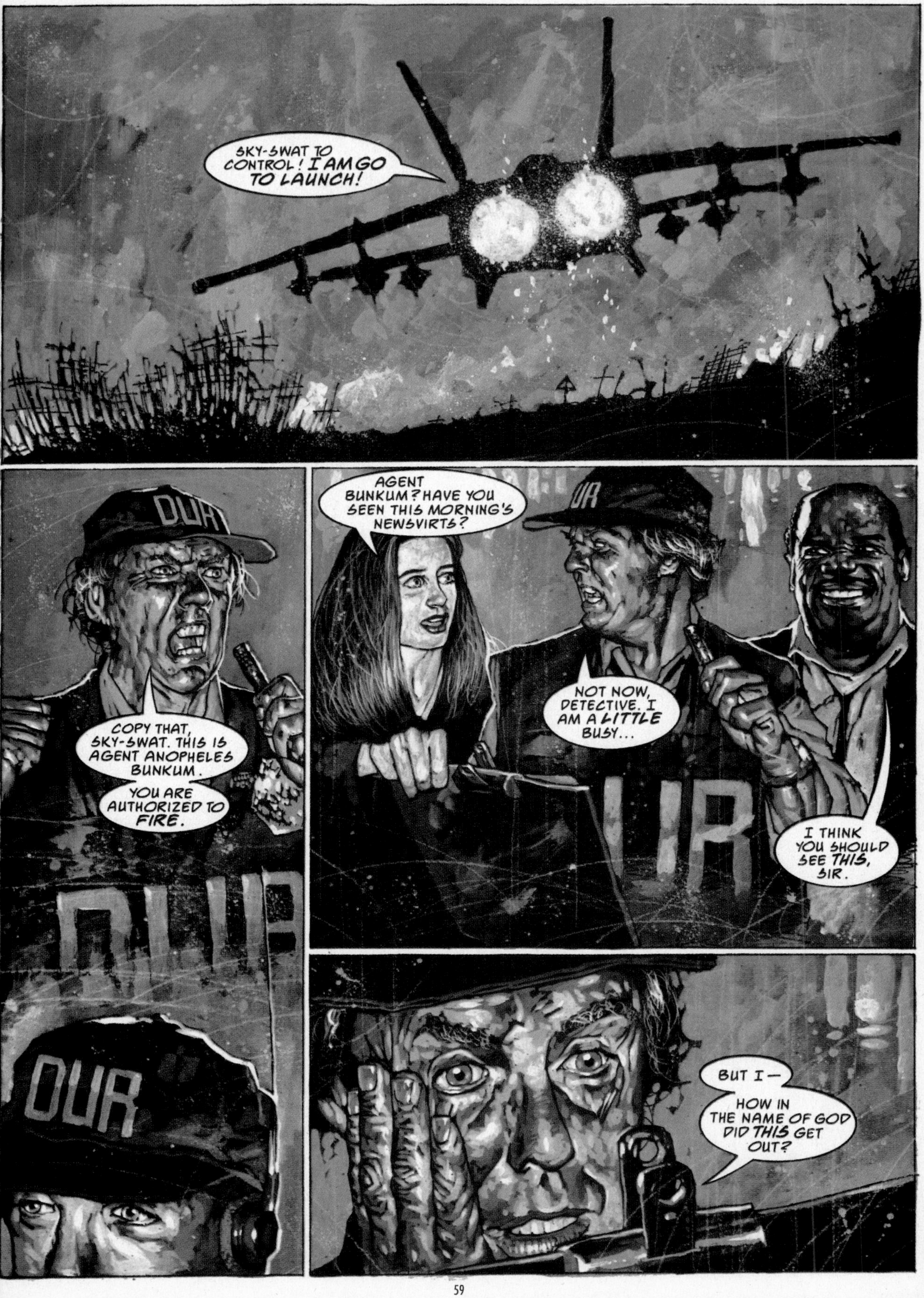
SKY-SWAT TO CONTROL! I AM GO TO LAUNCH!
COPY THAT, SKY-SWAT. THIS IS AGENT ANOPHELES BUNKUM.
YOU ARE AUTHORIZED TO FIRE.
DUR
AGENT BUNKUM? HAVE YOU SEEN THIS MORNING'S NEWSVIRTS?
NOT NOW, DETECTIVE. I AM A LITTLE BUSY...
I THINK YOU SHOULD SEE THIS, SIR.
BUT I—
HOW IN THE NAME OF GOD DID THIS GET OUT?

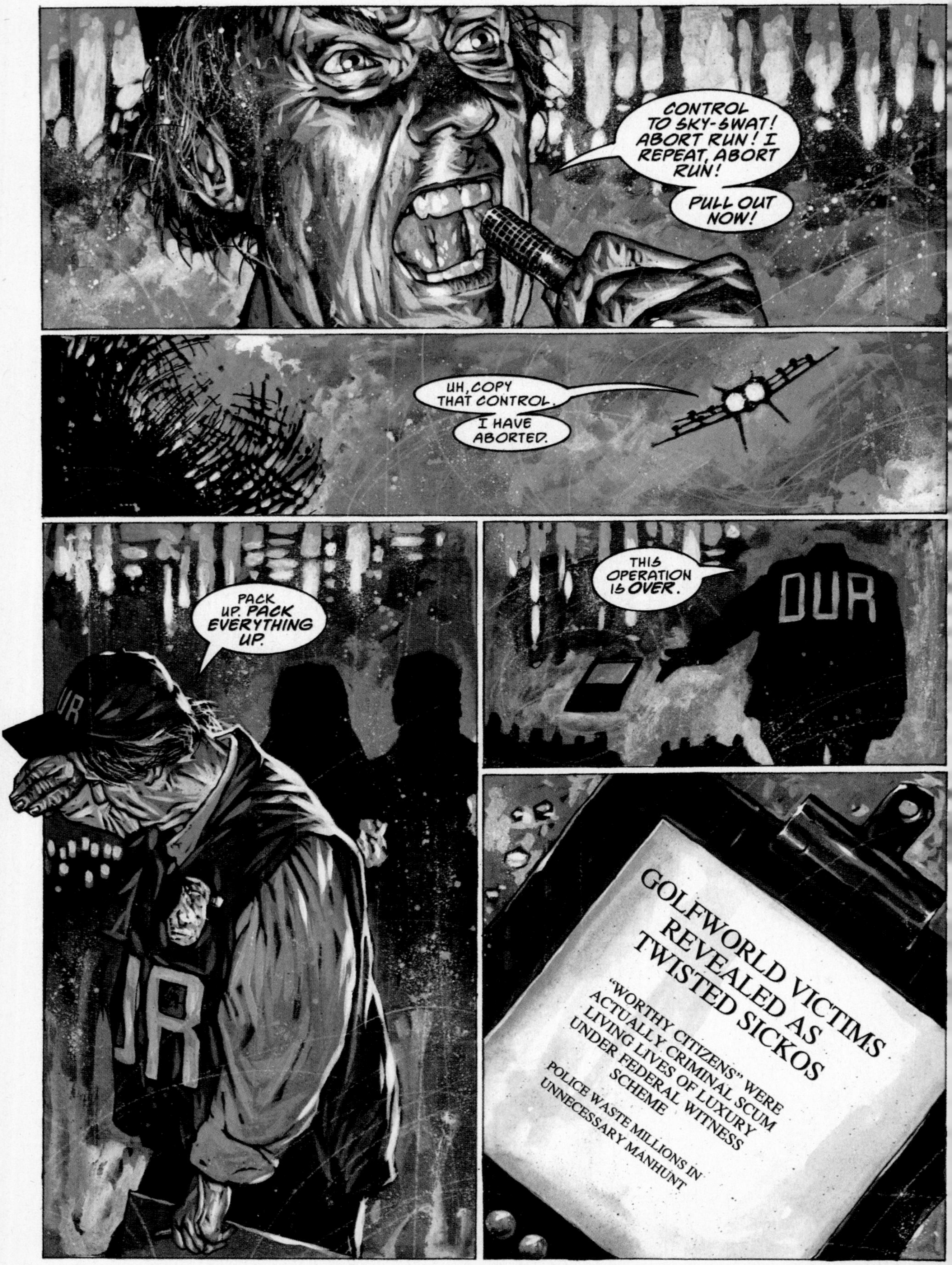
CONTROL TO SKY-SWAT! ABORT RUN! I REPEAT, ABORT RUN!
PULL OUT NOW!
UH, COPY THAT CONTROL.
I HAVE ABORTED.
PACK UP. PACK EVERYTHING UP.
THIS OPERATION IS OVER.
DUR
GOLFWORLD VICTIMS REVEALED AS TWISTED SICKOS
"WORTHY CITIZENS" WERE ACTUALLY CRIMINAL SCUM LIVING LIVES OF LUXURY UNDER FEDERAL WITNESS SCHEME
POLICE WASTE MILLIONS IN UNNECESSARY MANHUNT

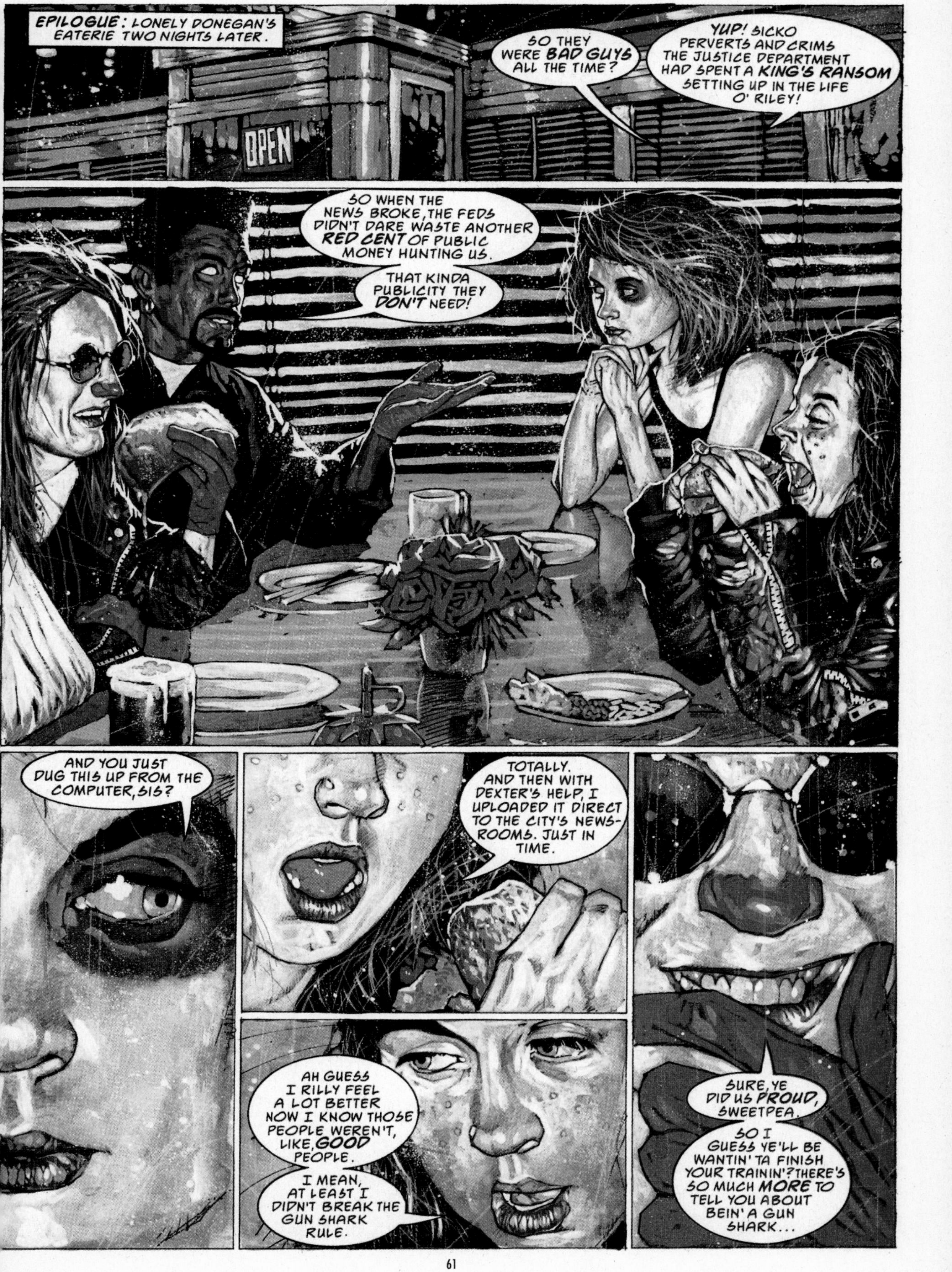
EPILOGUE: LONELY DONEGAN'S EATERIE TWO NIGHTS LATER.
SO THEY WERE BAD GUYS ALL THE TIME?
YUP! SICKO PERVERTS AND CRIMS THE JUSTICE DEPARTMENT HAD SPENT A KING'S RANSOM SETTING UP IN THE LIFE O' RILEY!
OPEN
SO WHEN THE NEWS BROKE, THE FEDS DIDN'T DARE WASTE ANOTHER RED CENT OF PUBLIC MONEY HUNTING US.
THAT KINDA PUBLICITY THEY DON'T NEED!
AND YOU JUST DUG THIS UP FROM THE COMPUTER, SIS?
TOTALLY. AND THEN WITH DEXTER'S HELP, I UPLOADED IT DIRECT TO THE CITY'S NEWS-ROOMS. JUST IN TIME.
AH GUESS I RILLY FEEL A LOT BETTER NOW I KNOW THOSE PEOPLE WEREN'T, LIKE, GOOD PEOPLE.
I MEAN, AT LEAST I DIDN'T BREAK THE GUN SHARK RULE.
SURE, YE DID US PROUD, SWEETPEA.
SO I GUESS YE'LL BE WANTIN' TA FINISH YOUR TRAININ'? THERE'S SO MUCH MORE TO TELL YOU ABOUT BEIN' A GUN SHARK...

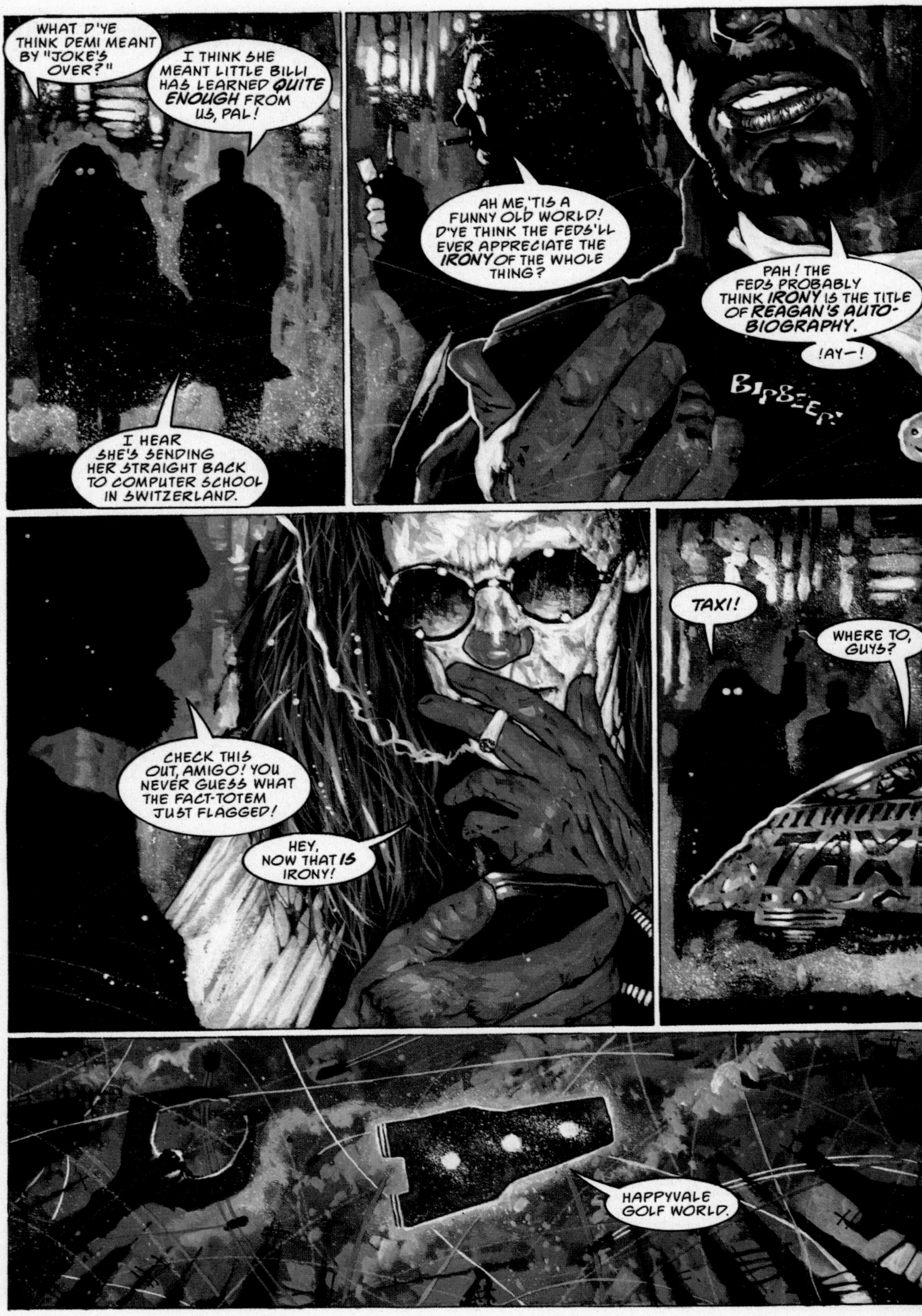
WHAT D'YE THINK DEMI MEANT BY "JOKE'S OVER?"
I THINK SHE MEANT LITTLE BILLI HAS LEARNED QUITE ENOUGH FROM US, PAL!
I HEAR SHE'S SENDING HER STRAIGHT BACK TO COMPUTER SCHOOL IN SWITZERLAND.
AH ME, 'TIS A FUNNY OLD WORLD! D'YE THINK THE FEDS'LL EVER APPRECIATE THE IRONY OF THE WHOLE THING?
PAH! THE FEDS PROBABLY THINK IRONY IS THE TITLE OF REAGAN'S AUTO-BIOGRAPHY.
!AY—!
BIPBEEP!
CHECK THIS OUT, AMIGO! YOU NEVER GUESS WHAT THE FACT-TOTEM JUST FLAGGED!
HEY, NOW THAT IS IRONY!
TAXI!
WHERE TO, GUYS?
TAXI
HAPPYVALE GOLF WORLD.

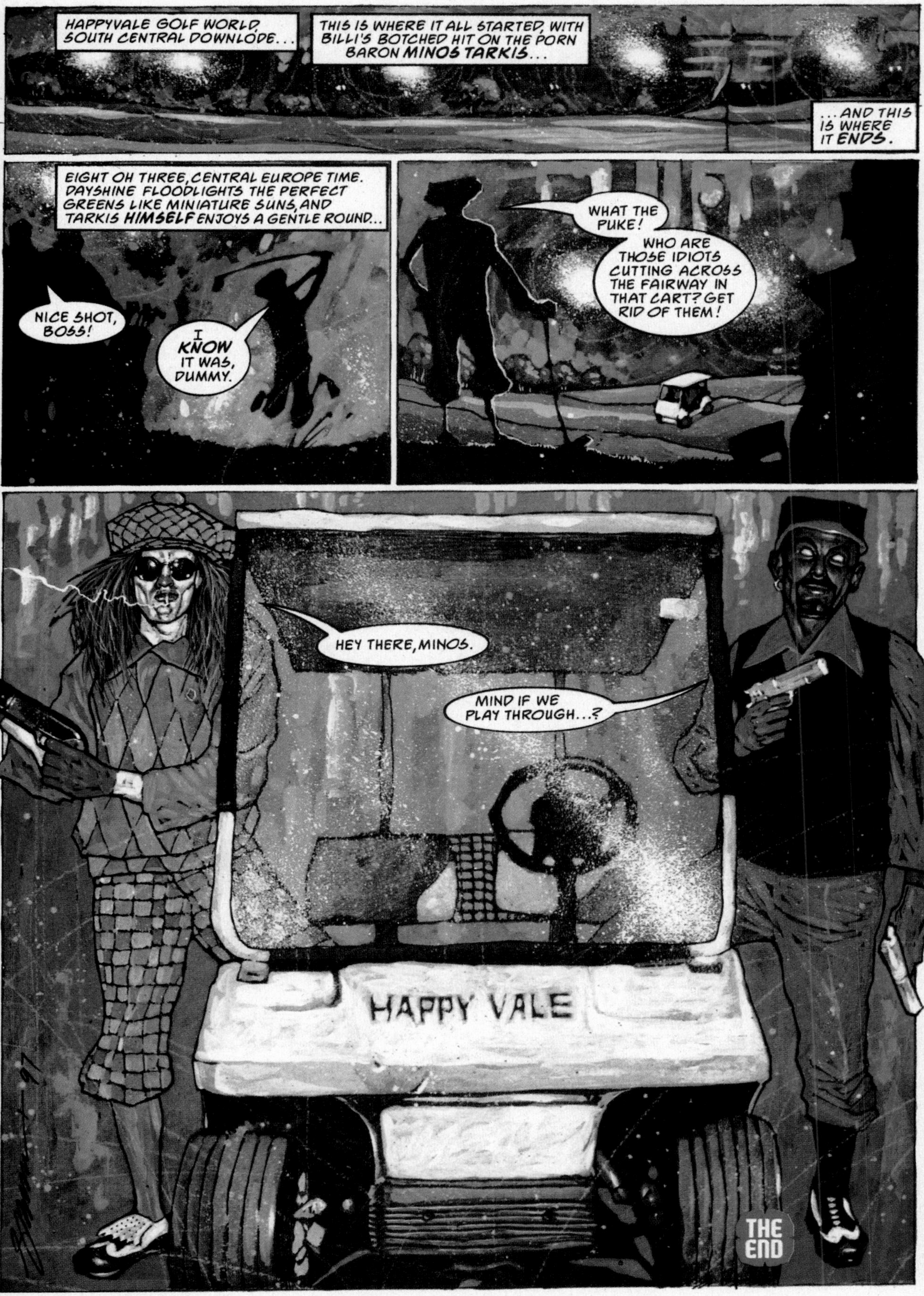

HAPPYVALE GOLF WORLD, SOUTH CENTRAL DOWNLODE...
THIS IS WHERE IT ALL STARTED, WITH BILLI'S BOTCHED HIT ON THE PORN BARON MINOS TARKIS...
...AND THIS IS WHERE IT ENDS.
EIGHT OH THREE, CENTRAL EUROPE TIME. DAYSHINE FLOODLIGHTS THE PERFECT GREENS LIKE MINIATURE SUNS, AND TARKIS HIMSELF ENJOYS A GENTLE ROUND...
NICE SHOT, BOSS!
I KNOW IT WAS, DUMMY.
WHAT THE PUKE!
WHO ARE THOSE IDIOTS CUTTING ACROSS THE FAIRWAY IN THAT CART? GET RID OF THEM!
HEY THERE, MINOS.
MIND IF WE PLAY THROUGH...?
HAPPY VALE
THE END

LUCK OF THE IRISH

Script: Dan Abnett

Art: Paul Johnson

Letters: Annie Parkhouse

Originally published in *2000 AD* Prog 1062

SINISTERDEXTER

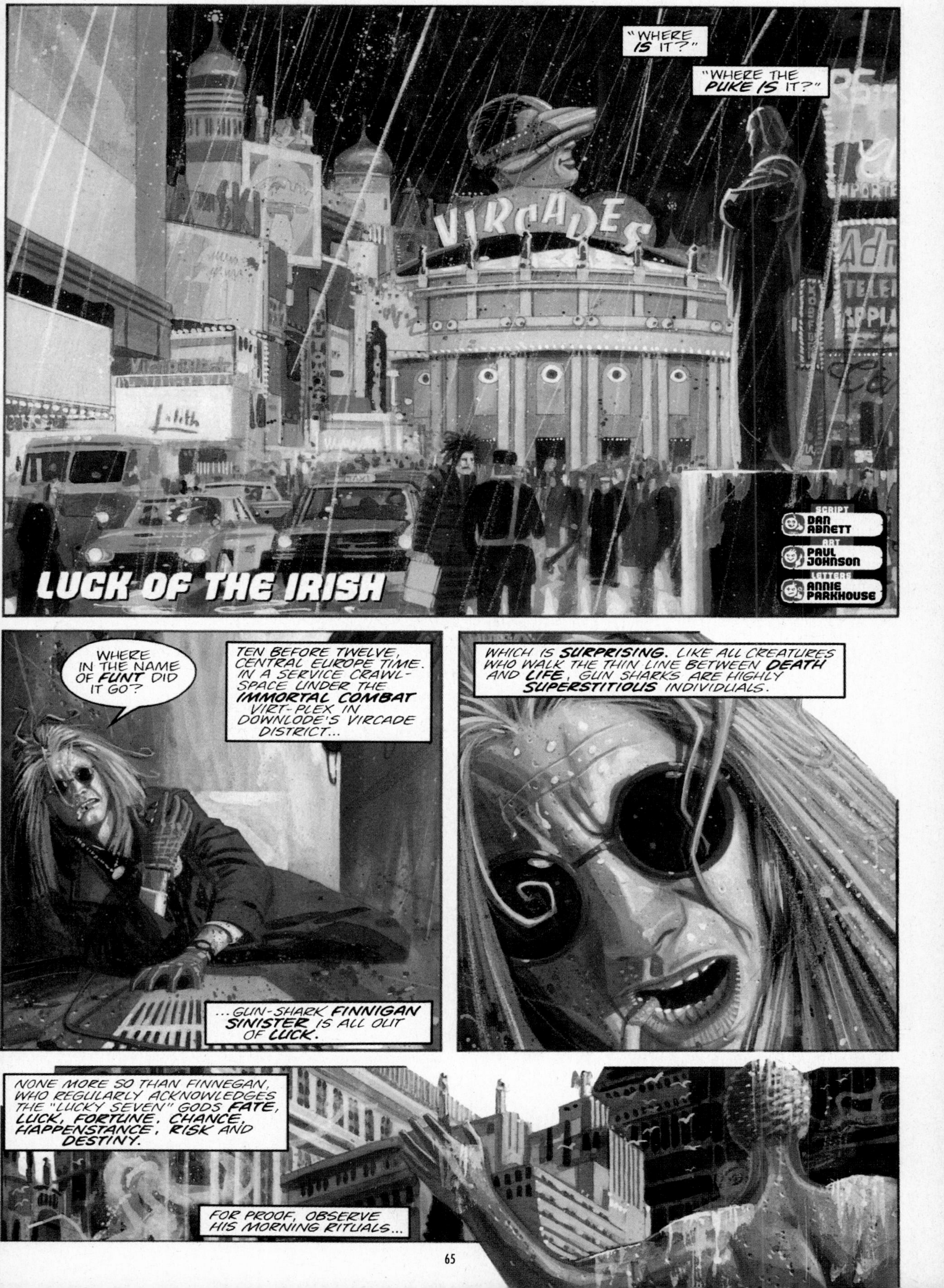
"WHERE IS IT?"
"WHERE THE PUKE IS IT?"
VIRCADES
LUCK OF THE IRISH
SCRIPT DAN ABNETT
ART PAUL JOHNSON
LETTERS ANNIE PARKHOUSE
WHERE IN THE NAME OF FUNT DID IT GO?
TEN BEFORE TWELVE, CENTRAL EUROPE TIME. IN A SERVICE CRAWL-SPACE UNDER THE IMMORTAL COMBAT VIRT-PLEX IN DOWNLODE'S VIRCADE DISTRICT...
...GUN-SHARK FINNIGAN SINISTER IS ALL OUT OF LUCK.
WHICH IS SURPRISING. LIKE ALL CREATURES WHO WALK THE THIN LINE BETWEEN DEATH AND LIFE, GUN SHARKS ARE HIGHLY SUPERSTITIOUS INDIVIDUALS.
NONE MORE SO THAN FINNEGAN, WHO REGULARLY ACKNOWLEDGES THE "LUCKY SEVEN" GODS FATE, LUCK, FORTUNE, CHANCE, HAPPENSTANCE, RISK AND DESTINY.
FOR PROOF, OBSERVE HIS MORNING RITUALS...

IT'S NOON! IT'S NOON! IT'S NOON! IT— SKRWWLLKKK!

WHAXK!

JESUS, WILL YE *SHUT UP?*

DOWNLODE "DO ZE R1n"

ON WAKING, HE SAYS A LITTLE PRAYER FOR *PROVIDENCE...*

...and as I get me up ta *whack*, I pray the Lord will watch me back, Amen.

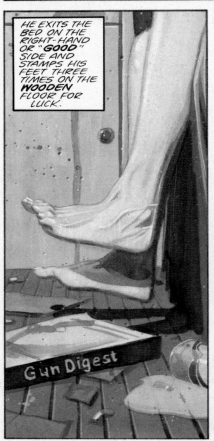

HE EXITS THE BED ON THE RIGHT-HAND OR *"GOOD"* SIDE AND STAMPS HIS FEET THREE TIMES ON THE *WOODEN* FLOOR FOR LUCK.

Gun Digest

HE USES A *FRESH BLADE* TO SHAVE, EVERY DAY.

AND HE ANOINTS ANY NICK WITH A DAB OF *HOLY WATER* FROM A BOTTLE HE GOT BLESSED AT THE ROMAN CHURCH ™.

WHEN HE COMES TO CLEAN HIS TEETH, HE LETS THE COLD FAWCET RUN FOR A FULL *THIRTY SECONDS* SO AS NOT TO GET THE UNLUCKY *"DEAD-WATER"* STANDING IN THE PIPE.

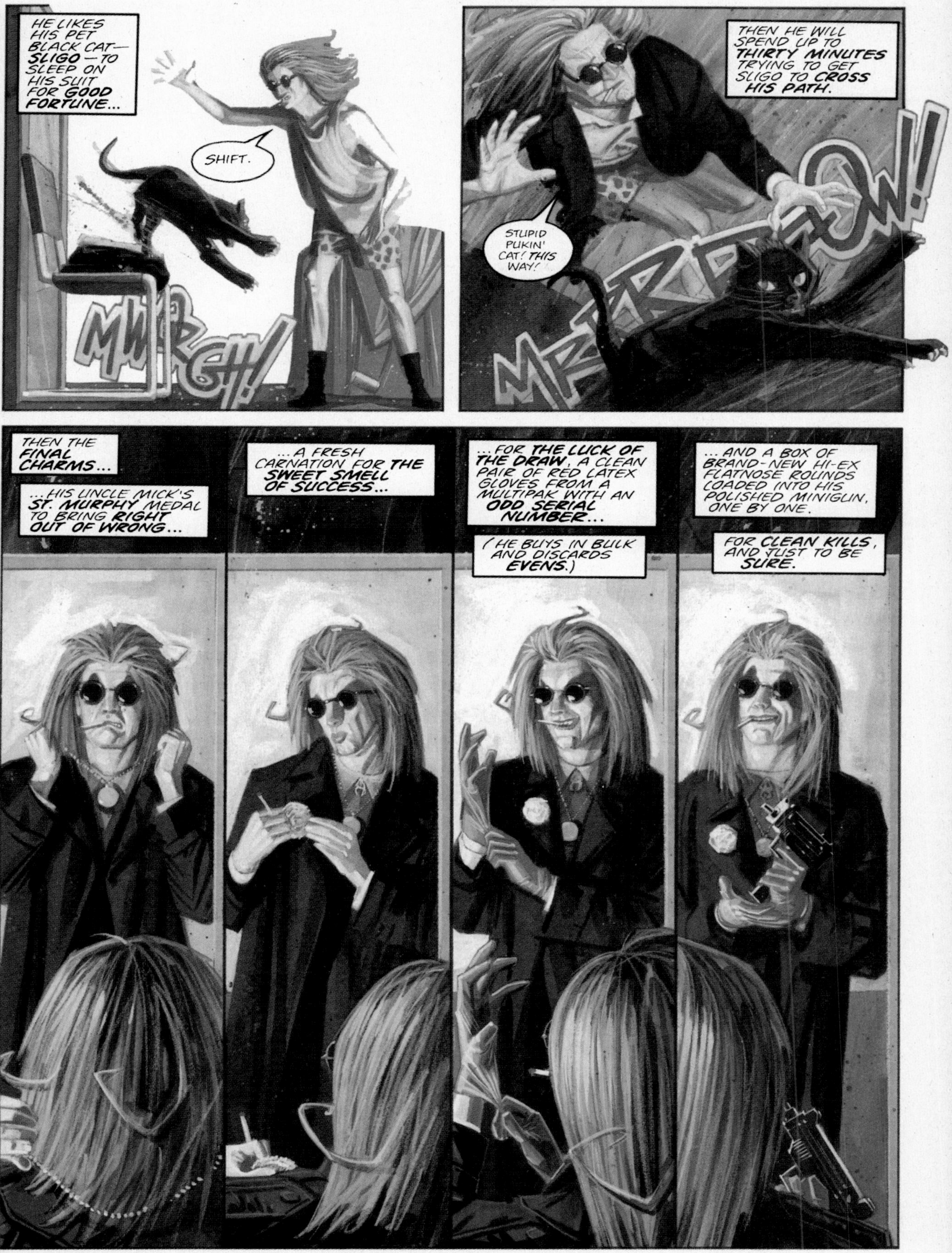
HE LIKES HIS PET BLACK CAT— SLIGO —TO SLEEP ON HIS SUIT FOR GOOD FORTUNE...
SHIFT.
MWRRGH!
THEN HE WILL SPEND UP TO THIRTY MINUTES TRYING TO GET SLIGO TO CROSS HIS PATH.
STUPID PUKIN' CAT! THIS WAY!
MRRROWW!
THEN THE FINAL CHARMS...
...HIS UNCLE MICK'S ST. MURPHY MEDAL TO BRING RIGHT OUT OF WRONG...
...A FRESH CARNATION FOR THE SWEET SMELL OF SUCCESS...
...FOR THE LUCK OF THE DRAW, A CLEAN PAIR OF RED LATEX GLOVES FROM A MULTIPAK WITH AN ODD SERIAL NUMBER...
(HE BUYS IN BULK AND DISCARDS EVENS.)
...AND A BOX OF BRAND-NEW HI-EX FLATNOSE ROUNDS LOADED INTO HIS POLISHED MINIGUN, ONE BY ONE.
FOR CLEAN KILLS, AND JUST TO BE SURE.

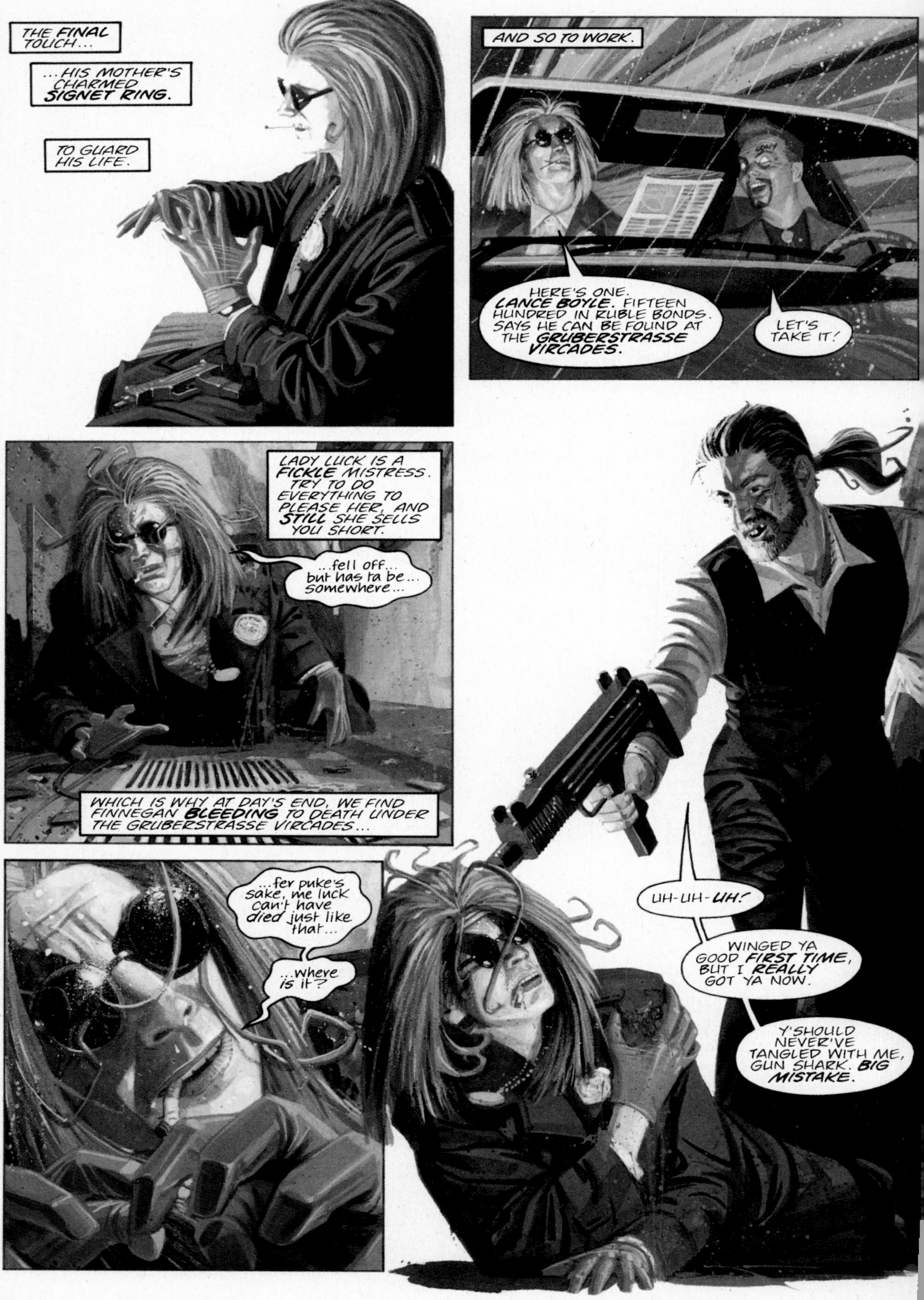

THE FINAL TOUCH...
...HIS MOTHER'S CHARMED SIGNET RING.
TO GUARD HIS LIFE.
AND SO TO WORK.
HERE'S ONE. LANCE BOYLE. FIFTEEN HUNDRED IN RUBLE BONDS. SAYS HE CAN BE FOUND AT THE GRUBERSTRASSE VIRCADES.
LET'S TAKE IT!
LADY LUCK IS A FICKLE MISTRESS. TRY TO DO EVERYTHING TO PLEASE HER, AND STILL SHE SELLS YOU SHORT.
...fell off... but has ta be... somewhere...
WHICH IS WHY AT DAY'S END, WE FIND FINNEGAN BLEEDING TO DEATH UNDER THE GRUBERSTRASSE VIRCADES...
...fer puke's sake, me luck can't have died just like that...
...where is it?
UH-UH-UH!
WINGED YA GOOD FIRST TIME, BUT I REALLY GOT YA NOW.
Y'SHOULD NEVER'VE TANGLED WITH ME, GUN SHARK. BIG MISTAKE.

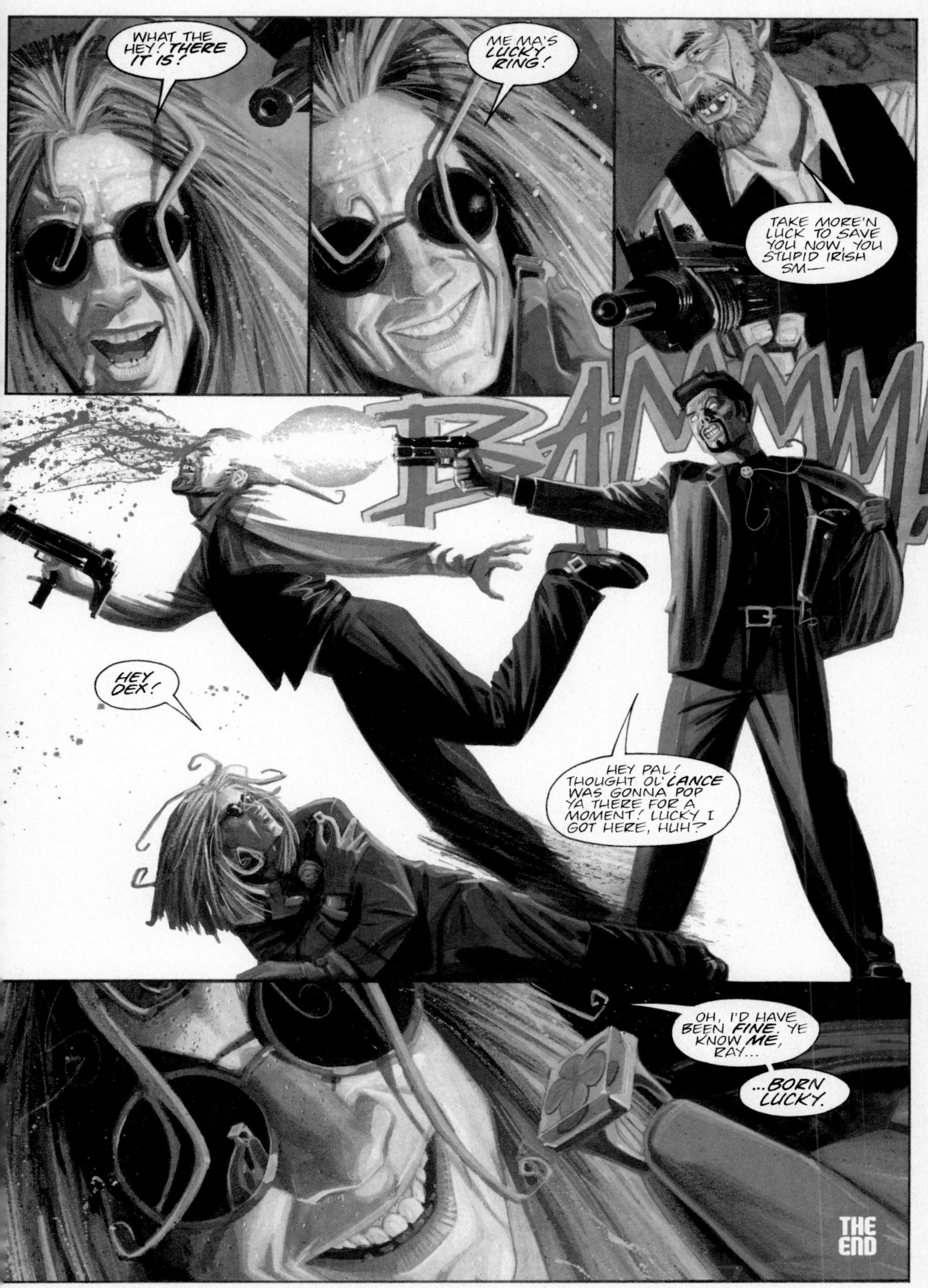
WHAT THE HEY! THERE IT IS!
ME MA'S LUCKY RING!
TAKE MORE'N LUCK TO SAVE YOU NOW, YOU STUPID IRISH SM—
BAMMM!
HEY DEX!
HEY PAL! THOUGHT OL' LANCE WAS GONNA POP YA THERE FOR A MOMENT! LUCKY I GOT HERE, HUH?
OH, I'D HAVE BEEN FINE. YE KNOW ME, RAY...
...BORN LUCKY.
THE END

WAITING FOR GOD KNOWS

Script: Dan Abnett

Art: Julian Gibson

Letters: Tom Frame

Originally published in *2000 AD* Prog 1063

SINISTERDEXTER

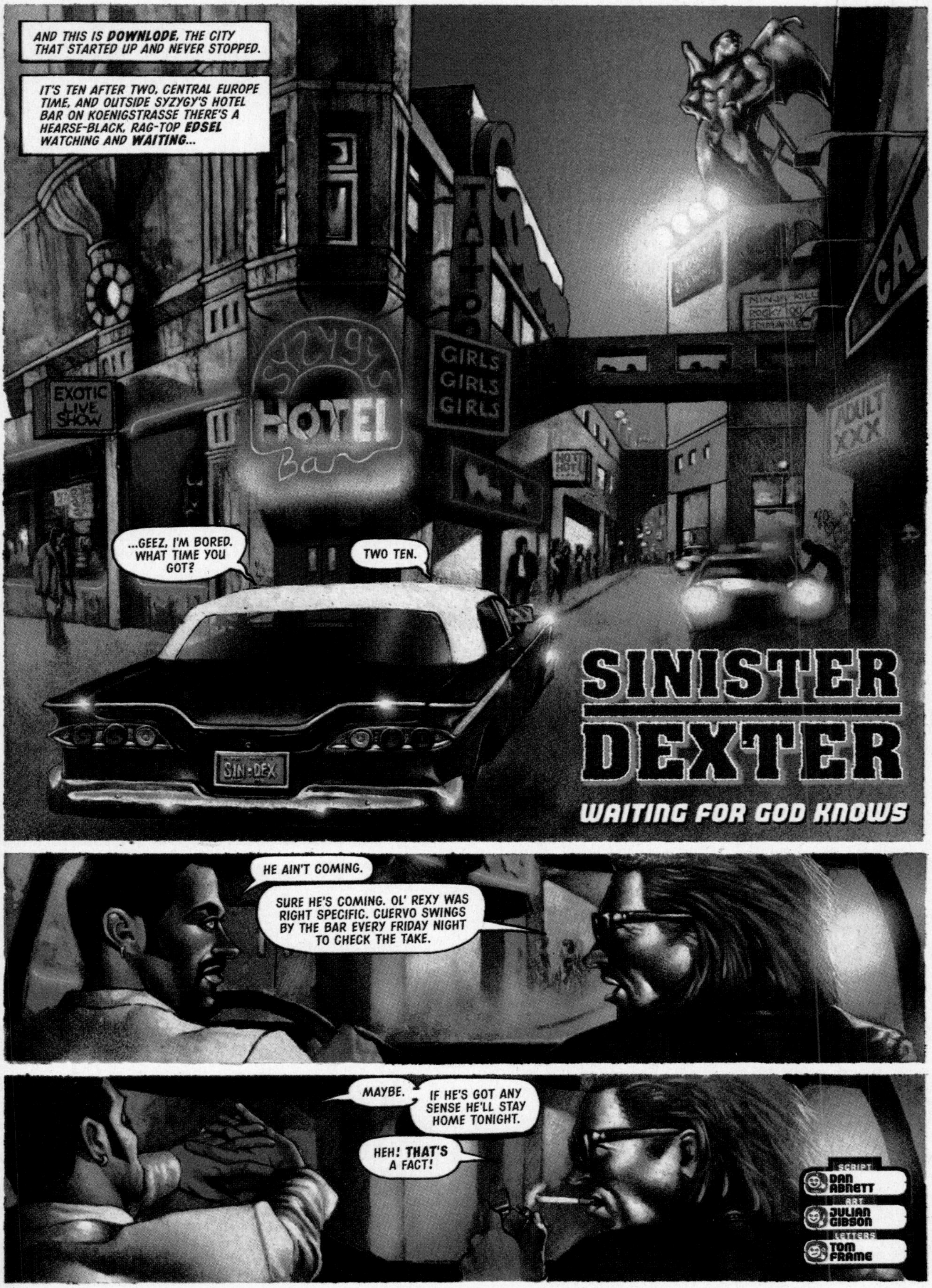
AND THIS IS DOWNLODE, THE CITY THAT STARTED UP AND NEVER STOPPED.
IT'S TEN AFTER TWO, CENTRAL EUROPE TIME, AND OUTSIDE SYZYGY'S HOTEL BAR ON KOENIGSTRASSE THERE'S A HEARSE-BLACK, RAG-TOP EDSEL WATCHING AND WAITING...
EXOTIC LIVE SHOW
HOTEL
Bar
GIRLS GIRLS GIRLS
ADULT XXX
...GEEZ, I'M BORED. WHAT TIME YOU GOT?
TWO TEN.
SIN-DEX
SINISTER DEXTER
WAITING FOR GOD KNOWS
HE AIN'T COMING.
SURE HE'S COMING. OL' REXY WAS RIGHT SPECIFIC. CUERVO SWINGS BY THE BAR EVERY FRIDAY NIGHT TO CHECK THE TAKE.
MAYBE.
IF HE'S GOT ANY SENSE HE'LL STAY HOME TONIGHT.
HEH! THAT'S A FACT!
SCRIPT DAN ABNETT
ART JULIAN GIBSON
LETTERS TOM FRAME

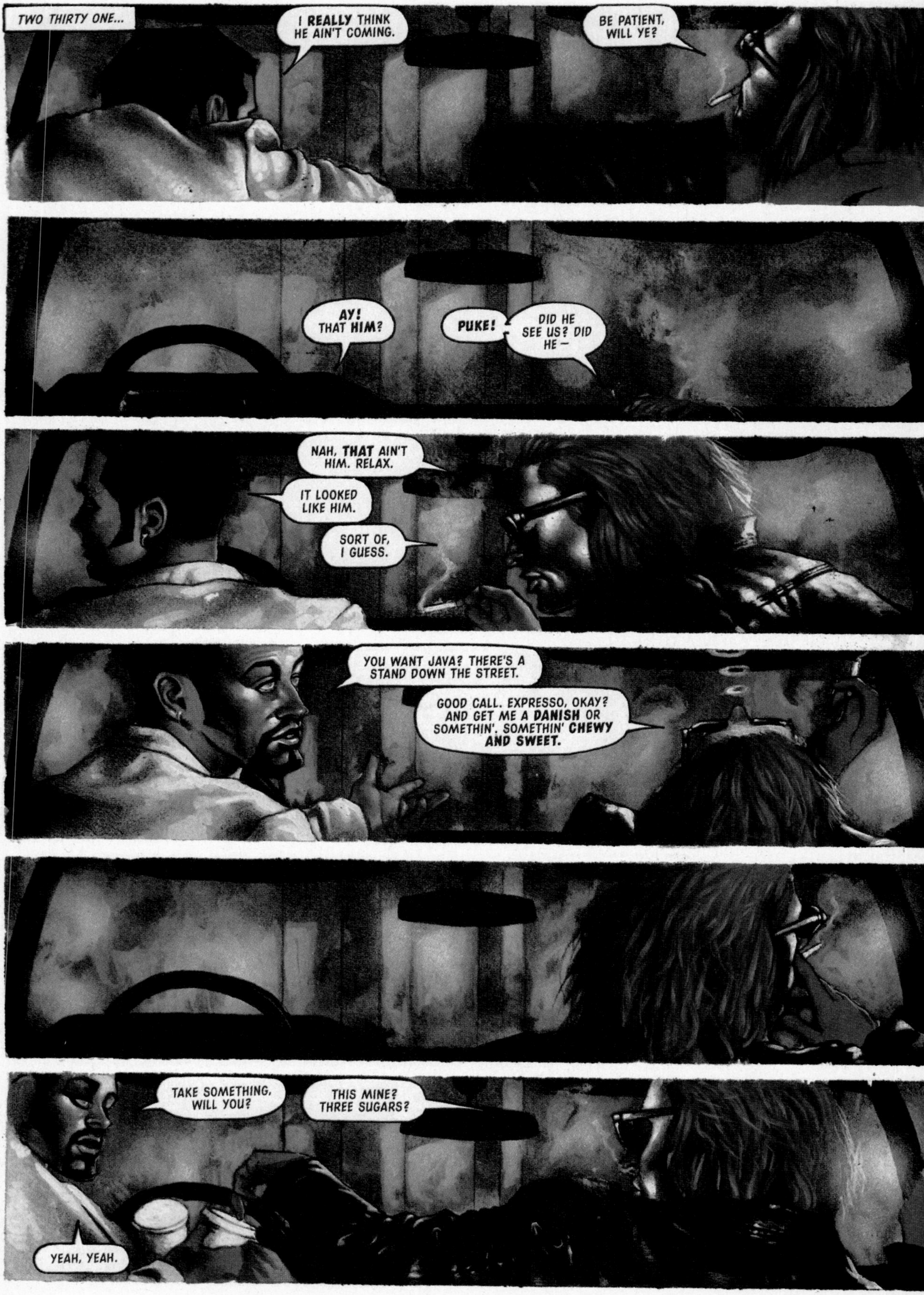

TWO THIRTY ONE...
I **REALLY** THINK HE AIN'T COMING.
BE PATIENT, WILL YE?
AY! THAT **HIM**?
PUKE!
DID HE SEE US? DID HE —
NAH, **THAT** AIN'T HIM. RELAX.
IT LOOKED LIKE HIM.
SORT OF, I GUESS.
YOU WANT JAVA? THERE'S A STAND DOWN THE STREET.
GOOD CALL. EXPRESSO, OKAY? AND GET ME A **DANISH** OR SOMETHIN'. SOMETHIN' **CHEWY AND SWEET.**
TAKE SOMETHING, WILL YOU?
THIS MINE? THREE SUGARS?
YEAH, YEAH.

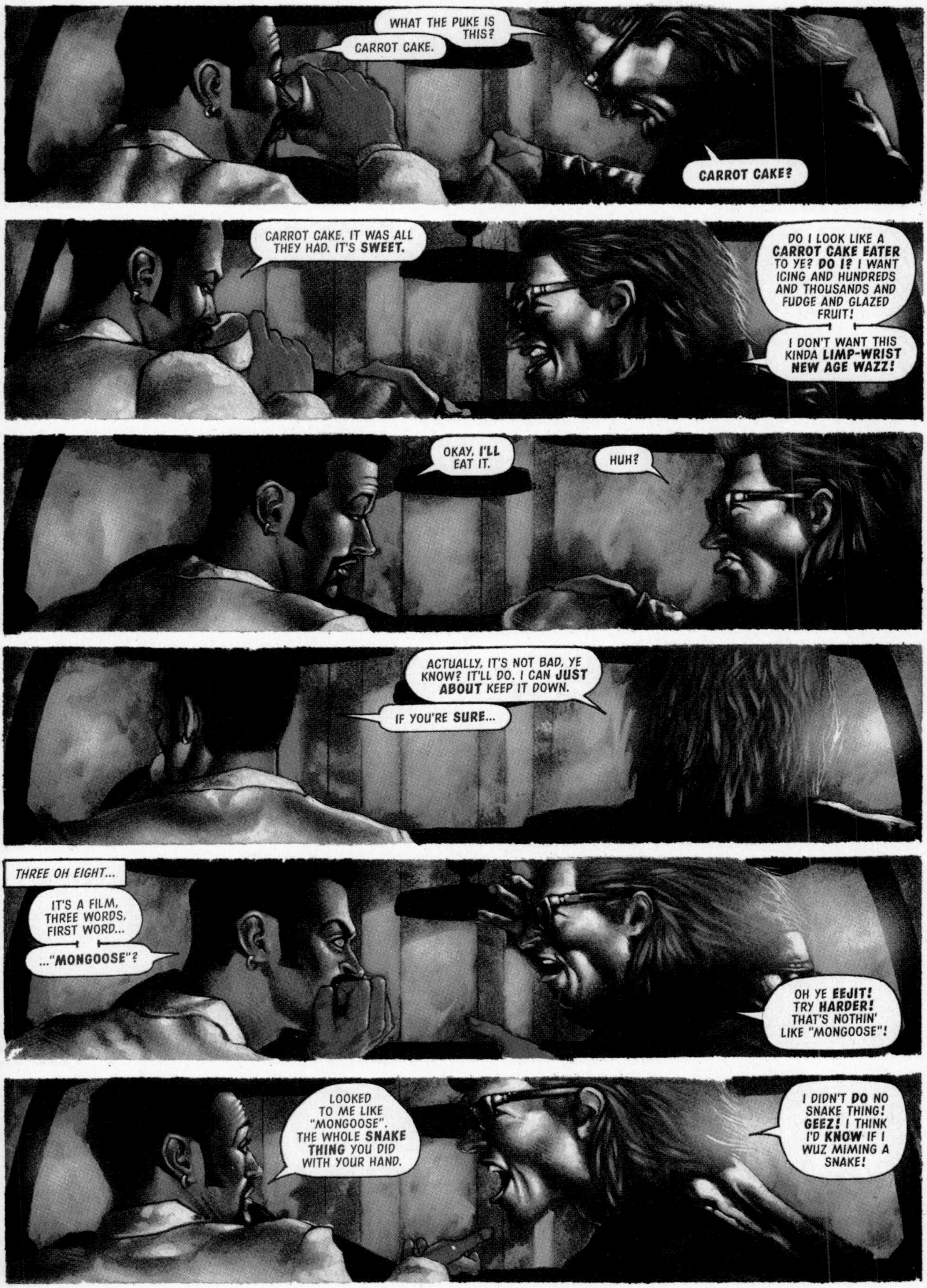
WHAT THE PUKE IS THIS?
CARROT CAKE.
CARROT CAKE?
CARROT CAKE. IT WAS ALL THEY HAD. IT'S SWEET.
DO I LOOK LIKE A CARROT CAKE EATER TO YE? DO I? I WANT ICING AND HUNDREDS AND THOUSANDS AND FUDGE AND GLAZED FRUIT!
I DON'T WANT THIS KINDA LIMP-WRIST NEW AGE WAZZ!
OKAY, I'LL EAT IT.
HUH?
ACTUALLY, IT'S NOT BAD, YE KNOW? IT'LL DO. I CAN JUST ABOUT KEEP IT DOWN.
IF YOU'RE SURE...
THREE OH EIGHT...
IT'S A FILM, THREE WORDS, FIRST WORD...
..."MONGOOSE"?
OH YE EEJIT! TRY HARDER! THAT'S NOTHIN' LIKE "MONGOOSE"!
LOOKED TO ME LIKE "MONGOOSE". THE WHOLE SNAKE THING YOU DID WITH YOUR HAND.
I DIDN'T DO NO SNAKE THING! GEEZ! I THINK I'D KNOW IF I WUZ MIMING A SNAKE!

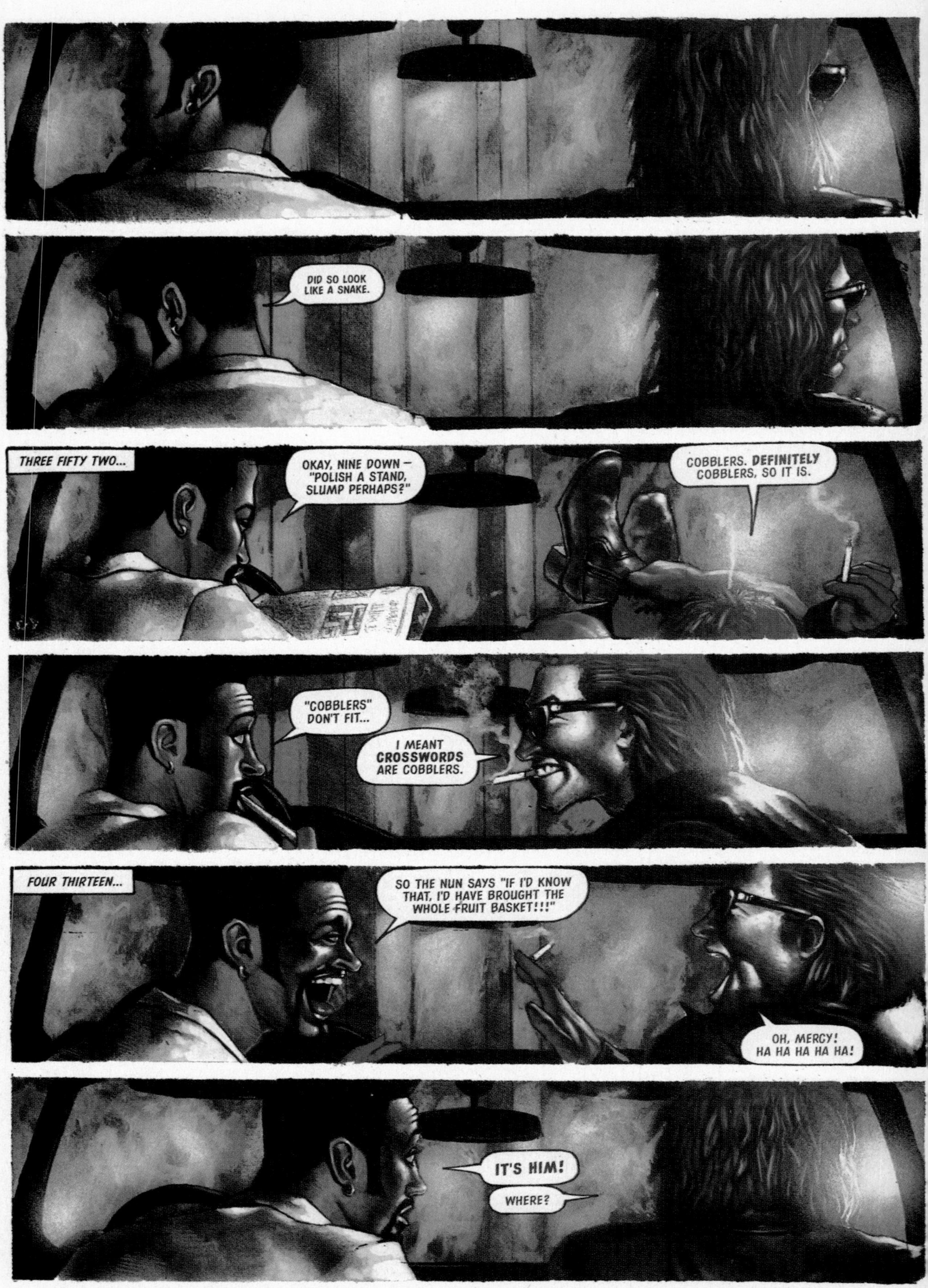
DID SO LOOK LIKE A SNAKE.
THREE FIFTY TWO...
OKAY, NINE DOWN — "POLISH A STAND, SLUMP PERHAPS?"
COBBLERS. DEFINITELY COBBLERS, SO IT IS.
"COBBLERS" DON'T FIT...
I MEANT CROSSWORDS ARE COBBLERS.
FOUR THIRTEEN...
SO THE NUN SAYS "IF I'D KNOW THAT, I'D HAVE BROUGHT THE WHOLE FRUIT BASKET!!!"
OH, MERCY! HA HA HA HA HA!
IT'S HIM!
WHERE?

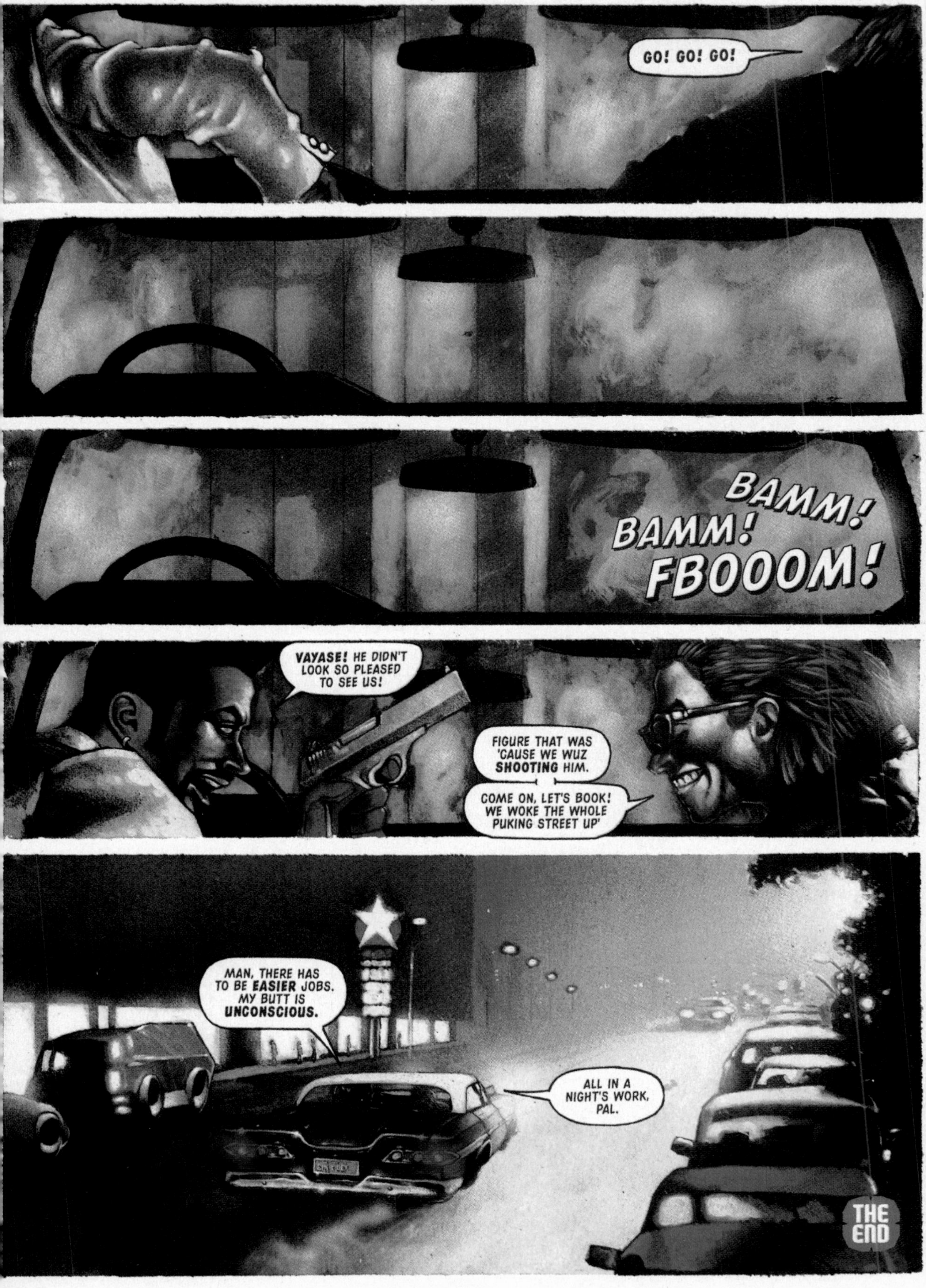
GO! GO! GO!
BAMM!
BAMM!
FBOOOM!
VAYASE! HE DIDN'T LOOK SO PLEASED TO SEE US!
FIGURE THAT WAS 'CAUSE WE WUZ SHOOTING HIM.
COME ON, LET'S BOOK! WE WOKE THE WHOLE PUKING STREET UP'
MAN, THERE HAS TO BE EASIER JOBS. MY BUTT IS UNCONSCIOUS.
ALL IN A NIGHT'S WORK, PAL.
THE END

60 SECONDS

Script: Dan Abnett

Art: Paul Johnson

Letters: Tom Frame

Originally published in *2000 AD* Prog 1064

SINISTERDEXTER

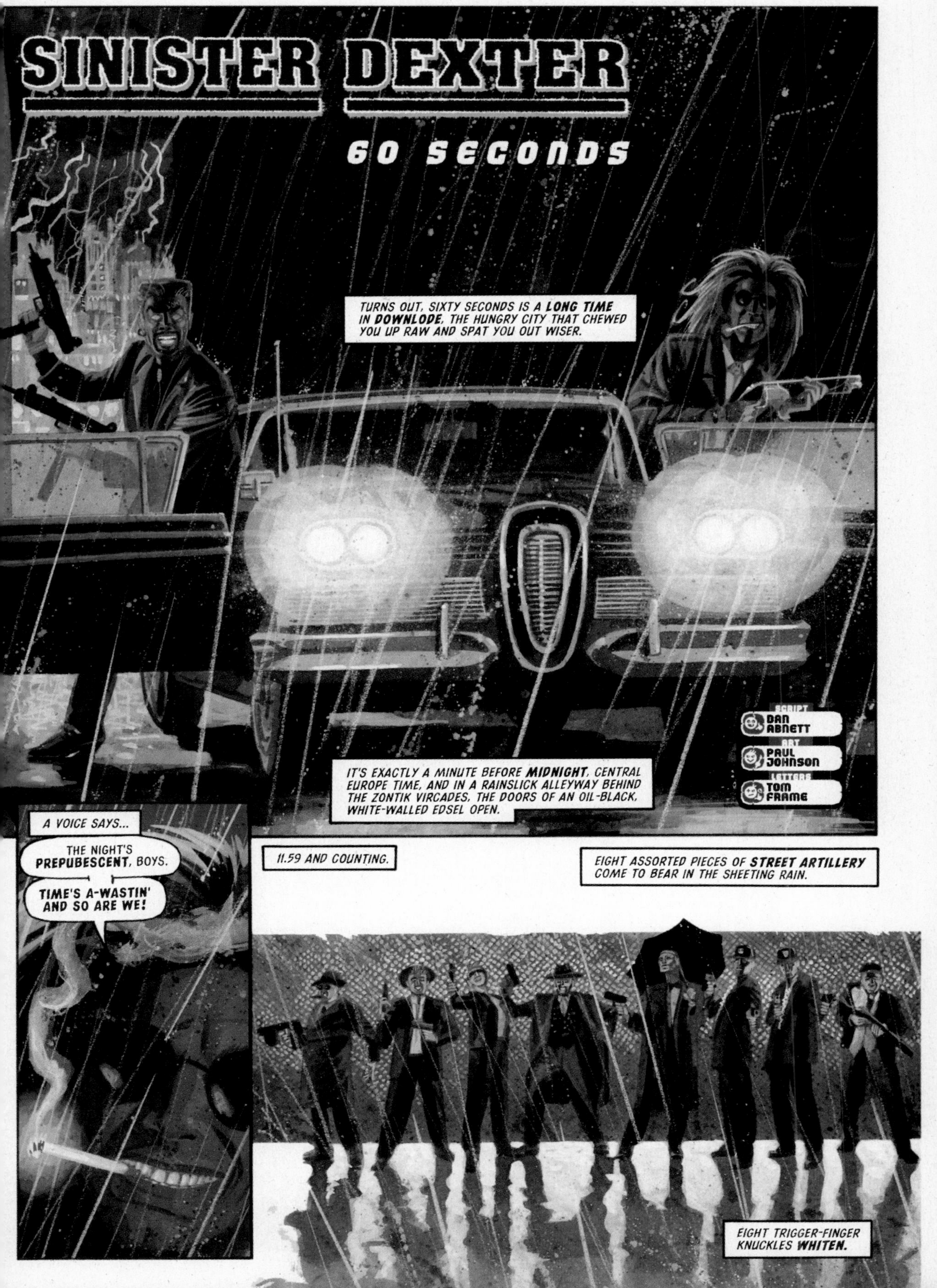
SINISTER DEXTER
60 SECONDS
TURNS OUT, SIXTY SECONDS IS A LONG TIME IN DOWNLODE, THE HUNGRY CITY THAT CHEWED YOU UP RAW AND SPAT YOU OUT WISER.
SCRIPT DAN ABNETT
ART PAUL JOHNSON
LETTERS TOM FRAME
IT'S EXACTLY A MINUTE BEFORE MIDNIGHT, CENTRAL EUROPE TIME, AND IN A RAINSLICK ALLEYWAY BEHIND THE ZONTIK VIRCADES, THE DOORS OF AN OIL-BLACK, WHITE-WALLED EDSEL OPEN.
A VOICE SAYS...
THE NIGHT'S PREPUBESCENT, BOYS.
TIME'S A-WASTIN' AND SO ARE WE!
11.59 AND COUNTING.
EIGHT ASSORTED PIECES OF STREET ARTILLERY COME TO BEAR IN THE SHEETING RAIN.
EIGHT TRIGGER-FINGER KNUCKLES WHITEN.

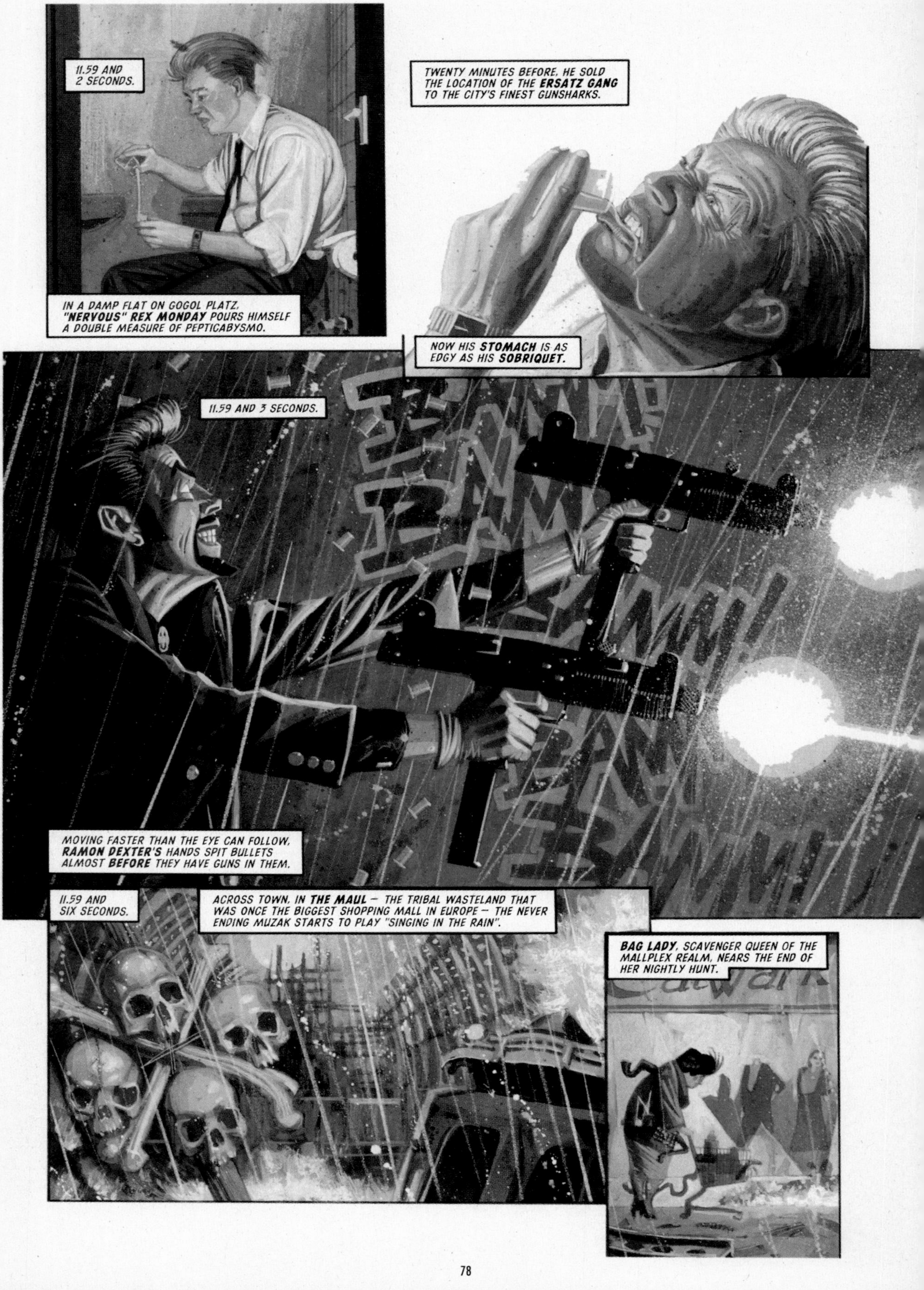
11.59 AND
2 SECONDS.
IN A DAMP FLAT ON GOGOL PLATZ,
"NERVOUS" REX MONDAY POURS HIMSELF
A DOUBLE MEASURE OF PEPTICABYSMO.
TWENTY MINUTES BEFORE, HE SOLD
THE LOCATION OF THE ERSATZ GANG
TO THE CITY'S FINEST GUNSHARKS.
NOW HIS STOMACH IS AS
EDGY AS HIS SOBRIQUET.
11.59 AND 3 SECONDS.
MOVING FASTER THAN THE EYE CAN FOLLOW,
RAMON DEXTER'S HANDS SPIT BULLETS
ALMOST BEFORE THEY HAVE GUNS IN THEM.
11.59 AND
SIX SECONDS.
ACROSS TOWN, IN THE MAUL – THE TRIBAL WASTELAND THAT
WAS ONCE THE BIGGEST SHOPPING MALL IN EUROPE – THE NEVER
ENDING MUZAK STARTS TO PLAY "SINGING IN THE RAIN".
BAG LADY, SCAVENGER QUEEN OF THE
MALLPLEX REALM, NEARS THE END OF
HER NIGHTLY HUNT.

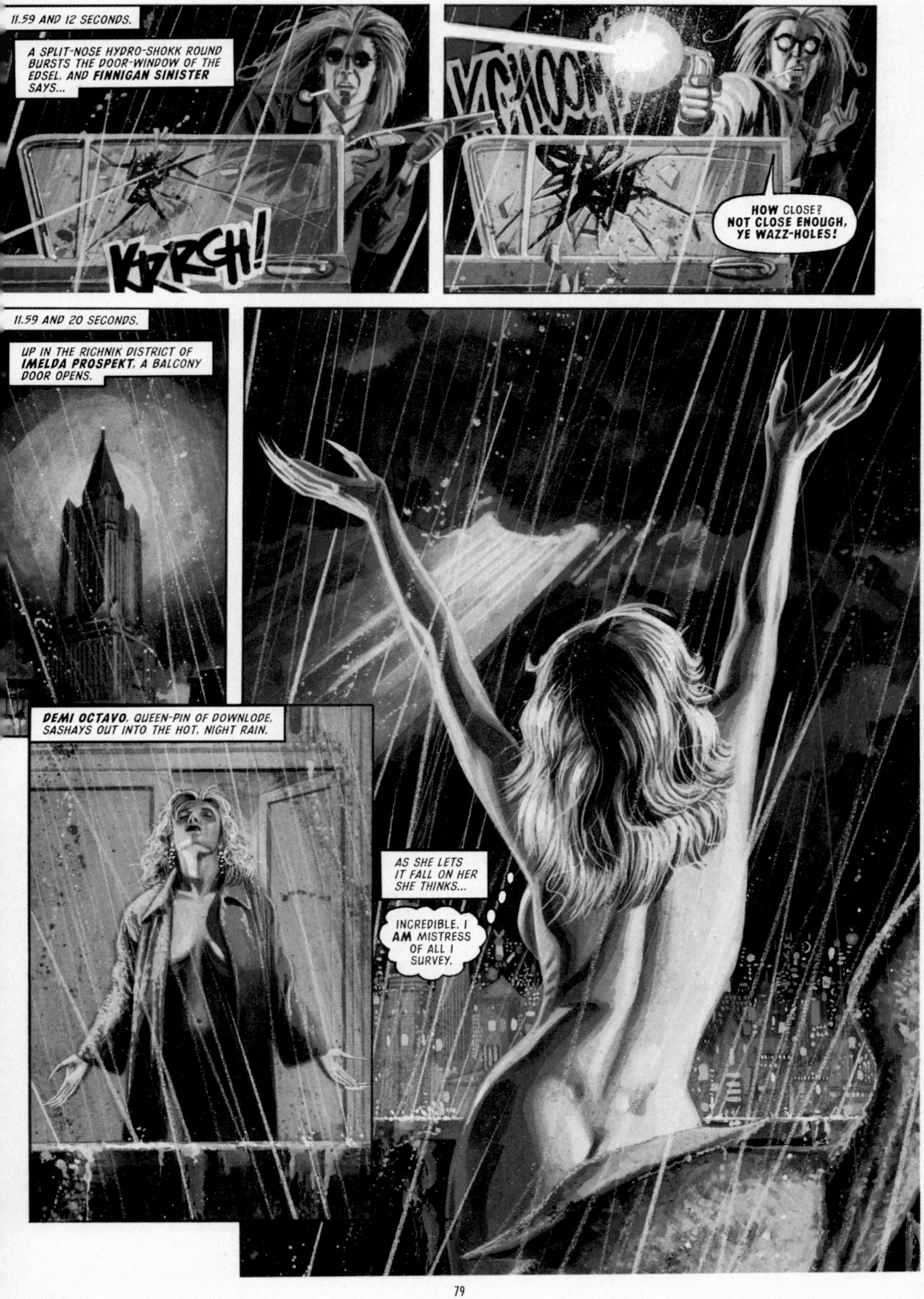
11.59 AND 12 SECONDS.
A SPLIT-NOSE HYDRO-SHOKK ROUND BURSTS THE DOOR-WINDOW OF THE EDSEL, AND FINNIGAN SINISTER SAYS...
KRRGH!
KCHOOM!
HOW CLOSE? NOT CLOSE ENOUGH, YE WAZZ-HOLES!
11.59 AND 20 SECONDS.
UP IN THE RICHNIK DISTRICT OF IMELDA PROSPEKT, A BALCONY DOOR OPENS.
DEMI OCTAVO, QUEEN-PIN OF DOWNLODE, SASHAYS OUT INTO THE HOT, NIGHT RAIN.
AS SHE LETS IT FALL ON HER SHE THINKS...
INCREDIBLE. I AM MISTRESS OF ALL I SURVEY.

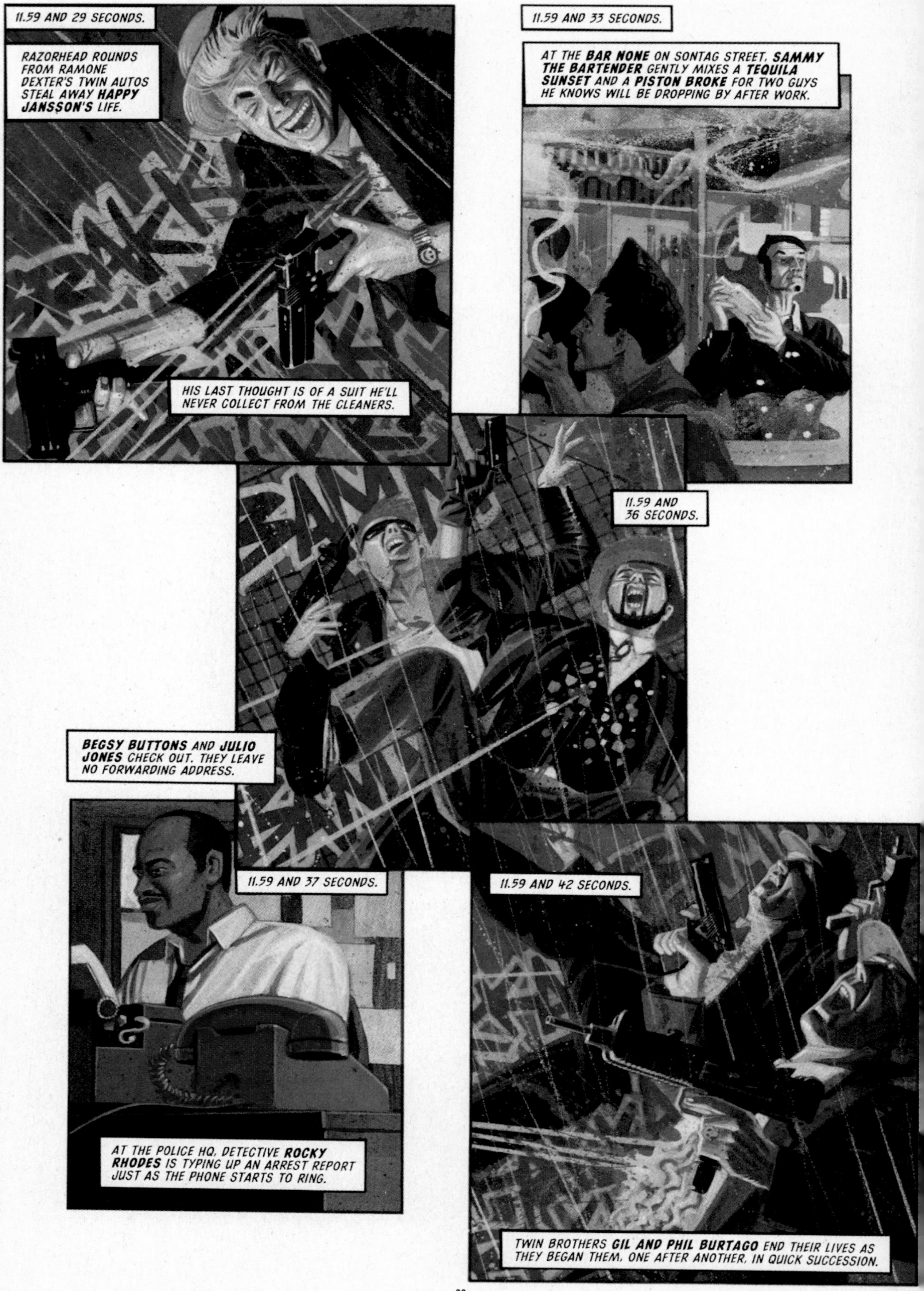
11.59 AND 29 SECONDS.
RAZORHEAD ROUNDS FROM RAMONE DEXTER'S TWIN AUTOS STEAL AWAY HAPPY JANSSON'S LIFE.
HIS LAST THOUGHT IS OF A SUIT HE'LL NEVER COLLECT FROM THE CLEANERS.
11.59 AND 33 SECONDS.
AT THE BAR NONE ON SONTAG STREET, SAMMY THE BARTENDER GENTLY MIXES A TEQUILA SUNSET AND A PISTON BROKE FOR TWO GUYS HE KNOWS WILL BE DROPPING BY AFTER WORK.
11.59 AND 36 SECONDS.
BEGSY BUTTONS AND JULIO JONES CHECK OUT. THEY LEAVE NO FORWARDING ADDRESS.
11.59 AND 37 SECONDS.
AT THE POLICE HQ, DETECTIVE ROCKY RHODES IS TYPING UP AN ARREST REPORT JUST AS THE PHONE STARTS TO RING.
11.59 AND 42 SECONDS.
TWIN BROTHERS GIL AND PHIL BURTAGO END THEIR LIVES AS THEY BEGAN THEM, ONE AFTER ANOTHER, IN QUICK SUCCESSION.

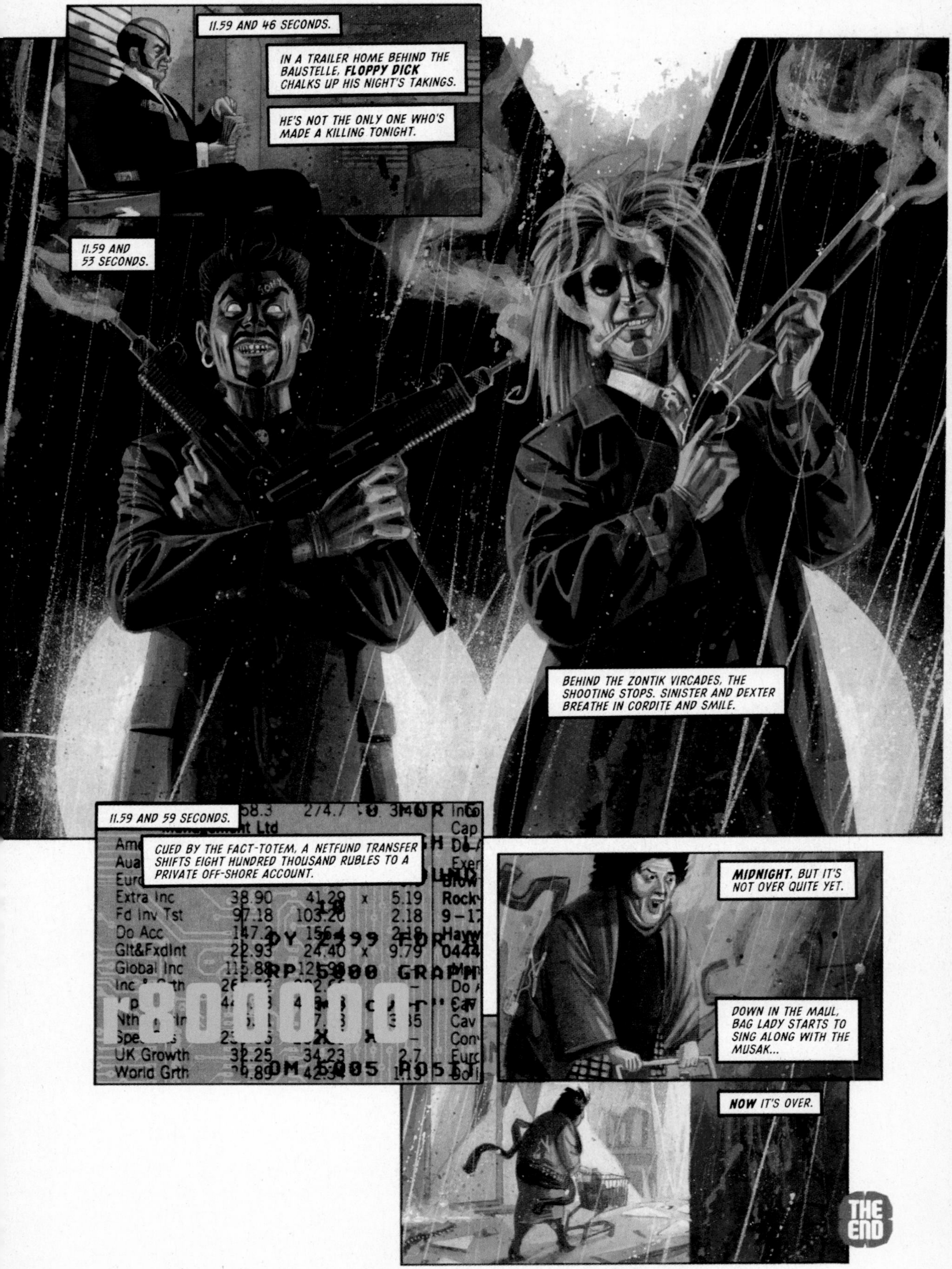
11.59 AND 46 SECONDS.
IN A TRAILER HOME BEHIND THE BAUSTELLE, FLOPPY DICK CHALKS UP HIS NIGHT'S TAKINGS.
HE'S NOT THE ONLY ONE WHO'S MADE A KILLING TONIGHT.
11.59 AND 53 SECONDS.
BEHIND THE ZONTIK VIRCADES, THE SHOOTING STOPS. SINISTER AND DEXTER BREATHE IN CORDITE AND SMILE.
11.59 AND 59 SECONDS.
CUED BY THE FACT-TOTEM, A NETFUND TRANSFER SHIFTS EIGHT HUNDRED THOUSAND RUBLES TO A PRIVATE OFF-SHORE ACCOUNT.
r800000
MIDNIGHT, BUT IT'S NOT OVER QUITE YET.
DOWN IN THE MAUL, BAG LADY STARTS TO SING ALONG WITH THE MUSAK...
NOW IT'S OVER.
THE END

THE WORST FIGHT WE WAS EVER IN

Script: Dan Abnett

Art: Julian Gibson

Letters: Steve Potter

Originally published in *2000 AD* Prog 1067

SINISTERDEXTER

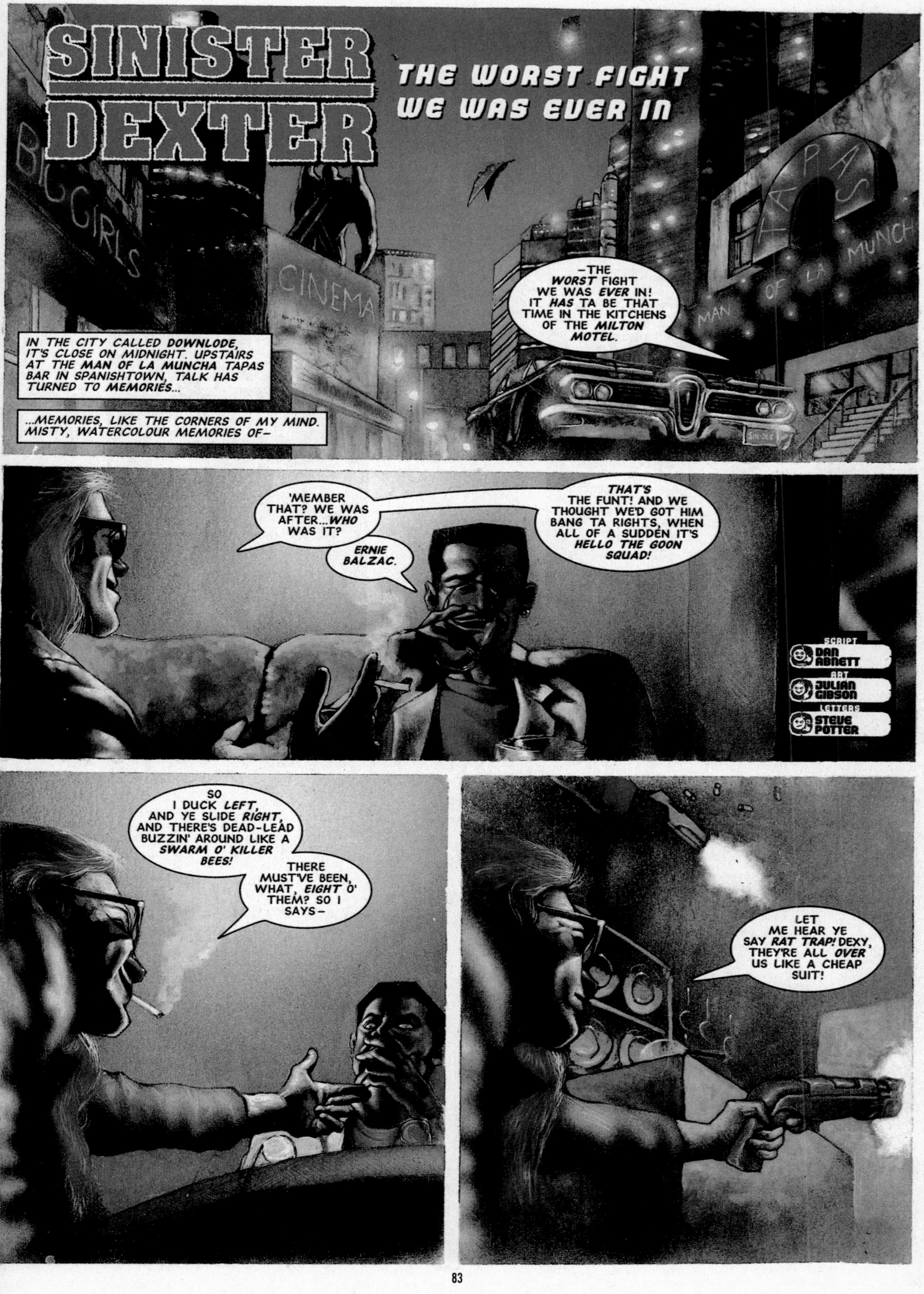
SINISTER DEXTER
THE WORST FIGHT WE WAS EVER IN
BIG GIRLS
CINEMA
TAPAS
MAN OF LA MUNCH
IN THE CITY CALLED DOWNLODE, IT'S CLOSE ON MIDNIGHT. UPSTAIRS AT THE MAN OF LA MUNCHA TAPAS BAR IN SPANISHTOWN, TALK HAS TURNED TO MEMORIES...
...MEMORIES, LIKE THE CORNERS OF MY MIND. MISTY, WATERCOLOUR MEMORIES OF–
–THE WORST FIGHT WE WAS EVER IN! IT HAS TA BE THAT TIME IN THE KITCHENS OF THE MILTON MOTEL.
'MEMBER THAT? WE WAS AFTER...WHO WAS IT?
ERNIE BALZAC.
THAT'S THE FUNT! AND WE THOUGHT WE'D GOT HIM BANG TA RIGHTS, WHEN ALL OF A SUDDEN IT'S HELLO THE GOON SQUAD!
SCRIPT DAN ABNETT
ART JULIAN GIBSON
LETTERS STEVE POTTER
SO I DUCK LEFT, AND YE SLIDE RIGHT, AND THERE'S DEAD-LEAD BUZZIN' AROUND LIKE A SWARM O' KILLER BEES!
THERE MUST'VE BEEN, WHAT, EIGHT O' THEM? SO I SAYS–
LET ME HEAR YE SAY RAT TRAP! DEXY, THEY'RE ALL OVER US LIKE A CHEAP SUIT!

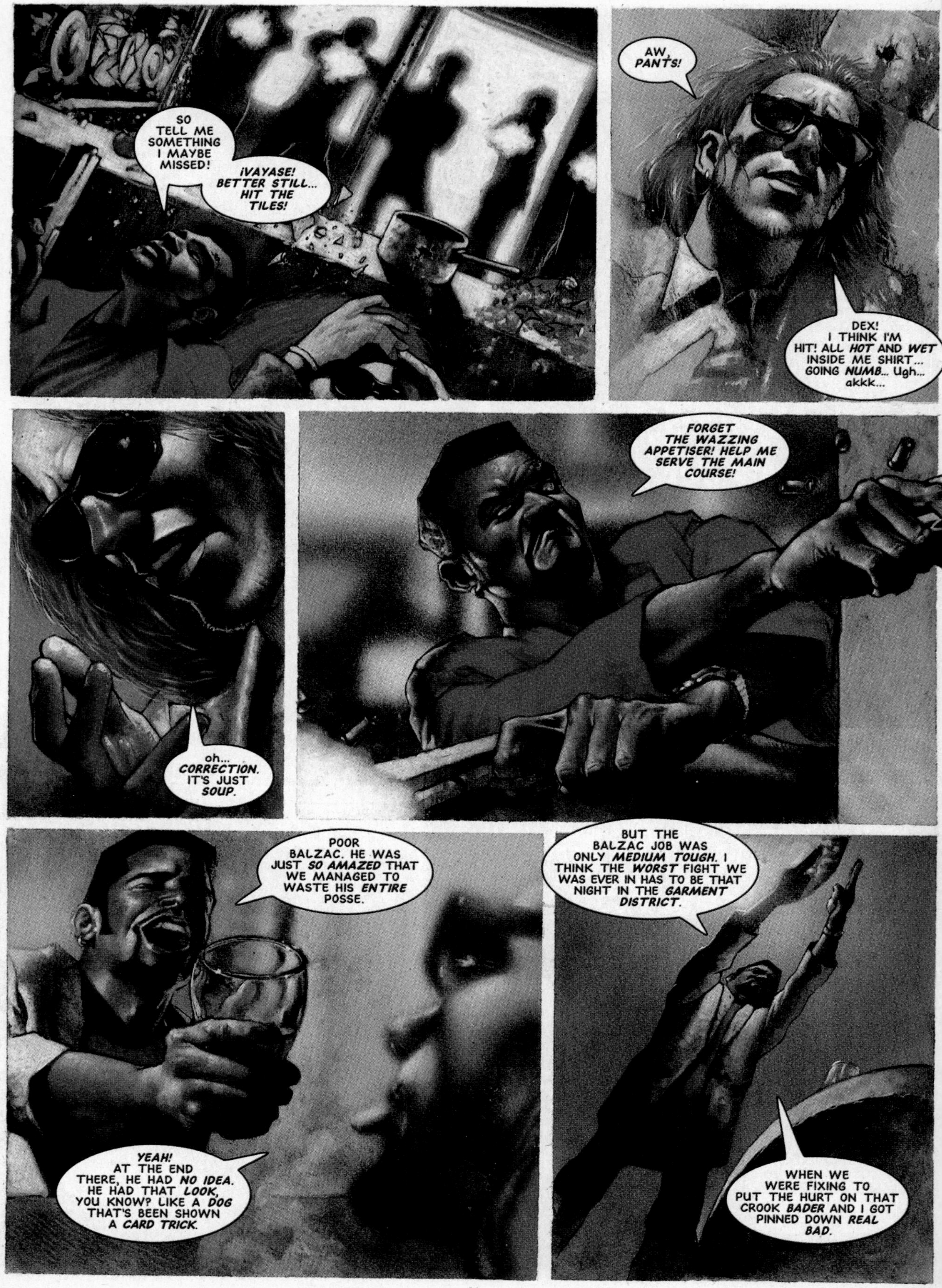

SO TELL ME SOMETHING I MAYBE MISSED!
¡VAYASE! BETTER STILL... HIT THE TILES!
AW, PANTS!
DEX! I THINK I'M HIT! ALL HOT AND WET INSIDE ME SHIRT... GOING NUMB... Ugh... akkk...
oh... CORRECTION. IT'S JUST SOUP.
FORGET THE WAZZING APPETISER! HELP ME SERVE THE MAIN COURSE!
POOR BALZAC. HE WAS JUST SO AMAZED THAT WE MANAGED TO WASTE HIS ENTIRE POSSE.
YEAH! AT THE END THERE, HE HAD NO IDEA. HE HAD THAT LOOK, YOU KNOW? LIKE A DOG THAT'S BEEN SHOWN A CARD TRICK.
BUT THE BALZAC JOB WAS ONLY MEDIUM TOUGH. I THINK THE WORST FIGHT WE WAS EVER IN HAS TO BE THAT NIGHT IN THE GARMENT DISTRICT.
WHEN WE WERE FIXING TO PUT THE HURT ON THAT CROOK BADER AND I GOT PINNED DOWN REAL BAD.

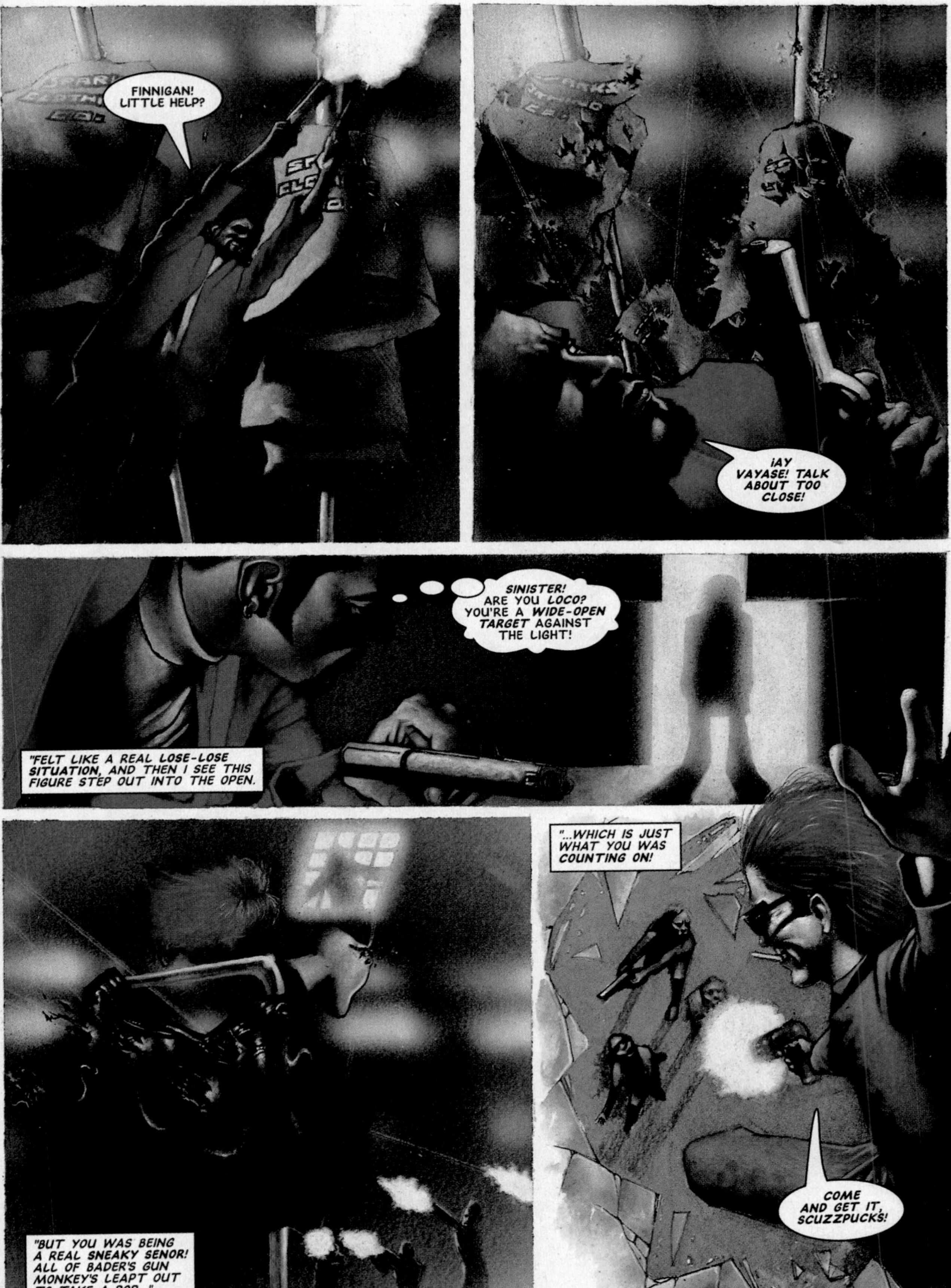
FINNIGAN! LITTLE HELP?
¡AY VAYASE! TALK ABOUT TOO CLOSE!
SINISTER! ARE YOU LOCO? YOU'RE A WIDE-OPEN TARGET AGAINST THE LIGHT!
"FELT LIKE A REAL LOSE-LOSE SITUATION, AND THEN I SEE THIS FIGURE STEP OUT INTO THE OPEN.
"BUT YOU WAS BEING A REAL SNEAKY SENOR! ALL OF BADER'S GUN MONKEY'S LEAPT OUT TO TAKE A POP..."
"...WHICH IS JUST WHAT YOU WAS COUNTING ON!
COME AND GET IT, SCUZZPUCKS!

YEAH, THAT WAS *BAD VOODOO*, NO QUESTION. RUINED A PERFECTLY GOOD *COAT*.

ANOTHER PITCHER HERE, POR FAVOR!

YE KNOW, I'M THINKING, MAYBE THE *WORST* FIGHT WE WAS EVER IN...

...WAS THAT TIME WE WENT CHASING OUT TO STOP THE *DE SOUZA GANG* FROM SCAMMIN' OFF WITH TWO MIL OF *HOLY MOSES'S* MONEY.

NEXT THING WE KNOW, *THEY'RE* CHASIN' *US* ACROSS ZEVSKY FIELDS IN A *STOLEN ARMOURED ASSAULT VEHICLE.*

JOHANN H. CRUFF ON A *PARALYSED PUFFIN!*

FASTER, DEX! IF THEY DON'T NAIL US WITH THE *CANNON,* THEY'LL MASH WITH THEIR ARMOURED *COW-CATCHER!*

LO SIENTO, AMIGO! THE *EDSEL* WASN'T BUILT TO *OFF-ROAD!*

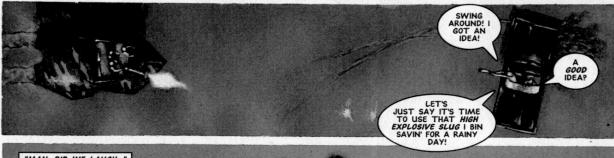

SWING AROUND! I GOT AN IDEA!

A *GOOD* IDEA?

LET'S JUST SAY IT'S TIME TO USE THAT *HIGH EXPLOSIVE SLUG* I BIN SAVIN' FOR A RAINY DAY!

"MAN, DID WE LAUGH..."

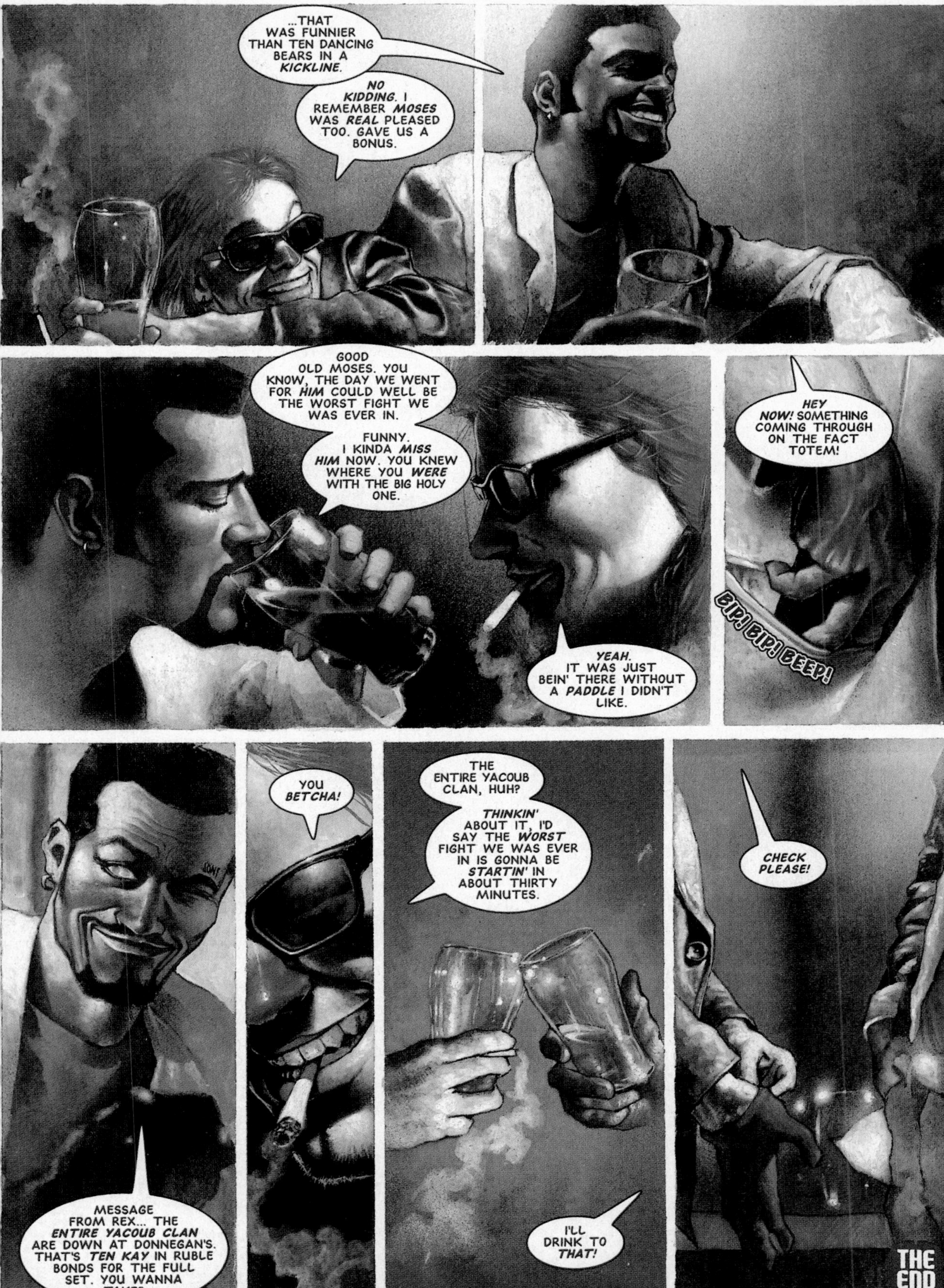
...THAT WAS FUNNIER THAN TEN DANCING BEARS IN A KICKLINE.
NO KIDDING. I REMEMBER MOSES WAS REAL PLEASED TOO. GAVE US A BONUS.
GOOD OLD MOSES. YOU KNOW, THE DAY WE WENT FOR HIM COULD WELL BE THE WORST FIGHT WE WAS EVER IN.
FUNNY. I KINDA MISS HIM NOW. YOU KNEW WHERE YOU WERE WITH THE BIG HOLY ONE.
YEAH. IT WAS JUST BEIN' THERE WITHOUT A PADDLE I DIDN'T LIKE.
HEY NOW! SOMETHING COMING THROUGH ON THE FACT TOTEM!
BIP! BIP! BEEP!
MESSAGE FROM REX... THE ENTIRE YACOUB CLAN ARE DOWN AT DONNEGAN'S. THAT'S TEN KAY IN RUBLE BONDS FOR THE FULL SET. YOU WANNA TAKE?
YOU BETCHA!
THE ENTIRE YACOUB CLAN, HUH?
THINKIN' ABOUT IT, I'D SAY THE WORST FIGHT WE WAS EVER IN IS GONNA BE STARTIN' IN ABOUT THIRTY MINUTES.
I'LL DRINK TO THAT!
CHECK PLEASE!
THE END

A BRIEF HISTORY OF GUNSHARKS

Script: Dan Abnett

Art: Robert McCallum

Colors: Dondie Cox

Letters: Steve Potter

Originally published in *2000 AD* Prog 1068

SINISTERDEXTER

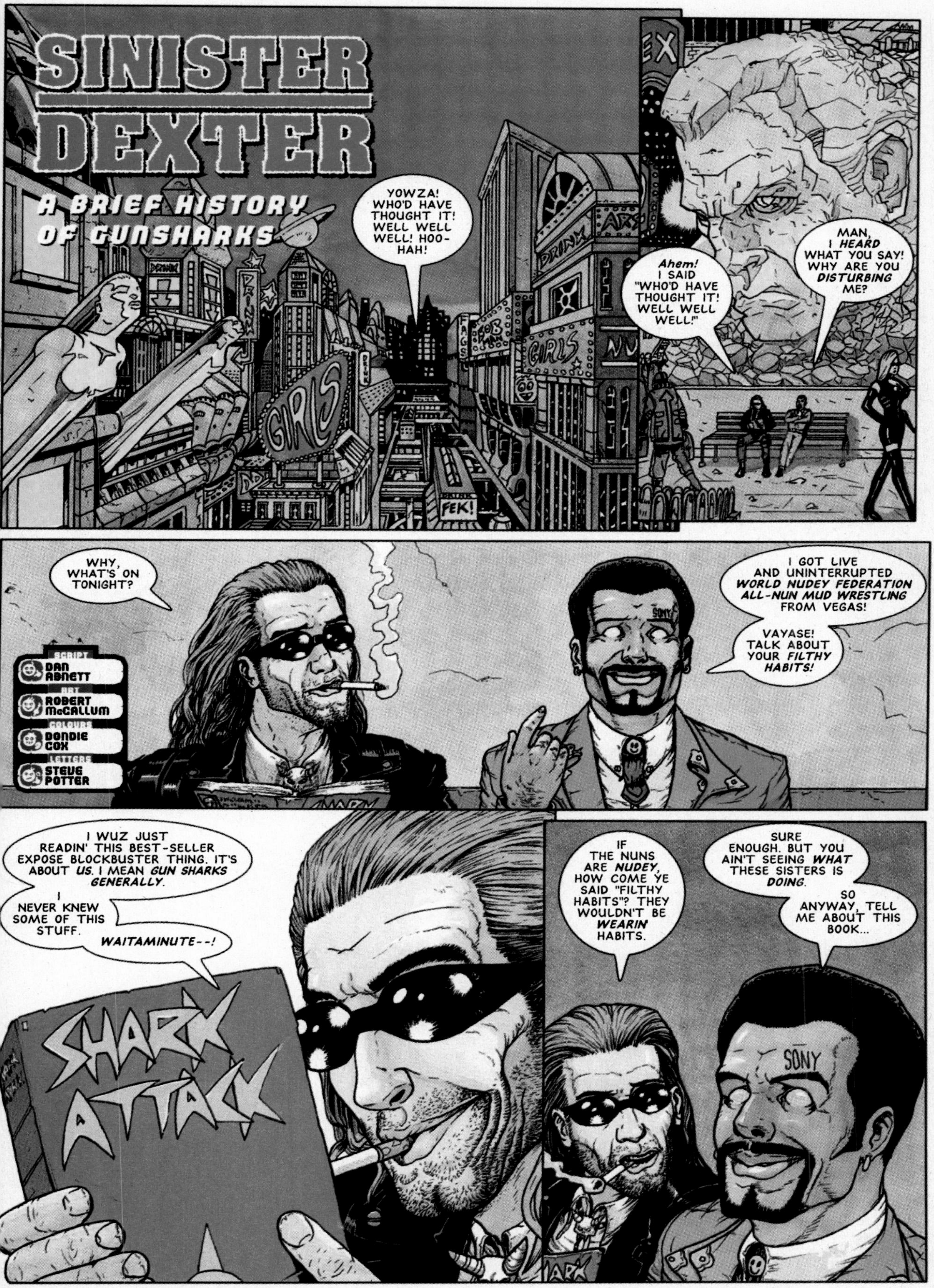
SINISTER DEXTER
A BRIEF HISTORY OF GUNSHARKS
YOWZA! WHO'D HAVE THOUGHT IT! WELL WELL WELL! HOO-HAH!
Ahem! I SAID "WHO'D HAVE THOUGHT IT! WELL WELL WELL!"
MAN, I HEARD WHAT YOU SAY! WHY ARE YOU DISTURBING ME?
WHY, WHAT'S ON TONIGHT?
I GOT LIVE AND UNINTERRUPTED WORLD NUDEY FEDERATION ALL-NUN MUD WRESTLING FROM VEGAS!
VAYASE! TALK ABOUT YOUR FILTHY HABITS!
SCRIPT DAN ABNETT
ART ROBERT McCALLUM
COLOURS DONDIE COX
LETTERS STEVE POTTER
I WUZ JUST READIN' THIS BEST-SELLER EXPOSE BLOCKBUSTER THING. IT'S ABOUT US. I MEAN GUN SHARKS GENERALLY.
I NEVER KNEW SOME OF THIS STUFF.
WAITAMINUTE--!
SHARK ATTACK
IF THE NUNS ARE NUDEY, HOW COME YE SAID "FILTHY HABITS"? THEY WOULDN'T BE WEARIN HABITS.
SURE ENOUGH. BUT YOU AIN'T SEEING WHAT THESE SISTERS IS DOING.
SO ANYWAY, TELL ME ABOUT THIS BOOK...
SONY

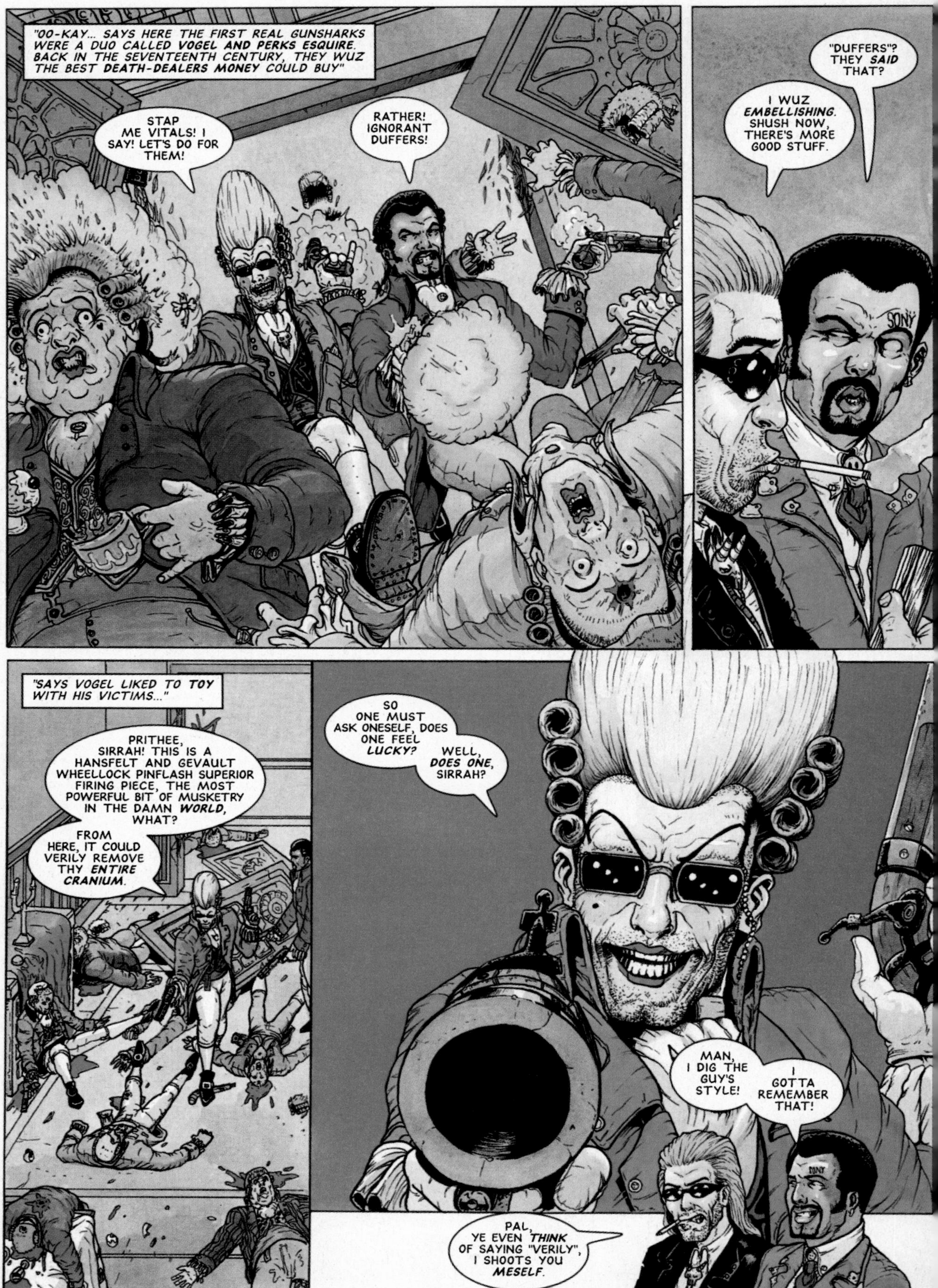
"OO-KAY... SAYS HERE THE FIRST REAL GUNSHARKS WERE A DUO CALLED VOGEL AND PERKS ESQUIRE. BACK IN THE SEVENTEENTH CENTURY, THEY WUZ THE BEST DEATH-DEALERS MONEY COULD BUY"
STAP ME VITALS! I SAY! LET'S DO FOR THEM!
RATHER! IGNORANT DUFFERS!
"DUFFERS"? THEY SAID THAT?
I WUZ EMBELLISHING. SHUSH NOW, THERE'S MORE GOOD STUFF.
SONY
"SAYS VOGEL LIKED TO TOY WITH HIS VICTIMS..."
PRITHEE, SIRRAH! THIS IS A HANSFELT AND GEVAULT WHEELLOCK PINFLASH SUPERIOR FIRING PIECE, THE MOST POWERFUL BIT OF MUSKETRY IN THE DAMN WORLD, WHAT?
FROM HERE, IT COULD VERILY REMOVE THY ENTIRE CRANIUM.
SO ONE MUST ASK ONESELF, DOES ONE FEEL LUCKY?
WELL, DOES ONE, SIRRAH?
MAN, I DIG THE GUY'S STYLE!
I GOTTA REMEMBER THAT!
SONY
PAL, YE EVEN THINK OF SAYING "VERILY", I SHOOTS YOU MESELF.

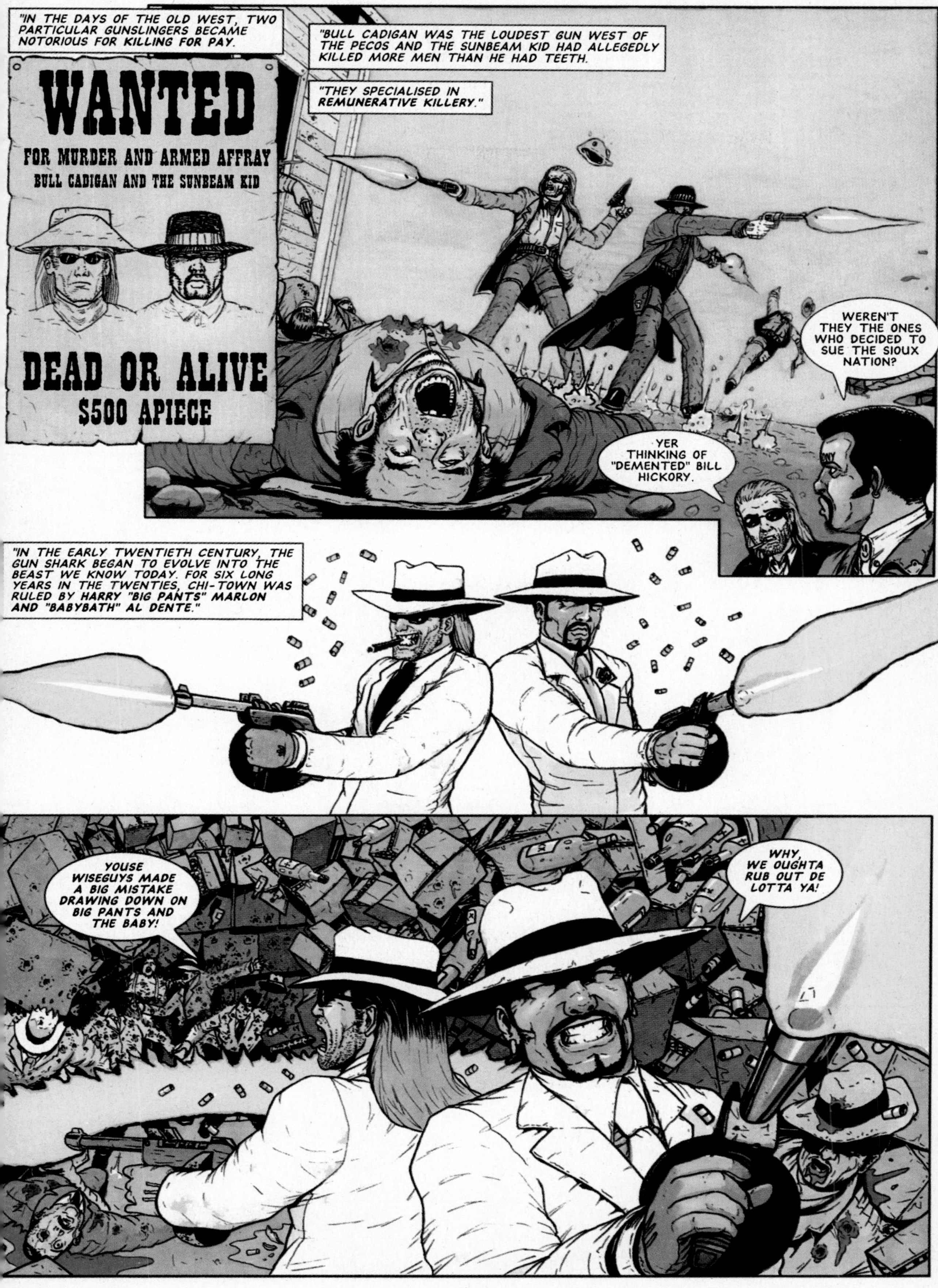
"IN THE DAYS OF THE OLD WEST, TWO PARTICULAR GUNSLINGERS BECAME NOTORIOUS FOR KILLING FOR PAY.
WANTED
FOR MURDER AND ARMED AFFRAY
BULL CADIGAN AND THE SUNBEAM KID
DEAD OR ALIVE
$500 APIECE
"BULL CADIGAN WAS THE LOUDEST GUN WEST OF THE PECOS AND THE SUNBEAM KID HAD ALLEGEDLY KILLED MORE MEN THAN HE HAD TEETH.
"THEY SPECIALISED IN REMUNERATIVE KILLERY."
WEREN'T THEY THE ONES WHO DECIDED TO SUE THE SIOUX NATION?
YER THINKING OF "DEMENTED" BILL HICKORY.
"IN THE EARLY TWENTIETH CENTURY, THE GUN SHARK BEGAN TO EVOLVE INTO THE BEAST WE KNOW TODAY. FOR SIX LONG YEARS IN THE TWENTIES, CHI-TOWN WAS RULED BY HARRY "BIG PANTS" MARLON AND "BABYBATH" AL DENTE."
YOUSE WISEGUYS MADE A BIG MISTAKE DRAWING DOWN ON BIG PANTS AND THE BABY!
WHY, WE OUGHTA RUB OUT DE LOTTA YA!

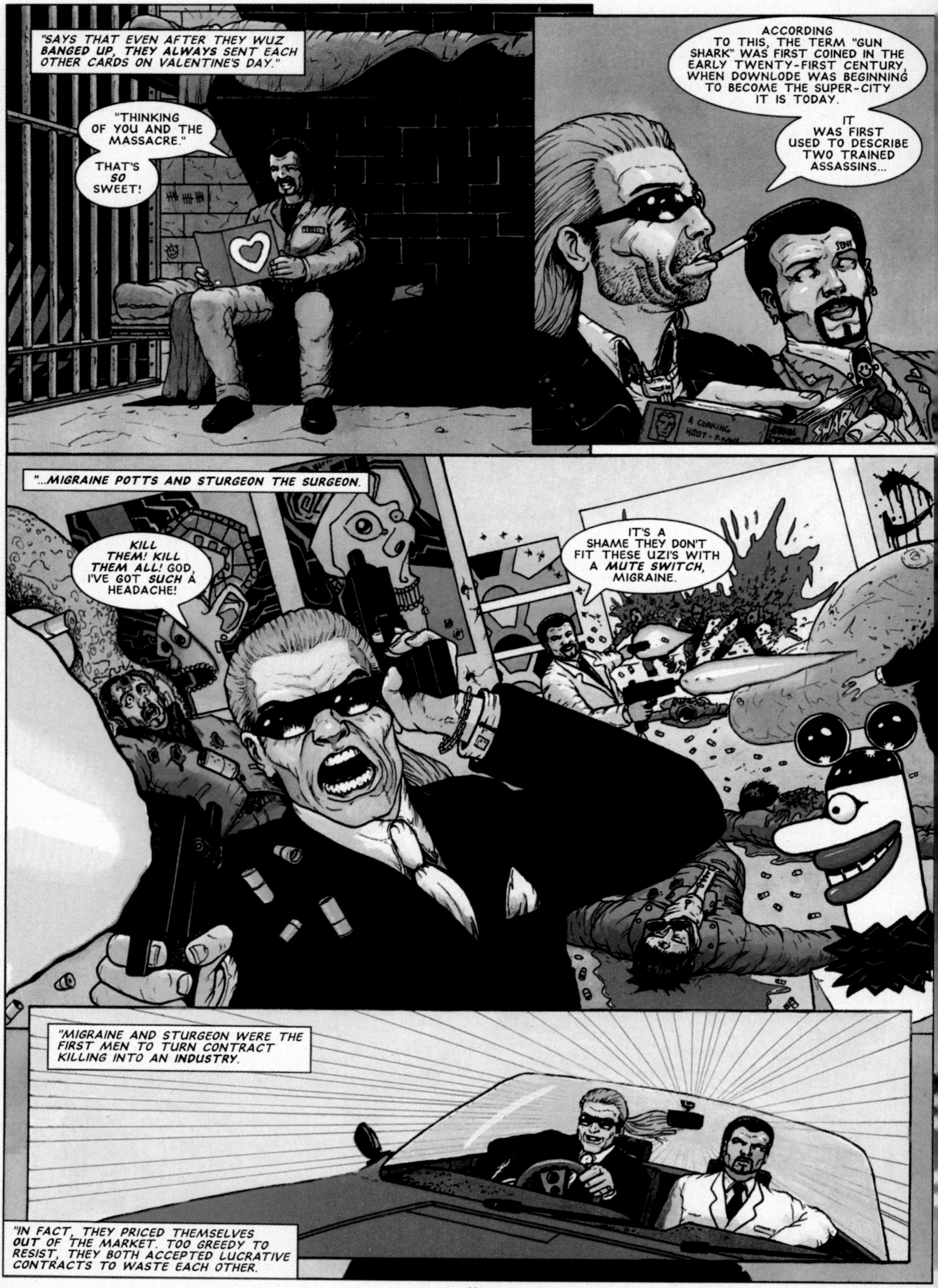
"SAYS THAT EVEN AFTER THEY WUZ BANGED UP, THEY ALWAYS SENT EACH OTHER CARDS ON VALENTINE'S DAY."
"THINKING OF YOU AND THE MASSACRE."
THAT'S SO SWEET!
ACCORDING TO THIS, THE TERM "GUN SHARK" WAS FIRST COINED IN THE EARLY TWENTY-FIRST CENTURY, WHEN DOWNLODE WAS BEGINNING TO BECOME THE SUPER-CITY IT IS TODAY.
IT WAS FIRST USED TO DESCRIBE TWO TRAINED ASSASSINS...
"...MIGRAINE POTTS AND STURGEON THE SURGEON.
KILL THEM! KILL THEM ALL! GOD, I'VE GOT SUCH A HEADACHE!
IT'S A SHAME THEY DON'T FIT THESE UZI'S WITH A MUTE SWITCH, MIGRAINE.
"MIGRAINE AND STURGEON WERE THE FIRST MEN TO TURN CONTRACT KILLING INTO AN INDUSTRY.
"IN FACT, THEY PRICED THEMSELVES OUT OF THE MARKET. TOO GREEDY TO RESIST, THEY BOTH ACCEPTED LUCRATIVE CONTRACTS TO WASTE EACH OTHER.

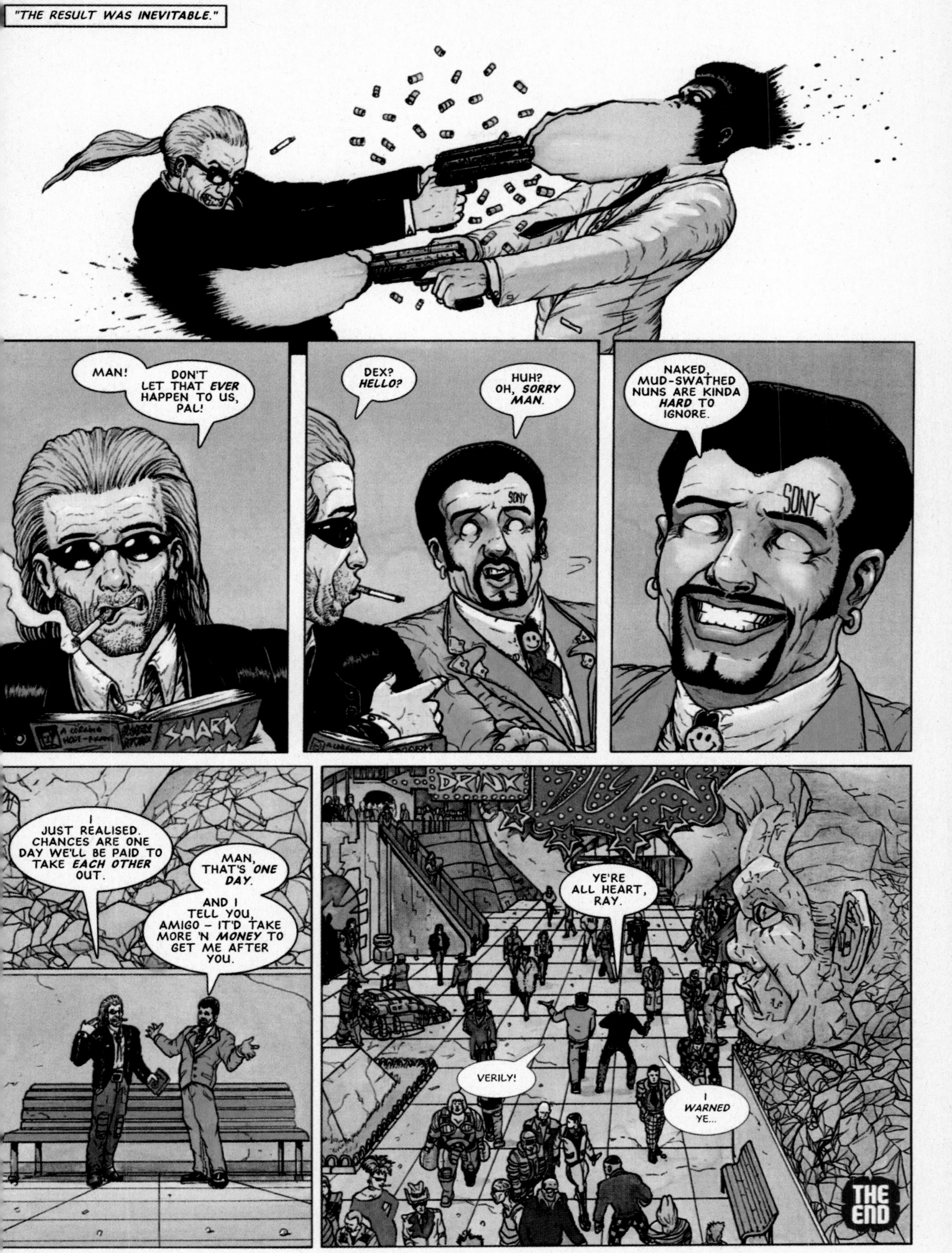
"THE RESULT WAS INEVITABLE."
MAN!
DON'T LET THAT EVER HAPPEN TO US, PAL!
DEX? HELLO?
HUH? OH, SORRY MAN.
NAKED, MUD-SWATHED NUNS ARE KINDA HARD TO IGNORE.
I JUST REALISED. CHANCES ARE ONE DAY WE'LL BE PAID TO TAKE EACH OTHER OUT.
MAN, THAT'S ONE DAY.
AND I TELL YOU, AMIGO – IT'D TAKE MORE 'N MONEY TO GET ME AFTER YOU.
YE'RE ALL HEART, RAY.
VERILY!
I WARNED YE...
THE END

PEDAL POWER

Script: Dan Abnett

Art: Andrew Currie

Colors: Alison Kirkpatrick

Letters: Steve Potter

Originally published in *2000 AD* Prog 1070

SINISTERDEXTEI

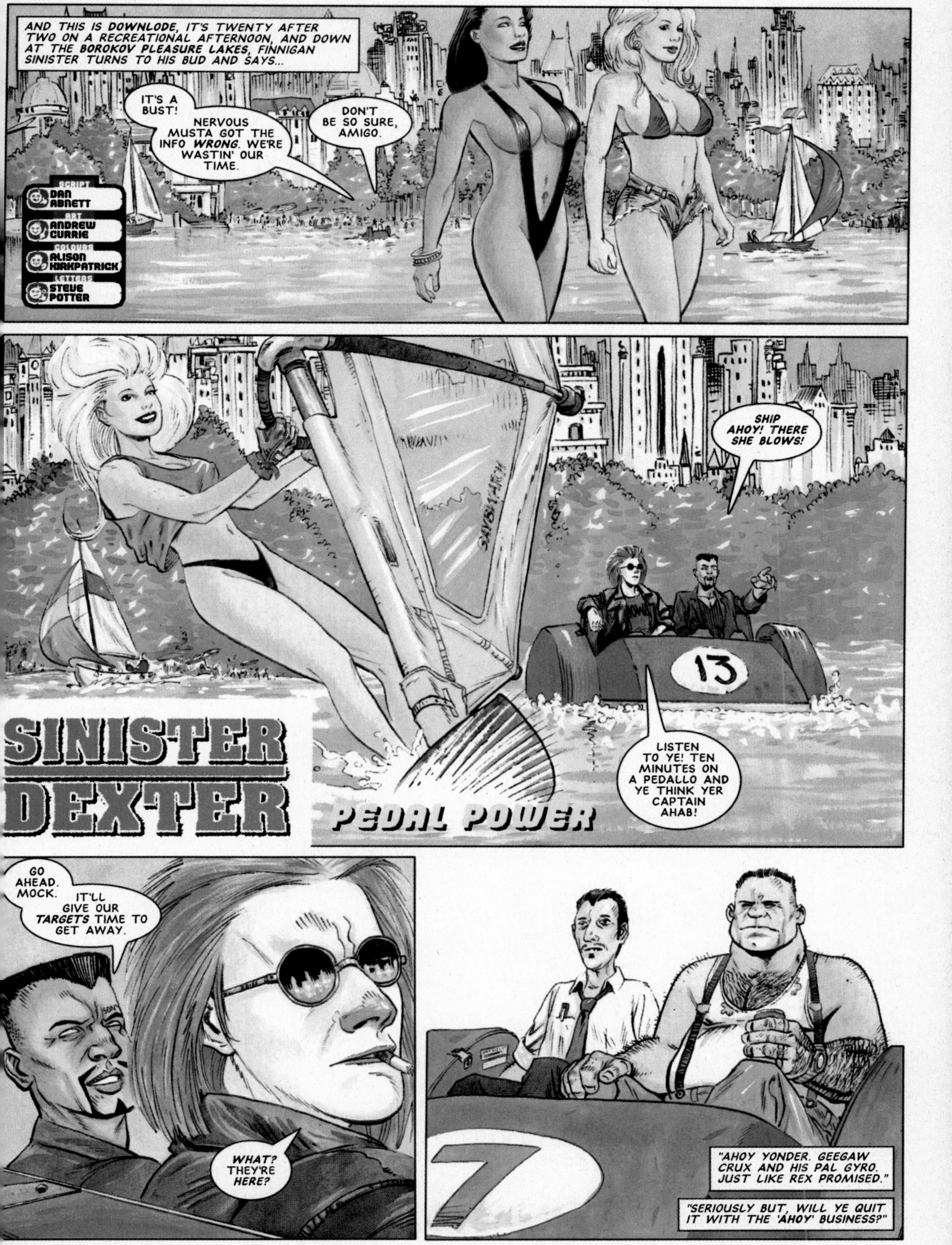
AND THIS IS DOWNLODE, IT'S TWENTY AFTER TWO ON A RECREATIONAL AFTERNOON, AND DOWN AT THE BOROKOV PLEASURE LAKES, FINNIGAN SINISTER TURNS TO HIS BUD AND SAYS...
IT'S A BUST!
NERVOUS MUSTA GOT THE INFO WRONG. WE'RE WASTIN' OUR TIME.
DON'T BE SO SURE, AMIGO.
SCRIPT DAN ABNETT
ART ANDREW CURRIE
COLOURS ALISON KIRKPATRICK
LETTERS STEVE POTTER
SHIP AHOY! THERE SHE BLOWS!
13
SINISTER DEXTER
PEDAL POWER
LISTEN TO YE! TEN MINUTES ON A PEDALLO AND YE THINK YER CAPTAIN AHAB!
GO AHEAD. MOCK.
IT'LL GIVE OUR TARGETS TIME TO GET AWAY.
WHAT? THEY'RE HERE?
7
"AHOY YONDER. GEEGAW CRUX AND HIS PAL GYRO. JUST LIKE REX PROMISED."
"SERIOUSLY BUT, WILL YE QUIT IT WITH THE 'AHOY' BUSINESS?"

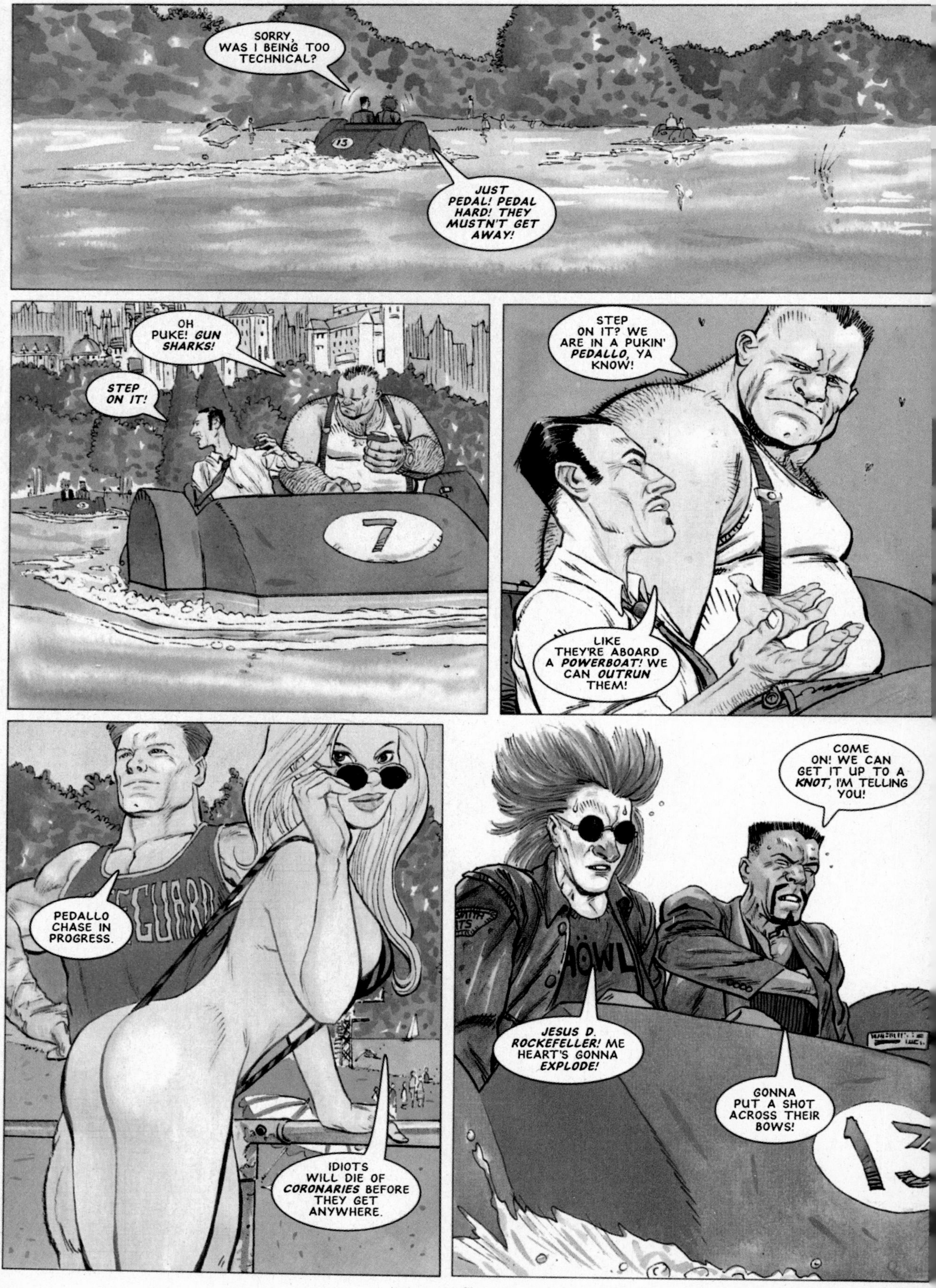
SORRY, WAS I BEING TOO TECHNICAL?
JUST PEDAL! PEDAL HARD! THEY MUSTN'T GET AWAY!
OH PUKE! GUN SHARKS!
STEP ON IT!
STEP ON IT? WE ARE IN A PUKIN' PEDALLO, YA KNOW!
LIKE THEY'RE ABOARD A POWERBOAT! WE CAN OUTRUN THEM!
PEDALLO CHASE IN PROGRESS.
IDIOTS WILL DIE OF CORONARIES BEFORE THEY GET ANYWHERE.
COME ON! WE CAN GET IT UP TO A KNOT, I'M TELLING YOU!
JESUS D. ROCKEFELLER! ME HEART'S GONNA EXPLODE!
GONNA PUT A SHOT ACROSS THEIR BOWS!

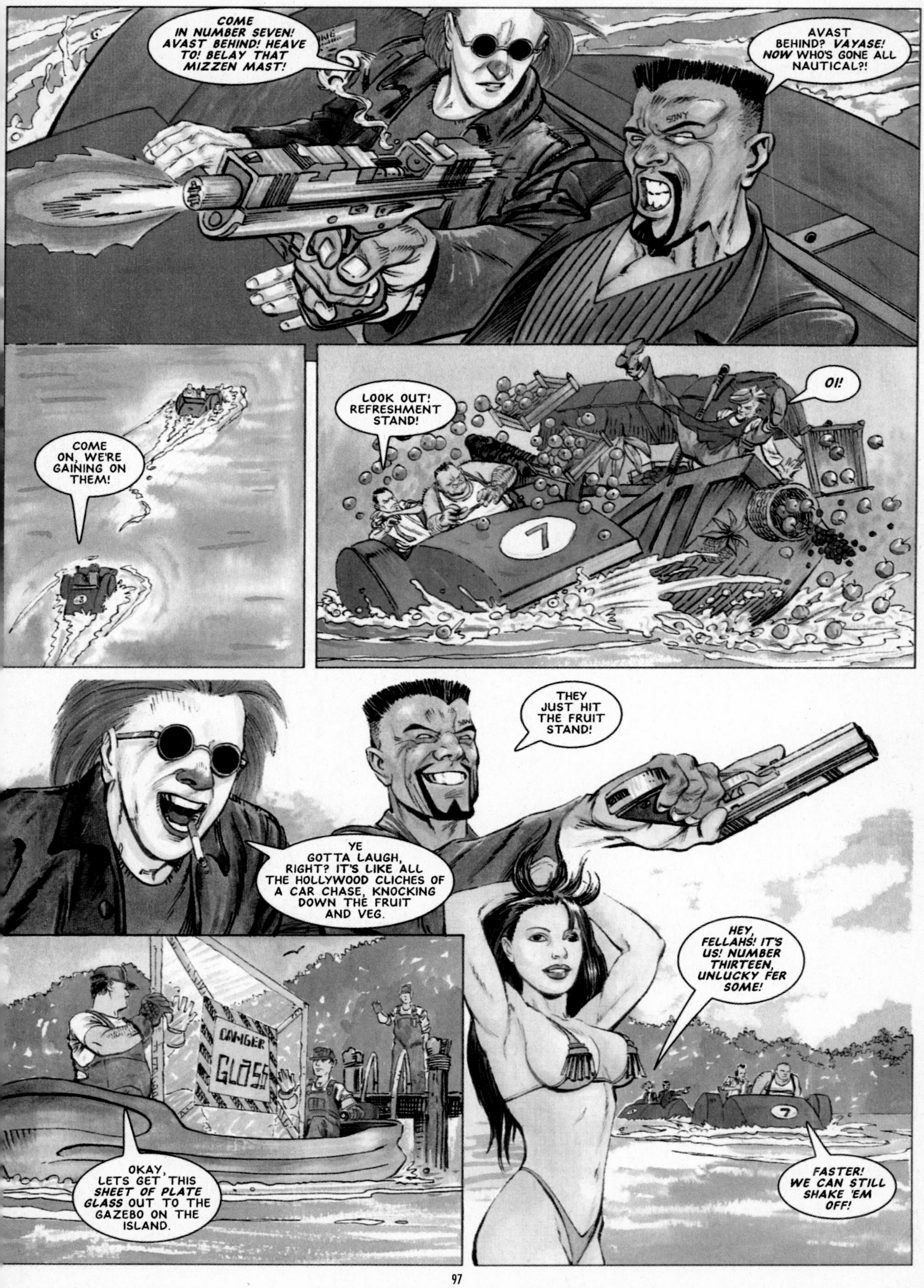
COME IN NUMBER SEVEN! AVAST BEHIND! HEAVE TO! BELAY THAT MIZZEN MAST!
AVAST BEHIND? VAYASE! NOW WHO'S GONE ALL NAUTICAL?!
COME ON, WE'RE GAINING ON THEM!
LOOK OUT! REFRESHMENT STAND!
OI!
7
THEY JUST HIT THE FRUIT STAND!
YE GOTTA LAUGH, RIGHT? IT'S LIKE ALL THE HOLLYWOOD CLICHES OF A CAR CHASE, KNOCKING DOWN THE FRUIT AND VEG.
HEY, FELLAHS! IT'S US! NUMBER THIRTEEN, UNLUCKY FER SOME!
DANGER GLASS
OKAY, LETS GET THIS SHEET OF PLATE GLASS OUT TO THE GAZEBO ON THE ISLAND.
FASTER! WE CAN STILL SHAKE 'EM OFF!

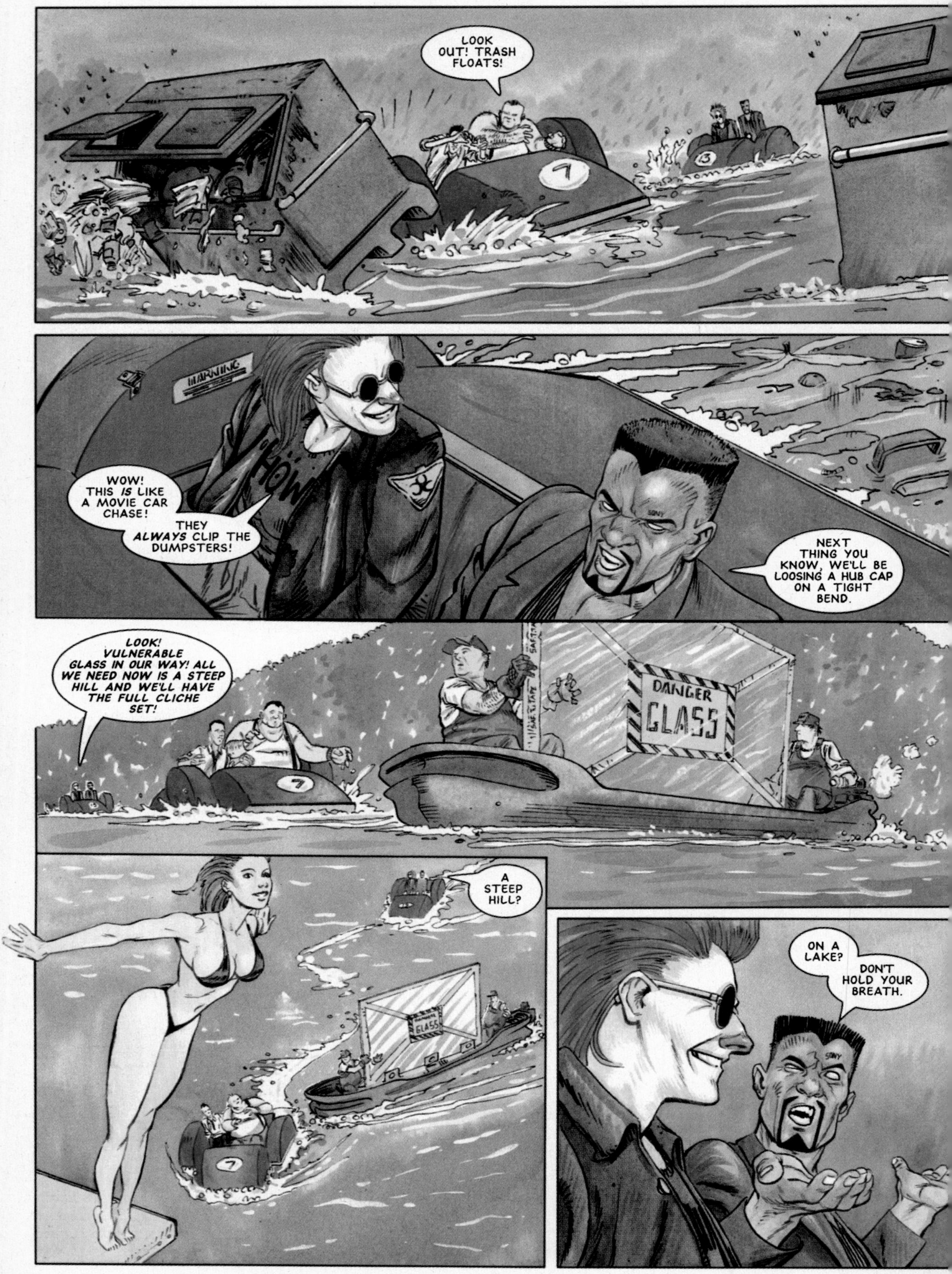
LOOK OUT! TRASH FLOATS!
WOW! THIS IS LIKE A MOVIE CAR CHASE!
THEY ALWAYS CLIP THE DUMPSTERS!
NEXT THING YOU KNOW, WE'LL BE LOOSING A HUB CAP ON A TIGHT BEND.
LOOK! VULNERABLE GLASS IN OUR WAY! ALL WE NEED NOW IS A STEEP HILL AND WE'LL HAVE THE FULL CLICHE SET!
DANGER GLASS
A STEEP HILL?
ON A LAKE?
DON'T HOLD YOUR BREATH.

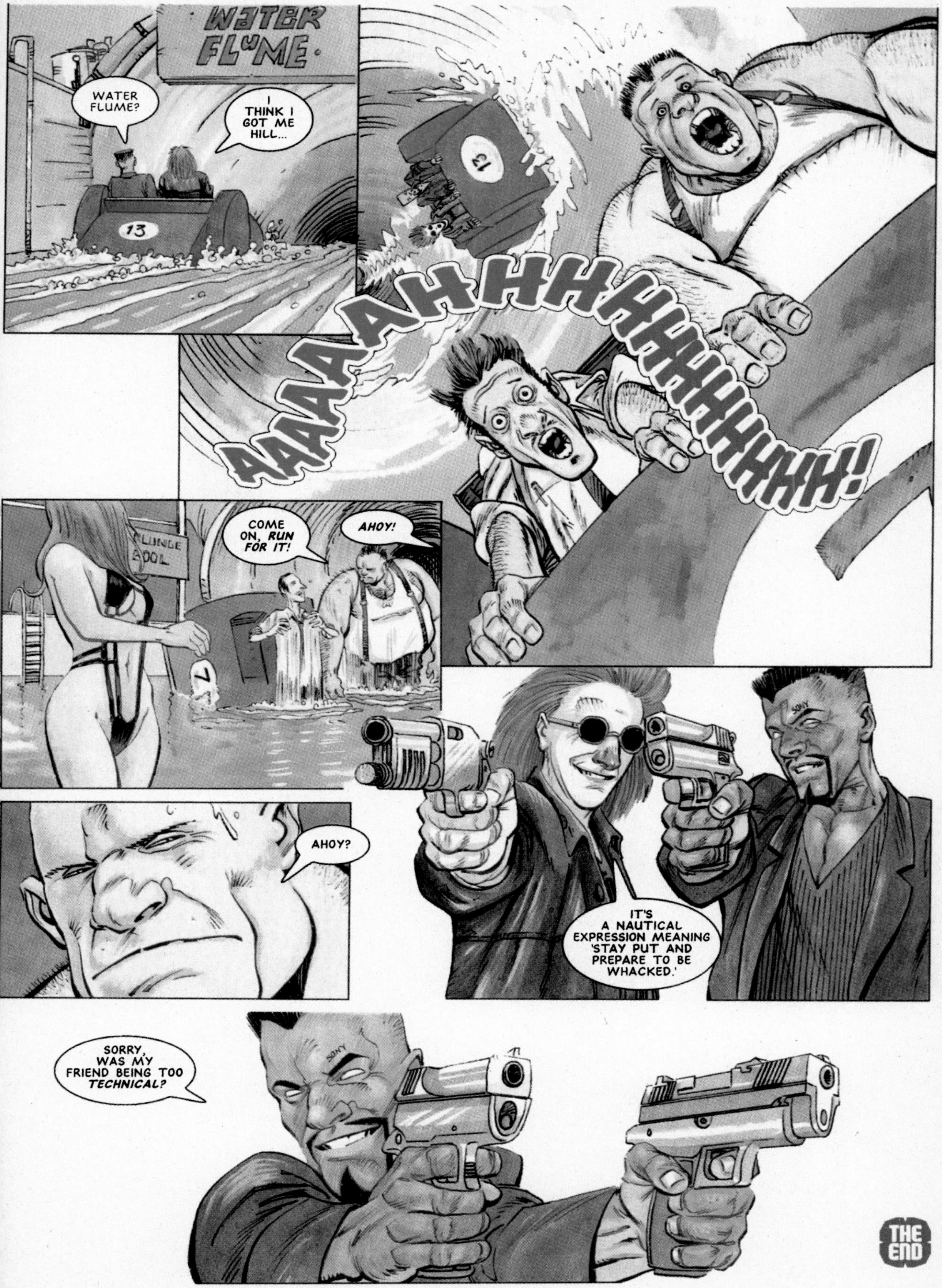
WATER FLUME
WATER FLUME?
I THINK I GOT ME HILL...
AAAAAHHHHHHHHHHHHHHHHH!
PLUNGE POOL
COME ON, RUN FOR IT!
AHOY!
AHOY?
IT'S A NAUTICAL EXPRESSION MEANING 'STAY PUT AND PREPARE TO BE WHACKED.'
SORRY, WAS MY FRIEND BEING TOO TECHNICAL?
THE END

THINGS TO DO IN DOWNLODE WHEN YOU'RE DEAD

Script: Dan Abnett

Art: Julian Gibson

Letters: Steve Potter

Originally published in *2000 AD* Prog 1071

SINISTERDEXTER

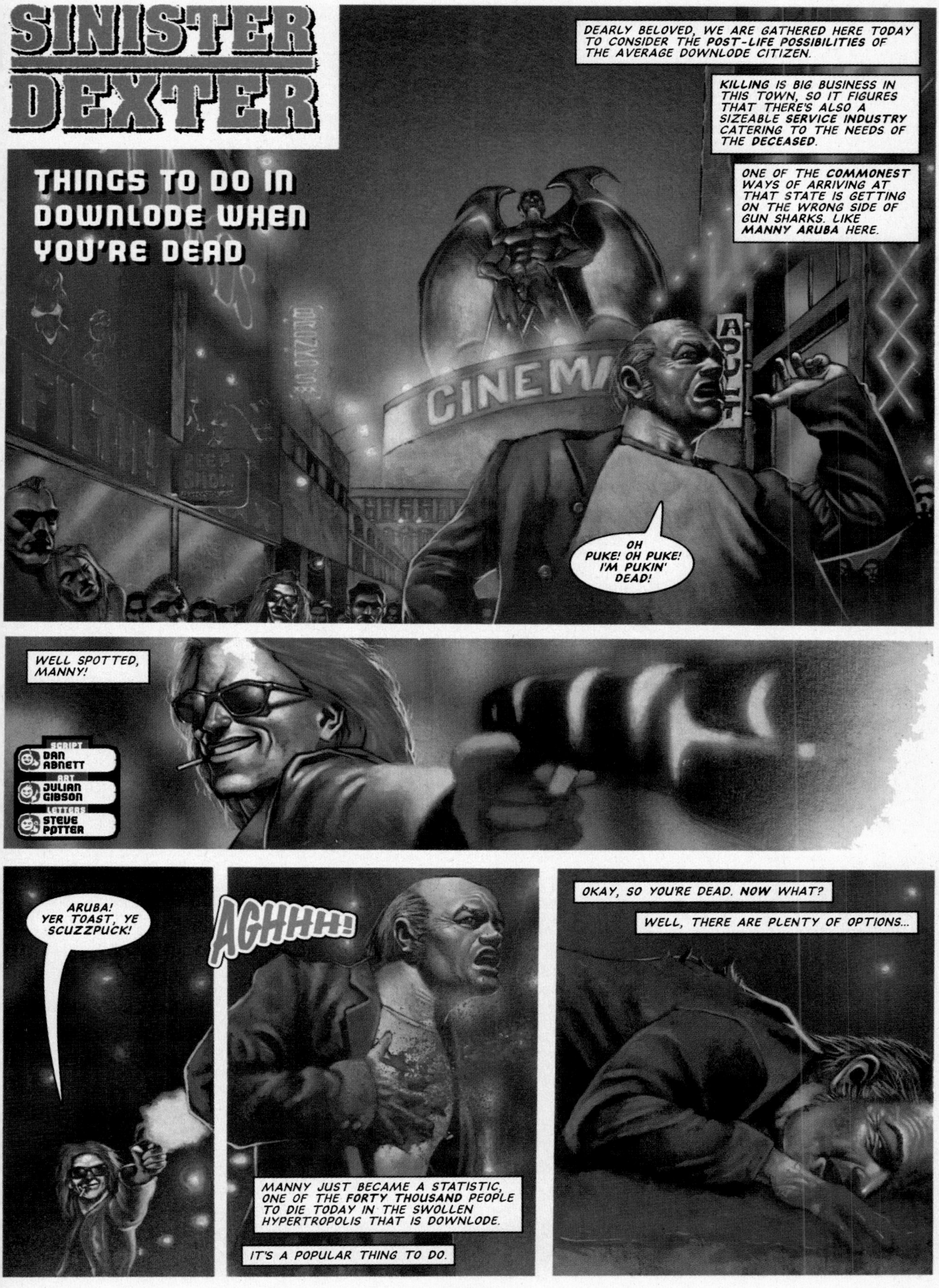
SINISTER DEXTER
THINGS TO DO IN DOWNLODE WHEN YOU'RE DEAD
DEARLY BELOVED, WE ARE GATHERED HERE TODAY TO CONSIDER THE POST-LIFE POSSIBILITIES OF THE AVERAGE DOWNLODE CITIZEN.
KILLING IS BIG BUSINESS IN THIS TOWN, SO IT FIGURES THAT THERE'S ALSO A SIZEABLE SERVICE INDUSTRY CATERING TO THE NEEDS OF THE DECEASED.
ONE OF THE COMMONEST WAYS OF ARRIVING AT THAT STATE IS GETTING ON THE WRONG SIDE OF GUN SHARKS. LIKE MANNY ARUBA HERE.
CINEMA
ADULT
OH PUKE! OH PUKE! I'M PUKIN' DEAD!
WELL SPOTTED, MANNY!
SCRIPT DAN ABNETT
ART JULIAN GIBSON
LETTERS STEVE POTTER
ARUBA! YER TOAST, YE SCUZZPUCK!
AGHHH!
MANNY JUST BECAME A STATISTIC, ONE OF THE FORTY THOUSAND PEOPLE TO DIE TODAY IN THE SWOLLEN HYPERTROPOLIS THAT IS DOWNLODE.
IT'S A POPULAR THING TO DO.
OKAY, SO YOU'RE DEAD. NOW WHAT?
WELL, THERE ARE PLENTY OF OPTIONS...

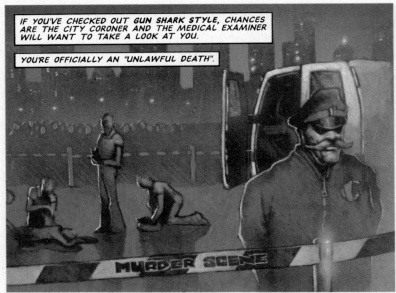

IF YOU'VE CHECKED OUT GUN SHARK STYLE, CHANCES ARE THE CITY CORONER AND THE MEDICAL EXAMINER WILL WANT TO TAKE A LOOK AT YOU.
YOU'RE OFFICIALLY AN "UNLAWFUL DEATH".
MURDER SCENE
YOU GET YOUR OWN CHALK OUTLINE, A WHOLE LOT OF ATTENTION FROM THE SOUTH CENTRAL HOMICIDE DIVISION, AND A SET OF UNUSUALLY CANDID PRINTS FOR THE ALBUM.
YOU MAY EVEN GET AN AUTOPSY.
A USEFUL TIP... IF YOU'RE JUST PLAYING DEAD, THIS WOULD BE A GOOD TIME TO OWN UP. BEFORE THEY BRING IN THE BONE SAW.
AFTER THAT, YOUR FAMILY GET YOU BACK AND IT'S TIME TO CHOOSE HOW YOU WANT TO BE LAID TO REST.
YOU GET AN OPEN CASKET IF YOU'RE IN OKAY SHAPE.
Kristian Dire.
DON'T SWEAT THOUGH, EVEN IF YOU HAVE DONE TEN ROUNDS WITH A ROAD TRAIN.
TRAINED BEAUTY MORTICIANS AT "KRISTIAN DIRE" CAN PATCH YOU UP, EMBALM YOU, MEND WOUNDS INVISIBLY WITH PLASTIC FLESH, AND ADD FOUNDATION, BLUSHER AND MUTED WARM TONES.
MAN, YOU'LL LOOK BETTER THAN YOU DID WHEN YOU WERE BREATHING!

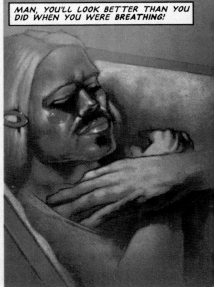

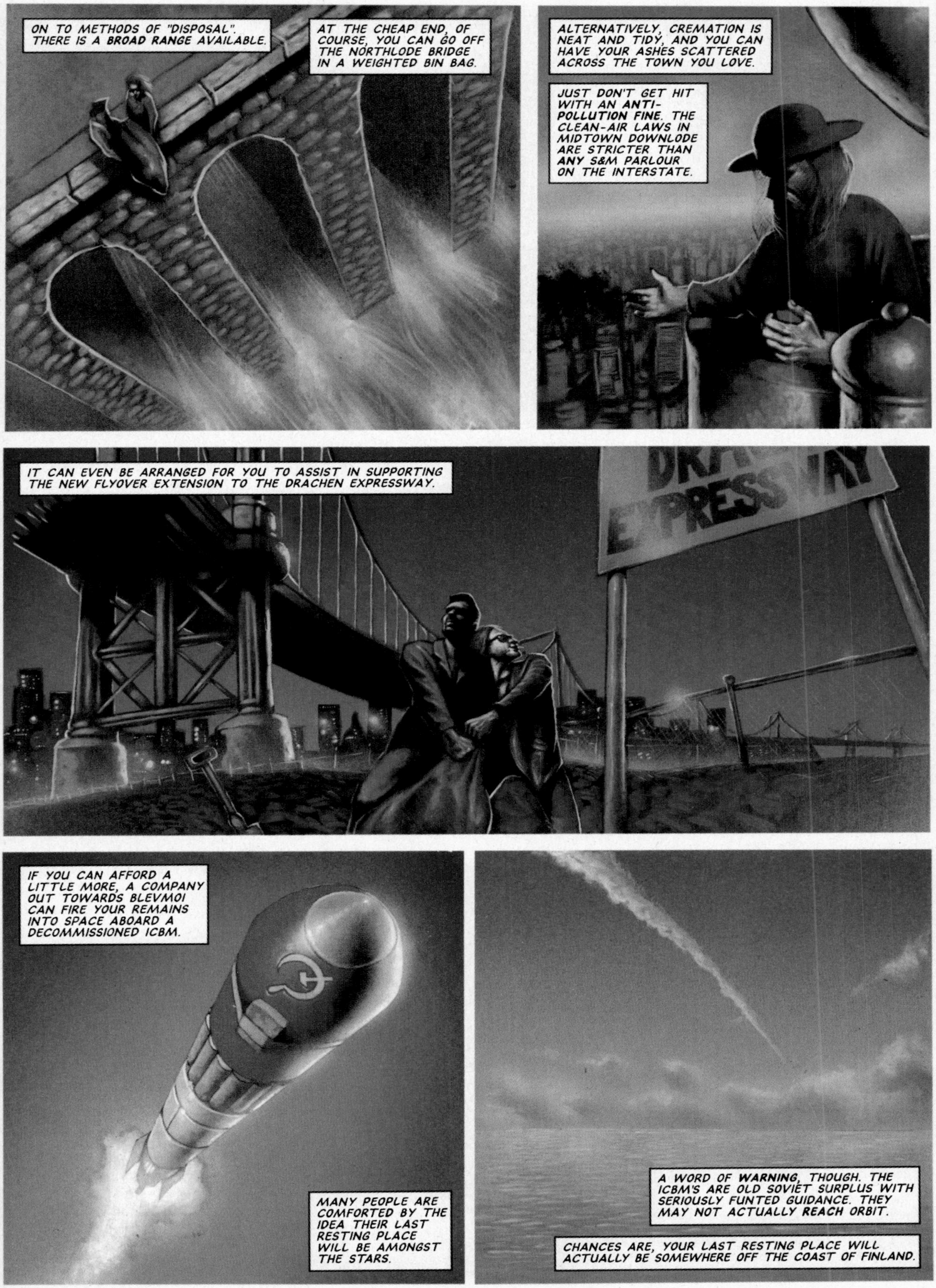
ON TO METHODS OF "DISPOSAL". THERE IS A BROAD RANGE AVAILABLE.
AT THE CHEAP END, OF COURSE, YOU CAN GO OFF THE NORTHLODE BRIDGE IN A WEIGHTED BIN BAG.
ALTERNATIVELY, CREMATION IS NEAT AND TIDY, AND YOU CAN HAVE YOUR ASHES SCATTERED ACROSS THE TOWN YOU LOVE.
JUST DON'T GET HIT WITH AN ANTI-POLLUTION FINE. THE CLEAN-AIR LAWS IN MIDTOWN DOWNLODE ARE STRICTER THAN ANY S&M PARLOUR ON THE INTERSTATE.
IT CAN EVEN BE ARRANGED FOR YOU TO ASSIST IN SUPPORTING THE NEW FLYOVER EXTENSION TO THE DRACHEN EXPRESSWAY.
IF YOU CAN AFFORD A LITTLE MORE, A COMPANY OUT TOWARDS BLEVMOI CAN FIRE YOUR REMAINS INTO SPACE ABOARD A DECOMMISSIONED ICBM.
MANY PEOPLE ARE COMFORTED BY THE IDEA THEIR LAST RESTING PLACE WILL BE AMONGST THE STARS.
A WORD OF WARNING, THOUGH. THE ICBM'S ARE OLD SOVIET SURPLUS WITH SERIOUSLY FUNTED GUIDANCE. THEY MAY NOT ACTUALLY REACH ORBIT.
CHANCES ARE, YOUR LAST RESTING PLACE WILL ACTUALLY BE SOMEWHERE OFF THE COAST OF FINLAND.

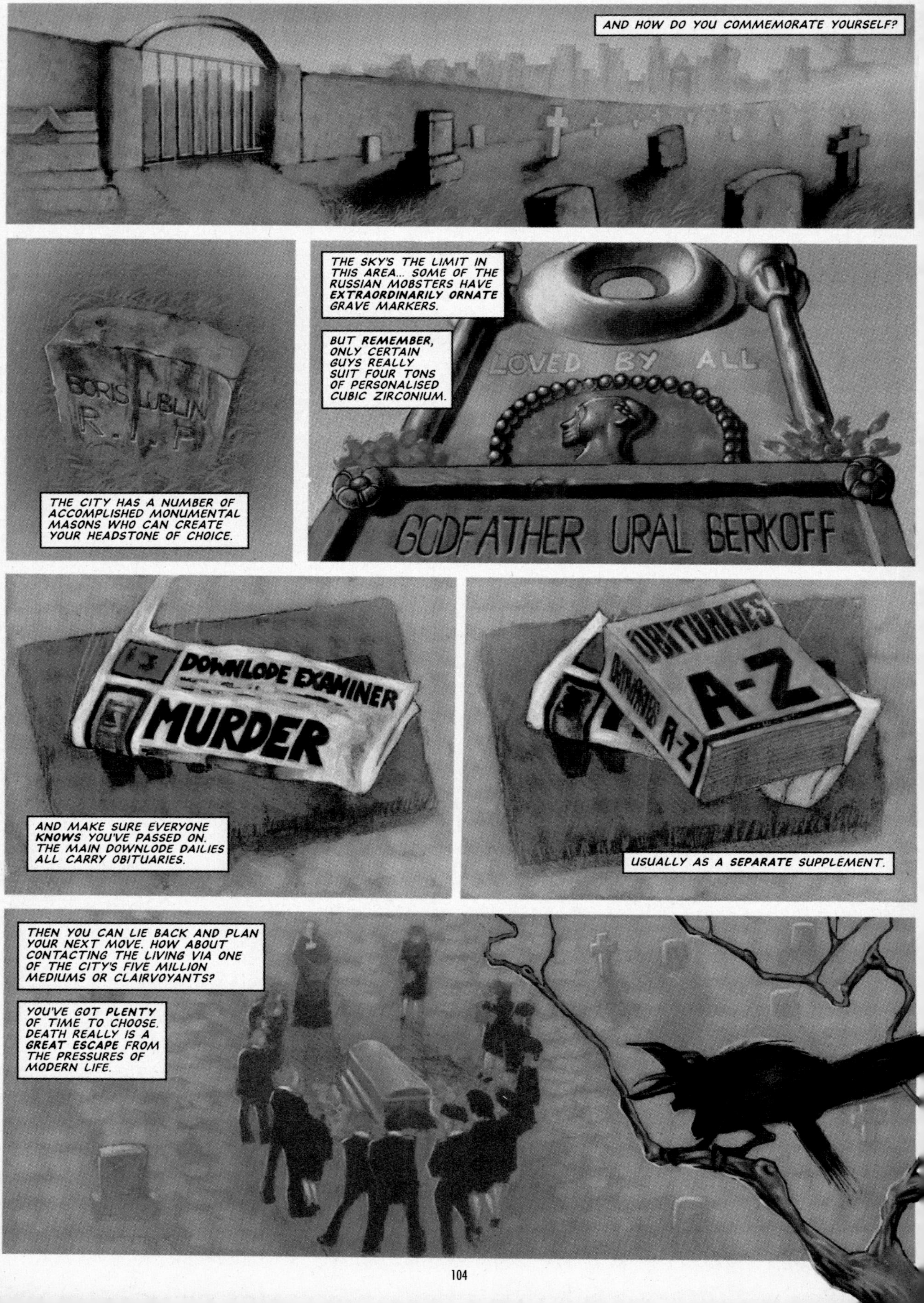
AND HOW DO YOU COMMEMORATE YOURSELF?
BORIS LUBLIN R.I.P
THE CITY HAS A NUMBER OF ACCOMPLISHED MONUMENTAL MASONS WHO CAN CREATE YOUR HEADSTONE OF CHOICE.
THE SKY'S THE LIMIT IN THIS AREA... SOME OF THE RUSSIAN MOBSTERS HAVE EXTRAORDINARILY ORNATE GRAVE MARKERS.
BUT REMEMBER, ONLY CERTAIN GUYS REALLY SUIT FOUR TONS OF PERSONALISED CUBIC ZIRCONIUM.
LOVED BY ALL
GODFATHER URAL BERKOFF
DOWNLODE EXAMINER
MURDER
AND MAKE SURE EVERYONE KNOWS YOU'VE PASSED ON. THE MAIN DOWNLODE DAILIES ALL CARRY OBITUARIES.
OBITUARIES
A-Z
OBITUARIES A-Z
USUALLY AS A SEPARATE SUPPLEMENT.
THEN YOU CAN LIE BACK AND PLAN YOUR NEXT MOVE. HOW ABOUT CONTACTING THE LIVING VIA ONE OF THE CITY'S FIVE MILLION MEDIUMS OR CLAIRVOYANTS?
YOU'VE GOT PLENTY OF TIME TO CHOOSE. DEATH REALLY IS A GREAT ESCAPE FROM THE PRESSURES OF MODERN LIFE.

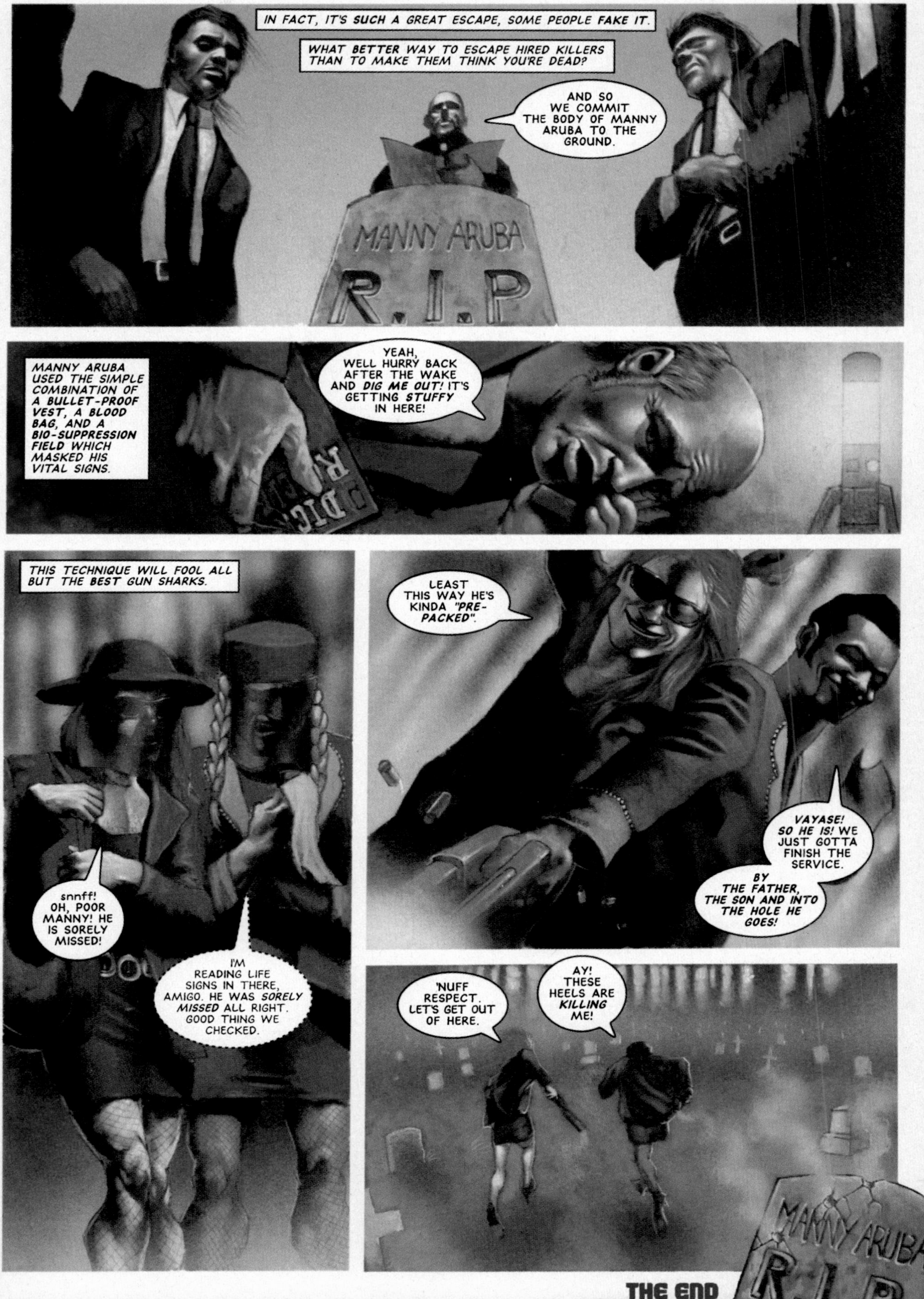
IN FACT, IT'S SUCH A GREAT ESCAPE, SOME PEOPLE FAKE IT.
WHAT BETTER WAY TO ESCAPE HIRED KILLERS THAN TO MAKE THEM THINK YOU'RE DEAD?
AND SO WE COMMIT THE BODY OF MANNY ARUBA TO THE GROUND.
MANNY ARUBA R.I.P
MANNY ARUBA USED THE SIMPLE COMBINATION OF A BULLET-PROOF VEST, A BLOOD BAG, AND A BIO-SUPPRESSION FIELD WHICH MASKED HIS VITAL SIGNS.
YEAH, WELL HURRY BACK AFTER THE WAKE AND DIG ME OUT! IT'S GETTING STUFFY IN HERE!
THIS TECHNIQUE WILL FOOL ALL BUT THE BEST GUN SHARKS.
snnff! OH, POOR MANNY! HE IS SORELY MISSED!
I'M READING LIFE SIGNS IN THERE, AMIGO. HE WAS SORELY MISSED ALL RIGHT. GOOD THING WE CHECKED.
LEAST THIS WAY HE'S KINDA "PRE-PACKED".
VAYASE! SO HE IS! WE JUST GOTTA FINISH THE SERVICE.
BY THE FATHER, THE SON AND INTO THE HOLE HE GOES!
'NUFF RESPECT. LET'S GET OUT OF HERE.
AY! THESE HEELS ARE KILLING ME!
MANNY ARUBA R.I.P
THE END

LONG TO RAIN OVER US

Script: Dan Abnett

Art: Paul Johnson

Letters: Steve Potter

Originally published in *2000 AD* Prog 1072

SINISTERDEXTER

SINISTER DEXTER

LONG TO RAIN OVER US

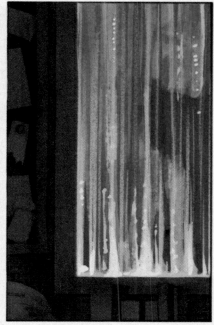

MONSOON SEASON, DOWNLODE CITY.

IT'S ALMOST TOO LATE, CENTRAL EUROPE TIME, AND STORMY CLOUDS HAVE CHASED EVERY ONE FROM THE PLACE.

SCRIPT
DAN ABNETT

ART
PAUL JOHNSON

LETTERS
STEVE POTTER

SKWAP!

THIS LOOKS LIKE THE PLACE.

SOMEONE'S UPSTAIRS.

LET'S GET INSIDE BEFORE I SPONTANEOUSLY DEVELOP GILLS.

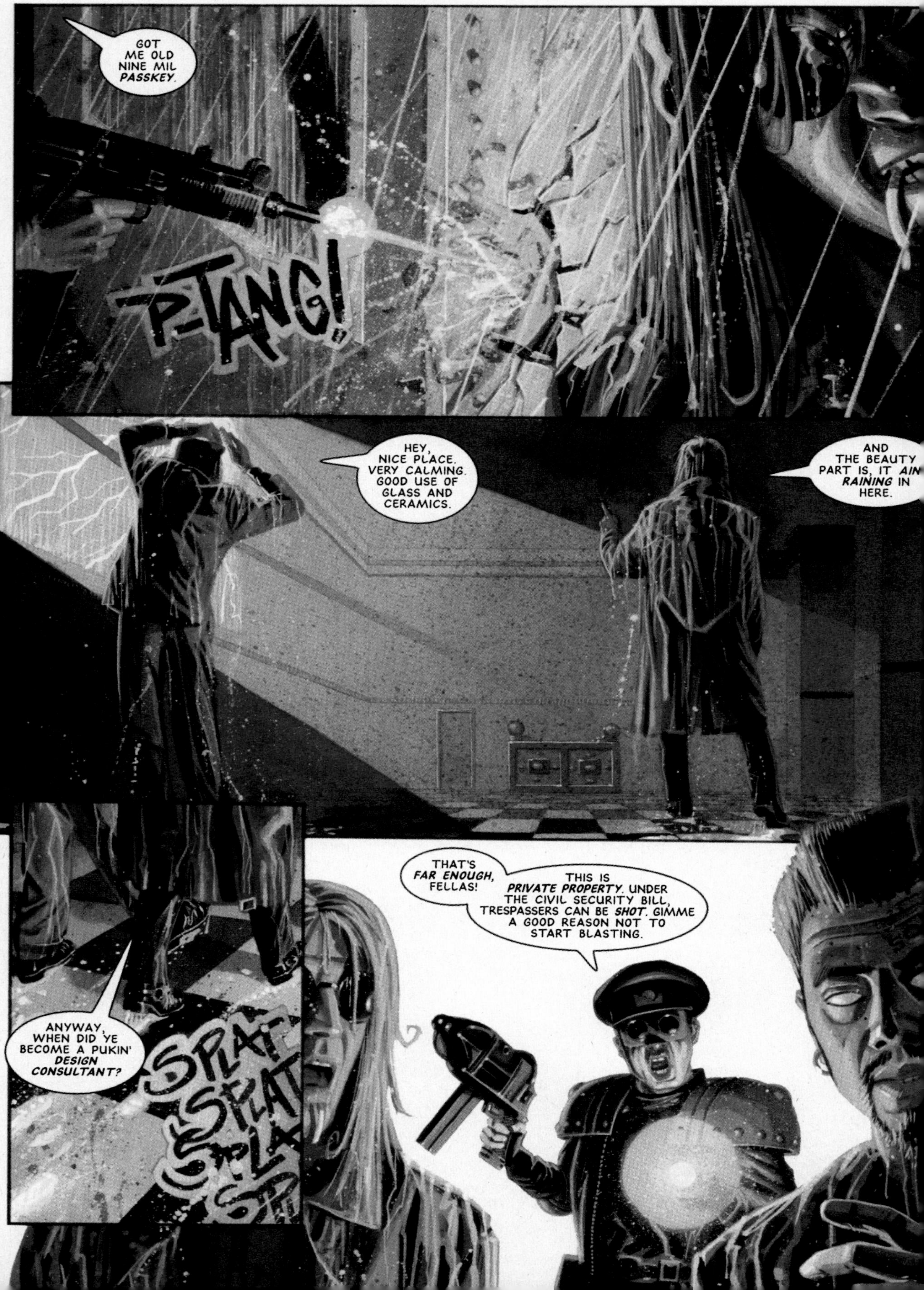
GOT ME OLD NINE MIL *PASSKEY*.
P-TANG!
HEY, NICE PLACE. VERY CALMING. GOOD USE OF GLASS AND CERAMICS.
AND THE BEAUTY PART IS, IT *AIN RAINING* IN HERE.
ANYWAY, WHEN DID 'YE BECOME A PUKIN' *DESIGN CONSULTANT?*
SPLAT
SPLAT
SPLA
THAT'S *FAR ENOUGH,* FELLAS!
THIS IS *PRIVATE PROPERTY*. UNDER THE CIVIL SECURITY BILL, TRESPASSERS CAN BE *SHOT*. GIMME A GOOD REASON NOT TO START BLASTING.

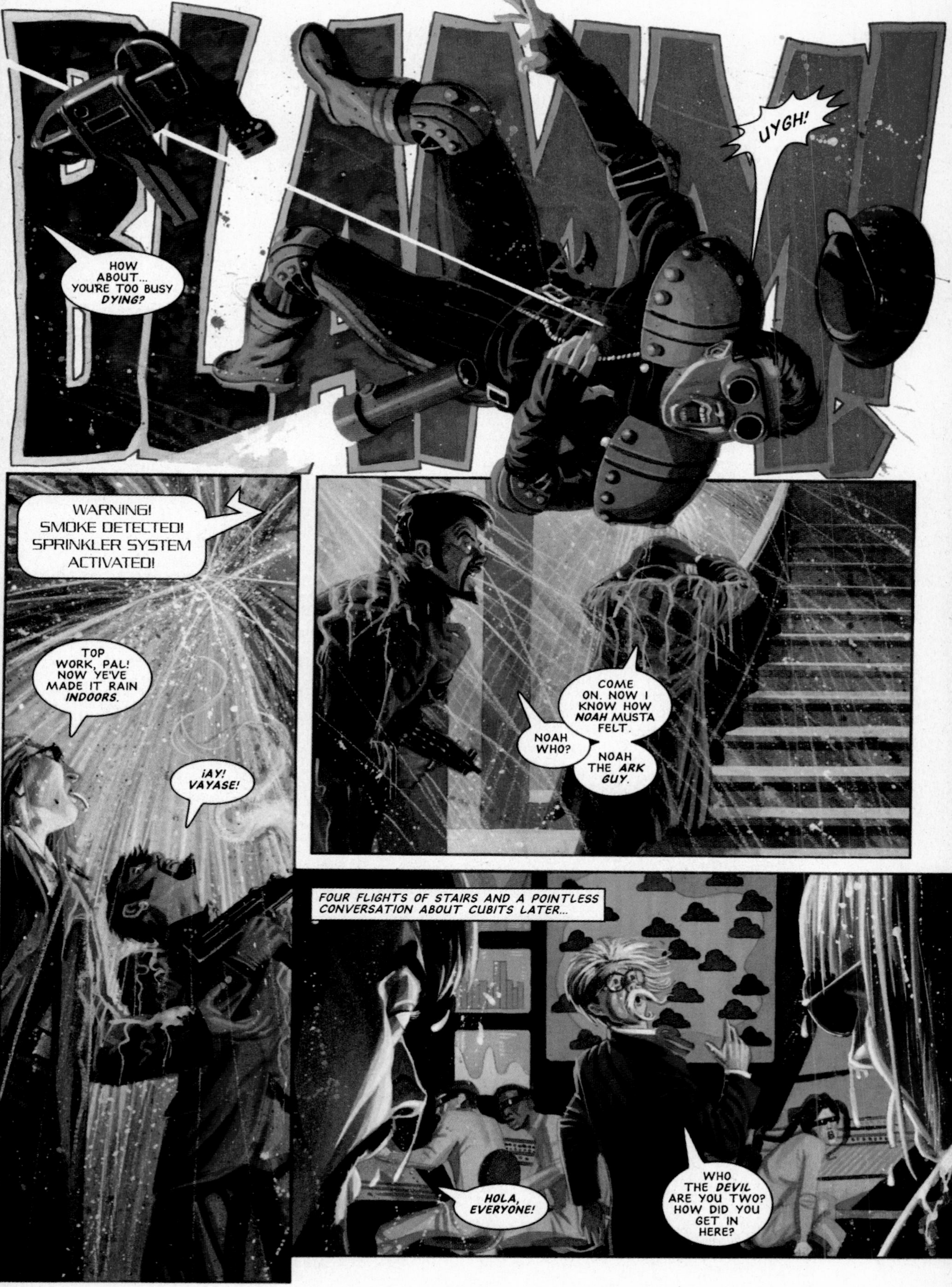
UYGH!
HOW ABOUT... YOU'RE TOO BUSY DYING?
WARNING! SMOKE DETECTED! SPRINKLER SYSTEM ACTIVATED!
TOP WORK, PAL! NOW YE'VE MADE IT RAIN INDOORS.
¡AY! VAYASE!
COME ON. NOW I KNOW HOW NOAH MUSTA FELT.
NOAH WHO?
NOAH THE ARK GUY.
FOUR FLIGHTS OF STAIRS AND A POINTLESS CONVERSATION ABOUT CUBITS LATER...
HOLA, EVERYONE!
WHO THE DEVIL ARE YOU TWO? HOW DID YOU GET IN HERE?

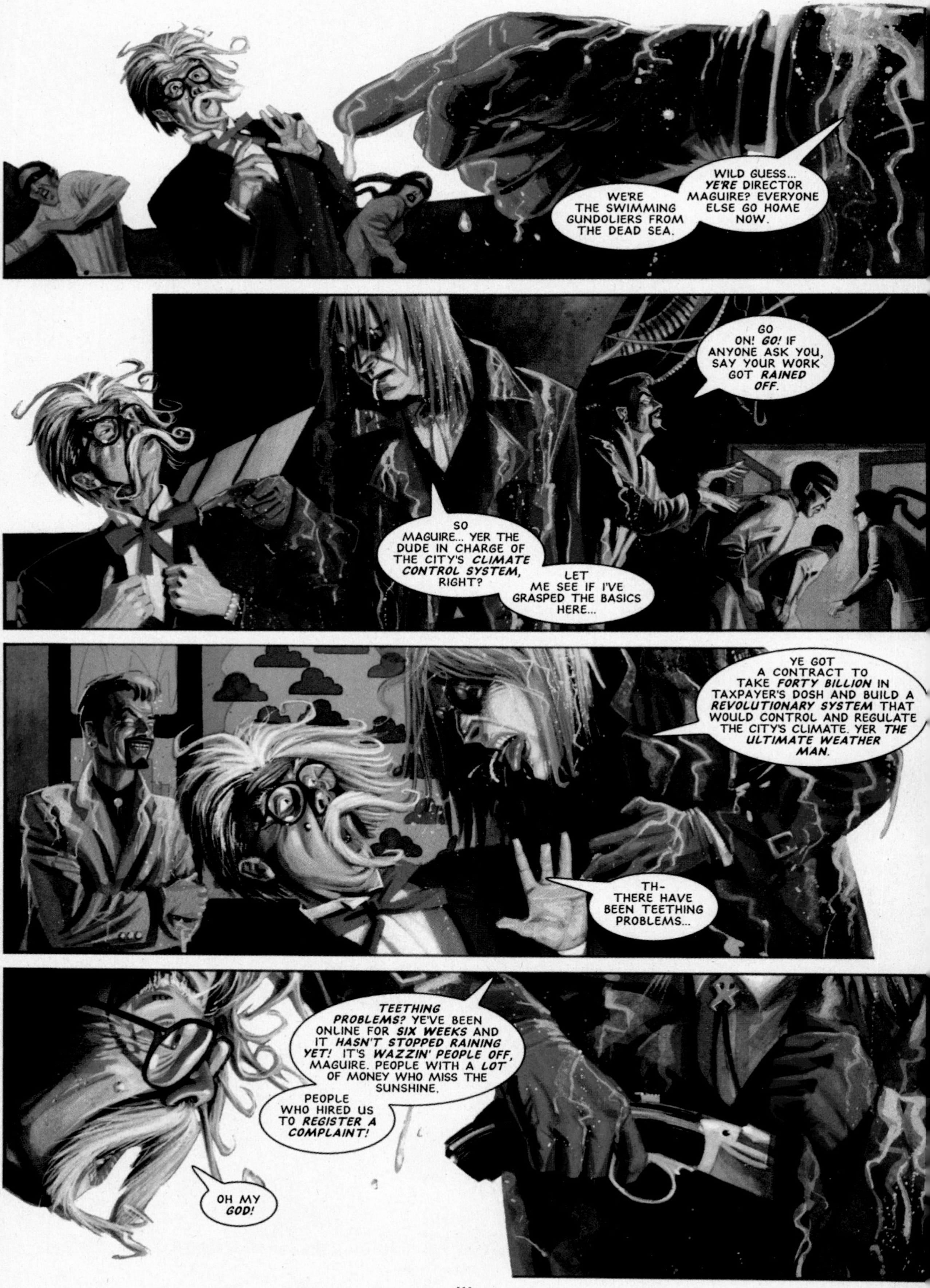

WE'RE THE SWIMMING GUNDOLIERS FROM THE DEAD SEA.
WILD GUESS... YE'RE DIRECTOR MAGUIRE? EVERYONE ELSE GO HOME NOW.
GO ON! GO! IF ANYONE ASK YOU, SAY YOUR WORK GOT RAINED OFF.
SO MAGUIRE... YER THE DUDE IN CHARGE OF THE CITY'S CLIMATE CONTROL SYSTEM, RIGHT?
LET ME SEE IF I'VE GRASPED THE BASICS HERE...
YE GOT A CONTRACT TO TAKE FORTY BILLION IN TAXPAYER'S DOSH AND BUILD A REVOLUTIONARY SYSTEM THAT WOULD CONTROL AND REGULATE THE CITY'S CLIMATE. YER THE ULTIMATE WEATHER MAN.
TH- THERE HAVE BEEN TEETHING PROBLEMS...
TEETHING PROBLEMS? YE'VE BEEN ONLINE FOR SIX WEEKS AND IT HASN'T STOPPED RAINING YET! IT'S WAZZIN' PEOPLE OFF, MAGUIRE. PEOPLE WITH A LOT OF MONEY WHO MISS THE SUNSHINE.
PEOPLE WHO HIRED US TO REGISTER A COMPLAINT!
OH MY GOD!

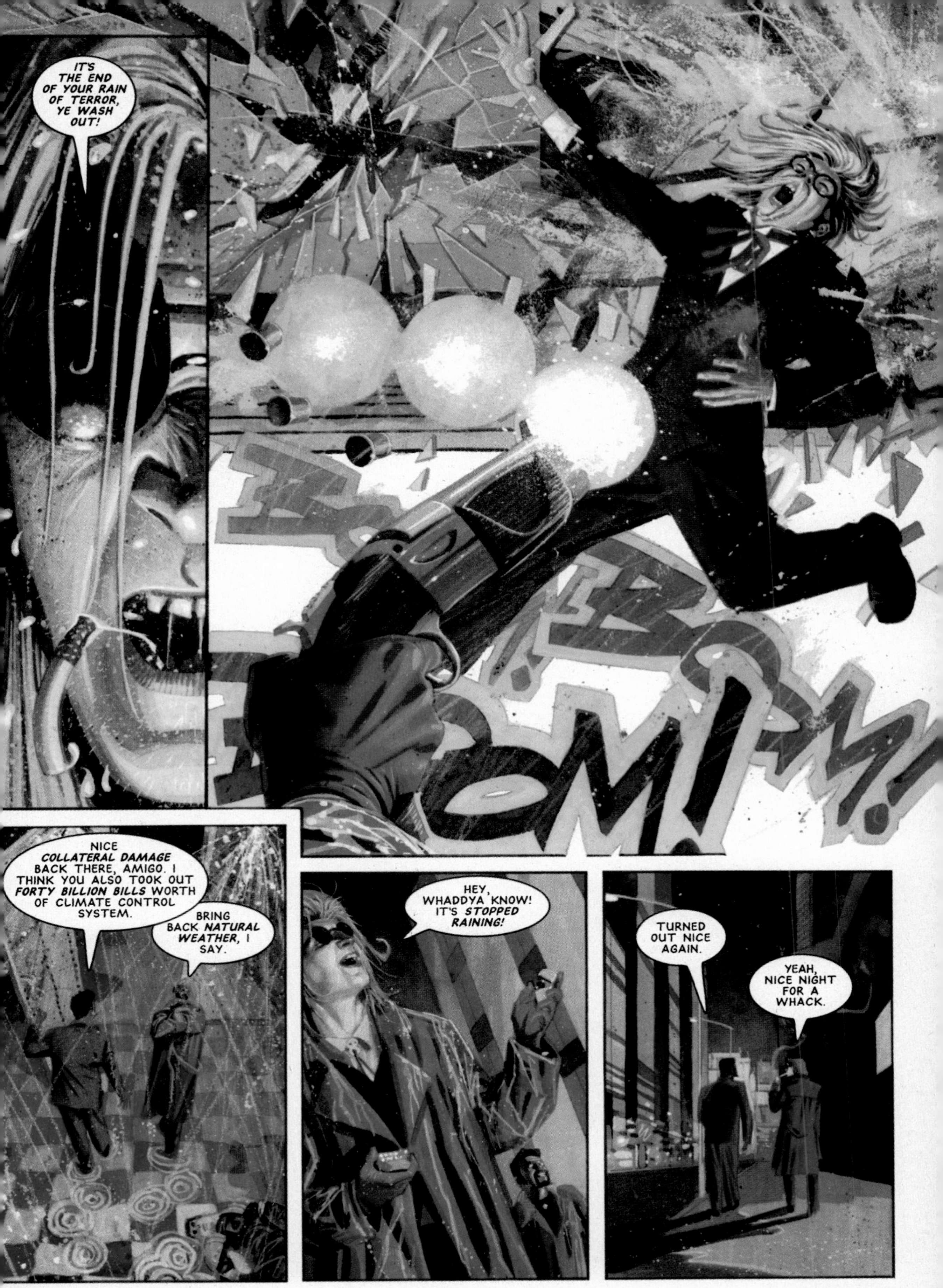
IT'S THE END OF YOUR RAIN OF TERROR, YE WASH OUT!
NICE *COLLATERAL DAMAGE* BACK THERE, AMIGO. I THINK YOU ALSO TOOK OUT *FORTY BILLION BILLS* WORTH OF CLIMATE CONTROL SYSTEM.
BRING BACK *NATURAL WEATHER*, I SAY.
HEY, WHADDYA KNOW! IT'S *STOPPED RAINING!*
TURNED OUT NICE AGAIN.
YEAH, NICE NIGHT FOR A WHACK.

THE END

ROLL WITH IT

Script: Dan Abnett

Art: Julian Gibson

Letters: Steve Potter

Originally published in *2000 AD* Prog 1073

SINISTERDEXTER

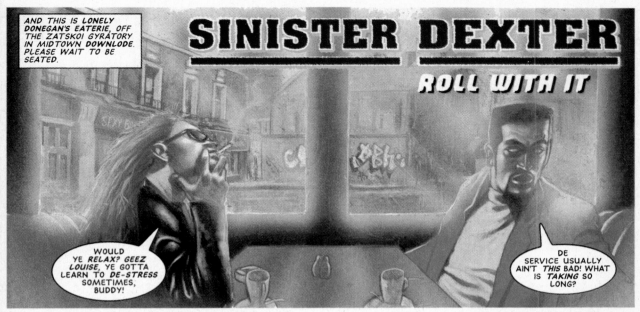

AND THIS IS LONELY DONEGAN'S EATERIE, OFF THE ZATSKOI GYRATORY IN MIDTOWN DOWNLODE. PLEASE WAIT TO BE SEATED.

SINISTER DEXTER
ROLL WITH IT

WOULD YE *RELAX*? *GEEZ LOUISE*, YE GOTTA LEARN TO *DE-STRESS* SOMETIMES, BUDDY!

DE SERVICE USUALLY AIN'T *THIS* BAD! WHAT IS *TAKING* SO LONG?

SO, THEY'RE A LITTLE *RUSHED*. MAKIN' A *FUSS* WON'T HELP.

IT'S BEEN *SO* LONG I'VE ALREADY *DRUNK* MY COFFEE! AND THERE'S BEEN NO SIGN OF NO *REFILL*!

HOW LONG DOES IT TAKE TO COOK *SOUP OF THE DAY*?

SCRIPT
DAN ABNETT

ART
JULIAN GIBSON

LETTERS
STEVE POTTER

WELL, DEPENDS ON THE SOUP. I MEAN... MINESTRONE, FIFTEEN MINUTES *MAX*.

MASTODON THOUGH. *PUKE!* YE'D HAVE TO CRACK THE LAWS O' TIME/SPACE, BUILD A VIABLE TIME MACHINE, TRAVEL BACK, STALK AND KILL YER MASTODON, PREPARE THE SOUP, *AND* BRING IT BACK, MAYBE PAUSING TO *REHEAT* BEFORE SERVING.

BUT THEN YE'D HAVE A *TIME MACHINE*, SO LIKE... IT WOULD BE *INSTANT SERVICE*. LIKE, "MASTODON SOUP? *BOOMF!* THERE YE GO, SIR! BON APPETITE!"

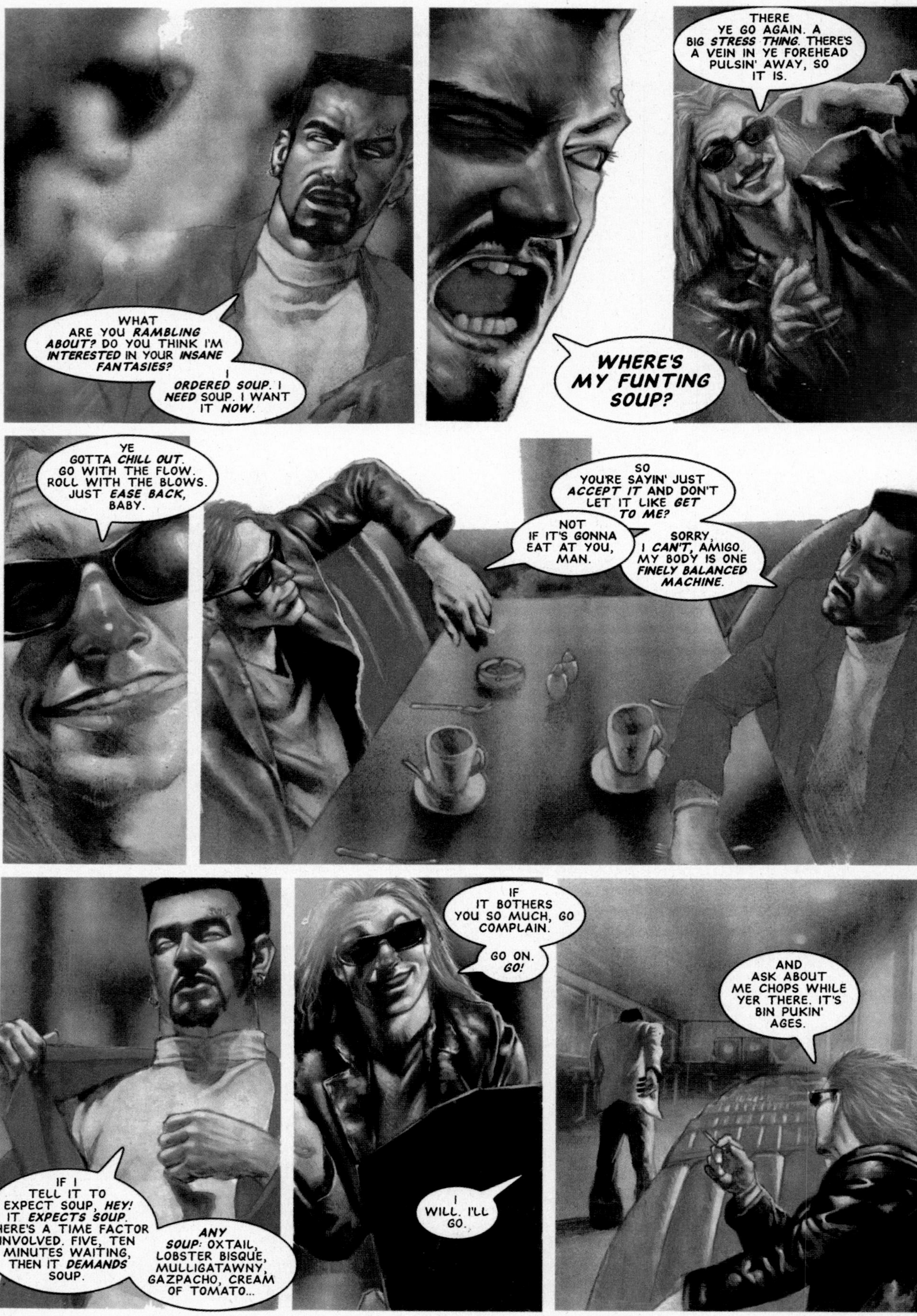

WHAT ARE YOU RAMBLING ABOUT? DO YOU THINK I'M INTERESTED IN YOUR INSANE FANTASIES?
I ORDERED SOUP. I NEED SOUP. I WANT IT NOW.
WHERE'S MY FUNTING SOUP?
THERE YE GO AGAIN. A BIG STRESS THING. THERE'S A VEIN IN YE FOREHEAD PULSIN' AWAY, SO IT IS.
YE GOTTA CHILL OUT. GO WITH THE FLOW. ROLL WITH THE BLOWS. JUST EASE BACK, BABY.
SO YOU'RE SAYIN' JUST ACCEPT IT AND DON'T LET IT LIKE GET TO ME?
NOT IF IT'S GONNA EAT AT YOU, MAN.
SORRY, I CAN'T, AMIGO. MY BODY IS ONE FINELY BALANCED MACHINE.
IF I TELL IT TO EXPECT SOUP, HEY! IT EXPECTS SOUP. THERE'S A TIME FACTOR INVOLVED. FIVE, TEN MINUTES WAITING, THEN IT DEMANDS SOUP.
ANY SOUP: OXTAIL, LOBSTER BISQUE, MULLIGATAWNY, GAZPACHO, CREAM OF TOMATO...
IF IT BOTHERS YOU SO MUCH, GO COMPLAIN.
GO ON. GO!
I WILL. I'LL GO.
AND ASK ABOUT ME CHOPS WHILE YER THERE. IT'S BIN PUKIN' AGES.

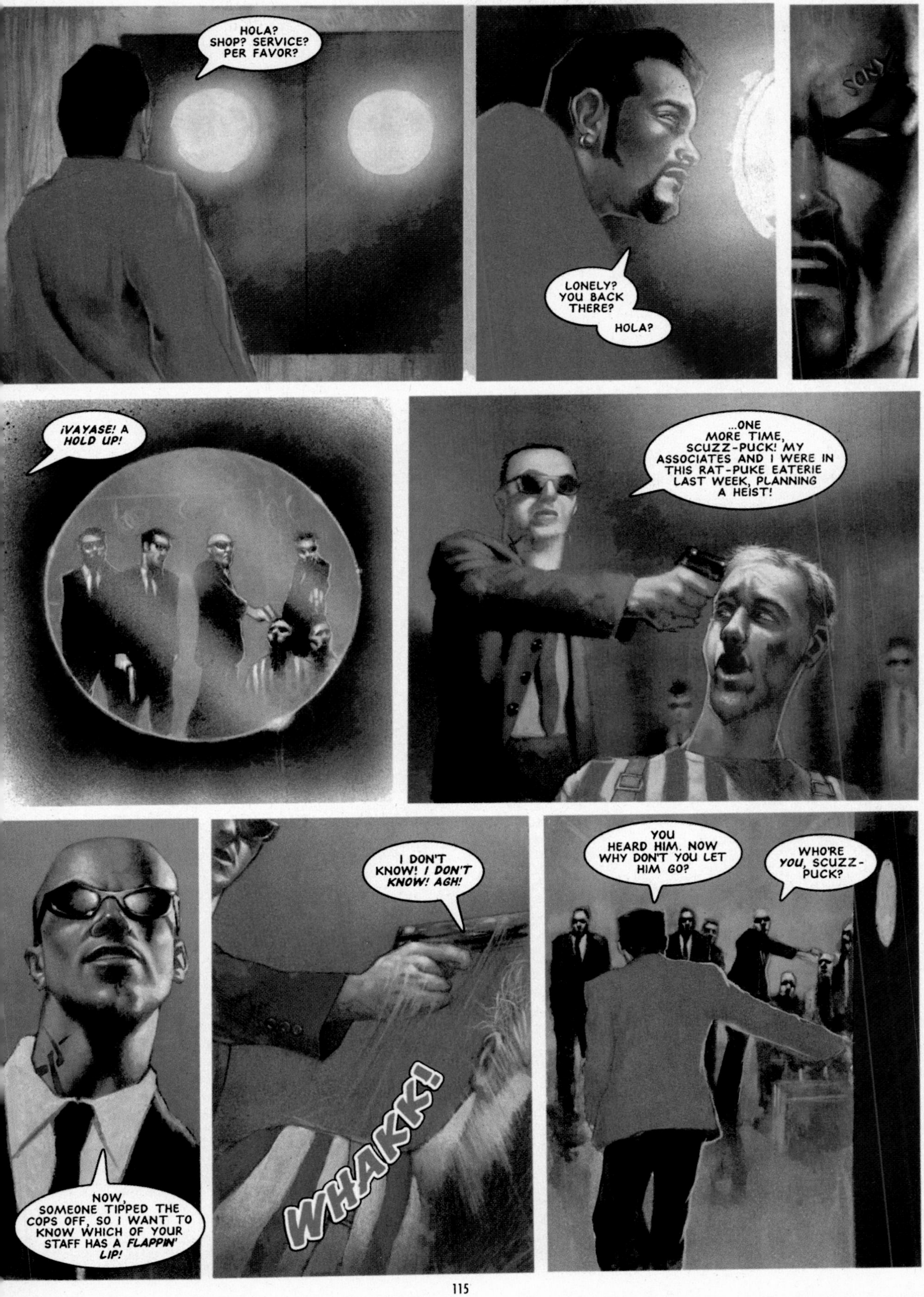
HOLA? SHOP? SERVICE? PER FAVOR?
LONELY? YOU BACK THERE?
HOLA?
¡VAYASE! A HOLD UP!
...ONE MORE TIME, SCUZZ-PUCK! MY ASSOCIATES AND I WERE IN THIS RAT-PUKE EATERIE LAST WEEK, PLANNING A HEIST!
NOW, SOMEONE TIPPED THE COPS OFF, SO I WANT TO KNOW WHICH OF YOUR STAFF HAS A *FLAPPIN'* *LIP!*
I DON'T KNOW! *I DON'T KNOW! AGH!*
WHAKK!
YOU HEARD HIM. NOW WHY DON'T YOU LET HIM GO?
WHO'RE *YOU*, SCUZZ-PUCK?

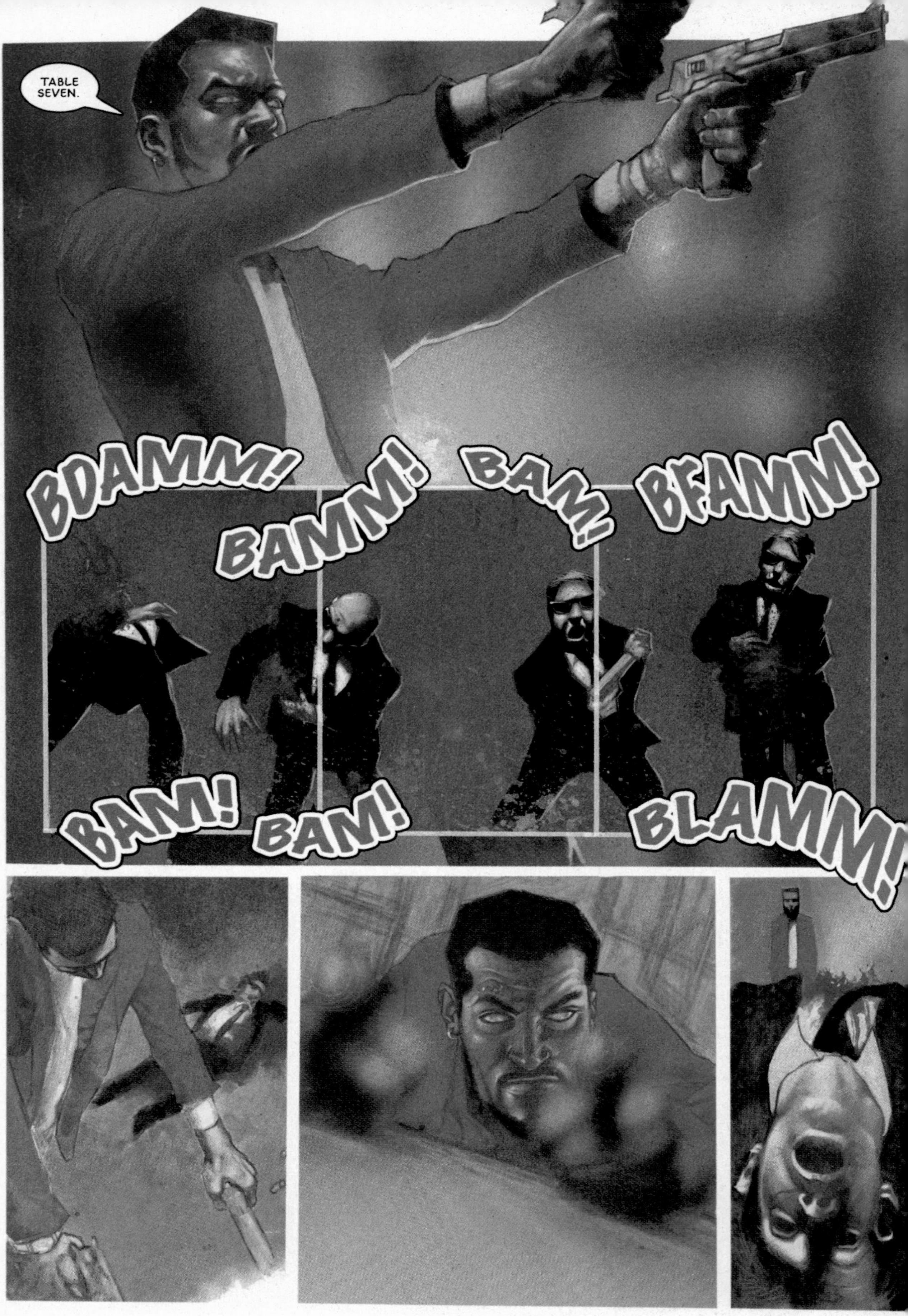
TABLE SEVEN.
BDAMM!
BAMM!
BAM!
BFAMM!
BAM!
BAM!
BLAMM!

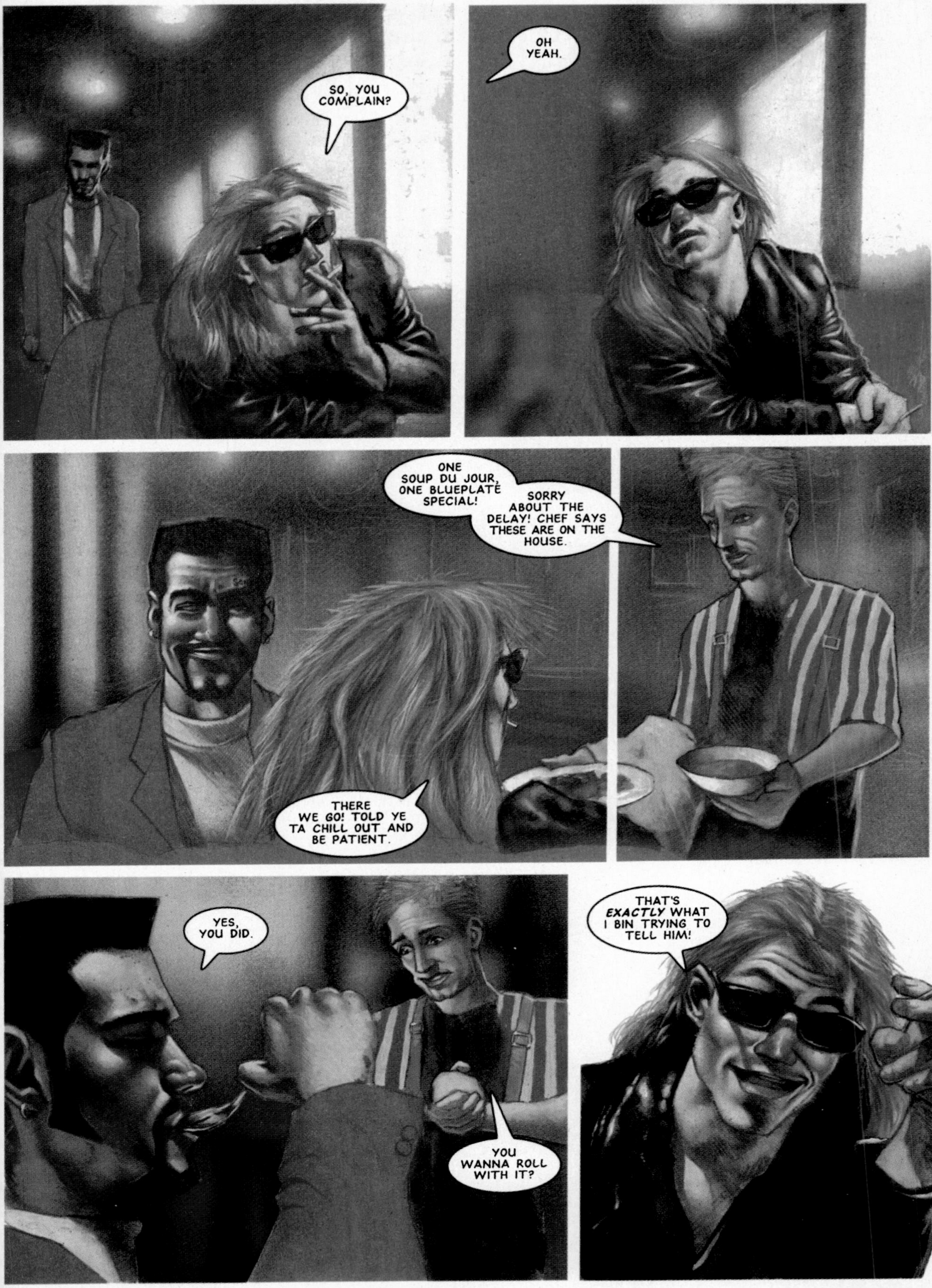
SO, YOU COMPLAIN?
OH YEAH.
ONE SOUP DU JOUR, ONE BLUEPLATE SPECIAL!
SORRY ABOUT THE DELAY! CHEF SAYS THESE ARE ON THE HOUSE.
THERE WE GO! TOLD YE TA CHILL OUT AND BE PATIENT.
YES, YOU DID.
YOU WANNA ROLL WITH IT?
THAT'S *EXACTLY* WHAT I BIN TRYING TO TELL HIM!

THE END

WHACK THE DINASAUR

Script: Dan Abnett

Art: Siku

Letters: Steve Potter

Originally published in *2000 AD* Prog 1075

SINISTERDEXTER

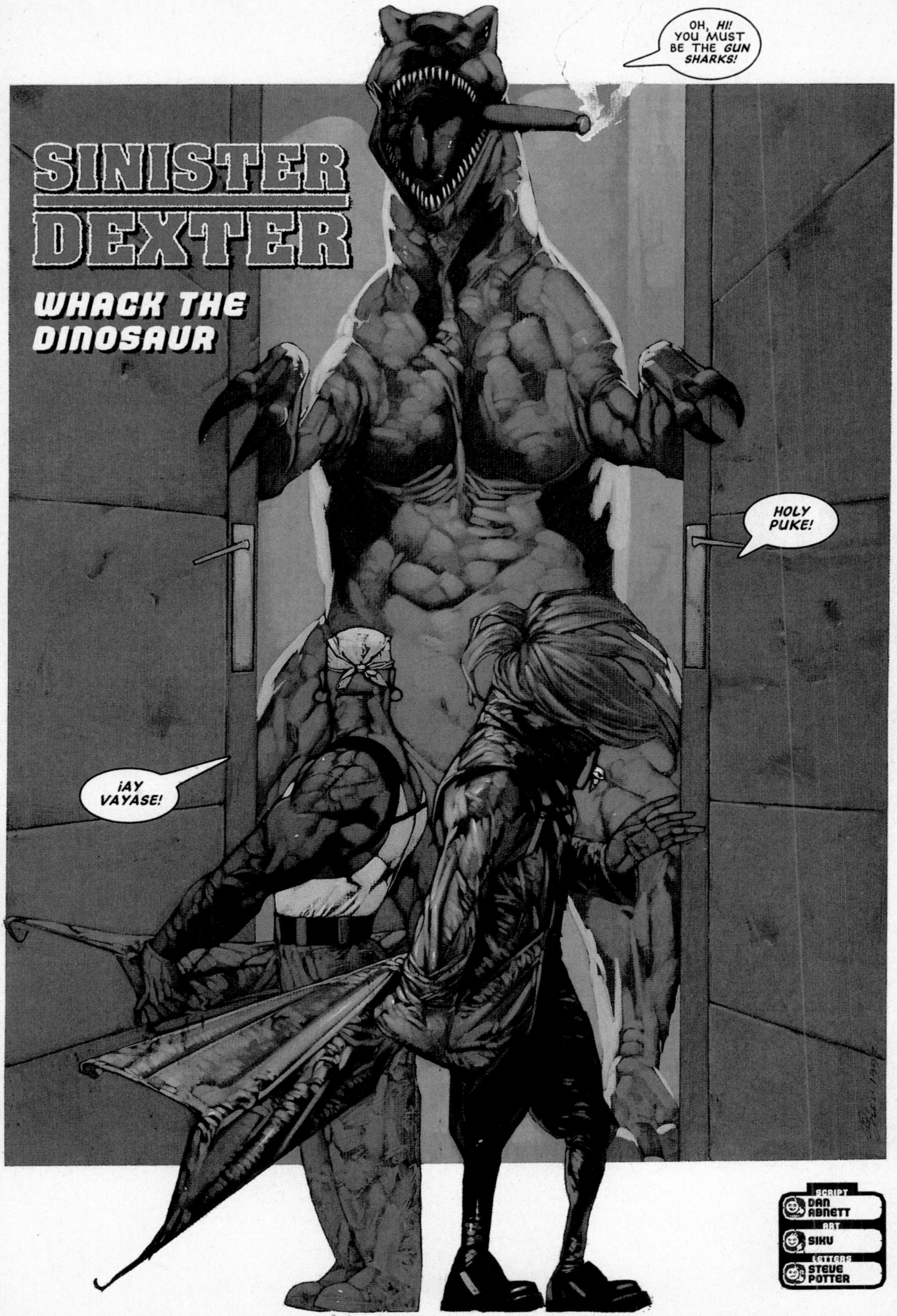
SINISTER DEXTER
WHACK THE DINOSAUR
OH, HI! YOU MUST BE THE GUN SHARKS!
¡AY VAYASE!
HOLY PUKE!
SCRIPT DAN ABNETT
ART SIKU
LETTERS STEVE POTTER

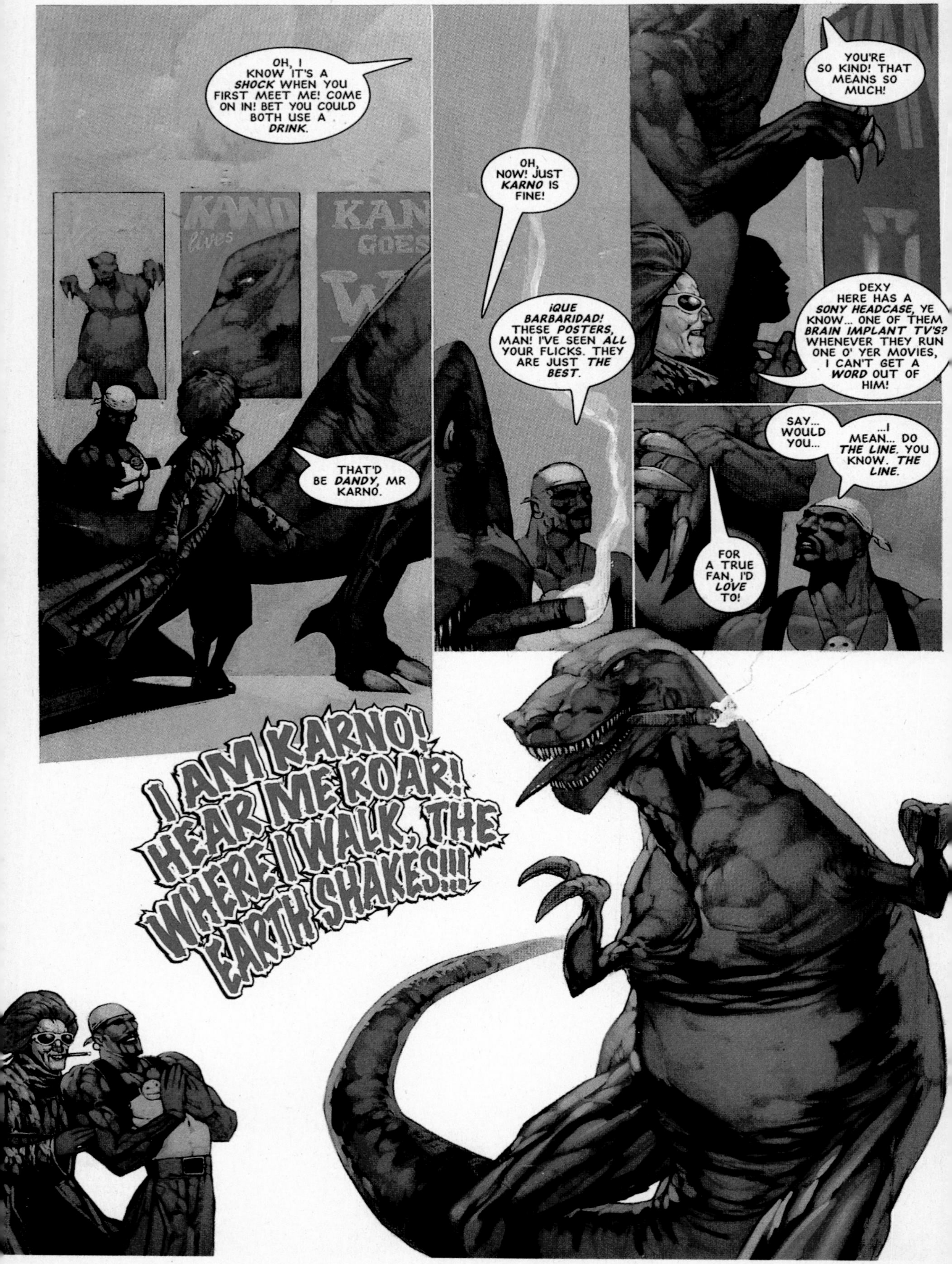
OH, I KNOW IT'S A SHOCK WHEN YOU FIRST MEET ME! COME ON IN! BET YOU COULD BOTH USE A DRINK.
KANO lives
KANO GOES
THAT'D BE DANDY, MR KARNO.
OH, NOW! JUST KARNO IS FINE!
¡QUE BARBARIDAD! THESE POSTERS, MAN! I'VE SEEN ALL YOUR FLICKS. THEY ARE JUST THE BEST.
YOU'RE SO KIND! THAT MEANS SO MUCH!
DEXY HERE HAS A SONY HEADCASE, YE KNOW... ONE OF THEM BRAIN IMPLANT TV'S? WHENEVER THEY RUN ONE O' YER MOVIES, I CAN'T GET A WORD OUT OF HIM!
SAY... WOULD YOU...
...I MEAN... DO THE LINE. YOU KNOW. THE LINE.
FOR A TRUE FAN, I'D LOVE TO!
I AM KARNO! HEAR ME ROAR! WHERE I WALK, THE EARTH SHAKES!!!

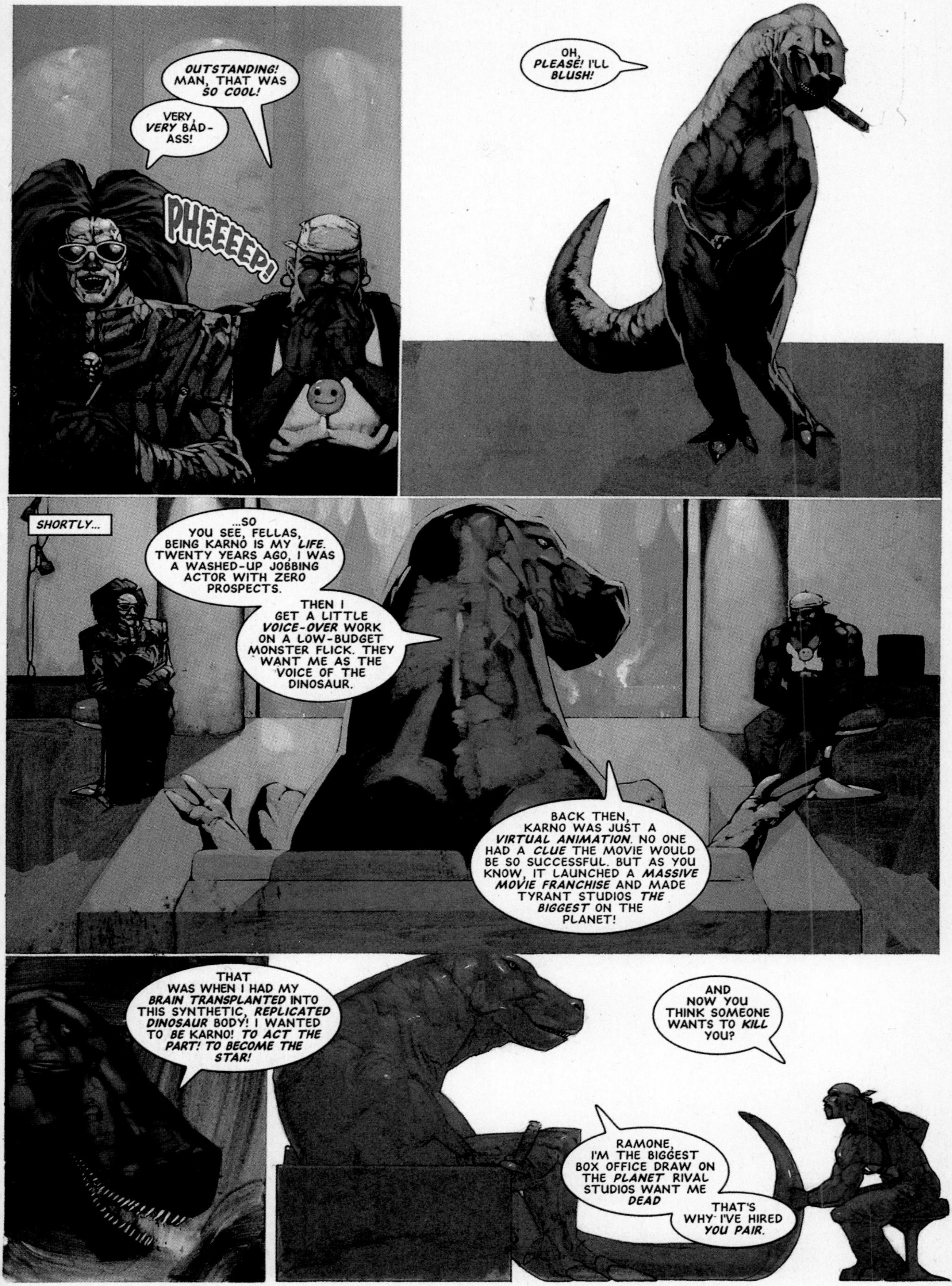

OUTSTANDING! MAN, THAT WAS SO COOL!
VERY, VERY BAD-ASS!
PHEEEEEP!
OH, PLEASE! I'LL BLUSH!
SHORTLY...
...SO YOU SEE, FELLAS, BEING KARNO IS MY LIFE. TWENTY YEARS AGO, I WAS A WASHED-UP JOBBING ACTOR WITH ZERO PROSPECTS.
THEN I GET A LITTLE VOICE-OVER WORK ON A LOW-BUDGET MONSTER FLICK. THEY WANT ME AS THE VOICE OF THE DINOSAUR.
BACK THEN, KARNO WAS JUST A VIRTUAL ANIMATION. NO ONE HAD A CLUE THE MOVIE WOULD BE SO SUCCESSFUL. BUT AS YOU KNOW, IT LAUNCHED A MASSIVE MOVIE FRANCHISE AND MADE TYRANT STUDIOS THE BIGGEST ON THE PLANET!
THAT WAS WHEN I HAD MY BRAIN TRANSPLANTED INTO THIS SYNTHETIC, REPLICATED DINOSAUR BODY! I WANTED TO BE KARNO! TO ACT THE PART! TO BECOME THE STAR!
AND NOW YOU THINK SOMEONE WANTS TO KILL YOU?
RAMONE, I'M THE BIGGEST BOX OFFICE DRAW ON THE PLANET RIVAL STUDIOS WANT ME DEAD
THAT'S WHY I'VE HIRED YOU PAIR.

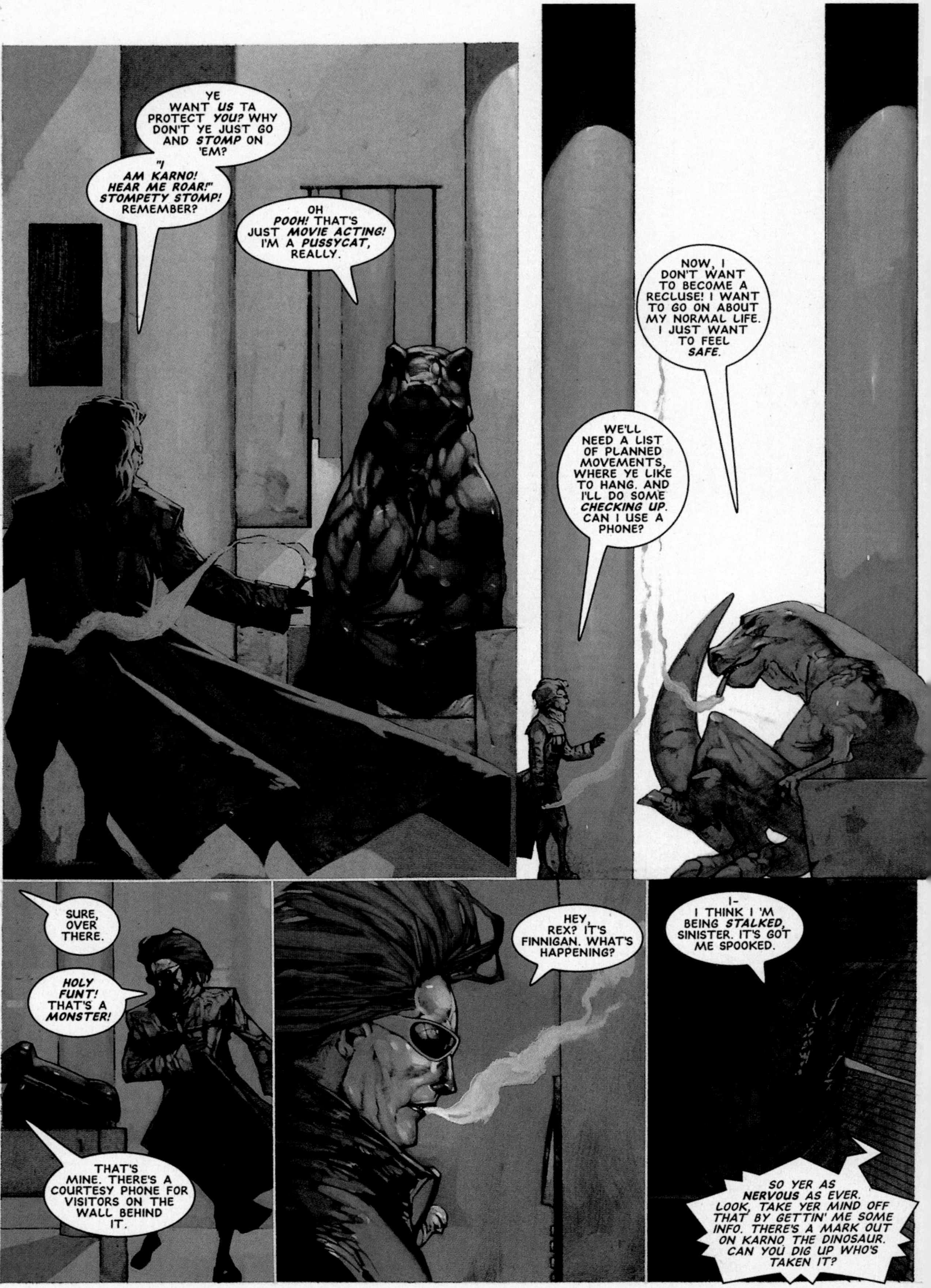
YE WANT US TA PROTECT YOU? WHY DON'T YE JUST GO AND STOMP ON 'EM?
"I AM KARNO! HEAR ME ROAR!" STOMPETY STOMP! REMEMBER?
OH POOH! THAT'S JUST MOVIE ACTING! I'M A PUSSYCAT, REALLY.
NOW, I DON'T WANT TO BECOME A RECLUSE! I WANT TO GO ON ABOUT MY NORMAL LIFE. I JUST WANT TO FEEL SAFE.
WE'LL NEED A LIST OF PLANNED MOVEMENTS, WHERE YE LIKE TO HANG. AND I'LL DO SOME CHECKING UP. CAN I USE A PHONE?
SURE, OVER THERE.
HOLY FUNT! THAT'S A MONSTER!
THAT'S MINE. THERE'S A COURTESY PHONE FOR VISITORS ON THE WALL BEHIND IT.
HEY, REX? IT'S FINNIGAN. WHAT'S HAPPENING?
I- I THINK I'M BEING STALKED, SINISTER. IT'S GOT ME SPOOKED.
SO YER AS NERVOUS AS EVER. LOOK, TAKE YER MIND OFF THAT BY GETTIN' ME SOME INFO. THERE'S A MARK OUT ON KARNO THE DINOSAUR. CAN YOU DIG UP WHO'S TAKEN IT?

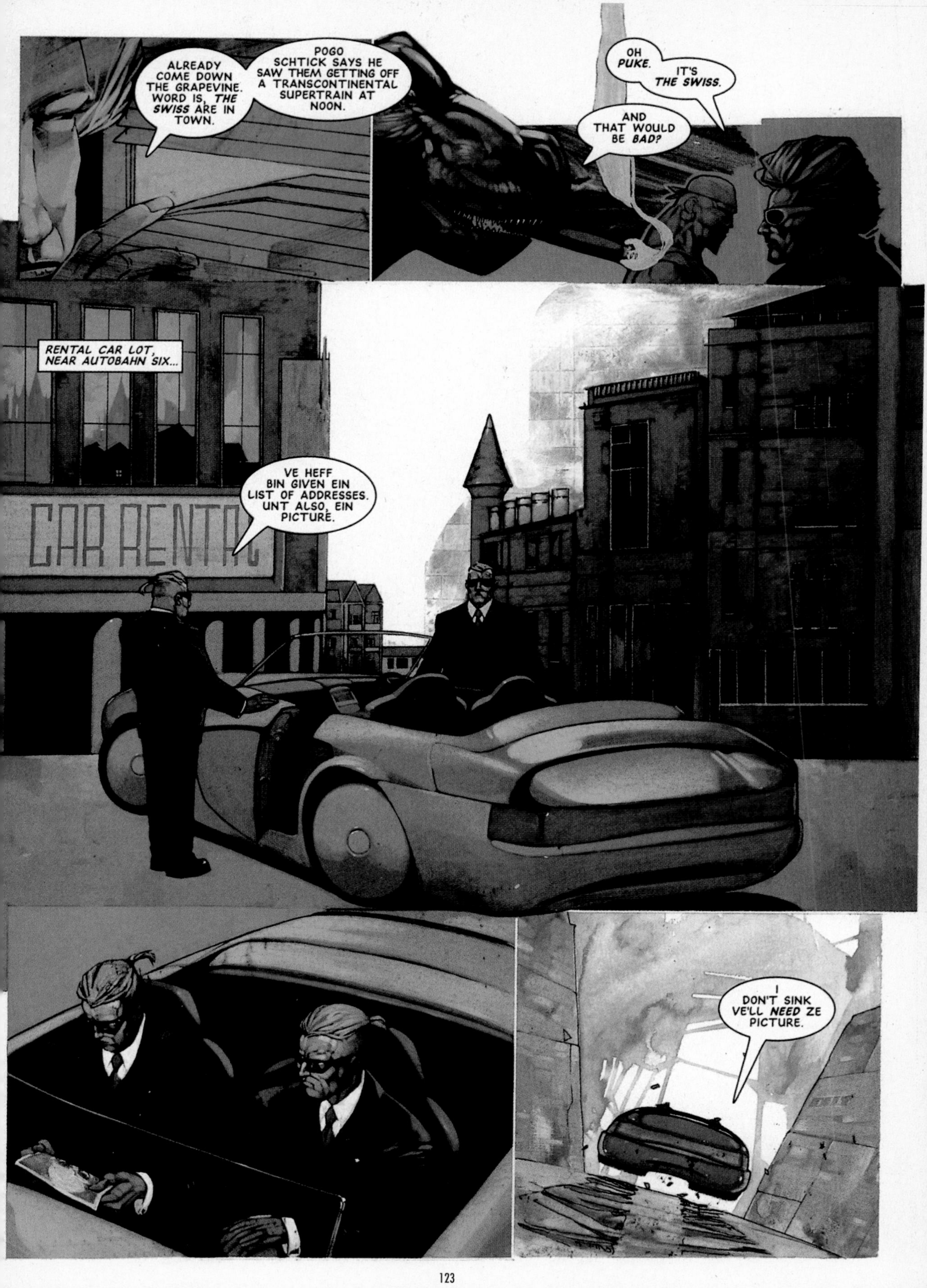
ALREADY COME DOWN THE GRAPEVINE. WORD IS, THE SWISS ARE IN TOWN.
POGO SCHTICK SAYS HE SAW THEM GETTING OFF A TRANSCONTINENTAL SUPERTRAIN AT NOON.
OH PUKE.
IT'S THE SWISS.
AND THAT WOULD BE BAD?
RENTAL CAR LOT, NEAR AUTOBAHN SIX...
VE HEFF BIN GIVEN EIN LIST OF ADDRESSES. UNT ALSO, EIN PICTURE.
CAR RENTAL
I DON'T SINK VE'LL NEED ZE PICTURE.

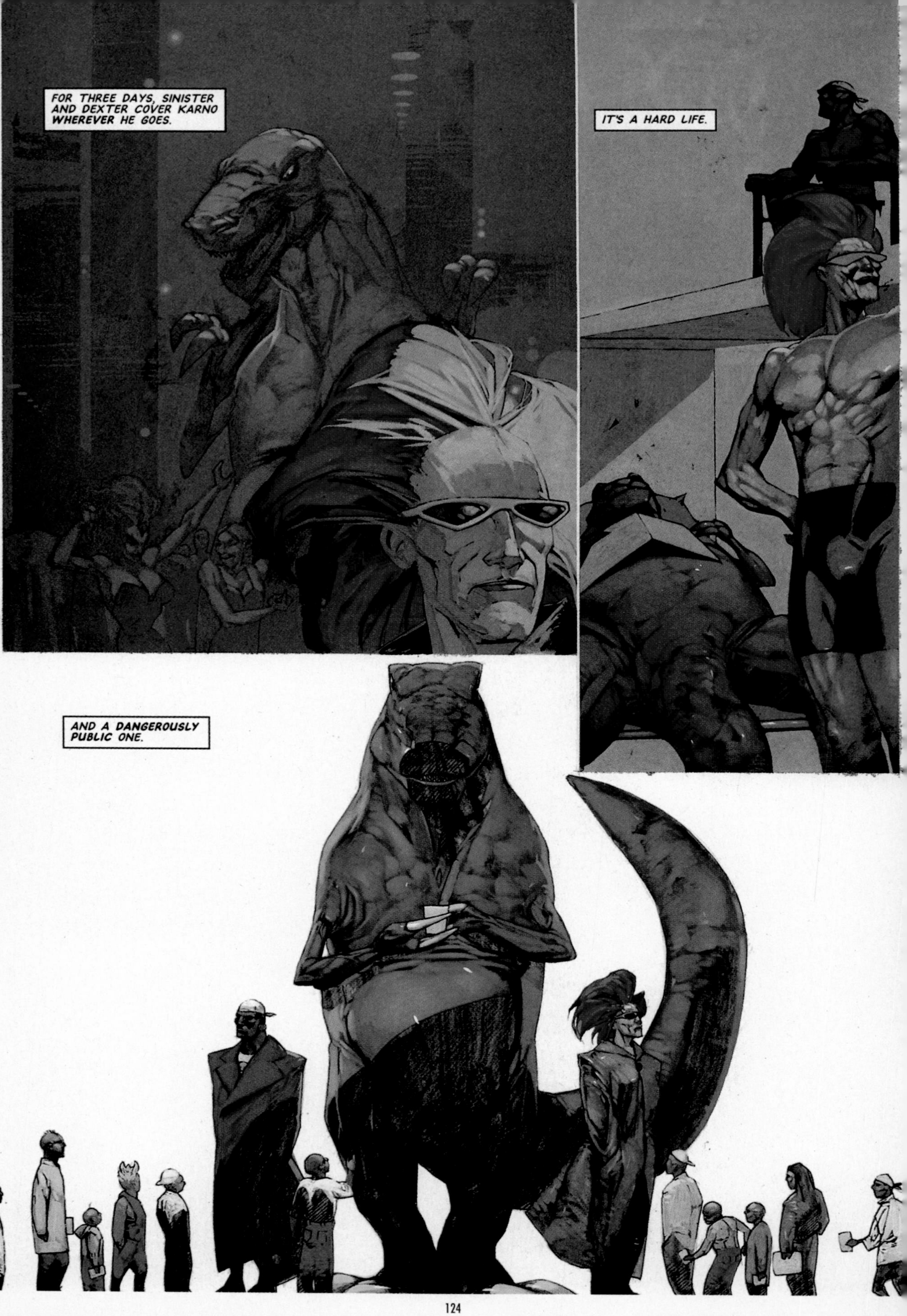
FOR THREE DAYS, SINISTER AND DEXTER COVER KARNO WHEREVER HE GOES.
IT'S A HARD LIFE.
AND A DANGEROUSLY PUBLIC ONE.

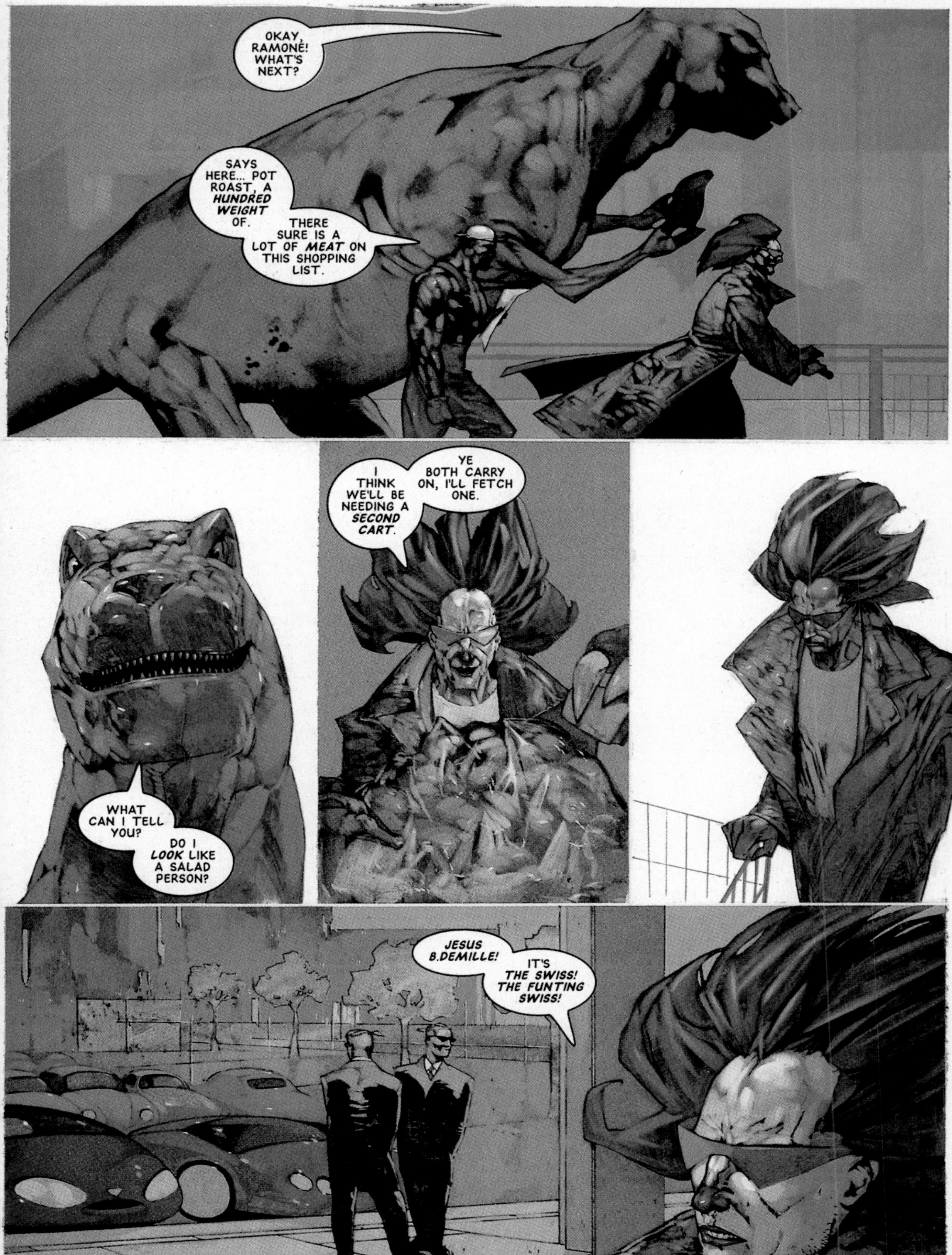
OKAY, RAMONÉ! WHAT'S NEXT?
SAYS HERE... POT ROAST, A HUNDRED WEIGHT OF.
THERE SURE IS A LOT OF MEAT ON THIS SHOPPING LIST.
WHAT CAN I TELL YOU?
DO I LOOK LIKE A SALAD PERSON?
I THINK WE'LL BE NEEDING A SECOND CART.
YE BOTH CARRY ON, I'LL FETCH ONE.
JESUS B.DEMILLE!
IT'S THE SWISS! THE FUNTING SWISS!

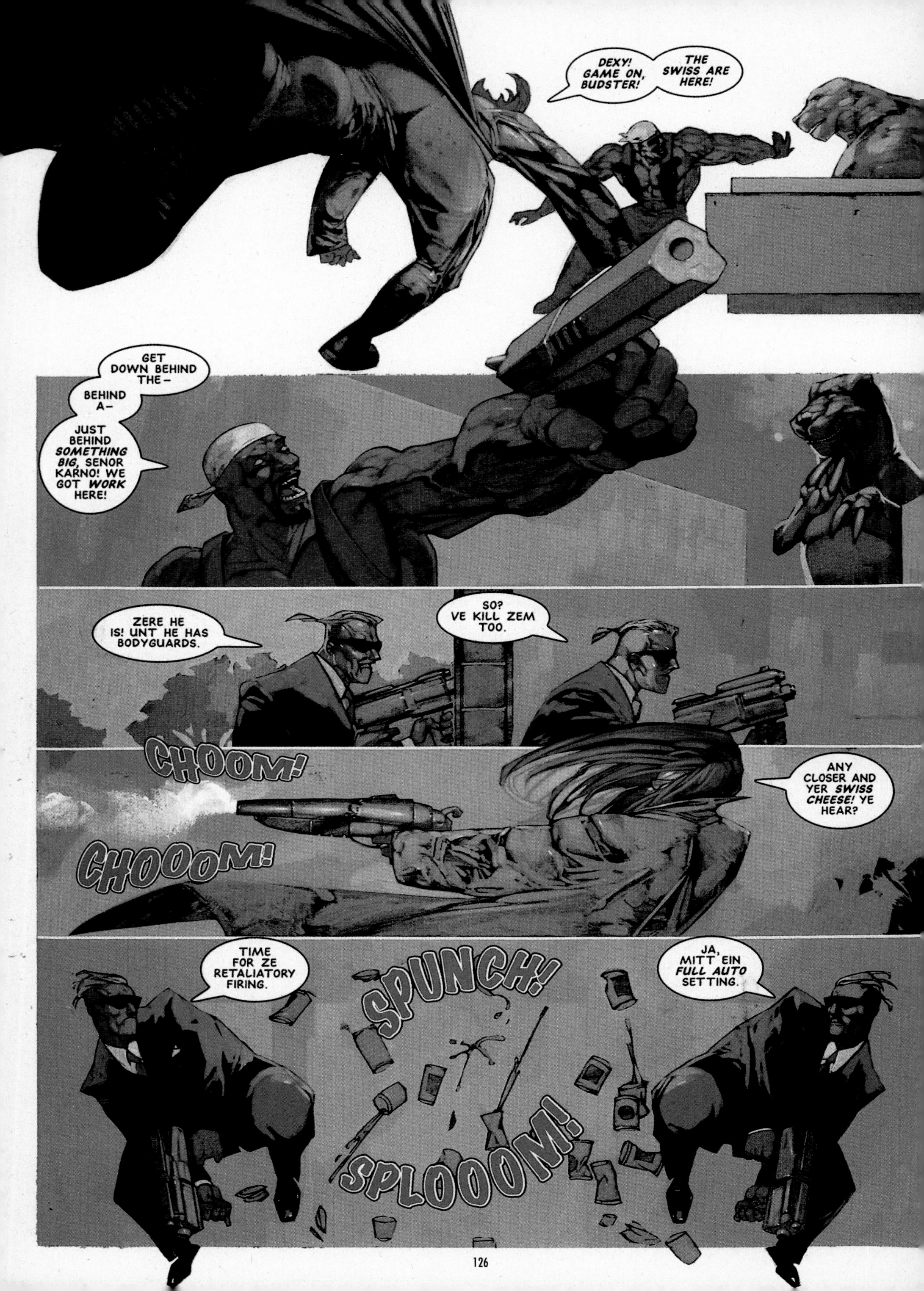
DEXY! GAME ON, BUDSTER!
THE SWISS ARE HERE!
GET DOWN BEHIND THE–
BEHIND A–
JUST BEHIND SOMETHING BIG, SENOR KARNO! WE GOT WORK HERE!
ZERE HE IS! UNT HE HAS BODYGUARDS.
SO? VE KILL ZEM TOO.
CHOOM!
CHOOOM!
ANY CLOSER AND YER SWISS CHEESE! YE HEAR?
TIME FOR ZE RETALIATORY FIRING.
SPUNCH!
JA, MITT EIN FULL AUTO SETTING.
SPLOOOM!

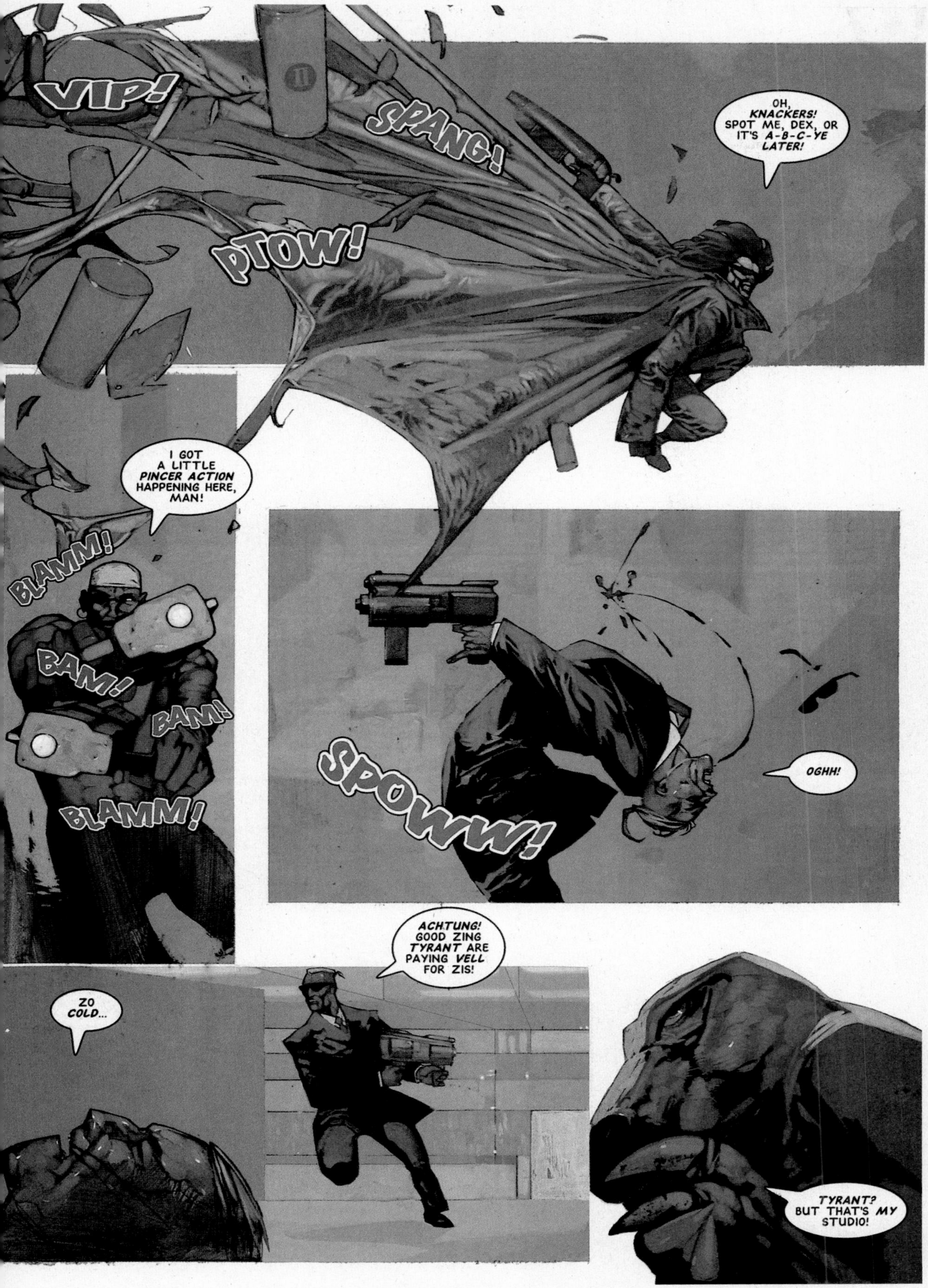

VIP!
SPANG!
PTOW!
OH, KNACKERS! SPOT ME, DEX, OR IT'S A-B-C-YE LATER!
I GOT A LITTLE PINCER ACTION HAPPENING HERE, MAN!
BLAMM!
BAM!
BAM!
BLAMM!
SPOWW!
OGHH!
ZO COLD...
ACHTUNG! GOOD ZING TYRANT ARE PAYING VELL FOR ZIS!
TYRANT? BUT THAT'S MY STUDIO!

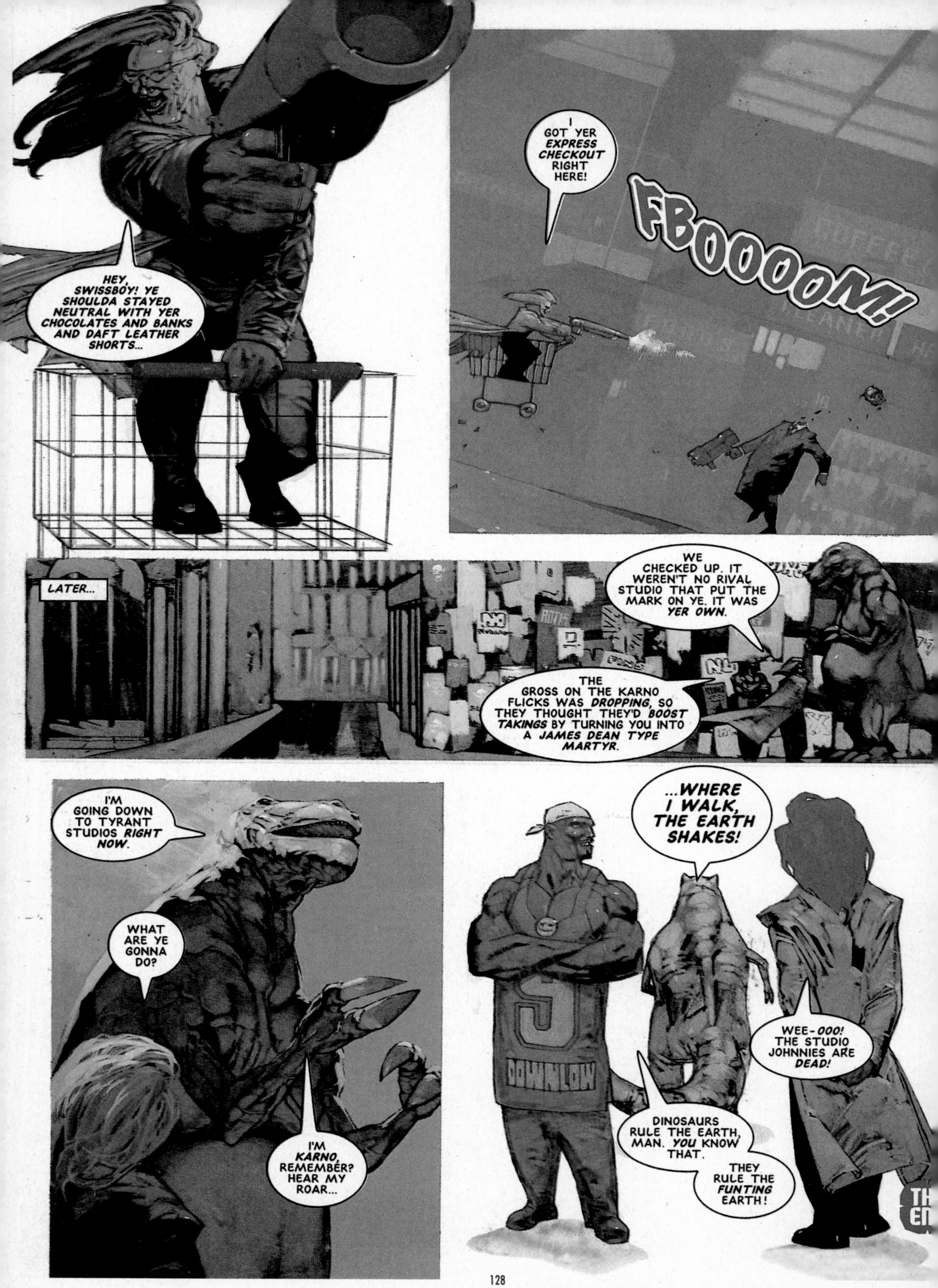
HEY, SWISSBOY! YE SHOULDA STAYED NEUTRAL WITH YER CHOCOLATES AND BANKS AND DAFT LEATHER SHORTS...
I GOT YER EXPRESS CHECKOUT RIGHT HERE!
FBOOOOM!
LATER...
WE CHECKED UP. IT WEREN'T NO RIVAL STUDIO THAT PUT THE MARK ON YE. IT WAS YER OWN.
THE GROSS ON THE KARNO FLICKS WAS DROPPING, SO THEY THOUGHT THEY'D BOOST TAKINGS BY TURNING YOU INTO A JAMES DEAN TYPE MARTYR.
I'M GOING DOWN TO TYRANT STUDIOS RIGHT NOW.
WHAT ARE YE GONNA DO?
I'M KARNO, REMEMBER? HEAR MY ROAR...
...WHERE I WALK, THE EARTH SHAKES!
WEE-OOO! THE STUDIO JOHNNIES ARE DEAD!
DOWNLOW
DINOSAURS RULE THE EARTH, MAN. YOU KNOW THAT.
THEY RULE THE FUNTING EARTH!

DOWNLODE BLUES

Script: Dan Abnett

Art: Alex Ronald

Colors: Dondie Cox

Letters: Ellie de Ville

Originally published in *2000 AD* Prog 1076

SINISTERDEXTER

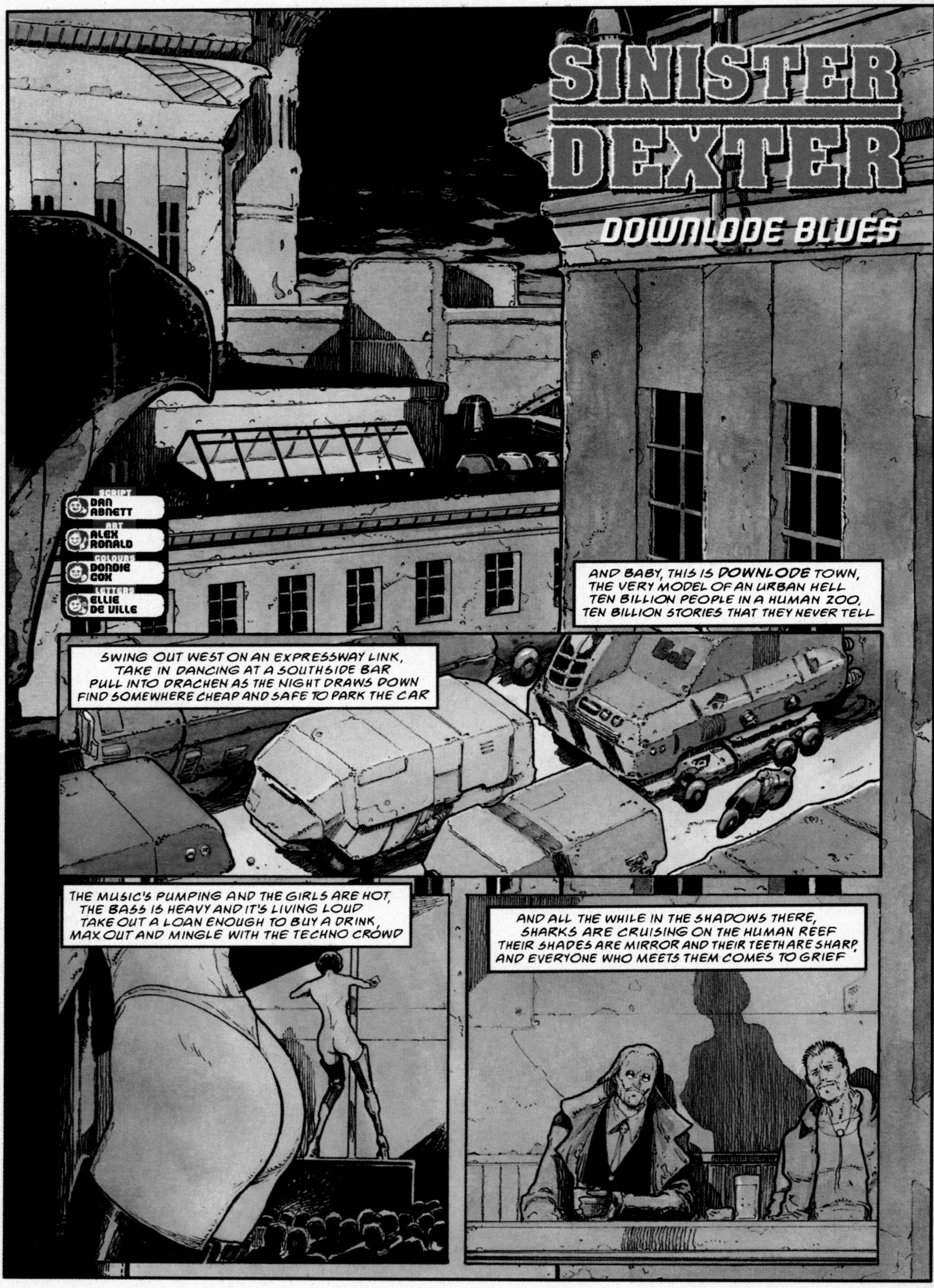
SINISTER DEXTER
DOWNLODE BLUES
SCRIPT DAN ABNETT
ART ALEX RONALD
COLOURS DONDIE COX
LETTERS ELLIE DE VILLE
AND BABY, THIS IS DOWNLODE TOWN, THE VERY MODEL OF AN URBAN HELL TEN BILLION PEOPLE IN A HUMAN ZOO, TEN BILLION STORIES THAT THEY NEVER TELL
SWING OUT WEST ON AN EXPRESSWAY LINK, TAKE IN DANCING AT A SOUTHSIDE BAR PULL INTO DRACHEN AS THE NIGHT DRAWS DOWN FIND SOMEWHERE CHEAP AND SAFE TO PARK THE CAR
THE MUSIC'S PUMPING AND THE GIRLS ARE HOT, THE BASS IS HEAVY AND IT'S LIVING LOUD TAKE OUT A LOAN ENOUGH TO BUY A DRINK, MAX OUT AND MINGLE WITH THE TECHNO CROWD
AND ALL THE WHILE IN THE SHADOWS THERE, SHARKS ARE CRUISING ON THE HUMAN REEF THEIR SHADES ARE MIRROR AND THEIR TEETH ARE SHARP, AND EVERYONE WHO MEETS THEM COMES TO GRIEF

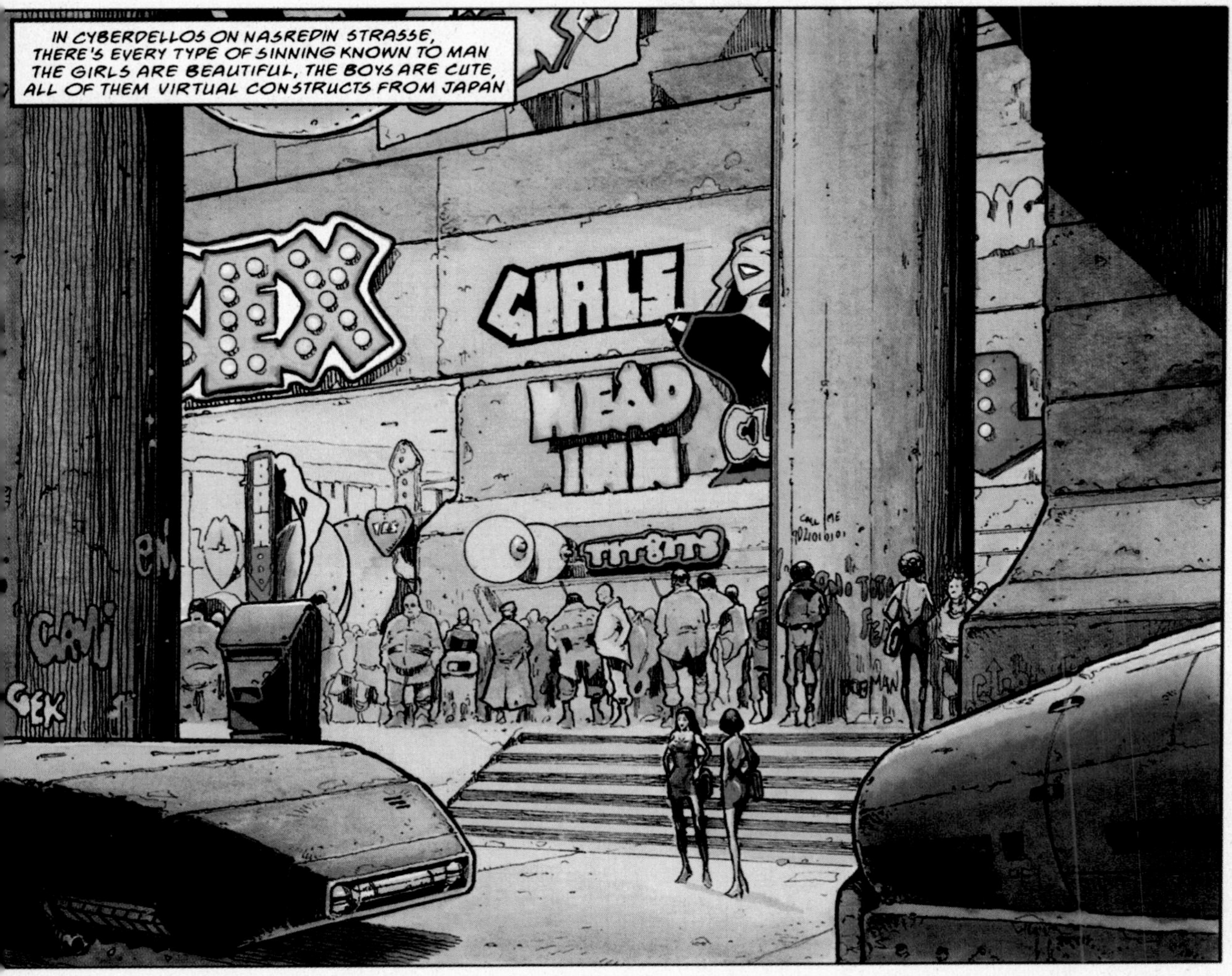
IN CYBERDELLOS ON NASREDIN STRASSE, THERE'S EVERY TYPE OF SINNING KNOWN TO MAN THE GIRLS ARE BEAUTIFUL, THE BOYS ARE CUTE, ALL OF THEM VIRTUAL CONSTRUCTS FROM JAPAN
GIRLS
HEAD INN

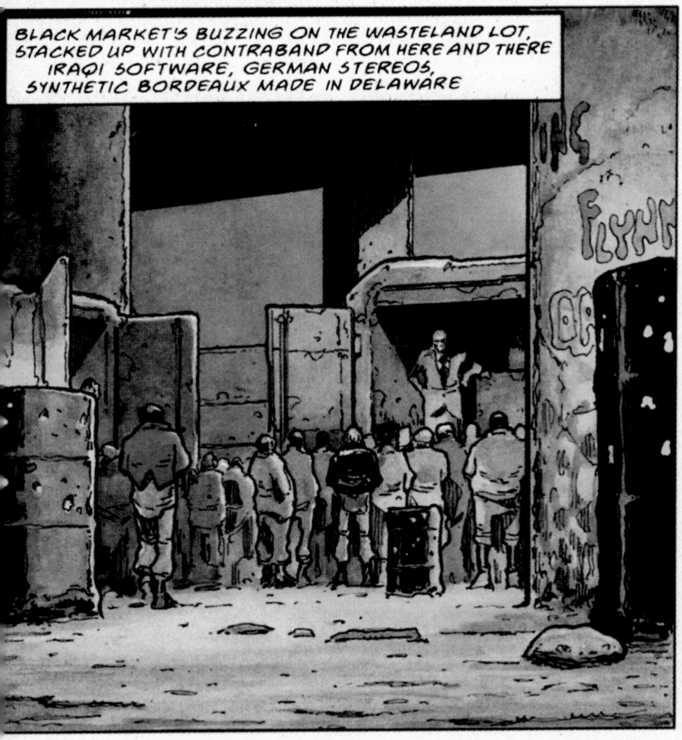
BLACK MARKET'S BUZZING ON THE WASTELAND LOT, STACKED UP WITH CONTRABAND FROM HERE AND THERE IRAQI SOFTWARE, GERMAN STEREOS, SYNTHETIC BORDEAUX MADE IN DELAWARE

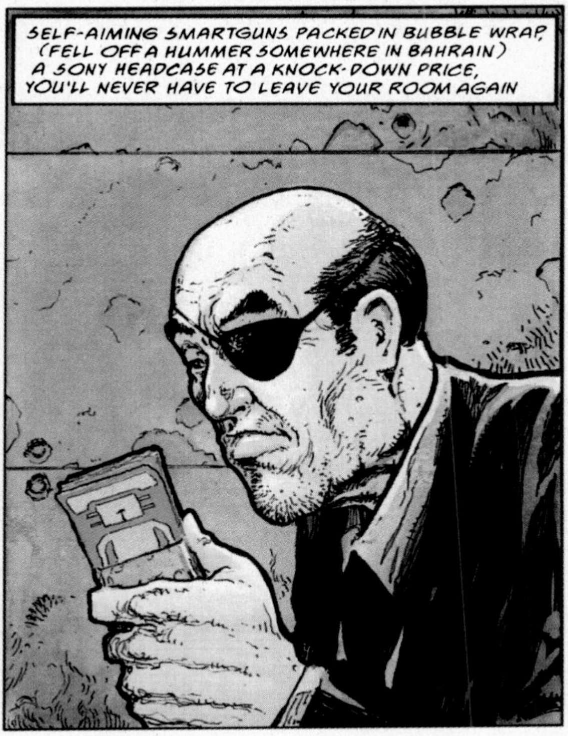
SELF-AIMING SMARTGUNS PACKED IN BUBBLE WRAP, (FELL OFF A HUMMER SOMEWHERE IN BAHRAIN) A SONY HEADCASE AT A KNOCK-DOWN PRICE, YOU'LL NEVER HAVE TO LEAVE YOUR ROOM AGAIN

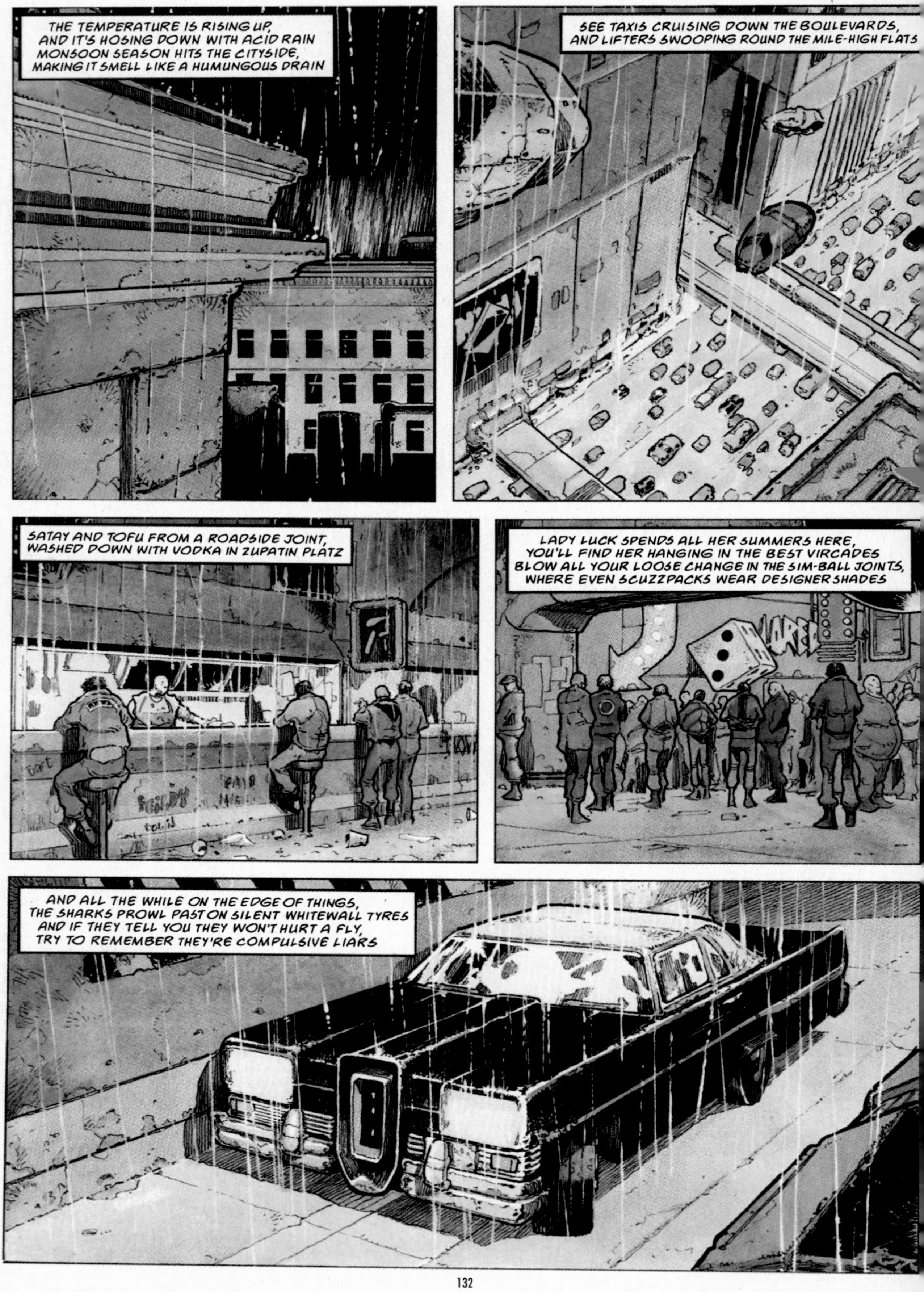
THE TEMPERATURE IS RISING UP, AND IT'S HOSING DOWN WITH ACID RAIN MONSOON SEASON HITS THE CITYSIDE, MAKING IT SMELL LIKE A HUMUNGOUS DRAIN
SEE TAXIS CRUISING DOWN THE BOULEVARDS, AND LIFTERS SWOOPING ROUND THE MILE-HIGH FLATS
SATAY AND TOFU FROM A ROADSIDE JOINT, WASHED DOWN WITH VODKA IN ZUPATIN PLATZ
LADY LUCK SPENDS ALL HER SUMMERS HERE, YOU'LL FIND HER HANGING IN THE BEST VIRCADES BLOW ALL YOUR LOOSE CHANGE IN THE SIM-BALL JOINTS, WHERE EVEN SCUZZPACKS WEAR DESIGNER SHADES
AND ALL THE WHILE ON THE EDGE OF THINGS, THE SHARKS PROWL PAST ON SILENT WHITEWALL TYRES AND IF THEY TELL YOU THEY WON'T HURT A FLY, TRY TO REMEMBER THEY'RE COMPULSIVE LIARS

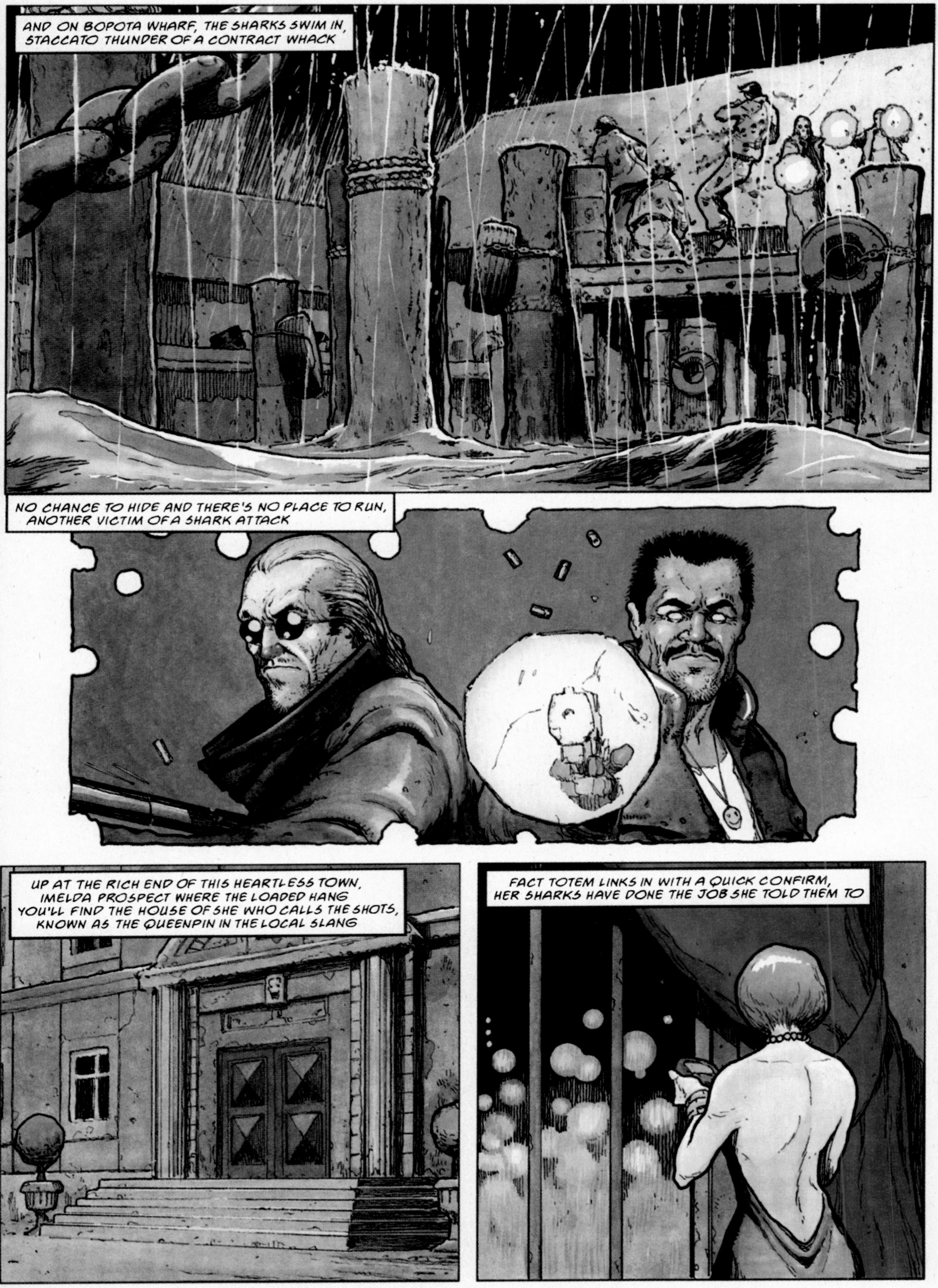
AND ON BOPOTA WHARF, THE SHARKS SWIM IN, STACCATO THUNDER OF A CONTRACT WHACK
NO CHANCE TO HIDE AND THERE'S NO PLACE TO RUN, ANOTHER VICTIM OF A SHARK ATTACK
UP AT THE RICH END OF THIS HEARTLESS TOWN, IMELDA PROSPECT WHERE THE LOADED HANG YOU'LL FIND THE HOUSE OF SHE WHO CALLS THE SHOTS, KNOWN AS THE QUEENPIN IN THE LOCAL SLANG
FACT TOTEM LINKS IN WITH A QUICK CONFIRM, HER SHARKS HAVE DONE THE JOB SHE TOLD THEM TO

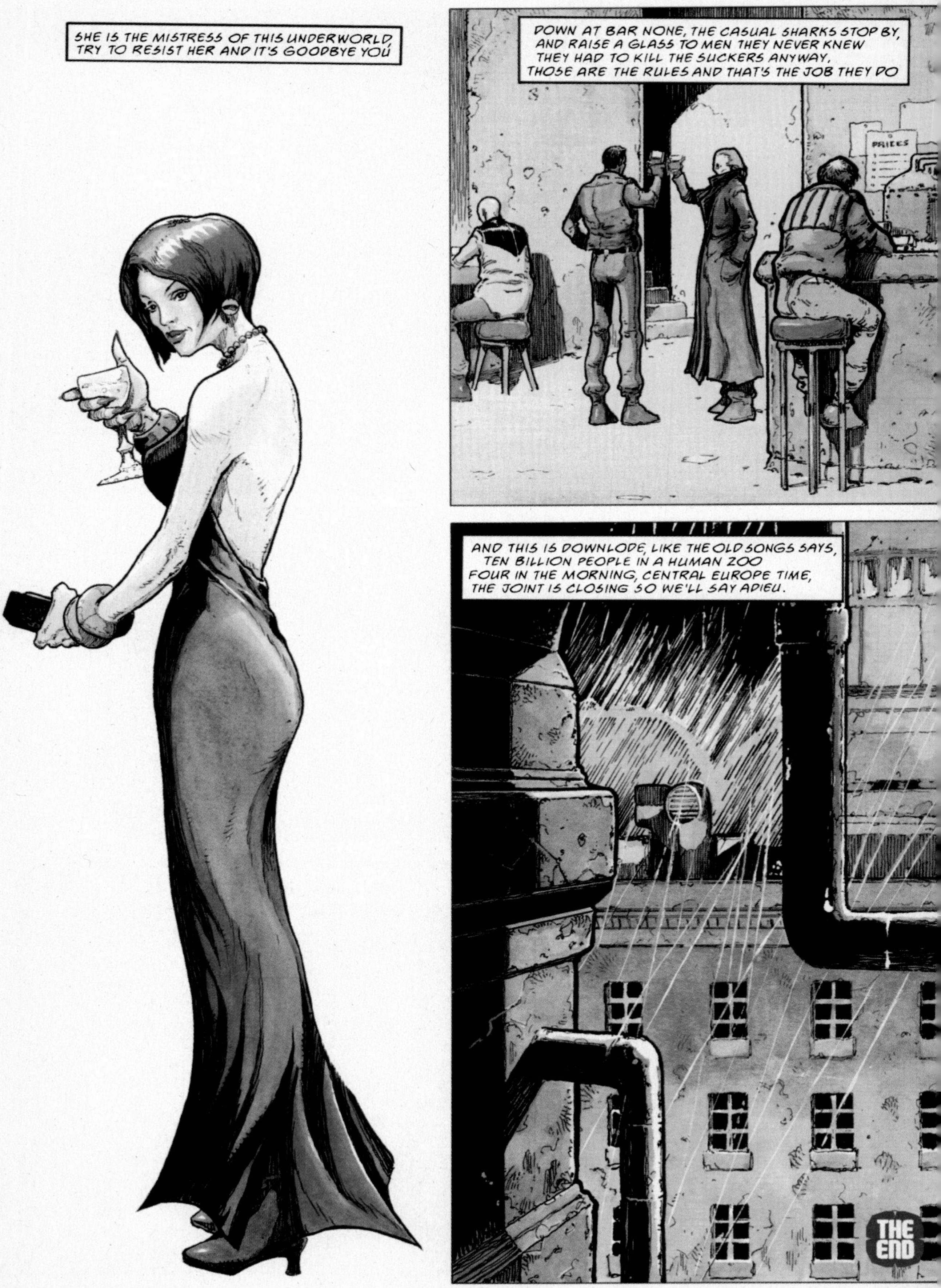
SHE IS THE MISTRESS OF THIS UNDERWORLD
TRY TO RESIST HER AND IT'S GOODBYE YOU
DOWN AT BAR NONE, THE CASUAL SHARKS STOP BY,
AND RAISE A GLASS TO MEN THEY NEVER KNEW
THEY HAD TO KILL THE SUCKERS ANYWAY,
THOSE ARE THE RULES AND THAT'S THE JOB THEY DO
PRICES
AND THIS IS DOWNLODE, LIKE THE OLD SONGS SAYS,
TEN BILLION PEOPLE IN A HUMAN ZOO
FOUR IN THE MORNING, CENTRAL EUROPE TIME,
THE JOINT IS CLOSING SO WE'LL SAY ADIEU.
THE END

TAKING THE MICK

Script: Dan Abnett

Art: Steve Yeowell

Letters: Ellie de Ville

Originally published in *2000 AD* Progs 1079-1082

SINISTERDEXTER

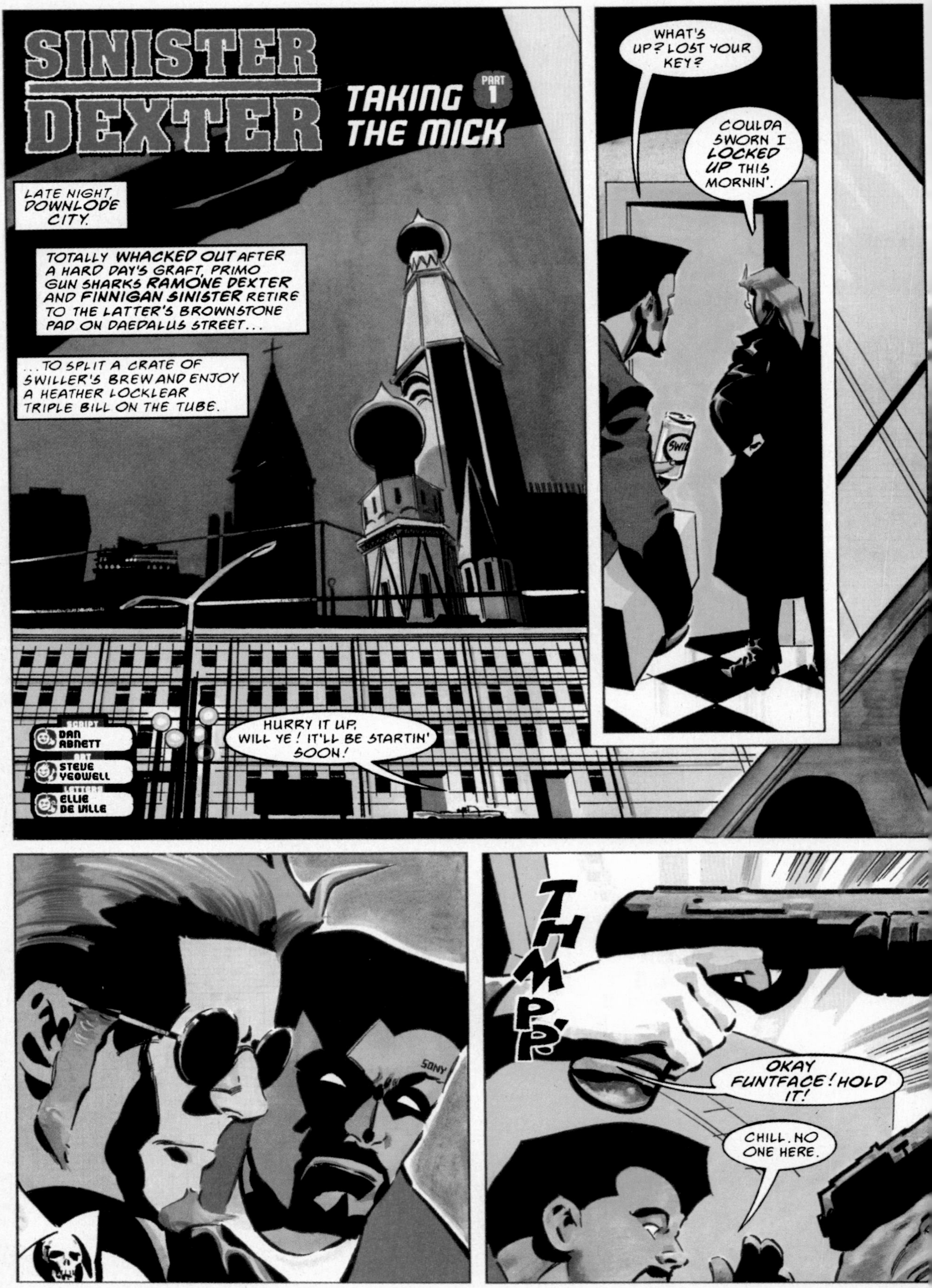
SINISTER DEXTER
TAKING THE MICK
PART 1
LATE NIGHT, DOWNLODE CITY.
TOTALLY WHACKED OUT AFTER A HARD DAY'S GRAFT, PRIMO GUN SHARKS RAMONE DEXTER AND FINNIGAN SINISTER RETIRE TO THE LATTER'S BROWNSTONE PAD ON DAEDALUS STREET...
...TO SPLIT A CRATE OF SWILLER'S BREW AND ENJOY A HEATHER LOCKLEAR TRIPLE BILL ON THE TUBE.
SCRIPT DAN ABNETT
ART STEVE YEOWELL
LETTERS ELLIE DE VILLE
HURRY IT UP, WILL YE! IT'LL BE STARTIN' SOON!
WHAT'S UP? LOST YOUR KEY?
COULDA SWORN I LOCKED UP THIS MORNIN'.
SONY
THMPP!
OKAY FUNTFACE! HOLD IT!
CHILL. NO ONE HERE.

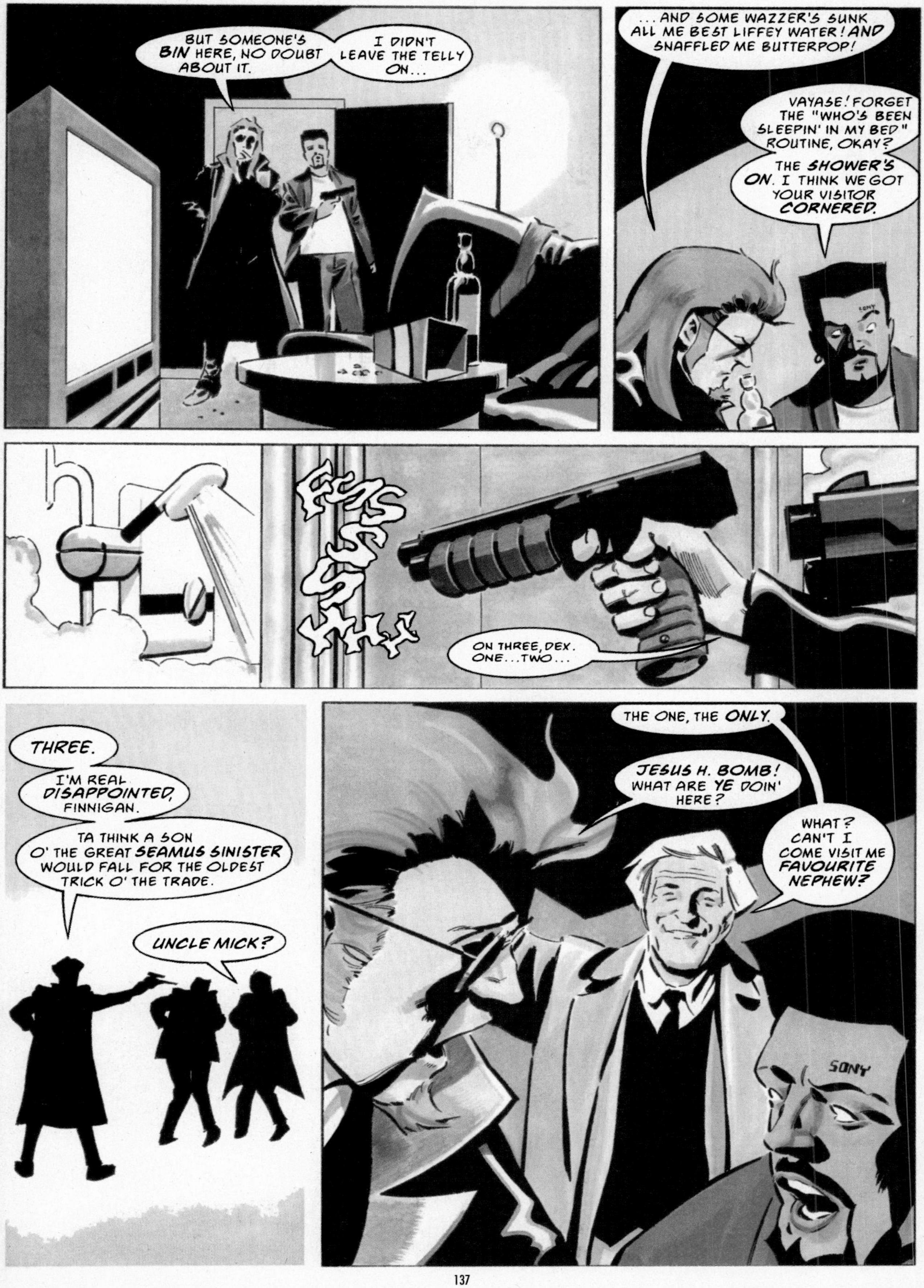
BUT SOMEONE'S BIN HERE, NO DOUBT ABOUT IT.
I DIDN'T LEAVE THE TELLY ON...
...AND SOME WAZZER'S SUNK ALL ME BEST LIFFEY WATER! AND SNAFFLED ME BUTTERPOP!
VAYASE! FORGET THE "WHO'S BEEN SLEEPIN' IN MY BED" ROUTINE, OKAY?
THE SHOWER'S ON. I THINK WE GOT YOUR VISITOR CORNERED.
SONY
ON THREE, DEX. ONE...TWO...
THREE.
I'M REAL DISAPPOINTED, FINNIGAN.
TA THINK A SON O' THE GREAT SEAMUS SINISTER WOULD FALL FOR THE OLDEST TRICK O' THE TRADE.
UNCLE MICK?
THE ONE, THE ONLY.
JESUS H. BOMB! WHAT ARE YE DOIN' HERE?
WHAT? CAN'T I COME VISIT ME FAVOURITE NEPHEW?
SONY

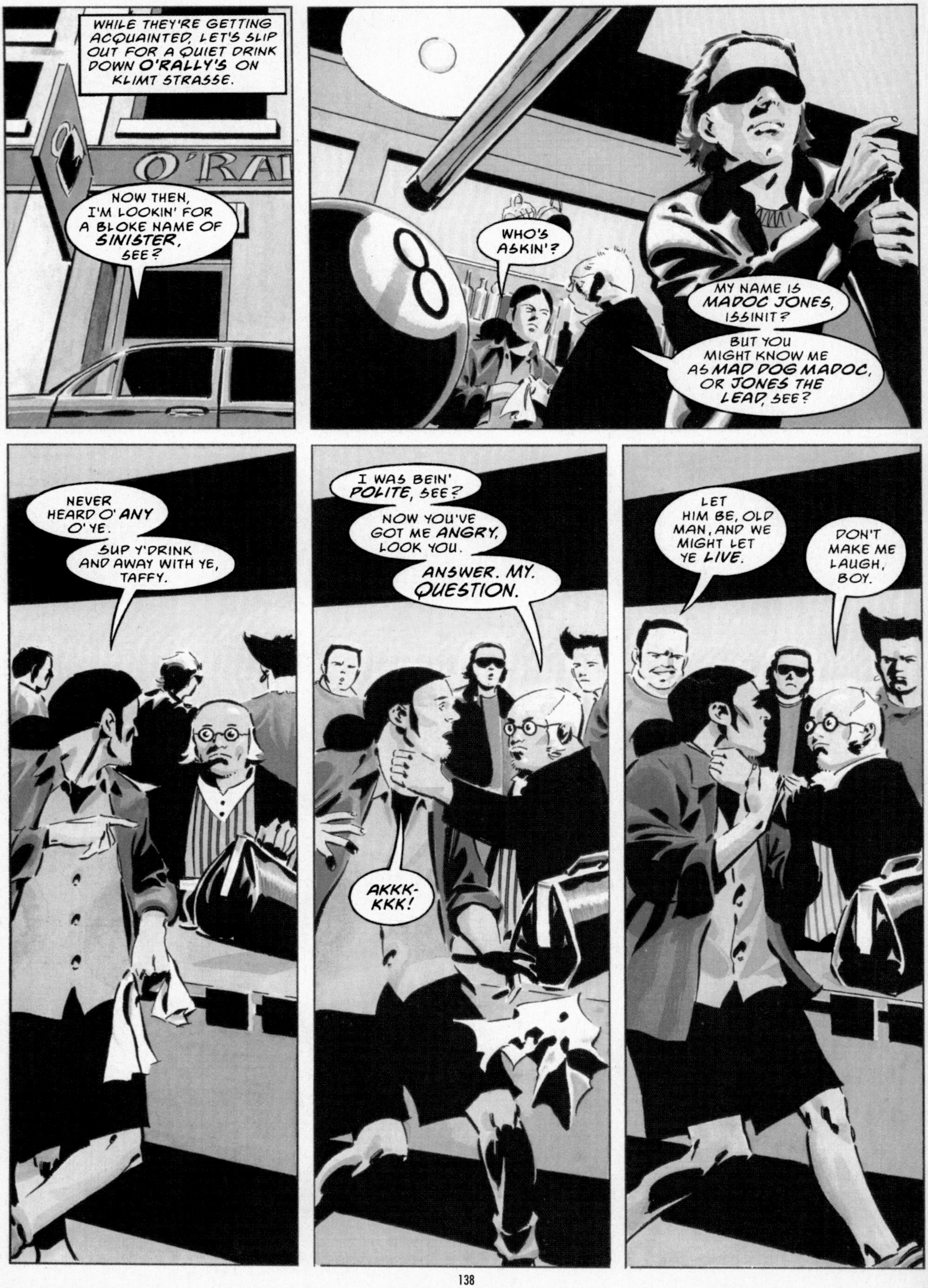
WHILE THEY'RE GETTING ACQUAINTED, LET'S SLIP OUT FOR A QUIET DRINK DOWN O'RALLY'S ON KLIMT STRASSE.
O'RA
NOW THEN, I'M LOOKIN' FOR A BLOKE NAME OF SINISTER, SEE?
WHO'S ASKIN'?
MY NAME IS MADOC JONES, ISSINIT?
BUT YOU MIGHT KNOW ME AS MAD DOG MADOC, OR JONES THE LEAD, SEE?
NEVER HEARD O' ANY O' YE.
SUP Y'DRINK AND AWAY WITH YE, TAFFY.
I WAS BEIN' POLITE, SEE?
NOW YOU'VE GOT ME ANGRY, LOOK YOU.
ANSWER. MY. QUESTION.
AKKK-KKK!
LET HIM BE, OLD MAN, AND WE MIGHT LET YE LIVE.
DON'T MAKE ME LAUGH, BOY.

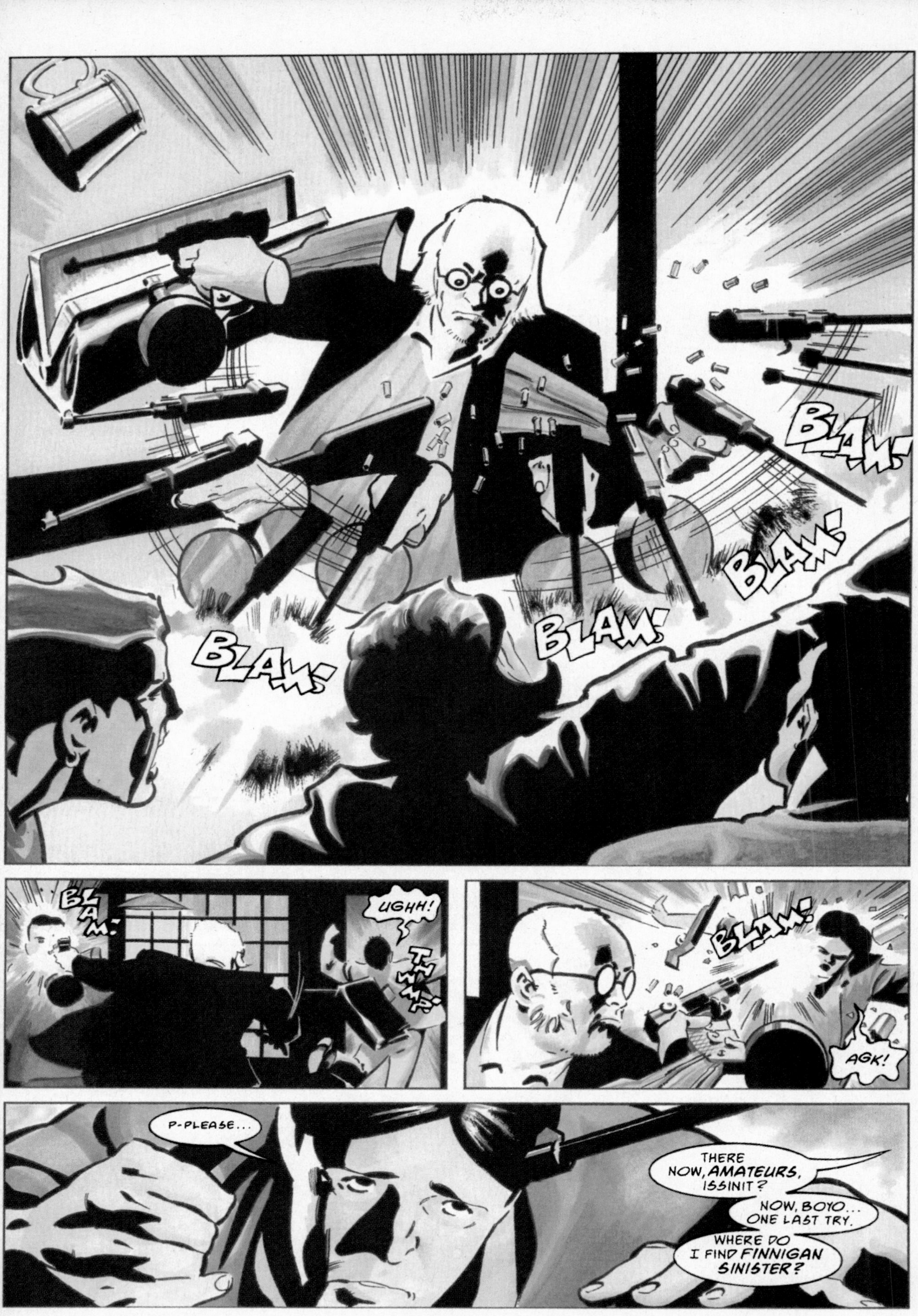
BLAM!
BLAM!
BLAM!
BLAM!
BLAM!
UGHH!
THWMP!
BLAM!
AGK!
P-PLEASE...
THERE NOW, AMATEURS, ISSINIT?
NOW, BOYO... ONE LAST TRY.
WHERE DO I FIND FINNIGAN SINISTER?

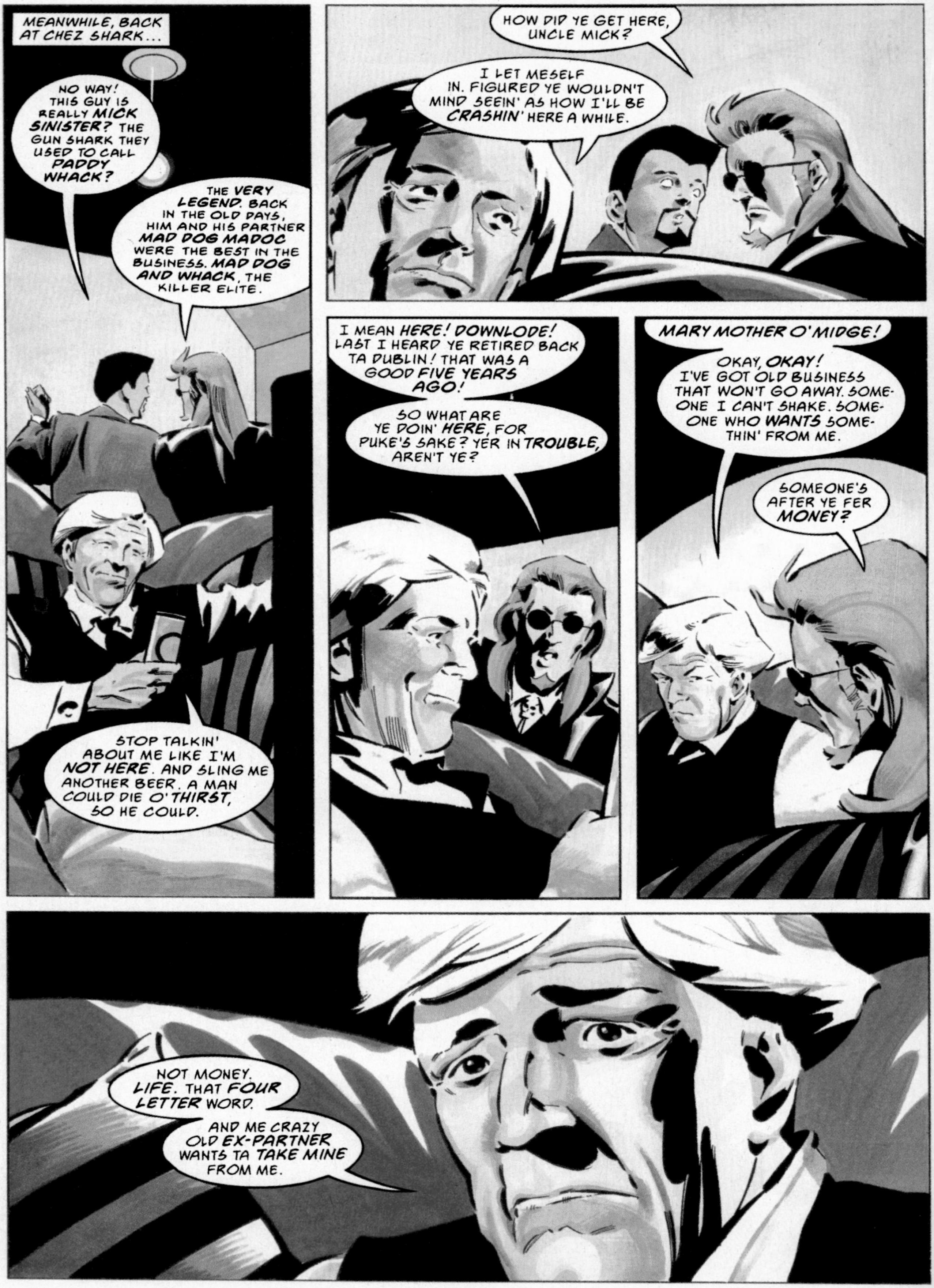

MEANWHILE, BACK AT CHEZ SHARK...
NO WAY! THIS GUY IS REALLY MICK SINISTER? THE GUN SHARK THEY USED TO CALL PADDY WHACK?
THE VERY LEGEND. BACK IN THE OLD DAYS, HIM AND HIS PARTNER MAD DOG MADOC WERE THE BEST IN THE BUSINESS. MAD DOG AND WHACK, THE KILLER ELITE.
STOP TALKIN' ABOUT ME LIKE I'M NOT HERE. AND SLING ME ANOTHER BEER. A MAN COULD DIE O' THIRST, SO HE COULD.
HOW DID YE GET HERE, UNCLE MICK?
I LET MESELF IN. FIGURED YE WOULDN'T MIND SEEIN' AS HOW I'LL BE CRASHIN' HERE A WHILE.
I MEAN HERE! DOWNLODE! LAST I HEARD YE RETIRED BACK TA DUBLIN! THAT WAS A GOOD FIVE YEARS AGO!
SO WHAT ARE YE DOIN' HERE, FOR PUKE'S SAKE? YER IN TROUBLE, AREN'T YE?
MARY MOTHER O' MIDGE!
OKAY, OKAY! I'VE GOT OLD BUSINESS THAT WON'T GO AWAY. SOMEONE I CAN'T SHAKE. SOMEONE WHO WANTS SOMETHIN' FROM ME.
SOMEONE'S AFTER YE FER MONEY?
NOT MONEY. LIFE. THAT FOUR LETTER WORD.
AND ME CRAZY OLD EX-PARTNER WANTS TA TAKE MINE FROM ME.

SINISTER DEXTER

TAKING THE MICK PART 2

SINISTER DELIVERS DEATH SO OFTEN, IT'S RARE FOR IT TO COME VISITING.

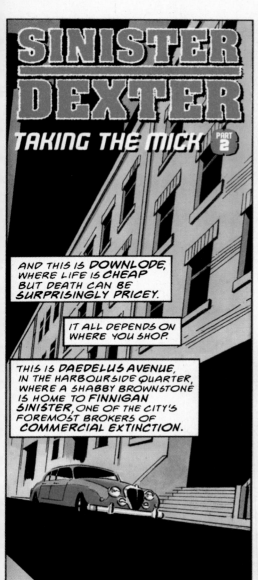

AND THIS IS DOWNLODE, WHERE LIFE IS CHEAP BUT DEATH CAN BE SURPRISINGLY PRICEY.

IT ALL DEPENDS ON WHERE YOU SHOP.

THIS IS DAEDELUS AVENUE, IN THE HARBOURSIDE QUARTER, WHERE A SHABBY BROWNSTONE IS HOME TO FINNIGAN SINISTER, ONE OF THE CITY'S FOREMOST BROKERS OF COMMERCIAL EXTINCTION.

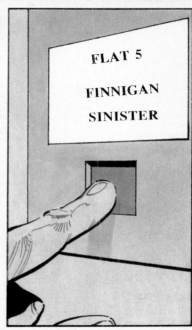

FLAT 5

FINNIGAN

SINISTER

SCRIPT
DAN ABNETT

ART
STEVE YEOWELL

LETTERS
ELLIE DE VILLE

THWMMMH!

DAMN. EMPTY, ISSINIT?

141

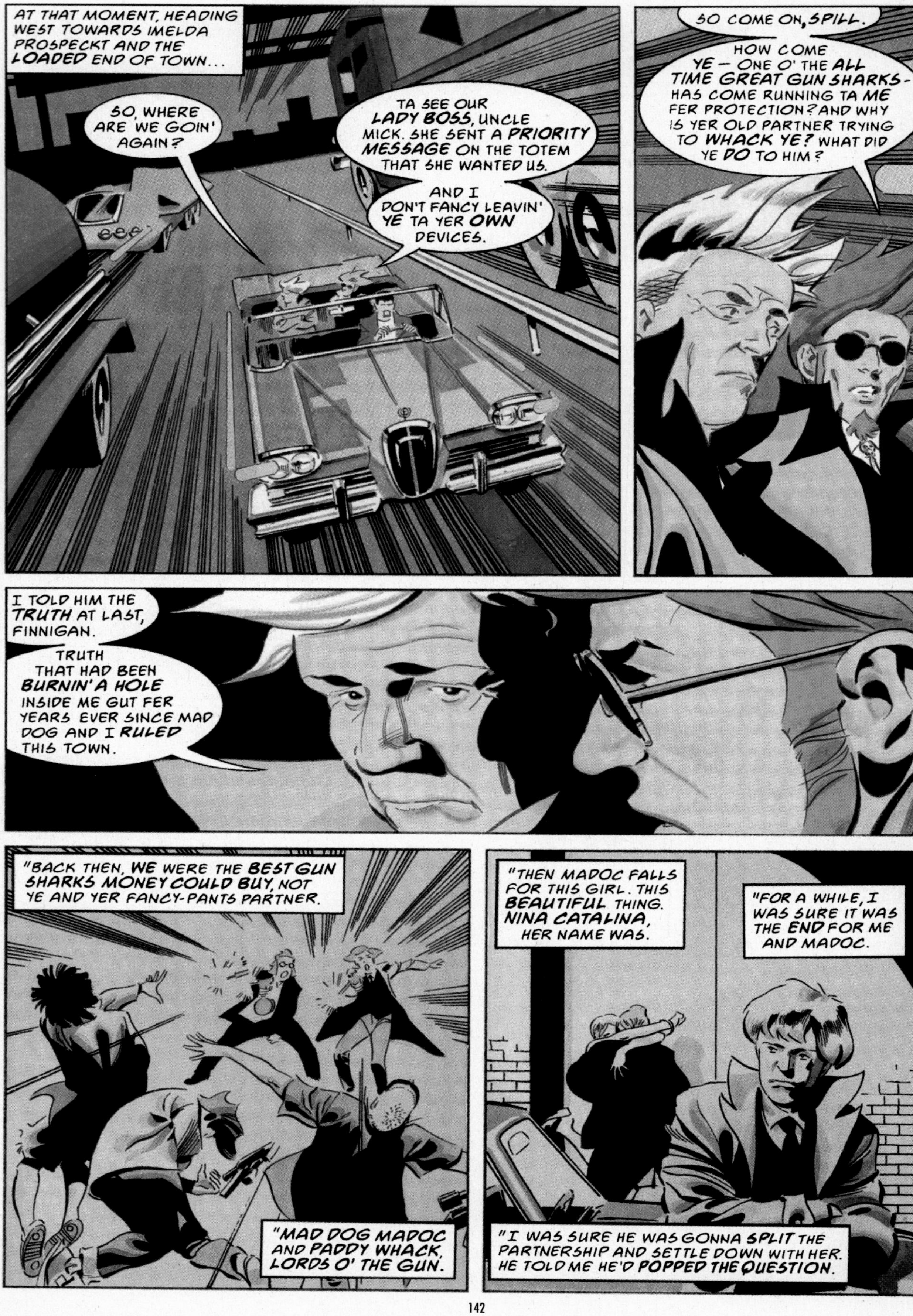
AT THAT MOMENT, HEADING WEST TOWARDS IMELDA PROSPECKT AND THE LOADED END OF TOWN...
SO, WHERE ARE 'WE GOIN' AGAIN?
TA SEE OUR LADY BOSS, UNCLE MICK. SHE SENT A PRIORITY MESSAGE ON THE TOTEM THAT SHE WANTED US.
AND I DON'T FANCY LEAVIN' YE TA YER OWN DEVICES.
SO COME ON, SPILL.
HOW COME YE — ONE O' THE ALL TIME GREAT GUN SHARKS - HAS COME RUNNING TA ME FER PROTECTION? AND WHY IS YER OLD PARTNER TRYING TO WHACK YE? WHAT DID YE DO TO HIM?
I TOLD HIM THE TRUTH AT LAST, FINNIGAN.
TRUTH THAT HAD BEEN BURNIN' A HOLE INSIDE ME GUT FER YEARS EVER SINCE MAD DOG AND I RULED THIS TOWN.
"BACK THEN, WE WERE THE BEST GUN SHARKS MONEY COULD BUY, NOT YE AND YER FANCY-PANTS PARTNER.
"MAD DOG MADOC AND PADDY WHACK, LORDS O' THE GUN.
"THEN MADOC FALLS FOR THIS GIRL. THIS BEAUTIFUL THING. NINA CATALINA, HER NAME WAS.
"FOR A WHILE, I WAS SURE IT WAS THE END FOR ME AND MADOC.
"I WAS SURE HE WAS GONNA SPLIT THE PARTNERSHIP AND SETTLE DOWN WITH HER. HE TOLD ME HE'D POPPED THE QUESTION.

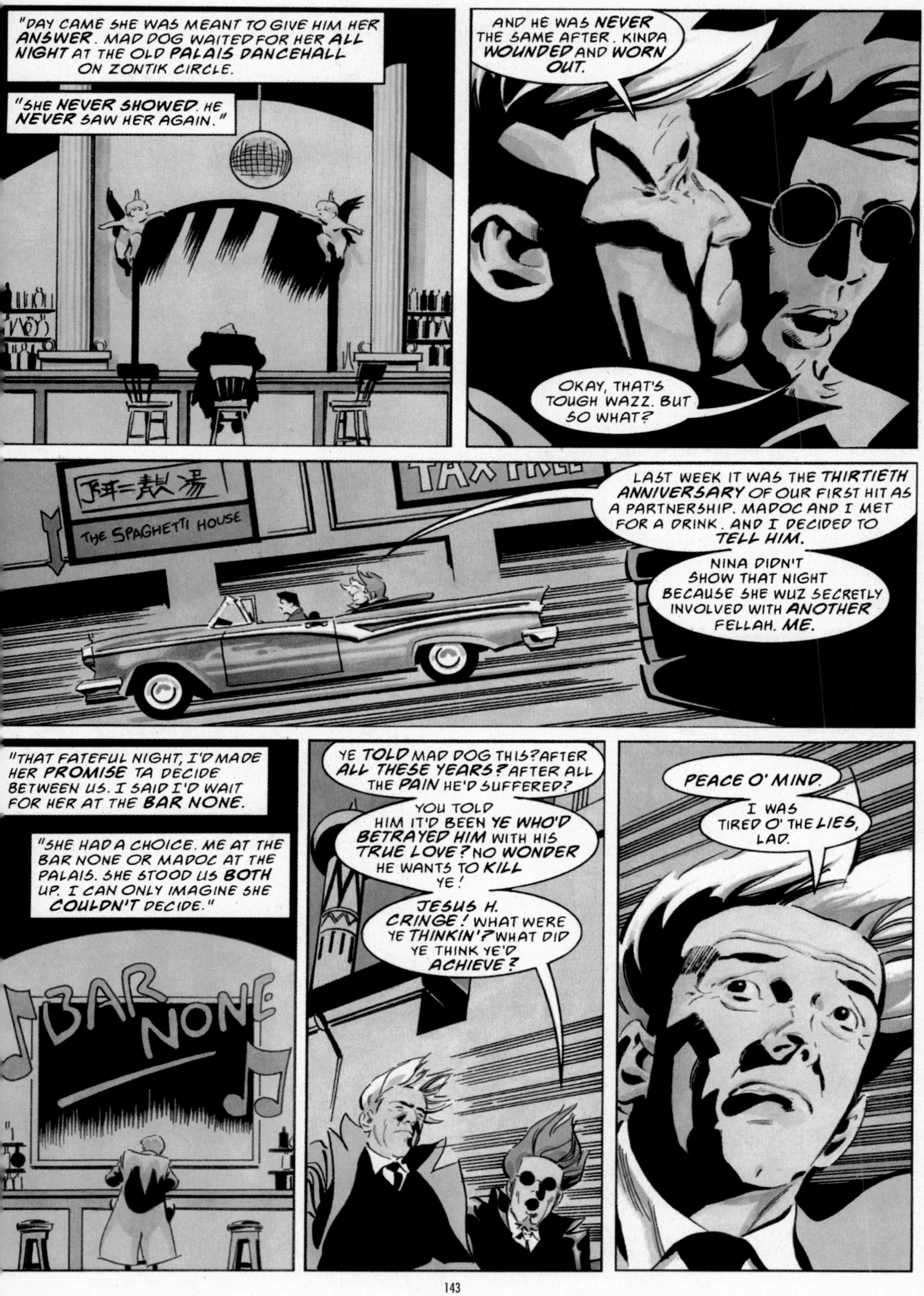
"DAY CAME SHE WAS MEANT TO GIVE HIM HER ANSWER. MAD DOG WAITED FOR HER ALL NIGHT AT THE OLD PALAIS DANCEHALL ON ZONTIK CIRCLE.
"SHE NEVER SHOWED. HE NEVER SAW HER AGAIN."
AND HE WAS NEVER THE SAME AFTER. KINDA WOUNDED AND WORN OUT.
OKAY, THAT'S TOUGH WAZZ. BUT SO WHAT?
TAX FREE
THE SPAGHETTI HOUSE
LAST WEEK IT WAS THE THIRTIETH ANNIVERSARY OF OUR FIRST HIT AS A PARTNERSHIP. MADOC AND I MET FOR A DRINK. AND I DECIDED TO TELL HIM.
NINA DIDN'T SHOW THAT NIGHT BECAUSE SHE WUZ SECRETLY INVOLVED WITH ANOTHER FELLAH. ME.
"THAT FATEFUL NIGHT, I'D MADE HER PROMISE TA DECIDE BETWEEN US. I SAID I'D WAIT FOR HER AT THE BAR NONE.
"SHE HAD A CHOICE. ME AT THE BAR NONE OR MADOC AT THE PALAIS. SHE STOOD US BOTH UP. I CAN ONLY IMAGINE SHE COULDN'T DECIDE."
BAR NONE
YE TOLD MAD DOG THIS? AFTER ALL THESE YEARS? AFTER ALL THE PAIN HE'D SUFFERED?
YOU TOLD HIM IT'D BEEN YE WHO'D BETRAYED HIM WITH HIS TRUE LOVE? NO WONDER HE WANTS TO KILL YE!
JESUS H. CRINGE! WHAT WERE YE THINKIN'? WHAT DID YE THINK YE'D ACHIEVE?
PEACE O' MIND.
I WAS TIRED O' THE LIES, LAD.

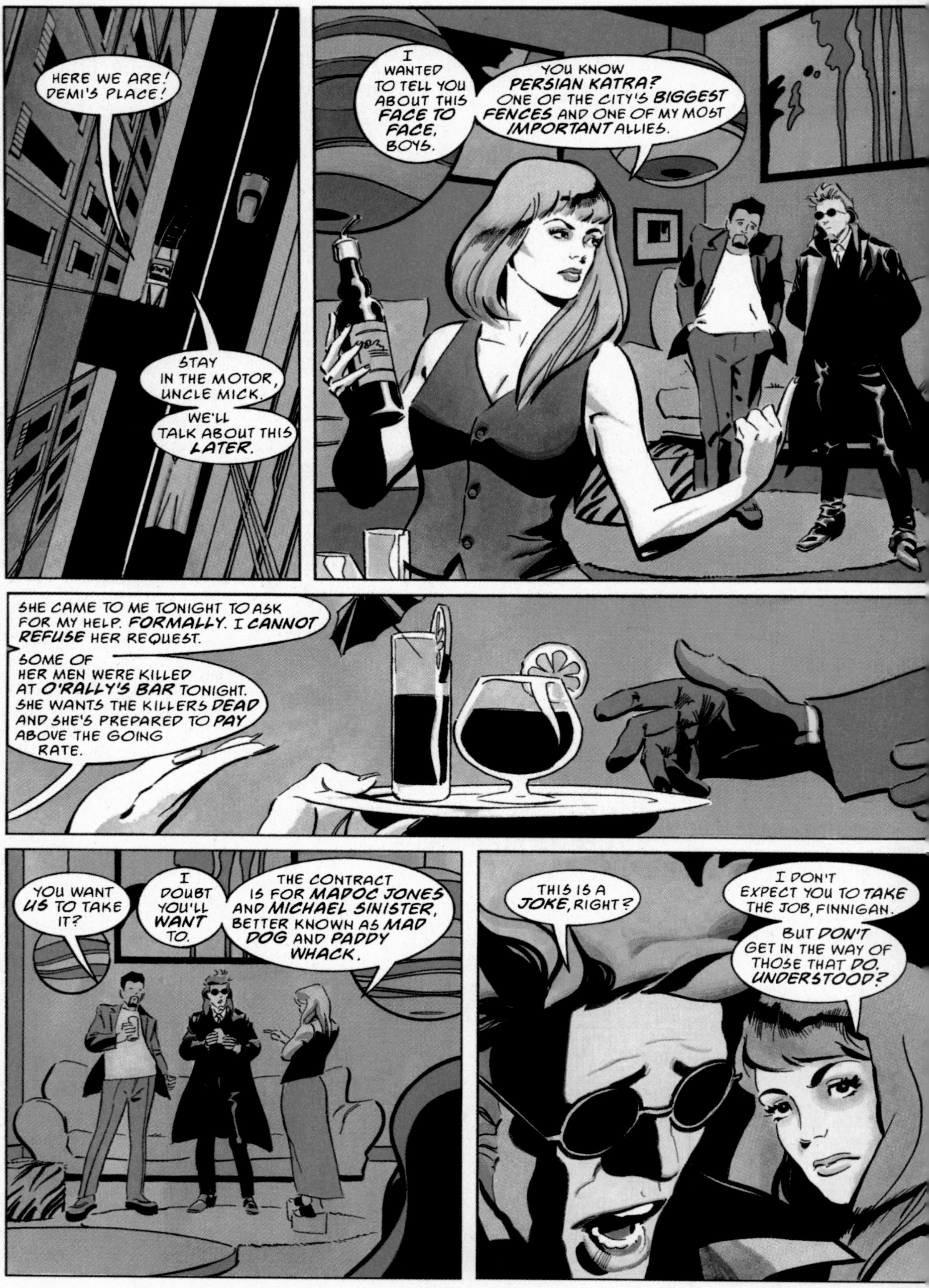
HERE WE ARE! DEMI'S PLACE!
STAY IN THE MOTOR, UNCLE MICK.
WE'LL TALK ABOUT THIS LATER.
I WANTED TO TELL YOU ABOUT THIS FACE TO FACE, BOYS.
YOU KNOW PERSIAN KATRA? ONE OF THE CITY'S BIGGEST FENCES AND ONE OF MY MOST IMPORTANT ALLIES.
SHE CAME TO ME TONIGHT TO ASK FOR MY HELP. FORMALLY. I CANNOT REFUSE HER REQUEST.
SOME OF HER MEN WERE KILLED AT O'RALLY'S BAR TONIGHT. SHE WANTS THE KILLERS DEAD AND SHE'S PREPARED TO PAY ABOVE THE GOING RATE.
YOU WANT US TO TAKE IT?
I DOUBT YOU'LL WANT TO.
THE CONTRACT IS FOR MADOC JONES AND MICHAEL SINISTER, BETTER KNOWN AS MAD DOG AND PADDY WHACK.
THIS IS A JOKE, RIGHT?
I DON'T EXPECT YOU TO TAKE THE JOB, FINNIGAN.
BUT DON'T GET IN THE WAY OF THOSE THAT DO. UNDERSTOOD?

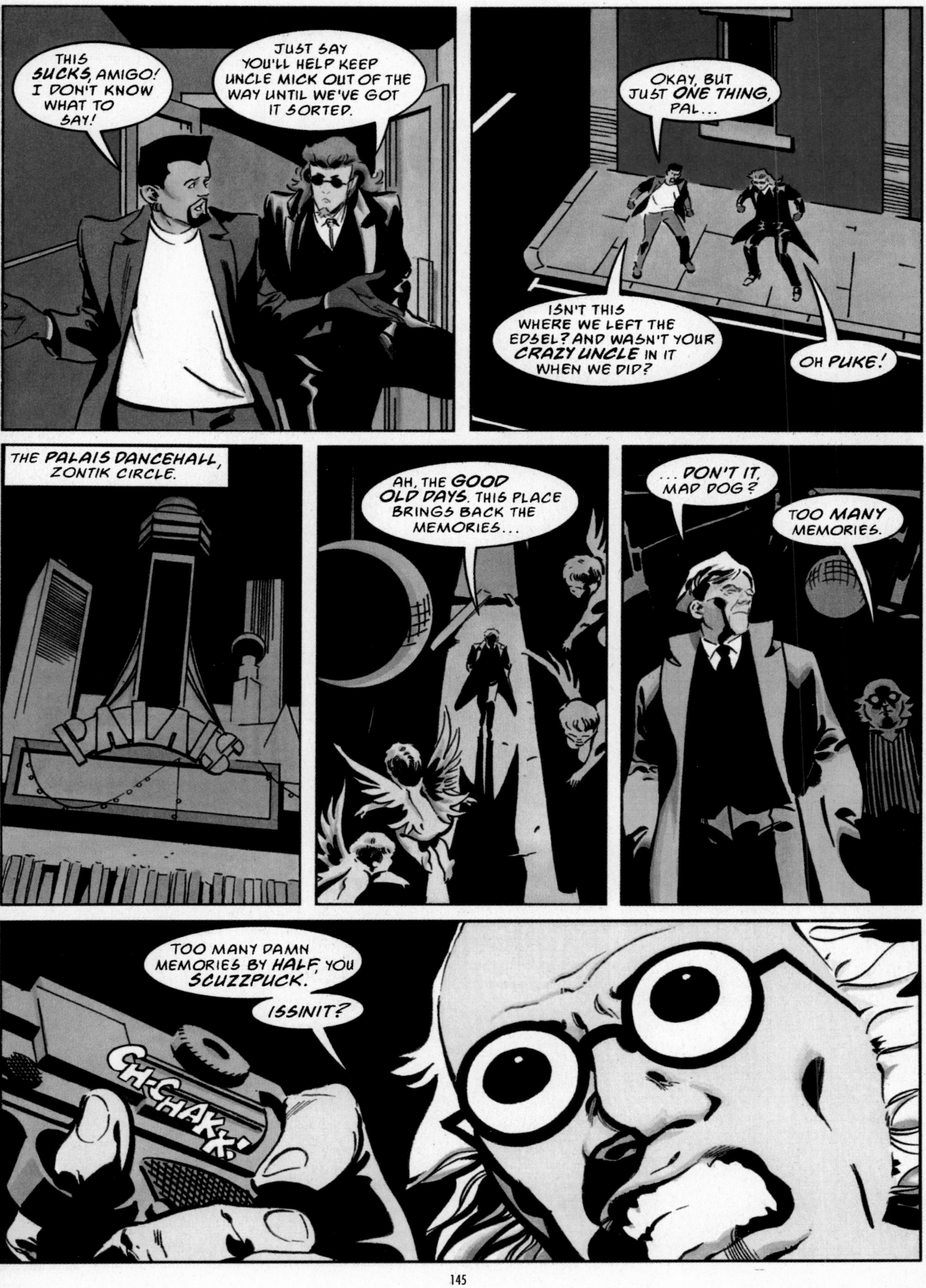
THIS SUCKS, AMIGO! I DON'T KNOW WHAT TO SAY!
JUST SAY YOU'LL HELP KEEP UNCLE MICK OUT OF THE WAY UNTIL WE'VE GOT IT SORTED.
OKAY, BUT JUST ONE THING, PAL...
ISN'T THIS WHERE WE LEFT THE EDSEL? AND WASN'T YOUR CRAZY UNCLE IN IT WHEN WE DID?
OH PUKE!
THE PALAIS DANCEHALL, ZONTIK CIRCLE.
PALAIS
AH, THE GOOD OLD DAYS. THIS PLACE BRINGS BACK THE MEMORIES...
... DON'T IT, MAD DOG?
TOO MANY MEMORIES.
TOO MANY DAMN MEMORIES BY HALF, YOU SCUZZPUCK.
ISSINIT?
CH-CHAKK!

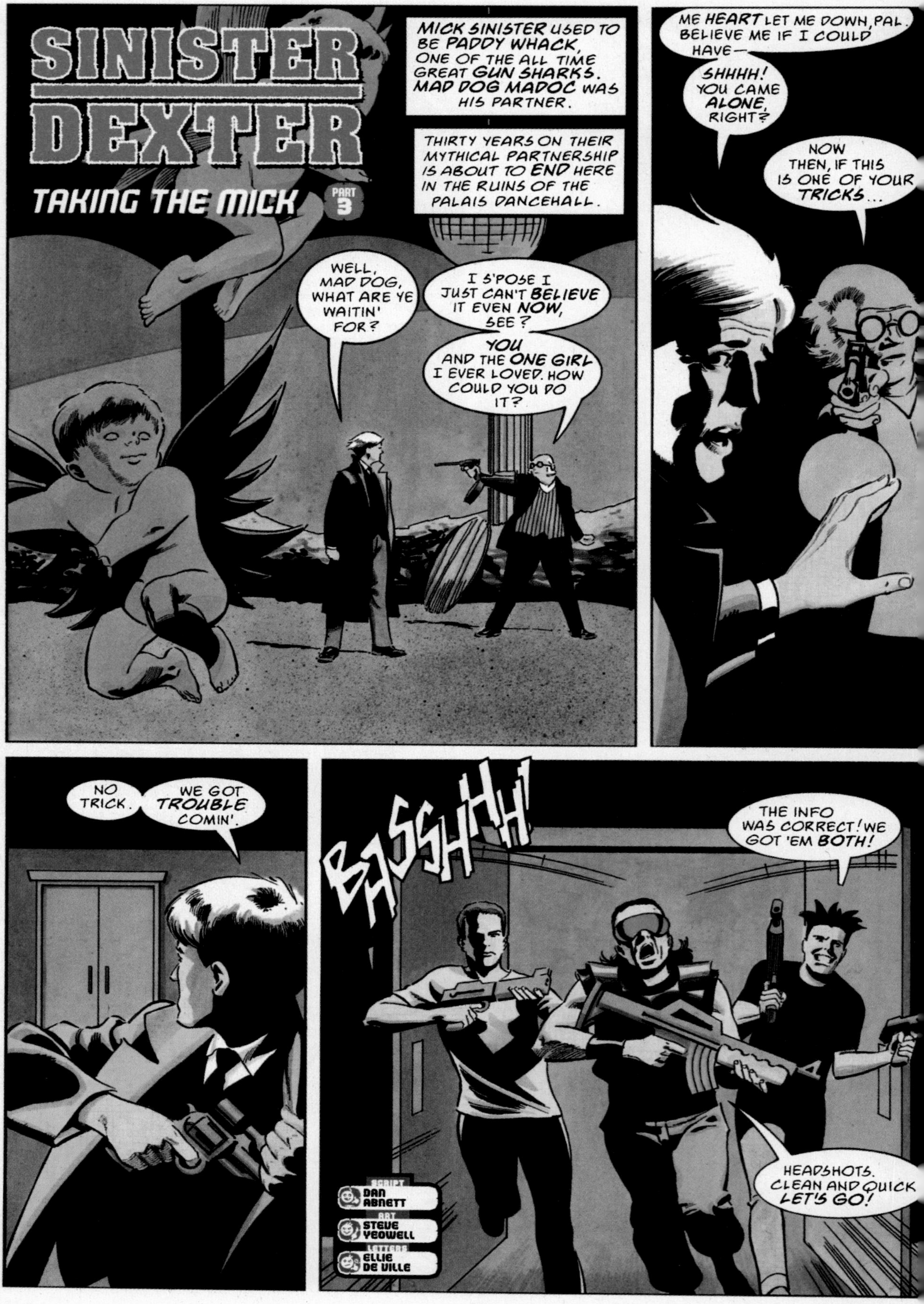
SINISTER DEXTER
TAKING THE MICK PART 3
MICK SINISTER USED TO BE PADDY WHACK, ONE OF THE ALL TIME GREAT GUN SHARKS. MAD DOG MADOC WAS HIS PARTNER.
THIRTY YEARS ON THEIR MYTHICAL PARTNERSHIP IS ABOUT TO END HERE IN THE RUINS OF THE PALAIS DANCEHALL.
WELL, MAD DOG, WHAT ARE YE WAITIN' FOR?
I S'POSE I JUST CAN'T BELIEVE IT EVEN NOW, SEE?
YOU AND THE ONE GIRL I EVER LOVED. HOW COULD YOU DO IT?
ME HEART LET ME DOWN, PAL. BELIEVE ME IF I COULD HAVE—
SHHHH! YOU CAME ALONE, RIGHT?
NOW THEN, IF THIS IS ONE OF YOUR TRICKS...
NO TRICK.
WE GOT TROUBLE COMIN'.
BASSHHH!
THE INFO WAS CORRECT! WE GOT 'EM BOTH!
HEADSHOTS. CLEAN AND QUICK LET'S GO!
SCRIPT DAN ABNETT
ART STEVE YEOWELL
LETTERS ELLIE DE VILLE

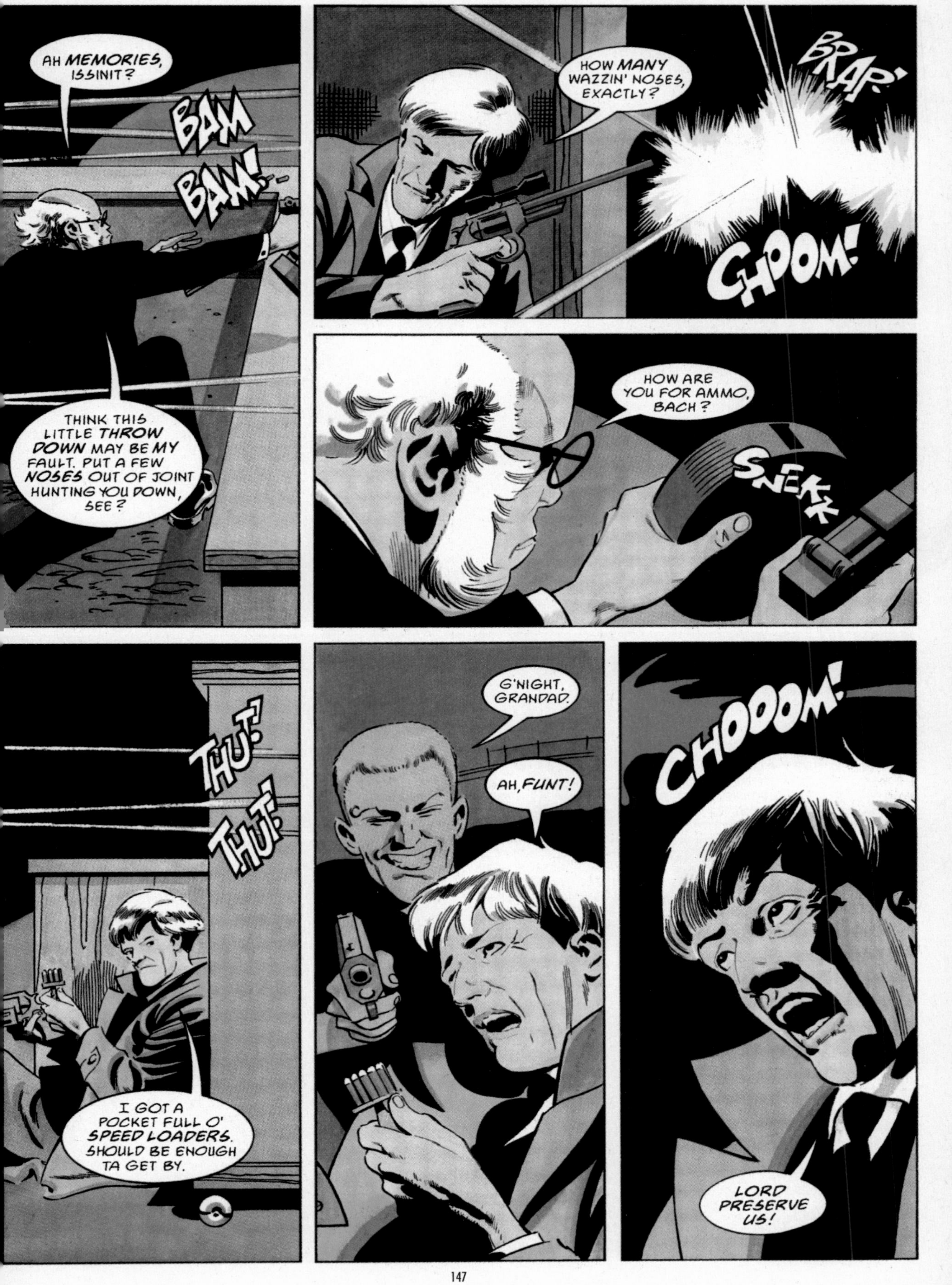

AH MEMORIES, ISSINIT?
BAM
BAM!
THINK THIS LITTLE THROW DOWN MAY BE MY FAULT. PUT A FEW NOSES OUT OF JOINT HUNTING YOU DOWN, SEE?
HOW MANY WAZZIN' NOSES, EXACTLY?
BRAP!
CHOOM!
HOW ARE YOU FOR AMMO, BACH?
SNEKK
THUT!
THUT!
I GOT A POCKET FULL O' SPEED LOADERS. SHOULD BE ENOUGH TA GET BY.
G'NIGHT, GRANDAD.
AH, FUNT!
CHOOOM!
LORD PRESERVE US!

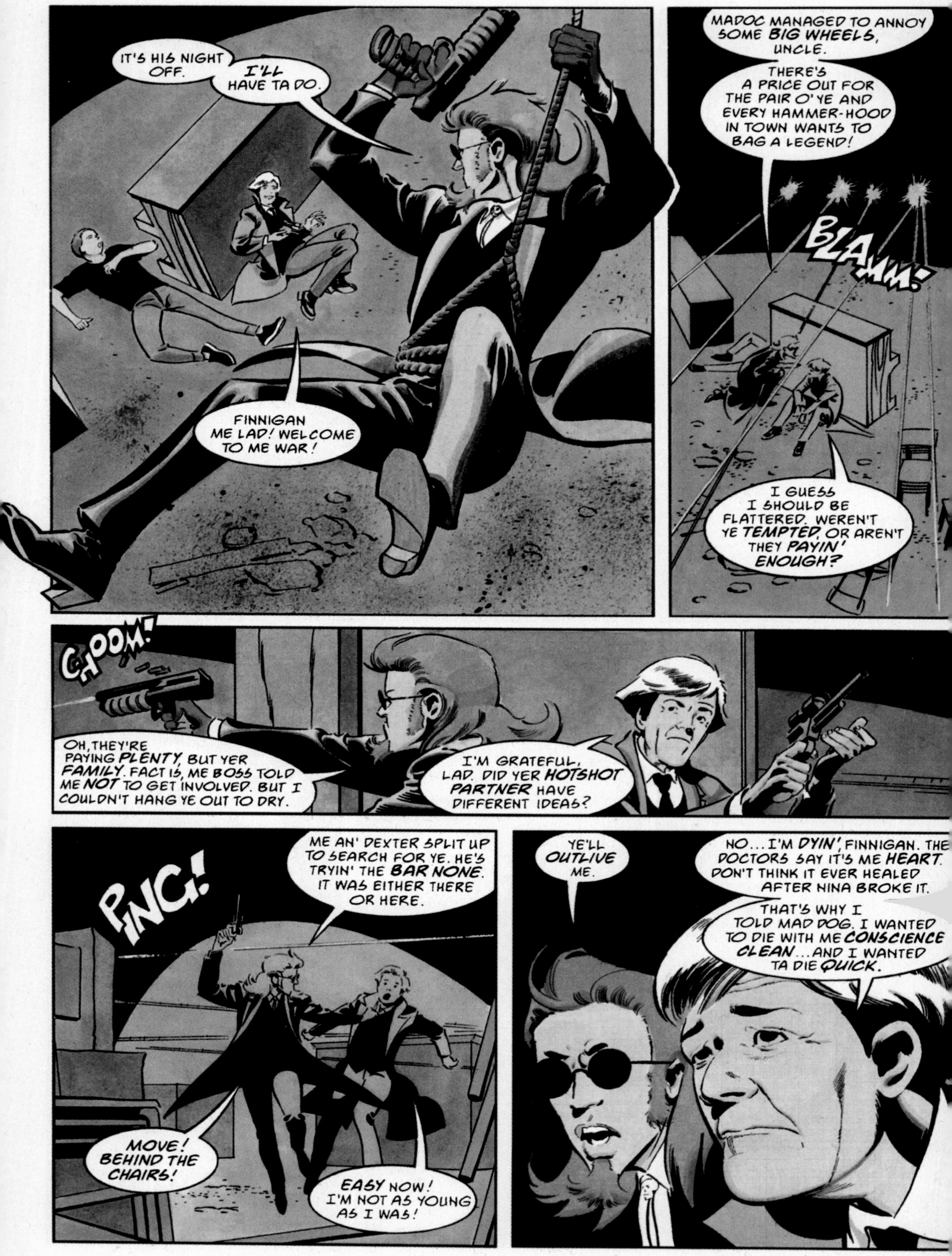

IT'S HIS NIGHT OFF.
I'LL HAVE TA DO.
FINNIGAN ME LAD! WELCOME TO ME WAR!
MADOC MANAGED TO ANNOY SOME BIG WHEELS, UNCLE.
THERE'S A PRICE OUT FOR THE PAIR O' YE AND EVERY HAMMER-HOOD IN TOWN WANTS TO BAG A LEGEND!
BLAMM!
I GUESS I SHOULD BE FLATTERED. WEREN'T YE TEMPTED, OR AREN'T THEY PAYIN' ENOUGH?
CHOOM!
OH, THEY'RE PAYING PLENTY, BUT YER FAMILY. FACT IS, ME BOSS TOLD ME NOT TO GET INVOLVED. BUT I COULDN'T HANG YE OUT TO DRY.
I'M GRATEFUL, LAD. DID YER HOTSHOT PARTNER HAVE DIFFERENT IDEAS?
PING!
ME AN' DEXTER SPLIT UP TO SEARCH FOR YE. HE'S TRYIN' THE BAR NONE. IT WAS EITHER THERE OR HERE.
MOVE! BEHIND THE CHAIRS!
EASY NOW! I'M NOT AS YOUNG AS I WAS!
YE'LL OUTLIVE ME.
NO... I'M DYIN', FINNIGAN. THE DOCTORS SAY IT'S ME HEART. DON'T THINK IT EVER HEALED AFTER NINA BROKE IT.
THAT'S WHY I TOLD MAD DOG. I WANTED TO DIE WITH ME CONSCIENCE CLEAN... AND I WANTED TA DIE QUICK.

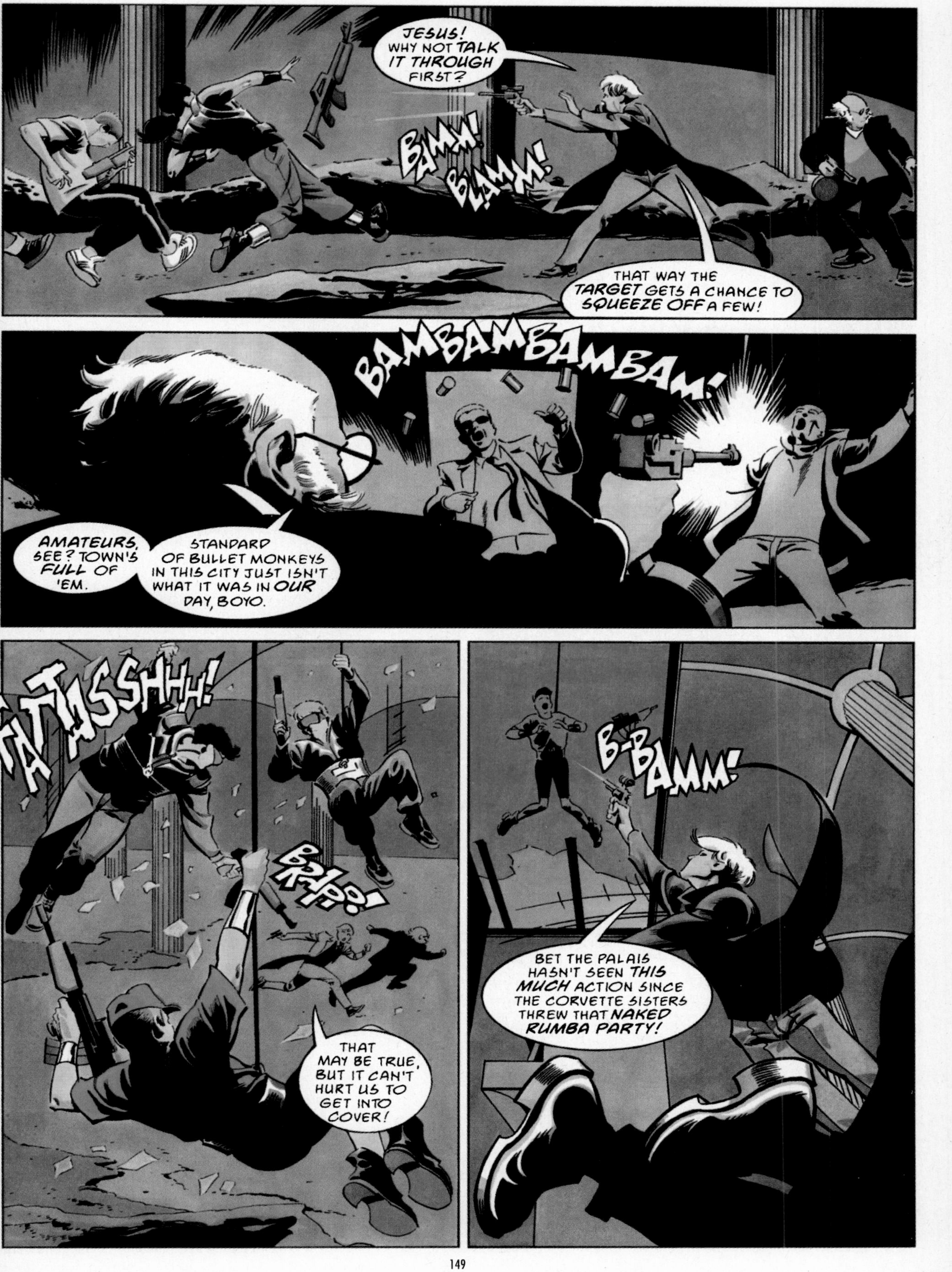
JESUS! WHY NOT TALK IT THROUGH FIRST?
BAMM! BAMM!
THAT WAY THE TARGET GETS A CHANCE TO SQUEEZE OFF A FEW!
BAMBAMBAMBAM!
AMATEURS, SEE? TOWN'S FULL OF 'EM.
STANDARD OF BULLET MONKEYS IN THIS CITY JUST ISN'T WHAT IT WAS IN OUR DAY, BOYO.
TATTASSHHH!
BRAPP!
THAT MAY BE TRUE, BUT IT CAN'T HURT US TO GET INTO COVER!
B-BAMM!
BET THE PALAIS HASN'T SEEN THIS MUCH ACTION SINCE THE CORVETTE SISTERS THREW THAT NAKED RUMBA PARTY!

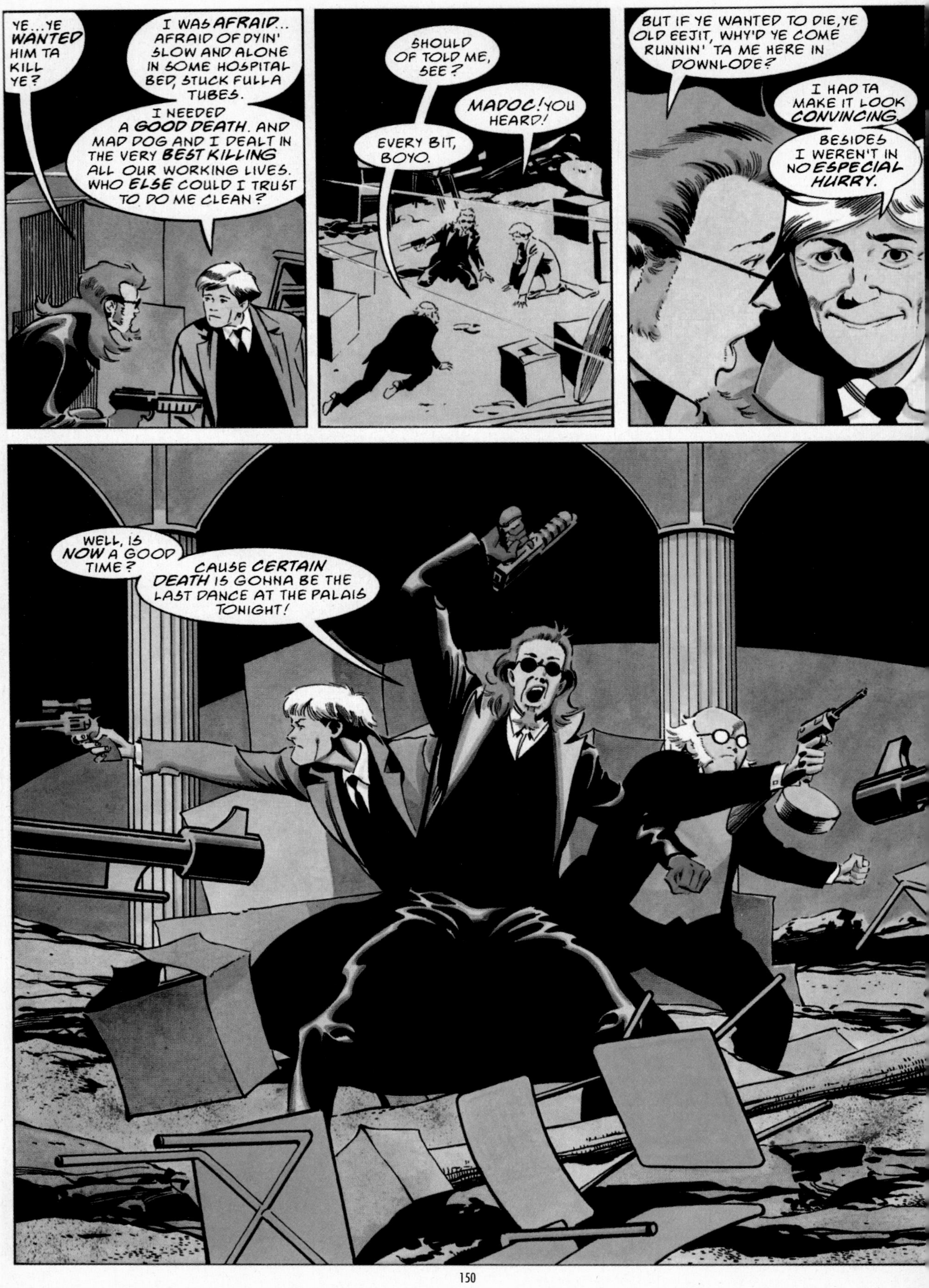
YE...YE WANTED HIM TA KILL YE?
I WAS AFRAID... AFRAID OF DYIN' SLOW AND ALONE IN SOME HOSPITAL BED, STUCK FULLA TUBES.
I NEEDED A GOOD DEATH. AND MAD DOG AND I DEALT IN THE VERY BEST KILLING ALL OUR WORKING LIVES. WHO ELSE COULD I TRUST TO DO ME CLEAN?
SHOULD OF TOLD ME, SEE?
MADOC! YOU HEARD!
EVERY BIT, BOYO.
BUT IF YE WANTED TO DIE, YE OLD EEJIT, WHY'D YE COME RUNNIN' TA ME HERE IN DOWNLODE?
I HAD TA MAKE IT LOOK CONVINCING.
BESIDES I WEREN'T IN NO ESPECIAL HURRY.
WELL, IS NOW A GOOD TIME?
CAUSE CERTAIN DEATH IS GONNA BE THE LAST DANCE AT THE PALAIS TONIGHT!

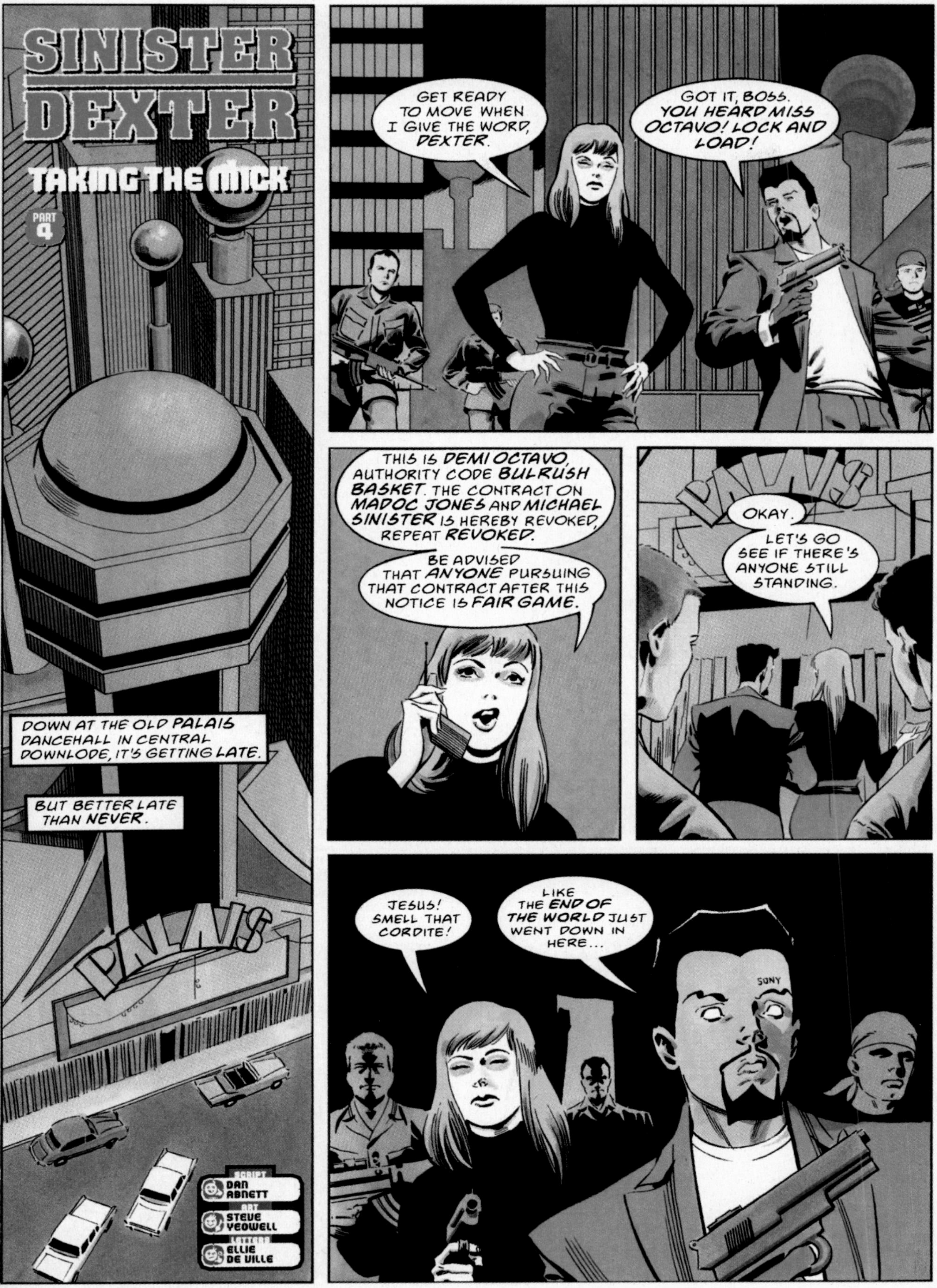
SINISTER DEXTER
TAKING THE MICK
PART 4
DOWN AT THE OLD PALAIS DANCEHALL IN CENTRAL DOWNLODE, IT'S GETTING LATE.
BUT BETTER LATE THAN NEVER.
PALAIS
SCRIPT DAN ABNETT
ART STEVE YEOWELL
LETTERS ELLIE DE VILLE
GET READY TO MOVE WHEN I GIVE THE WORD, DEXTER.
GOT IT, BOSS. YOU HEARD MISS OCTAVO! LOCK AND LOAD!
THIS IS DEMI OCTAVO, AUTHORITY CODE BULRUSH BASKET. THE CONTRACT ON MADOC JONES AND MICHAEL SINISTER IS HEREBY REVOKED, REPEAT REVOKED.
BE ADVISED THAT ANYONE PURSUING THAT CONTRACT AFTER THIS NOTICE IS FAIR GAME.
PALAIS
OKAY.
LET'S GO SEE IF THERE'S ANYONE STILL STANDING.
JESUS! SMELL THAT CORDITE!
LIKE THE END OF THE WORLD JUST WENT DOWN IN HERE...
SONY

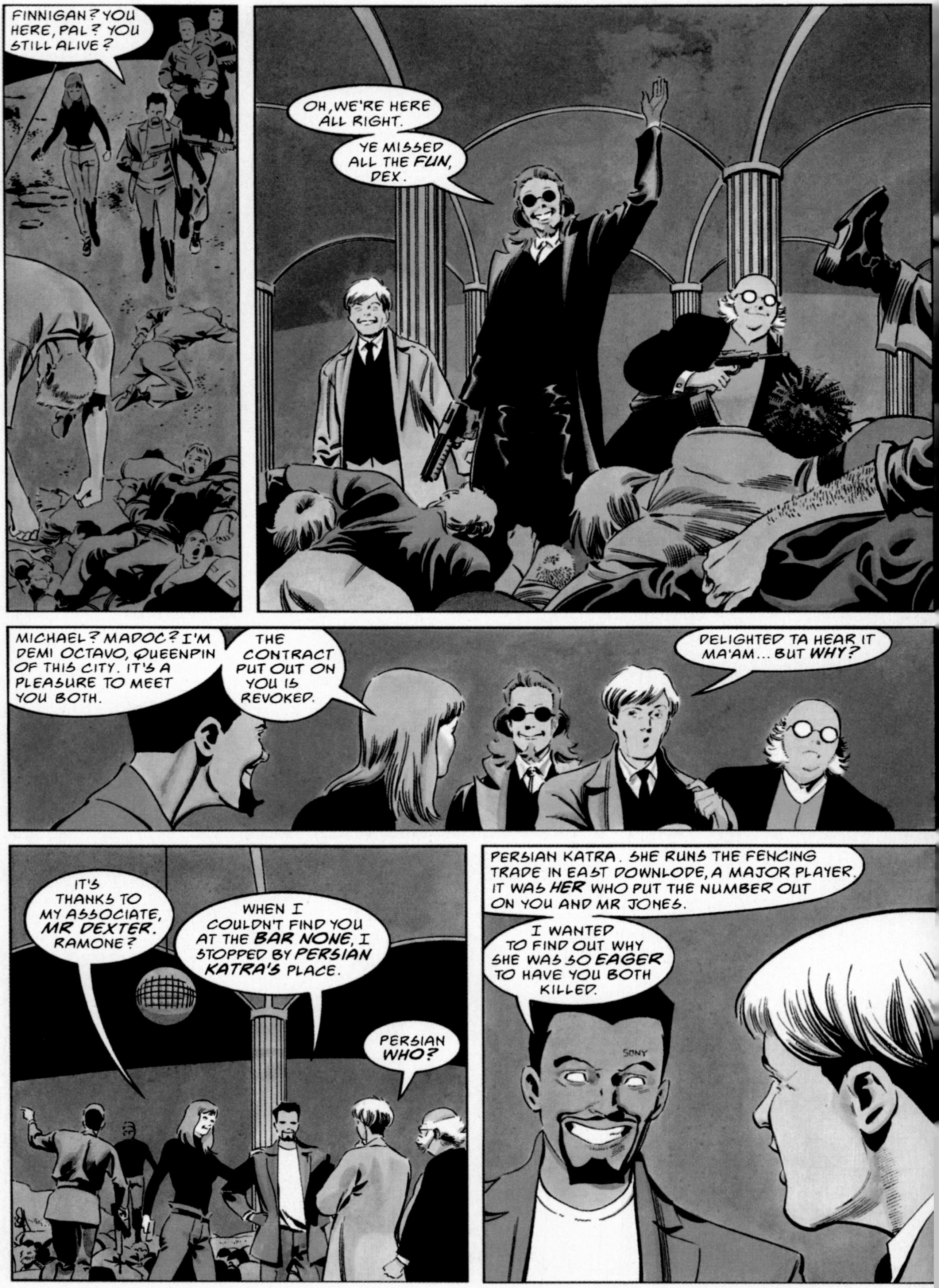
FINNIGAN? YOU HERE, PAL? YOU STILL ALIVE?
OH, WE'RE HERE ALL RIGHT.
YE MISSED ALL THE FUN, DEX.
MICHAEL? MADOC? I'M DEMI OCTAVO, QUEENPIN OF THIS CITY. IT'S A PLEASURE TO MEET YOU BOTH.
THE CONTRACT PUT OUT ON YOU IS REVOKED.
DELIGHTED TA HEAR IT MA'AM... BUT WHY?
IT'S THANKS TO MY ASSOCIATE, MR DEXTER. RAMONE?
WHEN I COULDN'T FIND YOU AT THE BAR NONE, I STOPPED BY PERSIAN KATRA'S PLACE.
PERSIAN WHO?
PERSIAN KATRA. SHE RUNS THE FENCING TRADE IN EAST DOWNLODE, A MAJOR PLAYER. IT WAS HER WHO PUT THE NUMBER OUT ON YOU AND MR JONES.
I WANTED TO FIND OUT WHY SHE WAS SO EAGER TO HAVE YOU BOTH KILLED.
SONY

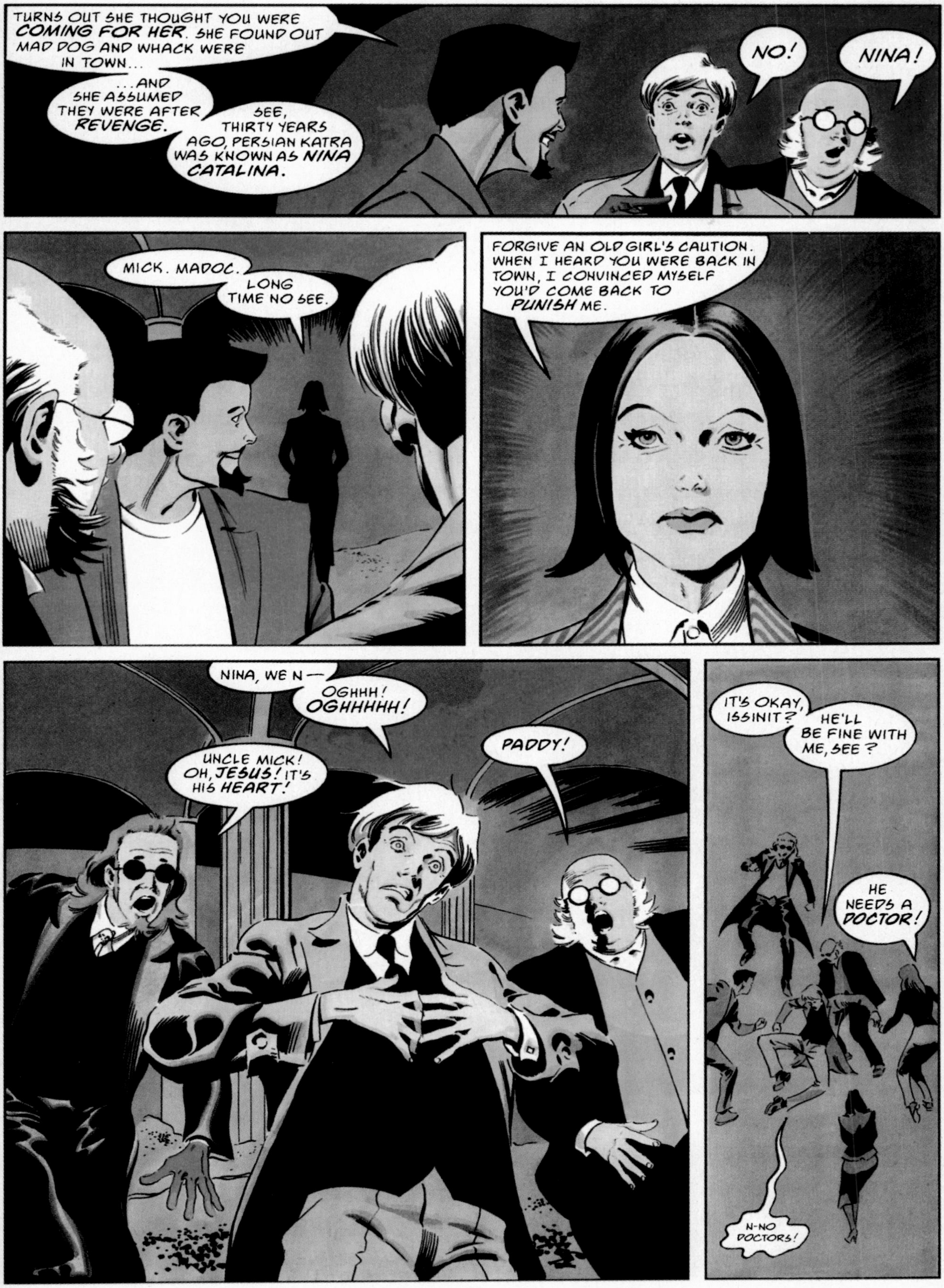
TURNS OUT SHE THOUGHT YOU WERE COMING FOR HER. SHE FOUND OUT MAD DOG AND WHACK WERE IN TOWN...
...AND SHE ASSUMED THEY WERE AFTER REVENGE.
SEE, THIRTY YEARS AGO, PERSIAN KATRA WAS KNOWN AS NINA CATALINA.
NO!
NINA!
MICK. MADOC.
LONG TIME NO SEE.
FORGIVE AN OLD GIRL'S CAUTION. WHEN I HEARD YOU WERE BACK IN TOWN, I CONVINCED MYSELF YOU'D COME BACK TO PUNISH ME.
NINA, WE N—
OGHHH! OGHHHHH!
UNCLE MICK! OH, JESUS! IT'S HIS HEART!
PADDY!
IT'S OKAY, ISSINIT?
HE'LL BE FINE WITH ME, SEE?
HE NEEDS A DOCTOR!
N-NO DOCTORS!

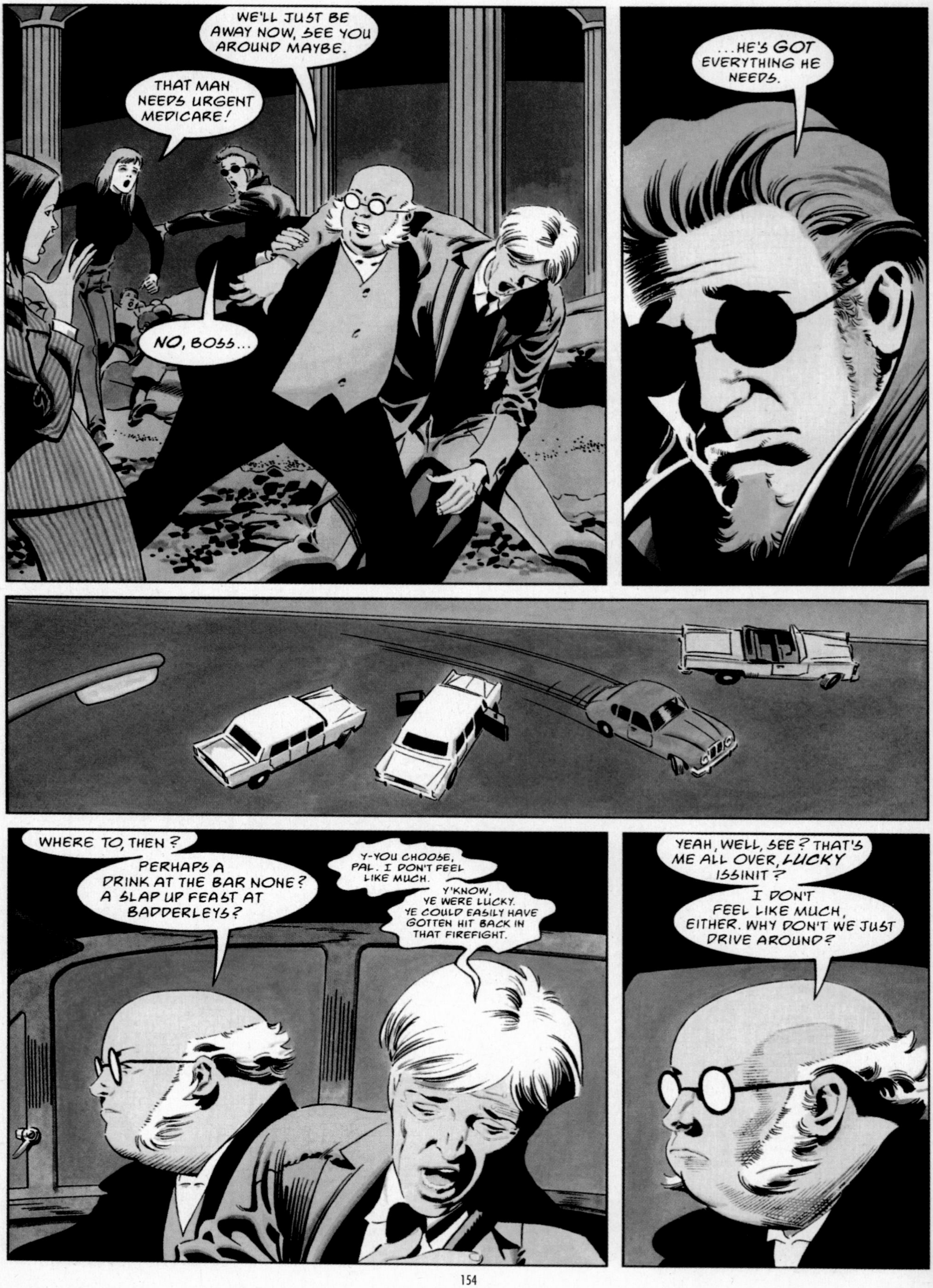

THAT MAN NEEDS URGENT MEDICARE!
WE'LL JUST BE AWAY NOW, SEE YOU AROUND MAYBE.
NO, BOSS...
...HE'S GOT EVERYTHING HE NEEDS.
WHERE TO, THEN?
PERHAPS A DRINK AT THE BAR NONE? A SLAP UP FEAST AT BADDERLEYS?
Y-YOU CHOOSE, PAL. I DON'T FEEL LIKE MUCH.
Y'KNOW, YE WERE LUCKY. YE COULD EASILY HAVE GOTTEN HIT BACK IN THAT FIREFIGHT.
YEAH, WELL, SEE? THAT'S ME ALL OVER, LUCKY ISSINIT?
I DON'T FEEL LIKE MUCH, EITHER. WHY DON'T WE JUST DRIVE AROUND?

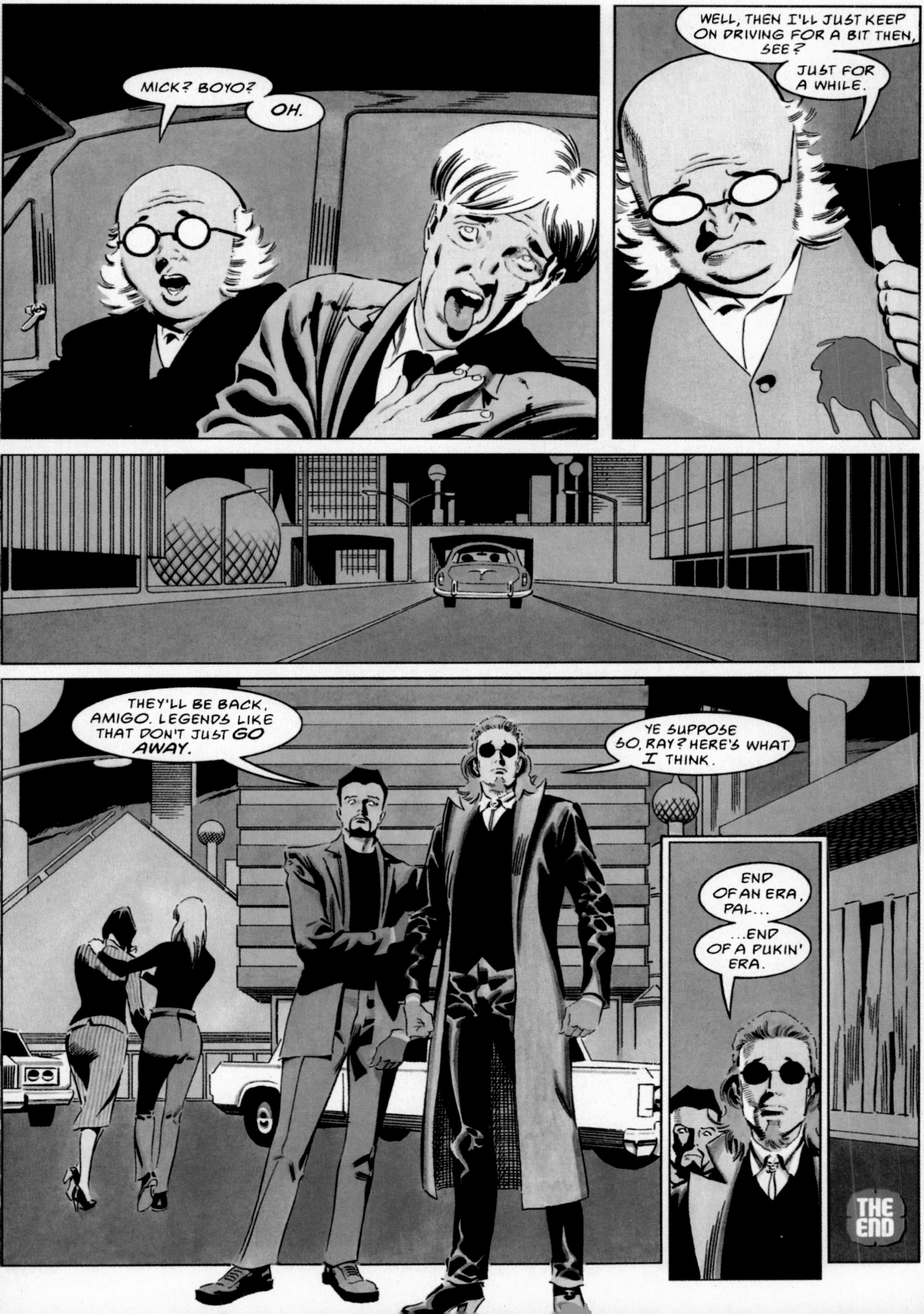
MICK? BOYO?
OH.
WELL, THEN I'LL JUST KEEP ON DRIVING FOR A BIT THEN, SEE?
JUST FOR A WHILE.
THEY'LL BE BACK, AMIGO. LEGENDS LIKE THAT DON'T JUST GO AWAY.
YE SUPPOSE SO, RAY? HERE'S WHAT I THINK.
END OF AN ERA, PAL...
...END OF A PUKIN' ERA.
THE END

Prog 1068 Cover by **Greg Staples**

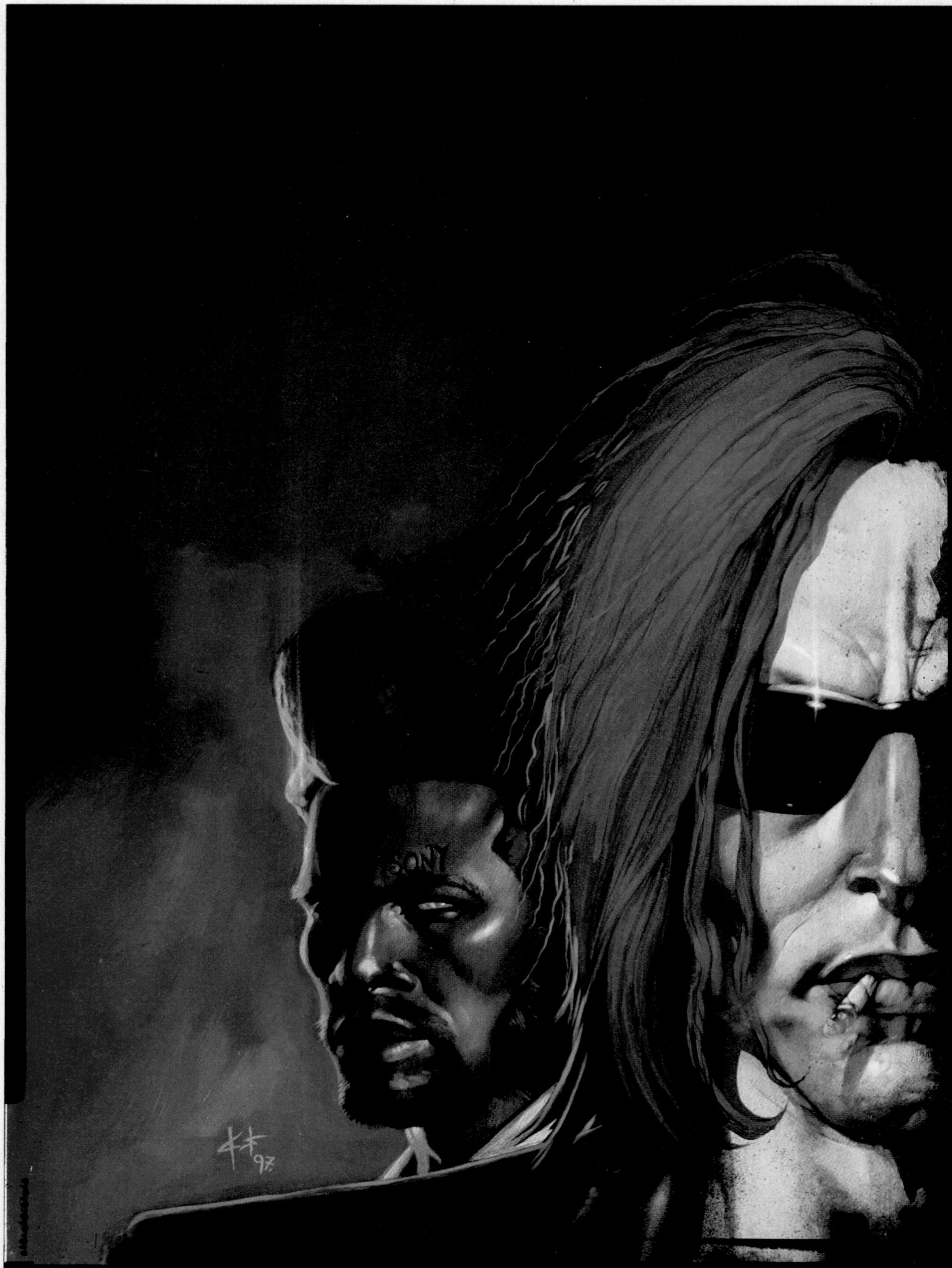
SONY

Prog 1070 Cover by **Steve Sampson**

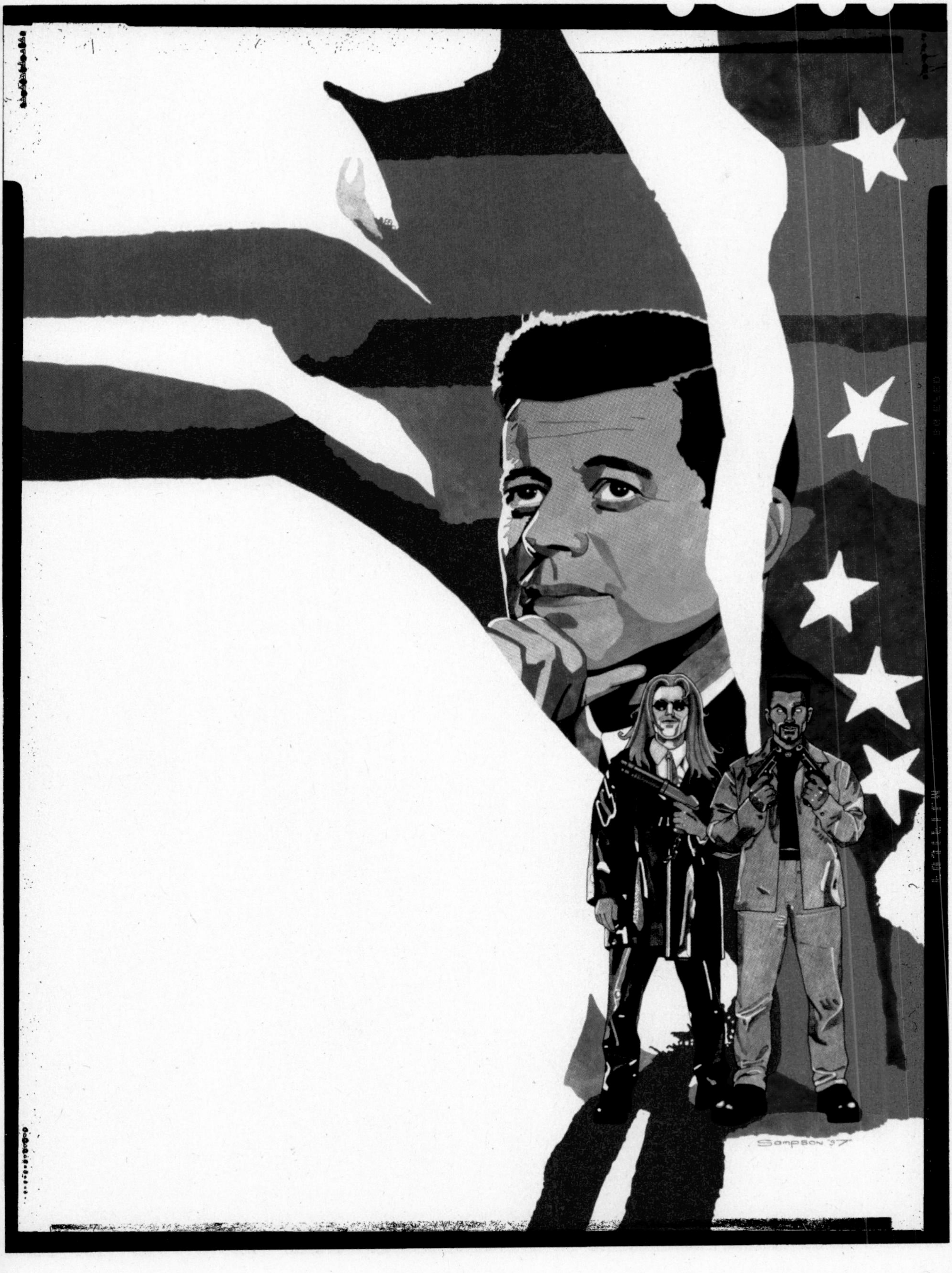
Sampson '97

Prog 1075 Cover by **Siku**

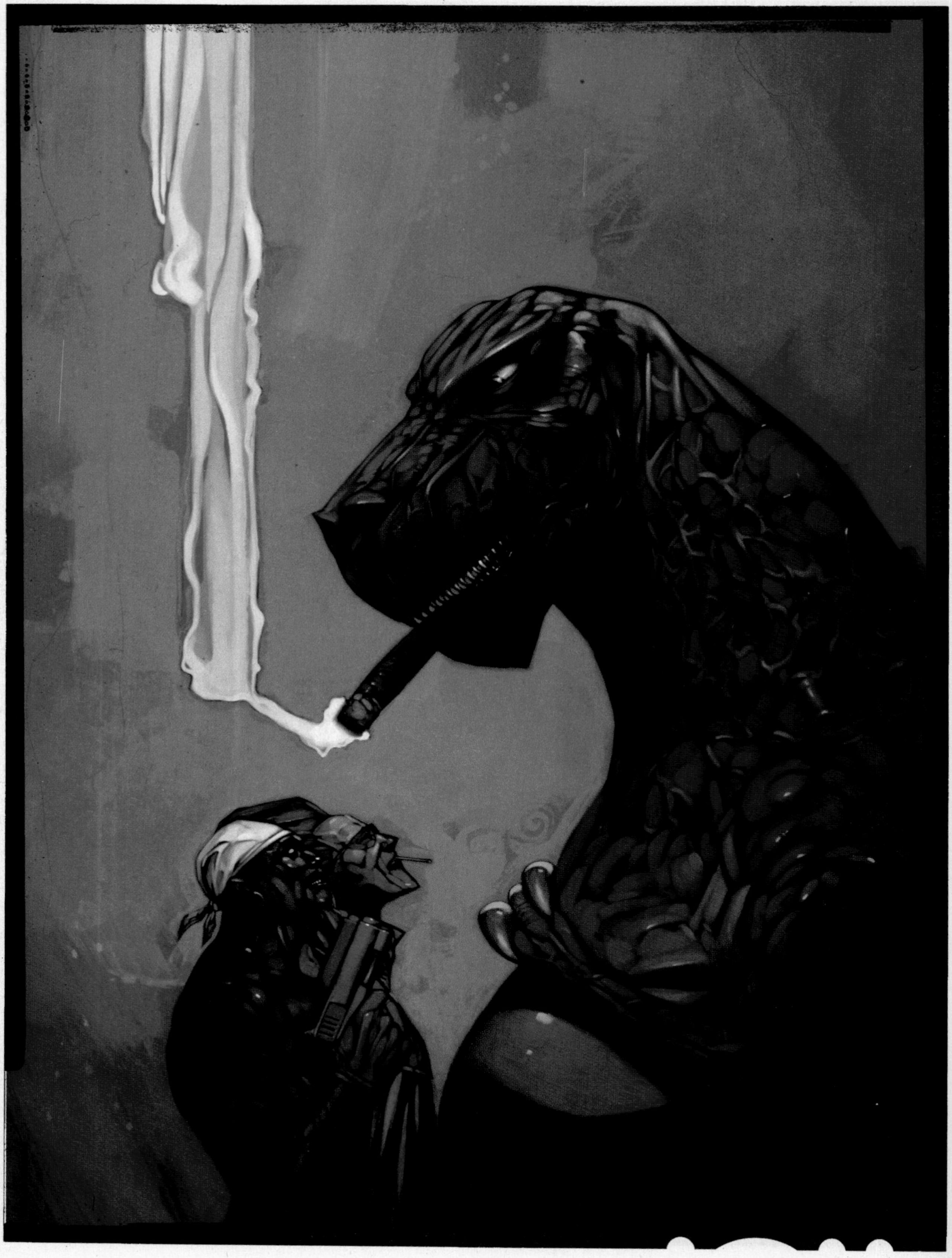

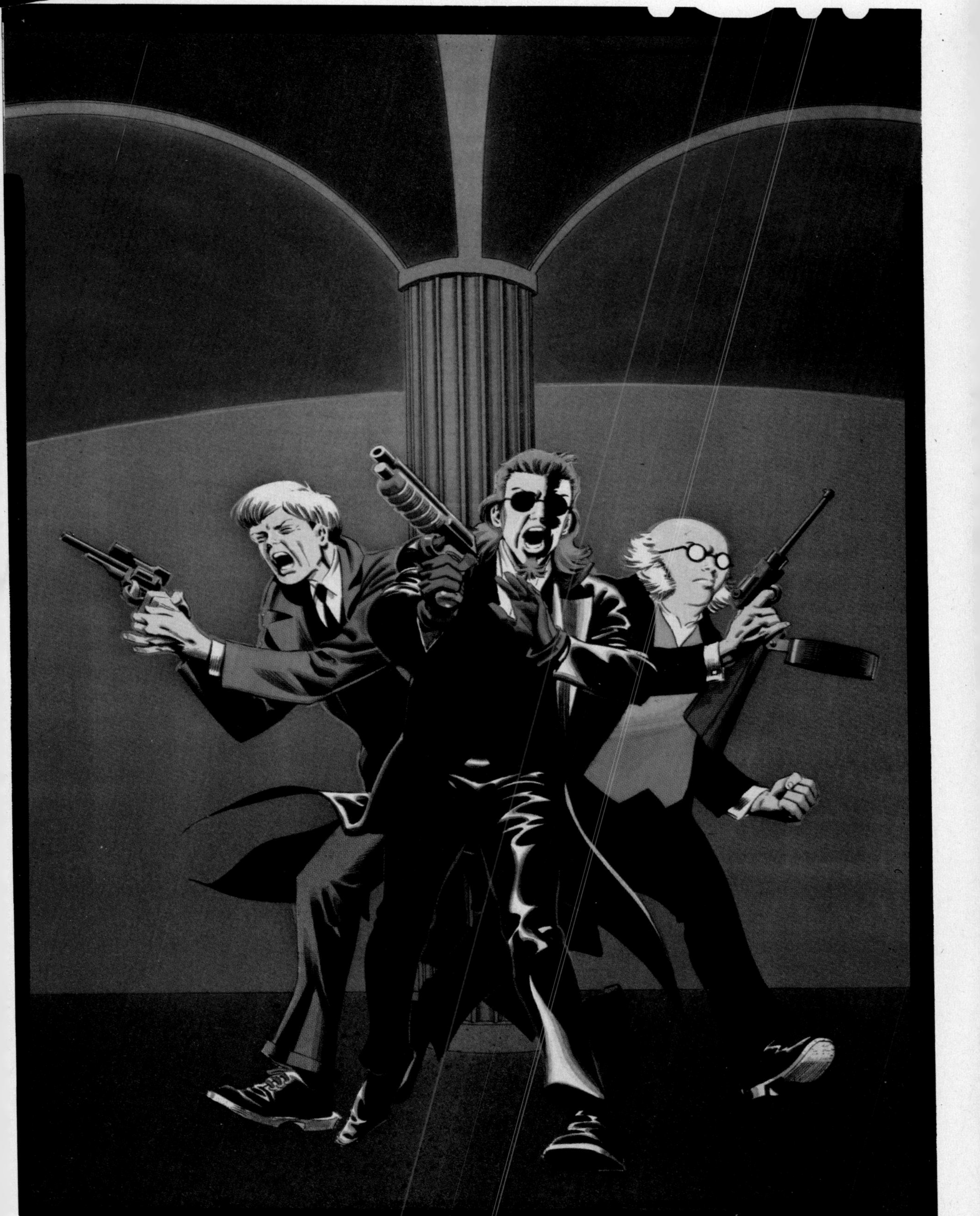

Dan Abnett is the co-creator of the *2000 AD* series ██████ also written *Black Light*, *Downlode Tales*, *Durham Red*, *Flesh*, *Future* ████ *Trooper*, *The V.C.'s*, *Vector 13* and *Venus Bluegenes*, as well as *The Scarlet Apoc* ████. A prolific creator, Abnett has also written for Marvel, Dark Horse and DC Comics, and he is the author of ██████ for the Black Library, including the bestselling *Gaunt's Ghosts* series. His most recent work outside the Galaxy's Greatest Comic is DC's *Legion* and *Superman*, and Wildstorm's *Mr. Majestic*. Dan Abnett was voted "Best Writer Now" at the 2003 National Comic Awards.

Simon Davis's unique, angular painted style has been a fixture of *Sinister Dexter* for some years now, since his *2000 AD* debut on the series. He has also found the time to create *B.L.A.I.R. 1* and *Black Siddha*, as well as contributing to *Downlode Tales*, *Judge Dredd*, *Missionary Man*, *Outlaw*, *Plagues of Necropolis*, *Tales of Telguuth*, *Tharg the Mighty* and *Vector 13*. His most recent non-*2000 AD* work was on DC's *JLA: Riddle of the Beast*.

Julian Gibson has illustrated *Judge Dredd* in addition to *Sinister Dexter*.

Paul Johnson is one of the UK's best-respected artists, having worked on comics as diverse as *Batman* and his own *London's Dark*. For *2000 AD*, he has illustrated *Downlode Tales*, *Future Shocks*, *Janus: Psi Division*, *Judge Dredd*, *Sinister Dexter*, *Tales of Telguuth*, *Terror Tales*, *Vector 13* and *Witchworld*.

Robert McCallum is the writer of *Mega-City Mania*, but he is perhaps better known as the artist of strips including *Judge Dredd*, *Maniac 5*, *Mean Machine*, *Shimura*, *Sinister Dexter* and *Vector 13*.

Alex Ronald has contributed to the series *Judge Dredd*, *Missionary Man*, *Rogue Trooper*, *Sinister Dexter* and *Vector 13*. His work has also been published in Caliber Comics' anthology *Negative Burn*.

Siku, a.k.a. Ajibayo Akinsiku, is the creator of the *Pan-African Judges*, and has illustrated *Downlode Tales*, *Future Shocks*, *Harlem Heroes*, *Judge Anderson*, *Judge Dredd*, *Judge Hershey*, *One-Offs*, *Pulp Sci-Fi*, *Sinister Dexter*, *Sláine*, *Tales of Telguuth* and *Witchworld*. He also contributed to Com. X's *Issue Zero*. Siku is currently Creative Director for the forthcoming video game *Evil Genius*.

Steve Yeowell has been a massively popular 2000 AD artist since his debut as penciller of the classic *Zenith*. He is also co-creator of *Maniac 5*, *Red Fang*, *Red Razors* and *The Red Seas*, and has pencilled *Armitage*, *Black Light*, *DeMarco*, *Devlin Waugh*, *Future Shocks*, *Judge Dredd*, *A Life Less Ordinary*, *Nikolai Dante*, *Pussyfoot 5*, *The Scarlet Apocrypha*, *Sinister Dexter*, *Tharg the Mighty* and *Vector 13*.

His work outside the Galaxy's Greatest Comic includes *Batman*, *Doom Patrol*, *The Invisibles*, *Sebastian O*, *Skrull Kill Krew*, *Starman* and *X-Men*.